The Denver Westerners

Golden Anniversary

Brand Book

1945 - 1995

Volume XXXII

This edition is limited to

1000 copies, of which this is

No. 8 3

LIBRARY OF CONGRESS CATALOG CARD NUMBER: 95-70291

ISBN: 0-9647302-0-0

The Denver Westerners
Golden Anniversary
Brand Book

Volume XXXII

*A collection of papers
presented before the
Denver Posse of the Westerners
from 1975 through 1994*

**Edited by Alan J. Stewart, P.M.
and Lee D. Olson, P.M.**

**Illustrations by
Max Smith, P.M.
William J. Barker, P.M.
Ralph M. Botter, C.M.
Gerard Curtis Delano**

THE DENVER POSSE OF THE WESTERNERS — 1995

Officers

The 1995 Officers of

The Denver Posse of The Westerners

Sheriff . . . . Theodore P. Krieger
Deputy Sheriff, Program Chairman . . . . . . Kenneth L. Gaunt
Past Sheriff . . . . John M. Hutchins
Roundup Foreman (Secretary) . . . . Earl McCoy
Tallyman and Trustee (Treasurer) . . . . Robert D. Stull
Registrar of Marks & Brands; Publications
      Chairman (Editor) . . . . Alan J. Stewart
Chuck Wrangler . . . . Keith H. Fessenden
Rosenstock Awards Chairman . . . . Eugene J. Rakosnik
Archivist . . . . Mark E. Hutchins
Membership Chairman . . . . Edwin A. Bathke
Keeper of the Possibles Bag . . . . Robert Lane

Dedication

Vol. XXXII, the Denver Westerners' Golden Anniversary *Brand Book*, is dedicated to four long-time Posse Members, all deceased. They are honored for their records of hard work, support, and achievements in behalf of the Posse. In addition, their bequests and financial assistance have helped to make this *Brand Book* a reality. Tribute is hereby paid to:

      Dr. Loren F. Blaney (1912-1991)
      George P. Godfrey (1907-1993)
      Fred A. Rosenstock (1895-1986)
      William H. Van Duzer (1920-1989)

Denver Westerners Posse Members

Dan Abbott (Res.)
Robert L. Akerley (Res.)
Richard G. Akeroyd Jr. (Res.)
Jon R. Almgren
Francis M. Bain (Res.)
Edwin A. Bathke
Nancy E. Bathke
John F. Bennett
Fletcher W. Birney Jr.
Earl Boland
James F. Bowers (Res.)
Richard G. Bowman
Dr. Robert K. Brown
Robert L. Brown
Dr. Marvin N. Cameron
Carl E.C. Carlson
Richard Conn
Robert D. Consolver Sr. (Res.)
Richard A. Cook
John D. Dailey
David F. Emrich
Bernie S. Faingold
Keith H. Fessenden
Kenneth L. Gaunt
Eleanor M. Gehres
W. Bruce Gillis Jr.
David L. Hartman (Res.)
Edward S. Helmuth (Res.)
John Milton Hutchins
Ray E. Jenkins (Res.)
Mark E. Hutchins
Clyde W. Jones
Herbert I. Jones
Dorothy Krieger

Dr. George W. Krieger
Theodore P. Krieger
Bob Lane
Robert E.A. Lee
Merrill J. Mattes
Earl McCoy
Roger Michels
Jack L. Morison
Dr. Robert W. Mutchler
Thomas J. Noel
Lee D. Olson
James W. Osborn
Stephen W. Pahs (Res.)
Kenneth Pitman
Robert S. Pulcipher
Omar Quade Jr.
Patricia Quade
Eugene J. Rakosnik
Dolores C. Renze (Hon.)
Francis B. Rizzari (Hon.)
Hugo G. Rodeck
John M. Shannon
Dr. Robert H. Shikes (Res.)
Dale W. Smith
Max D. Smith
Wayne L. Smith
C.R. Staadt
Alan J. Stewart
Robert D. Stull
Jackson C. Thode
Dr. Henry W. Toll Jr.
Lee Whiteley
Dr. Lester L. Williams (Res.)
Robert E. Woodhams

(Res. — Reserve member; Hon. — Honorary member)

v

Foreword

Perhaps you have heard some of the rumors.

About a vigilante group of old white guys who guarded local history at secret meetings where women and revisionists were taboo. Nowadays, when it is fashionable to publicly confess all sorts of things, such as smoking, drinking caffeine, and other character flaws, I confess to being a past sheriff of the Denver Posse and a guilty party fond of cigars, scotch and other unmentionables.

The Denver Posse of Westerners is now 50 years old and it is time to come clean. I confess further to enjoying the Westerners and thinking that some good research, speaking, and writing have brightened our dinner meetings on the fourth Wednesday of every month. This book is a collection of some of the better papers presented since 1976 when Alan J. Stewart (this book's editor) and the late L. Coulson Hageman got out the last volumes (XXX, XXXI) of the original series of *Brand Books*. The old *Brand Books* provided, in a handsome, well-illustrated format, often original and well-documented research on characters, locales, and episodes in the U.S. West. We hope you will think the same of this volume.

Let us hope that this 1995 revival is the first of another series of *Brand Books*. For this year the Denver Posse has heard some papers eligible for future volumes, such as Marcia Goldstein's talk on how Colorado men were the first in the entire world (outside of New Zealand) to vote yes on full women's suffrage.

Another lively 1995 program was storyteller and singer Pat Mendoza's account, from an Indian perspective, of what happened at the Sand Creek Massacre, one of the darkest, sorriest events in Colorado history.

As the Denver Posse's 1995 programs may suggest, the organization has evolved from a bunch of old white guys addicted to off-color jokes. The Posse now admits any Western history buff to membership—even women and Indians! Still, Westerners tend to have a rosier view of the past than academic historians such as my friend Patty Limerick at CU-Boulder. Whereas the "New Western Historians" are usually looking for villains, we Westerners tend to spend more time looking for heroes. I, for one, think we live in an age that needs heroes more than villains. There is no shortage of villains, or of blame to be teaspooned out. Why not focus on finding and celebrating what is good in our past?

The Denver Posse hopes you enjoy this sampler. We also hope that you will consider membership, or coming as a visitor, or even sharing your research at our monthly meetings. Membership in the Denver Posse is open to anyone with an interest in Western History and a willingness to hear other people tell of their research, a sometimes tedious but usually rewarding experience, as you will find in the following pages.

Welcome, partner, to this anthology of some of the talks we have swallowed with our drinks, dinners, and camaraderie.

—**Thomas J. Noel, P.M., Denver, 1995**

Preface

The Denver Posse of the Westerners was organized in 1945, the second such group in the nation. Its stated objectives are ". . . to investigate, discuss, and publish the facts and color relative to the historic, social, political, economic, and religious background of the West" and "to . . . preserve a record of the cultural background and evolution of the Western region. . . ."

Since 1945, the Westerners movement has spread worldwide. There are active "posses" or "corrals" in England, France, Germany, Hungary, Japan, Mexico, and other countries. In Colorado, there are corrals in Denver, Boulder, Colorado Springs, Durango, Fort Collins, and Loveland; and nationally, in Chicago, Kansas City, Los Angeles, San Diego, Washington, D.C., and other cities. Local members often affiliate with Westerners International Inc., in Oklahoma City.

The Denver Westerners bimonthly *Roundup* magazine is received by all members. The publication includes papers presented at monthly meetings, plus book reviews and other information. In years past, *Roundup* articles were collected in annual editions of the *Brand Book*.

What is a *Brand Book*? The name borrows from the days when cattle growers kept a record of their livestock brands. Members of the Denver Posse of the Westerners have put their own "brand" on historical papers they have researched and presented before the organization. These articles, as well as some from other sources, were compiled in the annual *Brand Book* Series, Vol. I-XXIX. The 1976 *Brand Book* (copyright 1977) combined Vols. XXX and XXXI. No *Brand Book* has since been published by the Denver Westerners.

Now, after a nearly 20-year hiatus, the Denver Westerners has produced another *Brand Book*: Vol. XXXII, as part of the organization's 50th Anniversary observance. This Golden Anniversary volume comprises 25 chapters, chosen from more than 100 papers published in the *Roundup*. This entire field of articles was reduced to 46. Final selections for the 25 chapters were based upon the desire to present a broad perspective of Western life, starting in the earliest days of Spanish exploration in the Sangre de Cristos, on up to more modern times, e.g., the Pueblo flood of 1921, early-day auto trails, and fledgling motion-picture filmmaking in Colorado.

The articles in many cases represent material gathered in life-long pursuit of a particular subject, such as early trails or rail-roads. The ranks of *Brand Book* authors include professional historians and knowledgeable published writers. In addition, several articles are by qualified lay historians who have dug into the nooks and crannies of Western archives to uncover a particular subject.

Thirty years ago, the Denver Westerners' 1965 *Brand Book* (Vol. XXI) had 18 articles in 430 pages, including 8 full-color plates, 50 photos, numerous drawings and etchings, index and dust jacket. Price of the book was $12 plus tax. The 1976 *Brand Book* was priced around $25. Since those days, publishing costs have climbed higher than the Front Range!

Financing a book became an insurmountable obstacle for the Denver Westerners. However, a way was found around much of the cost through desktop publishing procedures and computerized type production. Composing camera-ready pages of type and graphics has cut costs sufficiently to make this 50th Anniversary *Brand Book* feasible.

The resulting 25-chapter book has 496 pages with index; 120 photos, and more than 50 maps and sketches; a full-color dust jacket, plus 16 full-color pages reproducing the Southwestern art of Gerard Curtis Delano.

The way has now been opened to publishing future *Brand Books*, and additional volumes are expected to appear in the series. But . . . there can never be another Golden Anniversary *Brand Book*. This one is for collectors. It belongs on your bookshelf !

Acknowledgments

The Denver Posse of the Westerners wishes first to thank those authors whose works appear in this 50th Anniversary *Brand Book* for their many hours spent in research, collecting data and illustrations, and in writing.

One of our authors, Posse Member Carl A. Blaurock ("Tragedy on on Longs Peak"), died in 1993. Another, Corresponding Member David L. Hieb ("We Lived at Ft. Laramie"), died in 1980.

Supporting our authors—always ready with help and encouragement—are two institutions which deserve much credit: the Western History Department of the Denver Public Library, and the Colorado Historical Society. These two organizations have nationwide—maybe worldwide—reputations for their inspiration and reliability. You will find ample evidence throughout this book of their assistance, in quoted text and photo credits.

In particular, we want to thank the family of Carl Blaurock for making his pictures of Longs Peak available. We also wish to thank Gary Candelaria, superintendent, and Steven Fullmer, historian, Fort Laramie National Historic Site (National Park Service), for their help in supplying pictures for the Hieb chapter on Ft. Laramie, and for checking our manuscript.

Coeditor and Posse Member Lee D. Olson rendered exceptional assistance in editing, proofreading, and indexing, and in promotion and sales.

Much help and counsel came from Posse Member Merrill J. Mattes, not only on his two chapters ("Seeing the Elephant" and "War Club and Parasol"), but in both subject matter and illustrations for other articles.

Posse Member Jackson C. Thode was of invaluable help in providing photos to go with two chapters: Robert LeMassena's "How and Why the Railroads Came to Colorado" (Thode's private collection), and Bernard Kelly's "The Great Pueblo Flood of 1921" (from the Denver & Rio Grande archives).

A very special thank-you is due Posse Member Richard G. Bowman for his generosity in allowing the Westerners use of color separations and black-and-white sketches from his privately published book (1990) on the life of artist Gerard Curtis Delano, *Walking With Beauty*. This art has become a centerpiece, not only in Bowman's chapter on Delano, but for the entire volume. Delano's black-and-white sketches have also added much in illustrating several chapters in the book.

Original illustrations were created for several chapters by Max Smith, Littleton Posse Member. In addition, some incidental illustrations by the late Ralph M. Botter, Corresponding Member of Socorro, N.M., were reprinted from the 1976 *Brand Book*. An original Glorieta Pass battle map by the late Posse Member William J. Barker is reprinted from the 1948 *Brand Book*. The map includes Barker's sketches of Union and Confederate leaders.

Dr. Thomas Noel, P.M., helped set the tone for the book with his Introduction. Tom also provided text and illustrations for his own chapter, "Moral Geography in Denver; Streetcars, Suburbs & Saloons."

We wish to thank our volunteer computer typesetters for lightening the production load: Nancy and Ed Bathke, Marge and Keith Fessenden, Gloria and Ed Helmuth, Bob Lane, Lee Olson, Lyn Ryder, and Elinor Stewart. Jim Krebs gave additional help, with the use of scanning equipment on some text. Proofreading by Lee Olson and Nancy and Ed Bathke was also greatly appreciated.

Bearing the brunt of much of the production work for the Golden Anniversary *Brand Book* was Elinor L. Stewart, wife of editor Alan Stewart. A graduate journalist and experienced paralegal, Elinor played an exceptional and essential role in editing, proofreading, typesetting, graphics, indexing, and assembly and coordination of the book's 25 chapters. It would not have been possible for the Denver Westerners to produce this Golden Anniversary *Brand Book* without her hard work, consultation, and cheerful assistance.

—**Alan J. Stewart, P.M. Broomfield, 1995.**

Table of Contents

Illustrations

"Trader and Trapper" by *Delano*

Sangre de Cristo:
Colorado's Forgotten Pass

By Edward S. Helmuth

*V*ARIOUS MOUNTAIN RANGES have been barriers to people and animals. Passes were used to breach these ranges, to allow movement from point to point in as little time as possible. Sangre de Cristo Pass was an early-day route that had extensive usage, and was the principal passage from Spanish Territory to the Arkansas River Valley. In today's world, Sangre de Cristo Pass is not familiar, and the remembrance of it is largely limited to historians.

No public road exists today over the pass. Other passes in the region have become more prominent in modern usage: La Veta and North La Veta—highway routes; Pass Creek Pass—road; Veta—railroad; Mosca—a trail. Access to Sangre de Cristo today is over land owned by the Forbes Land Co. The pass is virtually ignored by the many travelers who go by only a few hundred yards from the saddle of the pass. If the traveler looked upward, he could see traces of the pass in the old ruts along the slopes, where wagons once crossed from the Oak Creek area to Sangre de Cristo Creek, and southwest into the San Luis Valley.

By the early 1700s and for about 70 years, the Comanches used the pass to move from the High Plains of eastern Colorado through the San Luis Valley, on their way to New Mexico to plunder the Spanish villages and to trade with the Taos Pueblo Indians. They crossed the Sangre de Cristo Range at an angle, ascending a branch of the Huerfano River to the top of the pass, then descending along Sangre de Cristo Creek into the San Luis Valley. The trail was smooth, wide in most places, and had a gradual grade. Yutas (Utes) rode up from the south in the fall, to visit their cousins, the Comanches, and to hunt buffalo with them. By 1749 Louisiana French fur traders had reached the area and Comanches guided these traders through the valleys, up and over the pass.

During 1768 Governor de Mendenueta of New Mexico led a group of 546 men from Taos over the pass to the Arkansas River Valley on

New Mexico Gov. Juan Bautista de Anza named the Sangre de Cristo (Blood of Christ) Mountains and Pass in September 1779.

the way to retaliate against marauding Comanches.

In September 1779, then-Gov. Juan Bautista de Anza and hundreds of soldiers used the pass to return to New Mexico, after defeating a band of Comanches under Chief Cuerno Verde (Green Horn) in the Arkansas River Valley, near present-day Rye, Colorado. De Anza is credited with naming the pass when his party was camped in the willows near the Huerfano Butte. A brilliant sunset colored the mountain range to the west a bright blood-red. He could see a feeder branch of the river coming down from a smooth dip in the "Blood of Christ" range to his southwest. The next morning, de Anza followed his Ute guides up to that dip. By evening, they had climbed 3,000 feet over 20 miles of a trail that ran up South Oak Creek from Badito Cone. This trail brought him to the tree-covered top of the pass. On the other side was a grassy valley, ringed by aspen trees. De Anza named the place Sangre de Cristo Pass, and descended along a gradual drop into the San Luis Valley. He quickly recognized the importance of the pass as an easy path through the mountain ranges to the high-country valleys beyond. His mind on building a Spanish empire, he realized Sangre de Cristo Pass would help such a plan.

By the early 1800s, French and American trappers were using the pass to move from the plains to the beaver streams of the Southwest. James Pursley and Baptiste La Lande came from Missouri in 1804 and 1805, by way of the Arkansas River. It is believed they were escorted over the mountains by Indian guides through Sangre de Cristo Pass. In October 1806, New Mexico Gov. Facundo Melgares and 600 Spanish dragoons journeyed to the Arkansas River area, hoping to intercept the U.S. expedition of Zebulon Pike. They did not find Pike, and returned to Santa Fe, using Sangre de Cristo Pass.

Pike, with a band of 23 hardy souls, reached the area in January 1807. He reported finding some sort of civilization near the pass. This is the first indication of any settlement there. Pike's shivering party could see the Spanish Peaks, with the dip of Raton Pass off to the left, and the dip of Sangre de Cristo Pass and the San Luis Valley to the right. Pike endeavored to cross the dip of Sangre de Cristo Pass, but the party was turned back by heavy snows.

Reports indicate that Pike did not cross into the San Luis Valley through Sangre de Cristo Pass. Rather, he used one of the westerly crossings of the range. Spanish Governor Alencaster ordered lookouts placed on Sangre de Cristo Pass to capture Pike's party if they appeared. Later, they were captured in the San Luis Valley.

By 1810, American fur traders were using the pass regularly to cross from the upper Arkansas River to Taos. James McLanahan, Reuben Smith, and James Patterson from St. Louis were arrested in New Mexican territory after crossing with a Spanish guide. John McKnight, A.P. Chouteau, and Jules De Mun, trapping in 1816-1817 near the headwaters of the Rio Grande River, had their pelts confiscated.

In 1818 Lt. Jose Maria de Arce was sent with militia from Taos over the pass (called in his journal "The Gap of the Sierra Blanca") to search out hostile settlers in the Arkansas River Valley.

A Spanish officer, Luis de Onis, read a French report early in 1819, which described an "easy footpath" up South Oak Creek between Sheep and Dike mountains and over the Sangre de Cristo Pass into the valley, then south to Taos and Santa Fe. This report had actually been written by De Mun in 1818. Based on the information that the pass was a place where a handful of men could hold off an entire army, de Onis asked Governor Melgares to build a fort on the pass. Melgares reported back in May 1819 that one had been erected on the east side of the pass. Sometime within the next several months, the fort was destroyed by Indians, or whites dressed as Indians (according to a Spanish survivor). Three-hundred Spanish soldiers were sent to reinforce the fort; however, it was abandoned soon after. As a result of the Mexican revolution on Aug. 24, 1821, Iturbide Augustin I crowned himself emperor. Melgares continued on as governor in New Mexico, but he let his mud fort on the pass dissolve in rain.

The pass fortification was described by one source as a triangular stone enclosure on a hill about five miles east of the summit. Another source called it a small mud fort, half way down South Oak Creek, between the summit and Huerfano River, about five miles. The fort was positioned to protect one of the most vulnerable access points. It was built on a little plateau as the trail left Oak Creek, and commanded a good view of the Huerfano Valley where the Taos Trail wound from Badito Cone to Sangre de Cristo Pass. Six badly armed militiamen were assigned to the fort. They proved no match when attacked by 100 or so Indians, thought to be Comanches. Ensign Don Jose Antonio Valenzuela repulsed the attack, but was unable to counterattack with his small force. Five of the six troops were killed.

In 1934 a Colorado exploration party consisting of Dr. LeRoy Hafen, Mr. and Mrs. Tim Hudson of Gardner, and Emmet King of Walsenburg found the crumbling ruins of native rock walls which bounded the enclosure. They reported scrub oak grown up around the walls and much evidence of treasure hunting over the years.

By the time the fort was built, the route had become well established. Sangre de Cristo was a popular trail from the Arkansas to the Rio Grande. The route was known as the Taos Trail by 1820. In historical writings, the Taos Trail was sometimes confused with the Mountain Branch of the Santa Fe Trail. The main Santa Fe route did not enter what is now the state of Colorado, skirting to the southeast. The Mountain Branch of the Santa Fe Trail did enter the southeast corner, passed by Bent's Old Fort, and headed south, over Raton Pass.

In the 1820s, the Taos Trail was used to transport goods from the

Missouri River settlements into New Mexico. Mexican, American, and Canadian mountain men used the trail during the 1820s and 1830s, carrying trade goods to Indians and pelts back to Taos, Santa Fe, and the Arkansas River.

When Hugh Glenn, a trader, learned that Mexico had declared its independence, he was camped with a group of 20 men near Pueblo. He decided to seek permission to trap in the Rio Grande area, a part of the newly independent country. He and four of his party joined up with soldiers bound for Santa Fe. They traveled the well-worn Sangre de Cristo trail, following the Huerfano River, past Badito Cone, leaving the river valley, crossing the pass, going down Sangre de Cristo Creek, then along the east side of the San Luis Valley into Taos. This route was so often used by trappers that it became known as the "Trapper's Trail" as well as the Taos Trail.

New Mexico eased its trade policy. The Taos Trail led people over the pass and then onto the extensive Sangre de Cristo Land Grant, but settlers didn't stay. They moved on through to other opportunities in the south. In the winter of 1821-1822, 20 Americans arrived in the Arkansas and Huerfano rivers region, now part of Huerfano and Pueblo counties. They set up a camp next to Indian settlements, to trade with the Comanche, Kiowa, and Arapaho tribes. The group remained there until January then moved on to Taos over the Sangre de Cristo Pass.

Soldiers escorted Maj. Jacob Fowler—for whom the town of Fowler was named—over the pass. They left Pueblo on Jan. 29, 1822, en route to Taos. Crossing Sangre de Cristo Pass on Feb. 5, they entered the San Luis Valley, which they referred to as "an open plain of great Extent."

A diary kept by Fowler gives much detail and fact about travel over the pass. They went from the Arkansas to the St. Charles River, across to the Greenhorn River, then up the Huerfano River to the pass area. Fowler talked about the "Spanish Road" when he wrote that on Sunday, Feb. 3, 1822, they set out early, going south along the foot of the mountains for about 10 miles to a creek where they saw the remains of a Spanish fort. He reported it appeared to have been occupied about a year earlier. They camped at the old fort location and posted guards to watch over the horses, after making only 15 miles that day.

The following day they headed out into a high and very cold wind, going southwest about two miles to a mountain peak and along a ridge until they reached the saddle and started down the other side, along

Sangre de Cristo Creek for about ten miles to a good stopping point for the night. Again they made about fifteen miles.

In the 1830s virtually all travel between the Arkansas Valley and New Mexico was over Sangre de Cristo Pass. In 1832 John Gantt opened trade with Cheyenne and Arapaho Indians on the Arkansas, at the mouth of the Purgatoire River. He bought supplies in Taos, and used the pass to get back and forth. Later Gantt and Charles and William Bent built forts near the present site of Pueblo.

Settlements like Pueblo, Hardscrabble, and Greenhorn in the Arkansas Valley sprang up in the 1840s and travel between these communities and Taos increased. The *Trinidad Daily News* (Aug. 28, 1881) reported that in the 1840s, Lucien Maxwell, Kit Carson, and Timothy Goodale made a trip from Pueblo to Taos in one day, using the Sangre de Cristo Pass route.

Early travelers along the Mountain Branch of the Santa Fe Trail openly commented upon its difficulty; it is more likely that people working for Bent and Ceran St. Vrain took the easier Taos Trail over Sangre de Cristo, rather than the longer, rougher, Raton Pass route. In 1842 John Hawkins and Dick Wootton (who later developed Raton Pass) hauled a valuable mixed cargo of beaver pelts and Spanish silver across Sangre de Cristo Pass to Bent's Fort on the Arkansas River.

Dick Wootton tells this story about the pass:

> At one time when coming through Sangre de Christo *[sic]* Pass, with a small party of prospectors, I came near running into an Apache ambuscade, where my career as a gold hunter would have been very suddenly cut short, had I not discovered the presence of the Indians in the nick of time. I always made it a point never to ride into any place which looked like a good hiding place for the savages, without taking a careful survey of the situation in advance.
>
> That was what I did when we were about to enter a narrow defile in the Sangre de Christo, and a quick sharp eye, which has, no doubt, saved my scalp a good many times, enabled me to discover an Apache, lying flat on the rocks above, so close to the road we should have taken in going through the pass, that we should have been powder-burned when they fired on us.
>
> I could only see the one Indian—and though I knew there were more of them—and he had covered himself with dust and looked so much like a rock, that I think nine out of ten of the mountain men even would have passed along without noticing him.
>
> I didn't know how many Indians a shot would scare out, but I knew that the one I saw would be a dead one, and so I raised my gun and fired. At the crack of my rifle he sprang up, but only to tumble over, as dead as Julius Caesar, a second later.
>
> At the same instant the very rocks seemed to turn into Indians, and they jumped out of a score of places, where we could see no sign of them before.

Sketch by Richard Kern, an artist with the Fremont and Gunnison expeditions, is a view of Sangre de Cristo Pass looking northeast from a camp near the summit. Picture was dated Aug. 11, 1853.

My party commenced firing on them then and the Indians ran. They did not stop until they got out of reach of our guns, and we passed along in safety.

Rufus Sage recorded a trip he took from Lancaster Lupton's fort on the South Platte River to New Mexico using the Taos Trail.

Charles Autobees took mule pack trains over Sangre de Cristo Pass from Taos to El Pueblo in 1844, where goods such as buffalo robes and beaver pelts were loaded onto wagons and taken east. He also hauled flour and whiskey (in 10-gallon casks) to trade with the Indians.

Weather was sometimes severe in the mid-1800s. During the spring of 1843 a group of about 15 Canadian and American trappers left Taos for Ft. St. Vrain. They did not reach the northern outpost until around the last of June, as they were detained by severe late-spring snowstorms in crossing Sangre de Cristo Pass and the Arkansas-Platte Divide.

In late September 1844 George and Juana Simpson and their baby; Juana's sister Cruz; and Joe Coyle, Asa Estes, and three Mexican mule drivers left the settlement of Hardscrabble for Taos. On the first day they reached the St. Charles River just south of Pueblo, where they were caught in an unseasonable snow storm. For the next seven days, they traveled only 60 miles through wind and snow, nursing their campfires at night to keep the baby warm. After the storm subsided, they made the top of Sangre de Cristo Pass. Here the men had to dismount and beat a path through the snowdrifts. Juana's horse stumbled and fell, throwing her and the baby into a snowbank. Juana was unconcerned; she came up smiling with her baby intact in her arms, and resumed her place in the cavalcade as if nothing had happened. On the other side of the pass they saw a Ute village and several Indians moving along Sangre de Cristo Creek, with a large number of cattle and sheep.

In 1846, a Mormon party of 55 people went from Taos, over the pass on to Pueblo, under the leadership of a Lt. W.W. Willis.

Adventurers from all over the world were learning about this "new" country. In January 1847, a young Englishman, George F. Ruxton, started his journey back to United States territory from New Mexico, by way of the San Luis Valley, Sangre de Cristo Pass, and Pueblo. He comments on entering an exceptionally windy valley, called El Vallecito, known as the "Wind Trap" among mountain men. From this uncomfortable place his party climbed Sangre de Cristo Pass and exited the valley. His book, *Wild Life in the Rocky Mountains*, is a good representation of Colorado during the 1840s and gives a graphic description of a stormy crossing of the pass.

Some New Mexicans rebelled against American settlers in January 1847. Taos Pueblo Indians formed a mob and killed Gov. Charles Bent and every American they could find in Taos. John Albert, a Greenhorn resident, was near Taos at Arroyo Hondo (about 12 miles north of Taos), site of Simeon Turley's distillery—home of the famed "Taos Lighting." Turley and others escaped by digging a hole from the distillery into a granary. Albert reached a log fence and lay concealed underneath it as the mob rushed past. Under cover of darkness, he crept off into the piñon-covered hills and escaped to the north, passing through the San Luis Valley, over Sangre de Cristo Pass and on toward Pueblo. He shot a deer on the east side of the pass and wrapped its skin around him. This kept him from freezing until he reached Greenhorn.

Indian activity continued. During the winter of 1847-1848 a campaign led by Col. Benjamin Beall and guided by Kit Carson engaged

Apaches east of the pass, and two chiefs were taken captive.

A delegation of about 50 men left Greenhorn to look for gold on the western slope of the Sangre de Cristo Pass in 1849, but not enough quality ore was found to justify further exploration.

By 1852 the United States government had taken action to protect settlers. The Army built on Ute Creek—one stream north of lower Sangre de Cristo Creek near the west foot of Sangre de Cristo Pass—the first military base in Colorado: Ft. Massachusetts. Raiding Indians were deterred only slightly. As the northernmost of a string of forts along the Rio Grande from Texas through New Mexico, Ft. Massachusetts was nearly 50 miles from the settlements on Culebra and Costilla creeks and also several miles off the Sangre de Cristo Pass Trail, which the Army intended to protect.

Around the first of February 1853, Tom Autobees left the Rio Colorado with a train of 60 pack mules and 25 men. The snow was so deep on the west side of Sangre de Cristo Pass that the party traveled 10 miles in eight days. At the summit they spent another day stamping a path through a mammoth drift that lay across the trail. But on the eastern side of the pass, at the headwaters of the Huerfano, the climate changed to early spring and the snow disappeared.

Word went east about the availability of routes in the new country. Sen. Thomas Hart Benton of Missouri urged building a railroad along the Taos Trail. In 1849 he urged support of the rail line and indicated his knowledge of the principal geological feature of the area, when he remarked:

> When this mighty work shall have been completed and the commerce of the East is brought over it, and the iron bands connect the oceans, a grateful country will carve out of the granite pillars of the Huerfano Butte, a statue of Columbus, pointing to the West and exclaiming "There is the East! There are the Indies!"

Huerfano Butte, a little volcanic cone and the intersection of two only radiating volcanic dikes, is a landmark on the east side of Interstate 25, about 10 miles north of Walsenburg and 39 miles south of Pueblo.

There was much discussion in the East about developing a rail route along the 38th parallel. This demarcation line crosses the Sangre de Cristo Range near present-day Crestone. During the next four decades many explorations, both publicly and privately funded, would come through seeking the most advantageous route for the railroad. Army men and explorers were regular visitors to the Taos Trail.

Three competing expeditions looked for a route, and the question

(Photo by Author)

In 1779 Juan Bautista de Anza's forces camped at the foot of Huerfano Butte, a prominent landmark for the pass entrance.

of the Pacific Railroad was a hot issue. Congress authorized four surveys, and various governmental and private groups competed during the years of survey for the "best" route.

Of the three survey parties entering and crossing the San Luis Valley in 1853, two were backed by Senator Benton and one was authorized by the Army. All the passes in the Sangre de Cristo Range in the area were considered for a railroad crossing. Opinions differed on the advantages of the others over Sangre de Cristo Pass. In the end, no railroad was ever built through any of the four main passes on the east side of the valley.

In the first week of June 1853, a small, hard-riding party of 12, under the leadership of a retired naval officer, Lt. Edward F. Beale, came through. Beale was going to California where he had been appointed U.S. Commissioner of Indian Affairs. But he was also to make observations for Benton on the Central Route to the Pacific. Gwinn Harris Heap, Beale's cousin, took notes on their journey. Heap's account is considered one of the classic records of Western travel. He remarked on the clear icy streams, luxuriant grass, flowers, plentiful antelope and deer. The party stopped overnight on June 4 near the summit of the pass. The large mountain meadow, numerous springs, dark pines, and the views back out to the eastern plains are mentioned in his journal. They traveled 26 miles that day.

Heap reported that an excellent wagon road might be built over the mountains through Sangre de Cristo Pass, but believed a better road could be developed over Robidoux's Pass (today's Mosca Pass). He noted that Sangre de Cristo Pass was more suitable for travelers on horseback. Beale wrote a letter from Santa Fe on June 9, 1853, commenting, "The Pass Sangre de Cristo is an excellent one. . . ."

When Capt. John Gunnison approached the pass in August, looking for a railroad route, he used the Huerfano Butte as a landmark. He had been assigned the task of exploring the most central possible railroad route across the country. Marcelino Baca of Greenhorn was hired to lead part of the survey party to Ft. Massachusetts. Baca led the party over Sangre de Cristo Pass to the fort, then returned to his home. Gunnison and his party of U.S. topographical engineers—32 strong, with 18 wagons and an ambulance—went over the pass. They concluded it was acceptable for a rail crossing. They moved up the Huerfano several miles along its southern bank, then crossed to the north side to the ford of the Taos Trail. Their route lay from Huerfano Butte to the base of the Sierra Blanca; thence to the summit of Sangre de Cristo Pass; down Sangre de Cristo Creek and into the San Luis Valley. It took them four days to cross the pass, as much work had to be done on the six-mile trail, clearing away overgrowth to make future crossing easier. There was such a "sidle" in places that the mounted riflemen roped the wagons and hung on for dear life on the upside to keep them from toppling.

The astronomer Homans put the pass summit at 9,219 feet, only 240 feet under today's figure.

Gunnison pronounced the scenery to be, ". . . very fine, the views extending far back over the plains. . . . The bold peaks tower loftily above us, whitened here and there by lines of snow."

The abundance of grouse, pheasant, deer, bear, and trout impressed the explorers. They were also surprised at the loss of endurance experienced by both men and animals in the rarified atmosphere.

"Even though the number of mules per wagon was doubled to 12 on the summit of the pass, they could not accomplish what six mules could do under ordinary circumstances," Gunnison reported. "Likewise, the achievements of our strongest men were reduced to less than half their normal performance."

During the easy descent to the Army's new Ft. Massachusetts, Gunnison also explored southeast of the pass. Other possible routes into the San Luis Valley were surveyed before they left the area, but Sangre de Cristo was the only pass recommended by Gunnison for a railroad.

The third explorer in 1853 was John Charles Fremont. He was now 40 years old, leading his fifth expedition, a party of 21 men. They crossed Sangre de Cristo Pass in December without incident. Fremont's father-in-law, Senator Benton, was still very interested in the region. He wrote to the editors of the *National Intelligencer,* on July 26, 1853: "Fort Massachusetts is a new fort established two years ago at the creek Trinchera, in the valley of San Luis, nearly opposite the Pass of El Sangre de Cristo. . . ."

The survey parties' use of the pass confirms that the Taos Trail was

(Author's Collection)

Capt. John Gunnison, left, and John Charles Fremont both took exploration parties over Sangre de Cristo Pass in 1853. It was Fremont's fifth expedition through the Rockies; Gunnison was seeking a railroad route.

widely known and used.

At Christmastime in 1854, tragedy struck in a massacre of settlers at Pueblo along the Arkansas River. Utes were retaliating for the death of several Indians who died from smallpox. Farm plazas at Pueblo, and on the St. Charles and Huerfano rivers were attacked. Just after the first of the new year, J.W. Atwood, John Jurnegan and Gunnison's guide, Marcelino Baca, set out for Sangre de Cristo Pass and New Mexico to summon help. Immediately the commanders at Ft. Union, Ft. Marcy at Santa Fe, the camp at Taos, and Ft. Massachusetts began secret preparations for an all-out campaign in the spring against the Utes and their supposed allies, the Jicarilla Apaches.

Under the command of Col. Thomas Fauntleroy of Ft. Massachusetts and guided by Kit Carson, the Army attacked Indian encampments on Cochetopa Pass, Poncha Pass, and across the Sangre de Cristo onto the plains. The Utes surrendered in the summer. In the short period of two years, the pass was used by the Army for both peaceful and warring expeditions.

In 1858, Ft. Massachusetts was renamed Ft. Garland and relocated to the northern end of the San Luis Valley and the western entrance to the pass. A Colonel Francisco, an Army sutler, used the pass numerous times on business trips to Colorado City, Denver, and Pueblo, between 1856 and the early 1860s.

Albert D. Richardson crossed Sangre de Cristo Pass on Oct. 27 and 28, 1859, with his pony, Liliput. He later printed his thoughts of the West, maintaining that travel on the Taos Trail was safe, even for a man traveling alone, in his book *Beyond the Mississippi.* (However, a record of the area noted the death of an American on Oak Creek, killed at the hands of an early-day bandit, in July 1859.)

At Santa Fe, Richardson met up with Kit Carson. Together they rode to Taos, then Richardson continued alone across the pass. His book gives an interesting account of crossing the pass.

In early 1860, prospecting interest was stirring in the San Juan Mountains. Many notable pioneer names were prominent in a migration from Denver to the new mining area. That year, Sarah Chivington, daughter of the recently arrived Methodist clergyman, the Rev. John M. Chivington, married "Noisy" Tom Pollock, erstwhile executioner of pioneer Denver. The newly wedded Pollocks started for the San Juans, presumably traveling along with a wagon party headed up by Stephen B. Kellogg. The party had 11 sturdy wagons, each with either six or eight yoke of oxen. They went by way of Colorado City and Pueblo, then across Sangre de Cristo Pass. This passage, difficult at any time, was doubly treacherous under the added hardships incurred in a December ascent. The necessity of road building in places and a lack of forage for their stock were among the difficulties encountered in the 14 days required to cross.

The streams were frozen, forage was scarce, and the roadway had to be hacked out of the frozen ground to accommodate heavily laden wagons. Trees had to be cut to furnish browse for the cattle, which had to be guarded day and night to keep them from straying or stampeding. The draft animals were fed bread moistened with snow. The Pollocks finally reached the Silverton area by April.

In 1861, Charles Baker and other mining parties used the pass to go to the San Juans. These miners used the customary route, down the east side of the Front Range to the Huerfano, across Sangre de Cristo Pass, and on through the San Luis Valley. The Baker group encountered so much snow on the pass that they were forced to cut trees to supply food for their stock. Still they lost 12 yoke of oxen.

Through the first half of the nineteenth century the Sangre de Cristo area had become increasingly well traveled. Word of the Taos Trail and Sangre de Cristo Pass had spread to Denver.

On March 19, 1861, a military express from Santa Fe brought a March 9 edition of the *Santa Fe Express* to Denver in just 10 days, instead of the usual 40 the postal service needed to go to Missouri, then to Denver on the Platte River route. Faster delivery of newspapers was a boon to an editor, and the greatly shortened time was a convenience to people along the route from Denver to "the Mexican towns." The Denver express came up through Ft. Union and Ft. Wise. Another route went eastward over Sangre de Cristo Pass from Ft. Garland to Cañon City, where it made weekly connection with a private pony express link to Denver.

The Civil War touched Colorado and Sangre de Cristo Pass. A group of new Colorado Volunteers marched from Cañon City to be mustered in at Ft. Garland in December 1861. Their forced march through the winter snow was made to allow them to participate in the Civil War battle at Glorieta Pass (New Mexico) against the Confederate invasion from Texas, in March 1862.

Captain Dodds' Independent Company left Cañon City on Dec. 7, 1861, marching 110 miles to Ft. Garland via Sangre de Cristo Pass. Later, as Company A of the Second Colorado Infantry, they proceeded to New Mexico and on Feb. 21, 1862, they fought in the battle of

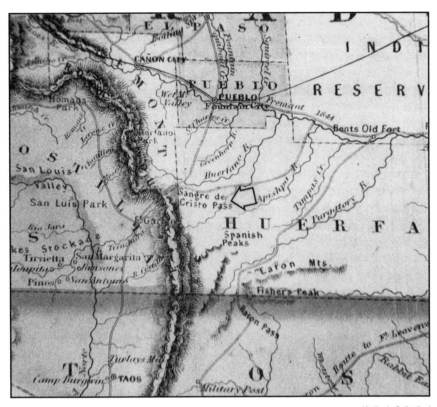

Sangre de Cristo Pass appears (arrow) on 1864 Johnson and Ward map.

Valverde under Col. Edward R.S. Canby against Southern forces commanded by Col. Henry H. Sibley.

Capt. Jim Ford's Independent Company left Cañon City on Dec. 12, and arrived at Ft. Garland Dec. 21, 1861. As Company B, it set out for Santa Fe, breaking snow a great part of the distance, and joined the garrison at Ft. Union.

Some miners on their way to the San Juans must have decided to prospect the Sangre de Cristo Range and surrounding areas. U.S. Surveyor General Case wrote on Dec. 12, 1863, "The Baca Grant No. 4 is located on the great line of travel between Denver and Santa Fe, and thousands of experienced miners have been traveling over the Sangre de Cristo, and have found no gold or other valuable minerals."

One of the few examples of crime on the pass is part of the Espinosa (or Espinoza) family story. In 1863 a series of crimes was committed by members of the Espinosa family against their enemies-at-large, newcomers into the Colorado Territory. One brother (his name may have been either Vivian or Felipio Nerio), murdered a man in Conejos. After a short stay with his family, he set out again, accompanied by a young nephew, toward Sangre de Cristo Pass, with a plan to ambush Gov. John Evans who had been in Conejos to meet with the Utes. The men were unsuccessful in attacking the Evans party. However, they did strike out at a man named Philbrook and a Mexican woman on the pass. The outlaws killed the mule team and captured the woman but the man escaped and walked to Ft. Garland to report the crime. One of the Espinosas was later killed near La Veta Pass.

In 1866 William (also called One-Arm) Jones procured a contract to transport mail weekly from Pueblo to Santa Fe by way of the mountain route, over Sangre de Cristo Pass and through the San Luis Valley. The points to be served en route by his two-mule buckboards (for mail, express freight, and passengers) were south from Pueblo to the settlement on the St. Charles River (called Rio San Carlos) and Hermosilla on the Huerfano River; from there they went west over the pass to Ft. Garland in the San Luis Valley. Jones publicized that his route was 150 miles and two days shorter than any other line. The Barlow and Sanderson route of that day went roundabout by way of Bent's Old Fort, 137 miles farther, according to distances published in Denver papers.

A *Rocky Mountain News* article on March 23, 1867, reported that the spring snow was much deeper than in other years and mule or wagon trains suffered severely and were compelled to put back. Fires and shovels were used to try to open passage for the wagons. Only pack animals could get through. The article indicated acceptance of the pass as a "regular route."

This period of history of the pass is represented by its use as a regular supply route to the San Juans, although the days of favor for the Sangre de Cristo route were fading. La Veta Pass was now under consideration for the Denver & Rio Grande Railway. Although Sangre de Cristo Pass remained the main route for mail, express, and passengers, interest was diverted as a shorter, more rugged toll road was built over Mosca Pass. The Denver and Santa Fe Stage Lines owned by Billy Jones ran until 1870 when Barlow and Sanderson bought the line and operated it for several years until the railroad over La Veta Pass gained prominence.

A popular route to the San Juans in the early 1870s involved taking the Rio Grande railroad from Denver to Colorado Springs. At this point the traveler was obliged to obtain his own conveyance, since there was no public transportation from there into the San Luis Valley. One road led through the Sangre de Cristo Pass and struck the valley at Ft. Garland.

Charles Richardson, a civil and mining engineer from Central City, reached Sangre de Cristo Pass just after noon on Oct. 3, 1872. He noted the magnificent views, brown sand-rippled formations, but saw no fossils. He sketched a view of the top of the pass, with the building he called the "Summit House." He visited with other travelers while staying overnight at the Summit House. Another traveler was from Cañon City, one from Pueblo, one from Chicago. His notes tell of a horse thief who had been tracked to the area, and his pending arrest.

The Army Corps of Engineers sent Lt. E.H. Ruffner and his expedition to the area in the summer of 1873. They noted in August that other passes in the vicinity are lower and far better suited for a wagon road to Ft. Garland than the Sangre de Cristo Pass, over which the road now passes.

Ruffner's report described the approach to Sangre de Cristo Pass, giving exact mileages.

> No profile was obtained of this pass, but others sufficiently demonstrate its uselessness as a railroad pass. For a wagon road between Pueblo and Ft. Garland, it is the most direct pass that can be obtained, and for that reason will probably not be abandoned for a lower route. . . . The best grade to be obtained, in the eastern ascent of the pass, is not less than 6 in 100 for certain distances of one-third of a mile, and it must be blocked by snow for a long season; otherwise, it presents no obstacles to a good wagon road; in fact, such a road already exists . . . and is in fair condition.

George M. Wheeler was the next widely known explorer to lead a government party over the pass. He was followed by a group assigned by Ferdinand V. Hayden. This U.S. Geographical and Geologic Survey party consisted of A.D. Wilson, Franklin Rhoda, and Frederich M. Endlich, constituting the southern or first division of Hayden's survey. They crossed the pass early in the summer of 1875.

The author of the "From the San Juan Country" column in the March 11, 1874, *Rocky Mountain News* reported a triweekly stage running from Pueblo to Del Norte.

> The morning I took transportation in one of these prairie schooners there were seven more passengers bound for Del Norte. . . . Two days later we reached Badito and as it was almost impossible to cross the range, must layover two or three days. . . . Snow lay 10 to 15 feet deep in places when we

finally started out. The pass is by no means easily traveled in summer and during winter it is as rough as going up a ladder feet first. I merely give an account of this in justice to the traveling public.

Alonzo Hubbard, a farmer, teamster, and businessman from Illinois, arrived in the San Luis Valley in 1874, by way of the Sangre de Cristo Pass road which now had a stage coming and going—with the help of the passengers, who usually had to push. It took his group four days, April 14 to 17, to travel from Badito to the summit and down to the Trinchera; a spring snow caught them just before they attained the summit.

The next March, Hubbard brought his family out to his new home. In writing down memories of the trip, a daughter related the story of crossing the pass.

> We caught up with a heavily loaded mule wagon train climbing the steep grades with a great deal of cracking of whips and other noise. A young bride, who, with her husband, was traveling with them, joined my mother and I who were walking. This was her first experience "roughing it" and she had been crying at the way they were beating the mules.

Lewis Barnum, the Pueblo superintendent of Barlow and Sanderson Stage Lines, died suddenly in January 1876, from pneumonia, at the Summit House atop Sangre de Cristo Pass. He had been at the pass working out preliminary plans for a stage route from the Huerfano River, by way of Badito, over Sangre de Cristo and across the San Luis Valley to the San Juans.

In 1877 the *Atlas of Colorado* was published. Among the roads shown in the atlas was one running 300 miles from civilization at Pueblo across Sangre de Cristo Pass and the San Luis Valley, then up the Rio Grande to a new silver camp in the San Juan Mountains, called Silverton.

In 1877 and 1878, the railroad was built over La Veta Pass. A group headed by railroad builder William Jackson Palmer decided to use the west side of Sangre de Cristo Pass as the west slope of the rail lines. However, in 1880 the railroad crossed over Raton Pass, making travel from the Front Range into New Mexico much easier. Sangre de Cristo Pass fell into disuse.

A March 1892 (reprinted 1920) Huerfano Park topographic map shows the trail over Sangre de Cristo Pass with a double solid-line designation to indicate a wagon road still existed at that time.

In March 1927, cowboys and ranchers used the pass to move cattle from winter range on the east slope, up and over Sangre de Cristo to summer range in the higher country near Alamosa. They did not find it a hard climb; they opened gates to get across the country and were able to travel more than 50 miles a day.

In the 1930s, Dr. LeRoy Hafen, accompanied by other historians, located possible remains of the old Spanish fort built on the pass. They felt the remains to be those of a corral. There was evidence the site had been ransacked by treasure and relic hunters prior to their arrival. They found several mounds which could have been graves, but they did no excavating. Later that decade, the Right Rev. Howard Delaney spent some time actively searching for the ruins. He noted that wagon ruts were still plainly evident from the air.

One legend has it that Spanish gold is buried near the site. Supposedly an early resident, when he needed money, would show up in stores at Gardner and offer as payment for goods, an eight-sided Spanish gold piece. The story was that this old man had found a cache of these coins inside the walls of the old fort or near it.

San Luis Valley historians searched out the pass in July 1968. They drove to North La Veta Pass, parked near some aspen trees, and climbed the hill toward where Sangre de Cristo Pass should be, judging by two maps—Hayden's 1877 and the Rio Grande National Forest of 1947. They found the old road. The panorama from the pass ridge was surprisingly open down to the High Plains to the northeast. It seemed a shockingly easy pass. Later the same year, members of the Huerfano County Historical Society and friends visited the pass and trail. They decided to investigate the route, to check mileages and sites in old records. This preliminary work led to an expedition of the San Luis Historical Society in 1972. This group was successful in putting together a "Taos Trail Walk." On June 25 that year, approximately 90 people walked the parts of the trails that were still accessible, in order to appreciate the ancient route.

In August 1990, the author visited the pass after obtaining permission from Forbes Ranch personnel. Various trails still exist in the summit area. Indications are that pass traffic followed a couple of different routes during the period of its heaviest use, although both routes cross the saddle within 200 yards of each other. The older and now unused trail drops from the pass, then makes a steep ascent of an adjacent ridge where it meets the newer trail. The new trail follows the ridge contours and shows modern use, probably for cattle movement. The point where the two trails meet provides scenic views to the north and east. Badito Cone and Huerfano Butte may be seen from this spot.

It is possible to get fairly close to the summit of the pass by using public roads. The east side of the pass can be ascended by taking ranch roads which run some miles up Oak Creek from Badito Cone. The west side of North La Veta Pass follows the old Sangre de Cristo Pass trail. Take the Pass Creek Pass road, just to the west, to visit some of the same ridge terrain as that of Sangre de Cristo Pass.

The old pass road is visible only as faint ruts on various parcels of fenced-off private land. Near the top of North La Veta Pass, on the west side, look to the north to see the old trail as it runs up the hill and down the valley. These ruts should be marked and preserved. Their history represents nearly a century or more of travel *before* the Santa Fe Trail. Sangre de Cristo Pass, though now nearly forgotten, is the true "old pass" of Colorado.

Sources and References

Bartlett, Richard A. "The Great Surveys in Colorado 1867-1879." Ph.D. diss., 1953.

Bean, Luther E. "Land of the Blue Sky People." *Monte Vista Journal*, Monte Vista, Colo., 1962.

Brown, Robert L. *An Empire of Silver*. Denver: Sundance Press, 1984.

Carhart, Arthur H. "Passes Over the Blood of Christ" from *Denver Westerners Brand Book*. Vol. XIII, 1957.

Colville, Ruth Marie. "The Sangre de Cristo Trail" from *The San Luis Valley Historian*. Vol. IV. No. 1, Winter 1972.

Conard, Howard Louis. *"Uncle Dick" Wootton—The Pioneer Frontiersman of the Rocky Mountain Region*. Chicago: W.E. Dibble & Co., 1890.

Cragin, Francis Whittemore. "Early Far West Notebook," November 1907.

LeCompte, Janet. *Essays & Monographs in Colorado History No. 6*. Denver: Colorado Historical Society, 1987.

LeCompte, Janet. *Pueblo, Hardscrabble, Greenhorn—The Upper Arkansas 1832-1856*. Norman: Univ. of Oklahoma Press, 1978.

Richardson, Charles S., civil and mining engineer of Central City, Colo., "Notebook No. 15," Oct. 3, 1872.

Rocky Mountain News. Denver, March 23, 1867.

Ibid., March 11, 1874.

Ibid., Dec. 1, 1875.

Ibid., Jan. 22, 1967.

Ruffner, Lt. E.H. U.S. Army Corps of Engineers, War Dept. *Report of a Reconnaissance in the Ute Country Made in the Year 1873*. Wash., D.C.: Government Printing Office, 1874.

Ruxton, George Frederick. *Wild Life in the Rocky Mountains*. New York: MacMillan Co., 1926.

Schiel, Jacob H. *Journey Through the Rocky Mountains and the Humboldt Mountains to the Pacific Ocean*. Norman: Univ. of Oklahoma Press, 1969.

Simmons, Virginia McConnell. *San Luis Valley*. Boulder, Colo.: Pruett Publishing Co., 1985.

Sprague, Marshall. *The Great Gates*. Lincoln: Univ. of Nebraska Press, 1964.

Taylor, Morris F. *First Mail West*. Albuquerque: Univ. of New Mexico Press, 1971.

About the Author

Edward S. Helmuth's interest in Colorado's mountain passes led to his paper, "Sangre de Cristo: Colorado's Forgotten Pass."

A native of Ohio, Ed worked for Marathon Oil Co. as an engineer/scientist for 30 years. He retired early in 1991 and, coincidentally, became a member of the Denver Posse of the Westerners. He was drawn to Colorado after a 1956 visit, but his interest in the state's history began in earnest in the early 1980s when he and his wife Gloria started a project of cataloging and visiting the mountain passes within Colorado. This project has led to extensive research of pass origins and uses. The culmination of the Helmuths' project has been publication of their book, *The Passes of Colorado* (Pruett Publishing, Boulder, Colo., 1994). Ed's research resulted in his paper on Sangre de Cristo Pass, one of Colorado's earliest used trails. He presented a paper on the subject for the Denver Westerners in October 1990.

Ed has begun working with the United States Geological Survey Board on Geographic Names to obtain recognition for many of the Colorado passes not yet officially designated.

Ed Helmuth holds a Business Statistics Bachelor of Science degree from University of Colorado and a Masters in Business Administration from Bowling Green State University (Ohio). He has been a member of the Society of Petroleum Engineers and has had papers published by the SPE.

In addition to the Denver Posse of the Westerners, Ed belongs to the Pikes Peak Posse, Colorado Springs; the Colorado Historical Society; and The Prospectors, a Chaffee County historical research group. He also participates in outdoor-oriented local groups, such as Audubon 62 Society and Trout Unlimited.

Ed and Gloria have two children: Ron Helmuth of Denver (along with two grandsons), and Kim Zehender of St. Croix, USVI.

"Emigrants Approaching South Pass," *Western Museum Laboratory, National Park Service*

Seeing the Elephant

By Merrill J. Mattes

*T*HE ELEPHANT WE ARE talking about is not the Indian elephant of your favorite zoo, or the rampaging African elephant which is becoming an endangered species. Neither is it the enormous but long-extinct mastodon or mammoth which roamed Nebraska in Pleistocene times. We are talking about a mythical Elephant which loomed very large in the minds of men and women who crossed the continent in covered wagons 100 years ago. Those who "saw the elephant," to use their own expression, were those who had been eyewitnesses to the hardships, dangers, and disasters of this 2,000-mile crossing and survived the rigors of the Nebraska-Wyoming-Utah-Nevada wilderness to become the exclusive fraternity of California pioneers.

I have yet to find a satisfactory explanation for the origin of the elephant metaphor which is so entangled with the great epic of the Gold Rush. Elephants appeared first in circuses in America in the 1840s and proved to be, along with flame-swallowers, leopard ladies, and dancing bears, one of the marvels of the age. Presumably because the strange giant was also conceived as deceptively sinister, capable of rampage, in frontier newspapers and gold-rush diaries, "seeing the elephant" became synonymous with the perilous crossing of the continent. Make note of the fact that this fantastic Elephant was not your everyday chained, placid, swaying behemoth pleading for peanuts. The scourge of the California Gold Rush was a fierce, threatening beast of gargantuan proportions who was apt to materialize every time danger threatened or disaster pounced. Thus we find expressions like, "I think I saw the tracks of the big elephant," or "the elephant must be in the neighborhood." One emigrant said that he "had seen the elephant and eaten its ears." Others felt "the brush of the elephant's tail" or "had a peep at his proboscis."

The trick was, having seen him or felt his hot breath, to get safely past him to the golden land where, promoters promised, nuggets lay on the ground in profusion to be had for the taking.

The main habitat of the Elephant in question was Nebraska where he haunted the Old Oregon Trail which in 1849 became the California Road. This followed both sides of the Platte River from Ft. Kearny after the several strands of migration came together from Kansas City, St. Joseph, and Council Bluffs. In 1854 Omaha first appeared on the map, the result of opening Indian Territory to settlement, as the geographic twin of Council Bluffs, and thus figured belatedly in the Gold Rush. Ft. Laramie on the North Platte, referred to often herein, was the great way-station of the trail, about 300 miles west of Ft. Kearny, and about 300 miles inside the present State of Wyoming.

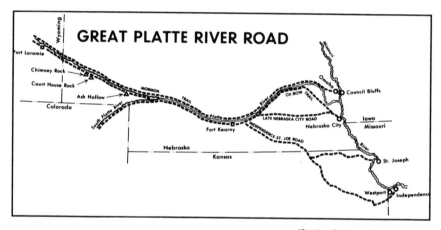

(Courtesy Nebraska Historical Society)
Oregon Trail routes started from at least four different cities.

In 1969, 100 years after the completion of the Union Pacific Railroad which marked the demise of the overland wagon trails, the Nebraska State Historical Society published my book, *The Great Platte River Road*, which was intended to contribute to the literature of the migration in two important ways. First, as the title suggests, it attempted to alleviate the confusion about all the trails that at various times followed the Platte River westward, by lumping them all together, geographically, and chronologically under one inclusive term. That this effort succeeded is apparent from the widespread use of this term today in signs, maps, and new publications.

Secondly, this was the first time any effort had been made to assemble all known overland journals and to collate them so that the data they revealed could be used comparatively—both horizontally along the trail, and vertically in an effort to construct a social history of the covered-wagon migrations. The success of this effort has been demonstrated by the considerable number of imitations of this book published by others since 1969.

Now, getting back to the "Elephants of the Platte," what were the various kinds of hazards which confronted the argonauts who collectively induced the frightening apparition of a gigantic beast on the horizon, which sometimes, indeed did destroy the frightened beholder? Countless graves along the Platte River testify to the fact that the overland crossing was in fact not a light-hearted adventure, but a grim running battle for survival. I conceive "the Elephant" as a psychological phenomenon, a focal image of collective troubles seen and unseen which enabled the traveler to confront the fears engendered by a strange, hostile environment. If he could give his fears a tangible identity, he could somehow cope—with bravado, with humor, or at least with resignation.

We can't review the whole catalog of emigrant adversity, but we can look briefly at some of the more common experiences, distilled from firsthand eyewitness reports of more than 800 travelers who wrote letters or diaries, or left reminiscences of their epic journeys. If I were required to categorize these misadventures—the Elephant's bag of dirty tricks—I would list Indians, Exhaustion, Antagonisms, Accidents, and Disease in ascending order of statistical severity.

Indians! We can imagine only faintly the fear that literary propaganda about the aborigines inspired in the covered-wagon communities. At the outset of the journey, at the jumping-off places, the emigrants visualized them as their Number One menace. Now it is true that an occasional straggler was victimized by a band of renegade Sioux or Pawnee braves. We have the dubious legend that Rawhide Creek got its name from a white man being skinned alive by natives in revenge for having wronged a tribal maiden. Actual attacks on emigrant trains in Hollywood-style corral formation were not unheard of but proven instances of such happenings are rare. The typical emigrant probably saw a few bedraggled Indians hanging around Ft. Kearny or Ft. Laramie or sometimes begging for handouts along the trail. There are at least two known instances of a chief offering to swap horses for an intriguingly blonde wife or daughter. Sometimes emigrants witnessed Indian bands stalking or fighting each other, but their fear for their own scalps was largely misplaced. The Elephant had other forms of mischief in mind.

A more deadly though less romantic danger was simple physical and mental exhaustion, something difficult to appreciate by we who

(Photo by Author)

Deeply eroded wagon wheel ruts scar the terrain on old Oregon Trail route across the North Platte River from Guernsey, Wyo.

can fly from Omaha to San Francisco in three hours, or drive comfortably in three days in contrast to the four or five months it took to escort stubborn or fractious oxen or mules drawing a clumsy wagon over virgin terrain—prairie rutted with buffalo tracks, draggy sandy soil, all uphill to the Continental Divide, then mountains, canyons, and burning deserts.

Much of the curse of primitive travel was the result of overly optimistic planning. Anticipated grass for the animals rapidly disappeared through drought and over-grazing. Game, scattered by the advancing hordes, was much scarcer than advertised. The teams couldn't pull the ridiculously overloaded wagons and the trail was strewn with jettisoned furniture, heirlooms, tools, anvils, mining machinery, and even precious food supplies. There were reports of flour, bacon, and sugar in great quantities abandoned to the wolves or to the grateful Pawnee. At Ft. Laramie it was commonplace to reduce wagons to handier size, or abandon wheels altogether in favor of pack trains, but too often these radical adjustments came too late, starving animals sickened and died, and more physical labor was heaped upon human survivors. The Mormons, with their famous handcarts, were the only companies who started out deliberately with the idea of human beings propelling their own freight; but others later fell in with the practice out of sheer brutal necessity.

Exhaustion led to frayed nerves and "wagon fever," that is, cabin fever on wheels. People who normally got along famously would quarrel over trivia. Husbands and wives, though circumstances prevented their legal separation, might not speak to each other clear across the continent. Sworn buddies would get mad, split their stock and provisions, and sometimes cut their wagon in half to make two carts, to avoid each other's company. Often peaceful coexistence was impossible and the result was assault and murder. I was amazed to learn about the number of homicides along the trail, sometimes followed by drumhead courts-martial and judicial lynching. A few miles west of Omaha a chance teenager was hanged for an axe murder committed by others. Near Green River a man was hanged from a gallows formed by two upturned wagon tongues for shooting another for molesting his wife. Near Chimney Rock a duel inspired by Demon Rum led to the knife killing of both antagonists and a common grave.

The Elephant thus assumed forms of hostility undreamed of by the emigrants when they first assembled their trains at the Missouri River. But his stock in trade took more predictable forms—accident and disease.

The safety record of the Great Migration was atrocious. The thousands of cripplings and deaths that resulted from simple violations of common sense are appalling. The most common cause of fatal accidents was the misuse of firearms, brought along in the first place to hunt buffalo (in decreasing supply after 1849), or to ward off the Indians who proved to be relatively peaceful. The arsenal of muskets, derringers, and pistols that was standard equipment for every train had few safety devices and evidently many amateur frontiersmen didn't know how to use them. Carelessness in handling the weapons, while in target practice or just showing off, resulted in a statistical massacre. More gravestone inscriptions told a sad story of companions, relatives or other innocent bystanders getting blasted by misfired guns than by any cause other than disease. Even trained soldiers heading west were not immune to this epidemic. At Scotts Bluff one Private Roby was buried after enduring nameless agonies from a gunshot wound accidentally inflicted upon himself instead of upon the antelope he had in mind.

Probably next in order of accidental death, was drownings. This factor is understandable enough. Since there were no roads there were no bridges. Every stream had to be crossed, whether the merest trickle or medium-sized stream like the Blue River, or an implacable torrent like the Platte itself in spring flood. This meant plunging in and getting wet and cold and exhausted, swimming your family, your stock, your wagons, and all your earthly possessions across to the other side. How often when I have zipped over the Platte on Interstate 80 have I marvelled that so many of our ancestors did cross safely under such shattering circumstances. Those who survived were revived, as often as not, with a jug of corn liquor. Those who did not, floated out of sight or were retrieved and buried on the melancholy shore.

There were, of course, other ways of committing self-destruction. Among recurring methods of record were falling under and getting crushed by the big ponderous wagon wheels, getting stomped by ornery horses or mules, or gored by oxen, or trampled by stampeding buffalo. When you were out in the open for several months on end, you were subject to vicissitudes of the weather, which included howling winds that upset wagons, blinding duststorms, deluges of rain that spoiled provisions and mired wagons, and hail that could kill and maim.

But the Elephant's secret weapon was Disease. This champion killer of them all was as relentless as it was invisible. For every accident or homicide victim, ten were laid low by organisms not yet exposed by microscope or challenged by effective medicine. From all causes, but mainly from disease, I calculate that during the 25-year migration period—1841 to 1866—there were some 20,000 deaths out of an estimated 350,000 emigrants up the Platte, or a ratio of one out of 17. Thus across the continent graves would average 10 to a mile, but in western Nebraska where the epidemics reached their climax, the ratio would have been greater. It is possible that more than 5,000, or one-fourth of the total, may have died between Ft. Kearny and Ft. Laramie in the three principal migration years, 1849-1852.

Dr. Tompkins, an emigrant of 1850, attributed the widespread contagion to camp food, "indigestible filth too crude even for the stomach of an ostrich, chilly night watches, sleeping on cold, wet ground, and the constant hard and exhausting toil." As early as 1846 an Oregon traveler said he was "unwell since coming upon the waters of the Nebraska, owing to mixed salts, alum, and magnesia." Among

(From Author's Collection)

Alcove Spring, painted by Dan Jacobson, was a heavily used campsite on
the Oregon Trail north of Blue Rapids, Kans. Rocks near the spring bear
initials and dates as early as 1846.

other villains most often accused were boiled beans, rancid bacon,
buffalo meat eaten right after a chase, lack of vegetables, and the all-
pervading lung-choking dust.

During the Gold Rush, vaccination was not unknown but it was
rarely practiced. The normal precaution was to take along a medicine
chest with an assortment of trusted home remedies for everything from
baldness to bubonic plague. Elizabeth Geer's inventory included "a
box of physicking pills, a box of castor oil, a quart of best rum, and a
vial of peppermint essence." The latter ingredient, combined with a
glass of brandy, would, according to John King, cure most ills. Another emigrant lady's portable apothecary included quinine for malaria, hartshorn for snakebite, citric acid for scurvy, and opium and
whiskey for everything else. Laudanum, morphine, calomel, and tinc-
ture of camphor were other potent drugs mentioned in the journals
which, doubtless, would do wonders for the symptoms if not for the
malady!

If you were a consumptive, it seems that Fate offered no middle ground: either you died before you reached the Platte or your stroll across the continent was so invigorating that you recovered and reached California in mint condition. Among other identifiable afflictions were whooping cough, measles, mumps, smallpox and malaria, usually called "fever and ague." So-called lung fever was presumably another name for pneumonia. "Bilious complaint" and "summer complaint" were evidently pseudonyms for diarrhea, the commonplace result of drinking the turbid waters of the Platte, or from shallow wells dug along its margin. "Mountain sickness," to judge from its symptoms, was probably scurvy resulting from a badly unbalanced diet.

Other routine complaints included rheumatism and toothache, the latter sometimes relieved by opium or amateur extractions. We encounter reports also of exotic illnesses, like delirium tremens, hydrophobia, bloody flux, and vertigo. But all of these ailments pale into insignificance beside the Asiatic cholera which raged along the Platte during the climax years of the Gold Rush. Brought to the seaport of New Orleans by ship rats, the epidemic arrived at the jumping-off places via Mississippi and Missouri river steamboats. It was the prime killer of emigrants; in the estimate of one journalist, "the Gold Rush caused more bereaved that the late Mexican War." Wrote another of the 1849 exodus, "The road from Independence to Ft. Laramie was a graveyard." In 1850 there are instances of children orphaned or entire families wiped out, leaving their prairie schooners adrift like derelict ships on the ocean.

In 1849 and 1850 the plague was evidently more severe on the south side of the Platte—the main California Road—and many escaped it by making early crossings. In 1852, however, it jumped to the north side. Ezra Meeker, who started from Omaha, found the north side healthful enough until opposite Ft. Kearny. Here he writes, "the epidemic struck our moving column where the throngs from the south side began crossing." From that point on, Meeker continues, it looked like a battlefield, with the dead laid out in rows.

A respectable number of medical doctors joined the Gold Rush. Many large trains made a point of having a doctor or surgeon along, and many of them kept journals. My favorite Gold Rush doctors are Dr. Israel Lord of New York and Dr. Reuben Knox of North Carolina, both of the 1850 migration, who not only kept meticulous diaries, but were tireless in their efforts to relieve the afflicted, including those of companies other than their own. Some like Dr. Caldwell, themselves, succumbed to the plague. While some doctors were saints and

(Painting by Vernon Demars, Scott's Bluff National Monument)
Emigrant train across the North Platte from Chimney Rock travels through Western Nebraska.

others were martyrs, there were also a few quacks. Two lady emigrants complained about a practice they deemed unethical; physicians painting signs on rocks or gravestones to advertise their services. Evidently for them the Gold Rush began before reaching California!

For the deceased, funeral services, if any, were a matter of chance. If you were fortunate enough to die during the first few weeks out, there might be trees available to construct a coffin and the observances would be well attended with all the ceremonial trimmings. However, as the migration moved along the Platte and emigrants began to die in wholesale lots, the spirit of gloom gave way to panic with the realization that members of laggard trains might starve or freeze to death in the Sierra Nevadas, like the Donner party in 1846, or the handcart people in 1856, with overtones of cannibalism. So burials and services came to be performed perfunctorily, sometimes with indecent haste. Sometimes a company would encamp waiting for a stricken member to die; more often he or she would be carried along in the wagon, suffering with every jolt until death mercifully intervened. Some trains moved on but left "watchers" to wait for the end and provide burial; but others simply abandoned hopeless cases by the roadside. According to one observer, "some were buried before life was extinct." Thus the emigration produced a numbing process of dehumanization, and the evil pachyderm which haunted the pilgrims must have bellowed in triumph.

If 5,000 died between Ft. Kearny and Laramie and gravestones became the highway markers of the Great Platte River Road, why can so few emigrant graves be identified today? Well, with scarce trees so precious for firewood or spare wagon parts, coffins were quite out of the question. The dear departed were hastily buried in shallow graves, and these were promptly ravished by wolves and coyotes, who displayed scant respect for the mortal remains. So prevalent were these ghoulish scavengers that one emigrant reported the disruption of a funeral service by converging coyotes, howling dismally as they impatiently waited for the train to move on. Counter-measures to protect loved ones with enclosing rock slabs proved of little avail. The ravenous prairie creatures simply tunneled their way to their objective.

Knowing that the Indians also robbed graves, survivors sometimes made efforts to conceal rather than mark them, by driving back and forth over the spot and replacing vegetation. When this ruse succeeded the deceased may have been preserved but his last resting place was forever lost to posterity. One emigrant also understood that some compatriots dug graves which were actually caches of goods, including casks of rum and brandy, for future reference! With most graves too shallow and destroyed by animals, some deliberately concealed, and some faked—-not to mention those obliterated by cultivation and road construction—it is small wonder that only a few identifiable emigrant graves survive today to remind us of the Gold Rush calamity. It seems that the rampaging Elephant is guilty not only of death and destruction on an epic scale, but of covering his tracks and disappearing into the historical woodwork like a Nazi war criminal.

Lest this recital of emigrant woes seems unduly morbid I would like to end on a cheerful note. Consider that if one of 17 emigrants died, and perhaps 10 percent of all who started changed their minds and returned home, then at least 85 percent made it to their destination.

The cholera was a sometime thing, which skipped around like lightning, and suddenly disappeared. Children were orphaned, but they themselves often seemed immune. West of Ft. Laramie the epidemic, for reasons unknown, seemed to disappear.

(W.H. Jackson sketch, Scott's Bluff National Monument)

Emigrant wagons line up for ferrying across the Missouri River (Big Muddy) at Kanesville Crossing near present Council Bluffs, Iowa.

Despite the hazards, life went on. People got married along the trail, though rarely enough, since men heavily outnumbered women during the Gold Rush. I think of two teenagers, at the Forks of the Platte in 1842, hitched by Parson Ezekiel Williams for the purpose—as he phrases it—of saving their immortal souls. And I think also of the young clerk at the Sutlers Store at Ft. Laramie who, in 1852, eloped with a girl from a Mormon train, escaping the wrath of relatives by blending into the landscape with friendly Indians.

People died, but people also had babies on the trail, which means there were a lot of pregnant women among the optimists jumping off from the Missouri River. There were turnarounds, those of faint heart, but if there were any suicides among the emigrants because of their hard lot I have yet to find a clear-cut documented case.

Most emigrants proved to be as tough-minded as they were hard-muscled. At Ash Hollow one wrote of his company that, despite the afflictions of Job, "we were a jolly crowd and laughed heartily at each other's experiences." The biggest ally of morale perhaps was innate good health, often improved by the rugged life. Many discovered new horizons within themselves, and were inspired to write paeans of prose in their diaries. If there was grief, there was also the exhilaration of high animal spirits, which expressed itself in the ability of the emigrants to entertain themselves or to celebrate despite fatigue. Dancing and merrymaking around campfires are recorded, as well as more somber occasions. The Fourth of July, which for most emigrants occurred between Chimney Rock and South Pass, was almost certain to produce joyous patriotic festivity—oratory, marching, feasting and, if any whiskey was left after extensive use for alleged medical purposes, drinking patriotic toasts until, as one journalist confided, "all hands got gentlemanly tite," climaxing their observances by rolling a wagon off the top of a high bluff!

Religion was another positive force or antidote to Elephant fever, perhaps as important as good health and certainly, for some, as potent as medicinal spirits. The great majority of emigrants were devout Bible-readers and Sabbath-observers. Who can deny that their simple Christian faith played a powerful role in sustaining them during their long ordeal? Consider that it was this healthy majority of Gold Rush emigrants, plus those who survived the sea voyage around Cape Horn, who became the first to settle the Far West. Their gold fever was transmuted into the energy and vision that spanned the continent and laid the foundations of modern America.

Today we face new and frightening frontiers our forebears never dreamed of, dangers far more lethal and devastating than "the arrow that flieth by night, or the pestilence that wasteth at noon day." We would scoff at the mythical Elephant and imagine that we have achieved a level of scientific sophistication that makes such childish symbolism unnecessary. But what of the courage, the resilient spirit, the perseverance under mortal stress, faith in God and reliance on themselves rather than government to attain their goals? These attributes of the covered-wagon pioneers we must revive, cherish, and emulate. If we do not, our civilizations, like those of ancient Babylon, Carthage, and Rome, will surely collapse, its ruins swept into the trash heap of history!

About the Author

Merrill J. Mattes is Denver's "oldest Westerner," having joined the Denver Posse as a Corresponding Member in 1945 while stationed on his first job with the National Park Service as superintendent of Scotts Bluff National Monument in western Nebraska. Merrill learned about the Westerners from Denver bookseller Fred Rosenstock.

Merrill later helped to organize the Omaha Westerners while stationed there as Regional Historian. When later transferred to San Francisco, he helped to organize the San Francisco Westerners, becoming its first Sheriff. With his final transfer to NPS Denver Service Center as Chief of Historic Preservation, he quickly became a Posse Member of the Denver Westerners. In the *Buckskin Bulletin* of Westerners International, Merrill Mattes has been described as a "living legend."

During his 40 years as a historian with the NPS, Merrill was involved in historic park planning and preservation, at such sites as Ft. Laramie and Bent's Old Fort, but his keenest personal interest has been in the westward migrations up the Platte River Valley corridor to South Pass and beyond to Oregon and California.

While still residing in Nebraska, he published *The Great Platte River Road* with the Nebraska State Historical Society. The book is now in its fourth edition. Retired in 1975, and aided by a grant from the National Endowment for the Humanities, he wrote his research masterpiece, *Platte River Road Narratives* (University of Illinois Press, 1988), a virtual encyclopedia of all known westering emigrants who left records of their journeys. Both of his books received the Wrangler Award from the National Cowboy Hall of Fame in Oklahoma City.

His *Colter's Hell and Jackson's Hole* (Yellowstone Nature Association) is the classic early history of Yellowstone and Grand Teton National Parks.

His paper, "Seeing the Elephant," was presented originally as a talk on Oct. 6, 1978, at a banquet of radiologists in convention at the University of Nebraska Medical Center, Omaha.

"Racing at the Rendezvous" by *Delano*

"We Lived at Fort Laramie"
Interviews with Old-Timers

By David L. Hieb

*W*HILE SERVING AS superintendent of the then Fort Laramie National Monument from May 1947 to June 1958, both my office and our living quarters were in the only partially rehabilitated Cavalry Barracks built in 1875. From that vantage point we not only learned to appreciate the conditions which the military and other earlier occupants of the Fort had endured, but also found a unique opportunity to interview on the ground former military-period residents of the Fort and its environs. These we called Old-Timers.

Since the major roles of Ft. Laramie in the pageant of the West from 1834 to 1890 are well documented and have been the subjects of thousand of pages by historians from Parkman to Hebard to Hafen and Mattes, the products of Old-Timer interviews are largely sidelights on history. They are sidelights, however, which deepen our perspective and whet our appetites to more fully appreciate that history. In this case they also provided information essential to accurate restoration of military buildings at the Fort.

Aside from some Old-Timers who were still local residents and will be mentioned later, the most productive of our interviews was among the first. We will never forget the portly, but still active gentleman who arrived at the Fort in a red Buick convertible on July 24, 1948, and introduced himself as Col. Louis Brechemin Jr., U.S. Army retired. Colonel Brechemin had lived at Ft. Laramie as a boy of 8 to 12, from 1885 to 1889 while his father, Capt. Louis Brechemin, Seventh Infantry, was Assistant Surgeon, the ranking post and regimental medical officer of that period. Moreover, the colonel was blessed with an almost photographic memory of the scenes and events of his happy boyhood years at the Fort. Having duplicated his father's career as an Army medical officer, he had had lifelong contact with the families of the then tiny officer corps which no doubt added to his retention of facts and stories about Ft. Laramie.

Colonel Brechemin had come back to the scenes of his boyhood,

Louis Brechemin Jr. took violin lessons at Ft. Laramie, where he lived as a boy, age 8 to 12.

and he was in no hurry. Nearly every day for 10 days he returned to the Fort and we had time to go over every building and ruin on the grounds together, discussing details of each structure and its usage. He helped us work out a complete floor plan of the ruined hospital, noting specifically as a doctor, that no special operating room was provided. He indicated that surgery, such as it was, was performed in his father's office or on one of the beds in a ward. He corrected some current misinformation and provided other data about the Sutler's Store and the Officers' Club therein which were later followed almost to the letter in the structural restoration and refurbishing of that interesting multi-purpose structure.

The colonel soon became practically a member of our family. He amazed us by naming virtually every man, woman, child, horse, and dog in group pictures from the 1880s in our collection. Later, as we corresponded with him at his homes in Deer Harbor, Wash., and Belfast, Me., he sent us many more fine photographs to copy. One of these depicts a group of three officers' daughters (one being his teenage sister) and two handsome young lieutenants and a young rancher who he said were around together all the time, and were nicknamed "The Kindergarten."

During our conversations Colonel Brechemin often alluded to stories he remembered from his years at the Fort and which he said he would write up and send to us. Finally, more than two years later, two batches of them arrived and, with a minimum of editing, here are the best.

"Barney, or Horse Racing at Fort Laramie in 1885"

There was no circular racetrack at the Post. The races that year were straight, on the flat, about a quarter of a mile, with the start at the Stage Barn and the finish in front of the Rustic Hotel. One day that fall there were a number of scrub races there. It was payday and soldiers and cowboys were down there betting. Suddenly a queer-looking man drove up in a rickety wagon with a horse tied behind. It was a woebegone skate covered with mud and long hair.

This man got to arguing around the crowd and wanted to enter the horse in the next race. He was laughed at, but he bet that his horse would not come in last. He was taken up on that and then went around again betting that his horse would come in second. Finally he went around betting that his horse would come in first. He was taken

Three officers' daughters and two handsome lieutenants and a young cowboy made up this 1880s social group, which became known as "The Kindergarten."

up on many bets and put up his money. After the betting was completed he went to his wagon and gave the horse a bath and grooming. This revealed a beautiful chestnut sorrel race horse and a jockey saddle and bridle. He himself appeared in jockey silks of brilliant colors. The crowd was astonished and of course the stranger cleaned up in the race, winning all bets.

Mr. Eli Hall, manager of the Post Trader's interests, was among those who lost on the race, but he agreed to let the man quarter the horse "Barney" in Mr. London's stable in the back yard of the Post Trader's house. Mr. Hall lived in that yard in a small house. About midnight Mr. Hall was awakened by the stranger who said he had lost all his money in a poker game with some soldiers and wanted to borrow $500 leaving the horse Barney as security. Mr. Hall loaned the man the money and never saw him again. However, he had the horse and soon put him up in a raffle. Lt. Tommy Tompkins won the raffle and in a month or so put Barney up for another raffle and Mr. Hall won him back. My father also put up his horse Larry in a raffle and Mr. Hall won him too. By that time the Post was somewhat suspicious but nothing was proved. Barney won every race except one at Ft. Laramie. The exception was losing to a cowpuncher horse and Mr. Hall rode Barney. The whole Post blamed Mr. Hall for not picking a real jockey.

Around the Fort, Barney was frequently ridden by Neeley Williams, the daughter of Capt. Constant Williams, who married Louis Kittson, son of Commodore Kittson of St. Paul. They were married in the Burt house next to the Post Trader's Store by Dr. Rafter, the Episcopal minister from Cheyenne. Mrs. Kittson then laid siege to Mr. Hall to buy Barney and he was finally shipped to St. Paul.

Colonel Brechemin's next story he dates November 1885 and titles:

"The Lachlin-Flannery Fight"

I was 8 years old and walking from the London house towards the Store and saw two soldiers and a huge cowpuncher standing by the back yard gate. They were quarreling violently and the cowpuncher drew his Colt's revolver and threatened one of the soldiers. Just then Mr. London came up the walk from his house and stepped into the road. He called to them, "Boys, stop that quarreling." Al Lachlin, the cowpuncher, walked towards Mr. London putting his revolver back in its holster. As he continued toward the Store, Flannery, one of the soldiers, called after him, "I'm not afraid of your so and so revolver" and continued cursing him. Lachlin said nothing and went into the Store. Flannery and the other soldier, Clements, both of H Company, followed to the steps of the Post Office talking loudly.

Lieutenant Tompkins came by, heard the men talking and ordered Flannery to "Go to his quarters." Flannery started for his quarters and disappeared until Lieutenant Tompkins walked on. Then Flannery returned to the Post Office steps and was storming with Clements when Al Lachlin came out of the Store with a package of sugar. He stopped in front of the Post Office and Flannery insulted him again. Then Lachlin pulled out his revolver and struck Flannery over the head with it. Flannery jumped on him and they both fell over the dirt from a small ditch. Flannery captured the revolver and beat Lachlin over the head with it. Clements told Flannery to take the revolver to the commanding officer and they started up the officer's walk, but met Lieutenant Kendrick and gave the gun to him. Flannery came back and found Lachlin standing on the Store steps and started cussing him out again when Lachlin reached down and smashed him in the face. Flannery was up like a flash and after Lachlin, but the Sergeant of the Guard stopped him and Kendrick ordered Lachlin taken to the Guardhouse.

My father was called to the Guardhouse and he took Lachlin to the Hospital and stitched up his scalp, for the man was in pretty bad shape. Father also had to stitch up Flannery's scalp. We boys were horrified at the fight and so much bloodshed.

The next morning Lachlin's revolver was returned to him and he left the Post. My father sent a cowboy after him about 10 days later to tell him to come back and get the stitches taken out. Then father heard that Al had an infected wound and concussion and had nearly died. However, we saw him many times later at the Post and he was all right.

Many years later in 1900 at Corregidor Hospital in Manila I was making ward rounds one morning and came to a new admission, Ordinance Sergeant Flannery, standing at his bunk. I told him to turn his head around and said to him, "There are the old Al Lachlin scars, Sergeant." Needless to say Flannery was somewhat astonished.

"The Tramp Sprinter"

In the summer and fall of 1887 the Post went wild about foot races. They were 100-yard dashes in front of the Rustic Hotel.

One day two men showed up dressed as awkward looking tramps. They talked around the Rustic Hotel and found out that our best sprinter was Duffy of the Band—the snare drummer and also the Post Barber. One of the tramps went to the Barber Shop to see Duffy and arranged a foot race between the two for the next morning. Everyone went to the Rustic and Duffy appeared in trunks and spiked shoes but the tramp wore his overalls and ran in stocking feet. From the start the tramp ran awkwardly and quit after a few steps claiming it was not a fair start and that he had hurt his foot. He was overruled and Duffy won the money.

Then the tramp challenged our next-best sprinter, Corporal Long, and his confederate circulated around the crowd making bets. After

(Courtesy Fort Laramie Historical Association)

View of Ft. Laramie as it is today—looking across the Laramie River.

the money was put up the tramp peeled off his clothes and appeared in running trunks and spiked shoes. At the starting gun the tramp jumped in front of Long and kept a yard ahead down the course winning by exactly one yard. Long couldn't pass him without running into his spike shoes. Of course the soldiers yelled foul and there was one of the hottest arguments you ever heard. Finally, Lt. D. L. Howell, our best umpire, came down and heard all sides. He ruled against Long and the tramp got all the money. Of course both the tramps made a hasty exit from the Post and were never seen again.

Here Colonel Brechemin added this comment: "You might think the soldiers would have learned to look with suspicion on all sporting strangers in that old Western time but they never did. Every summer some gambler appeared and took them in."

Our final story from Colonel Brechemin is quite different in that it details a documented historic event.

"The Sawmill Fire of 1857"

The Fort Laramie Fire Department was organized as follows with the following equipment: Seventh Infantry Band — Axes; Co. A Seventh Infantry — Hose Cart; Co. H Seventh Infantry — Hose Cart. These units were quartered in the upper garrison. In the Cavalry Barracks were: Co. D Seventh Infantry — Hook and Ladder; Co. F Seventh Infantry — Buckets. That was the entire garrison that year. The two hose carts were stored at the northeast corner of the parade and covered with tarpaulins. There was no hook-and-ladder truck so D Company carried the ladders on their shoulders.

On this memorable evening in May 1887, the entire battalion stood Dress Parade. The men in complete full dress, helmets, white gloves, etc., were all in formation. The Band was trooping down the center of the formation in helmets with white plumes. There were the usual spectators in the officers row: ladies, children, and housemaids. On the porch of the wooden Barracks east of the parade ground were a number of cowpunchers, ranchers, and other civilians watching the parade. Fire alarms at the Post consisted of a big locomotive bell at the Sawmill, Trumpeter of the Guard sounding the fire call, and Corporal of the Guard firing the evening gun.

I was on the porch of the house we lived in at that time—the old magazine now in ruins. Everybody was watching the parade when suddenly the Sawmill bell began to ring. Little Eddie Rain, the Commissary Sergeant's son, came running up wild with excitement yelling, "The Sawmill is on fire!" The cowpunchers started to run in front of the Trader's Store and turned into the road leading to the Sawmill and the Rustic Hotel. Then "Keno," the C Company dog, and "Shep," Mr. Eli Hall's dog, took it into their heads to stage the biggest dog-fight I ever saw in the midst of the running crowd. As we turned the corner by the Trader's Store we saw the Sawmill, an old wooden building, blazing from the roof with huge flames high up. Major Freeman was commanding the parade and was a long time understanding what was up. Then the Trumpeter blew Fire Call and he came to life. He dismissed the battalion and the men came off the parade ground whooping and hollering. They tore into the Barracks and tried to change from full-dress to overalls. They got the hose carts under way, but had hitched on to the hydrant at the corner and that cart's hose didn't reach and the second cart's hose was not the same size. They tried to couple the two hoses in the road in front of the saloon but no go! When the men got down to the Sawmill they were ordered away until Sergeant Wilson opened the steam valves. A boiler explosion was feared. The building burned to the ground destroying the pumps for our water supply and for some time afterwards the water wagon went around filling barrels until the new mill was built of concrete and made fireproof.

We boys had the wildest excitement and the best time you ever saw and I cannot forget any detail of that wild scene, the rush, the dog-fight and the fire. Mr. Sanderock was our Post Engineer until his death and he was the only man at the Post that was of the modern age or understood machinery or plumbing either. There was a soldier helper who lived at the mill but was standing parade that evening and the fire got started from sawdust.

(Fort Laramie Historical Association Picture)

"Old Bedlam," constructed in 1849, is the oldest surviving building on the Fort (restored to 1852-1868 era). It was at one time officers' quarters and post headquarters.

Colonel Brechemin's mention of Mr. Sanderock introduces the next of our interviewers, actually a family rather than one individual. When Thomas B. Sanderock died at the age of 42, he left a widow and eight children ranging in age from 4 months to 18 years. Widowed and with only two or three of her children old enough to work, Harriet Sanderock managed to live on at the Fort until its abandonment by the Army in 1890. At the auction of the Fort buildings in April of that year the other bidders saw to it that she should acquire a 12-room officer's quarters duplex for about $50. Later, she and her oldest son, George, were able to homestead the sites of that house and the Old Guardhouse and a sizeable tract extending from the Fort grounds across the Laramie River and up Deer Creek. Also, the widow soon became Postmistress, the Post Office fixtures being moved to a room in her home from the Sutler's Store. There, at the south end of the old parade ground, the Sanderock family grew up—the boys becoming cowboys or ranchers; the girls to marry and move away.

Harriet Sanderock lived at the Fort until her death in 1934 at the age of 88. She was preceded in death by George, and another son died in 1943. All the rest of the Sanderock children were well known to us and contributed much historical information during the years.

Mrs. Maime Robertson, the oldest daughter, had worked for several officers' families following her father's death, and provided considerable insight into the makeup of life of their households. She always recalled vividly the removal of the soldiers' bodies to Ft. McPherson National Cemetery from the Ft. Laramie Cemetery and the Gratton Massacre mass burial, probably because one of the contractor's workmen had given her a bent iron arrowhead from the skull of one of Gratton's men.

Stella, the youngest daughter, married Emery Bright, who as a young cowboy had helped bring one of the last big trail herds from Texas to the Powder River Valley and later settled in London Flats, east of Ft. Laramie and near the Gratton Massacre site. Emery had seen the last years of the Fort only as a cowboy on the outside, but Stella was able to provide helpful information about her old home, Officer's Quarters "A," before we began its restoration.

Oddly, it may seem to you, it was Mead, the youngest of the Sanderocks, who was to provide the most helpful information about the Fort. Born in 1886, only a few months before his father's death, he had grown up in Officer's Quarters "A" and then moved to his ranch two miles south. Thus he had seen all the changes in the Fort following its abandonment. He became a close friend and frequent companion on fishing and hunting trips and to community activities of varying kinds. He was blessed with an excellent memory and was always willing to stop in and help us determine the originality of a feature of any building we were restoring or planning to restore. A unique and amusing example relates to Officer's Quarters "A" which we restored in 1956 to 1958. The original long, straight, double stairway had been torn out and replaced with one winding stairway, for his mother, about 1916. But, from physical remains we had been able to duplicate the originals excepting one detail: newel posts. Mead stopped by and I posed the question to him. His response was quick and positive. "That side [west] had a plain ball-top post, but this side [east] had no post at all, just a nice smooth end on the rail. I remembered that because we boys would always slid down the rail on this side but couldn't on the other." To prove his point he proceeded to demonstrate stair rail sliding at age 70. Just to be sure, I checked Mead's story with two of his sisters who confirmed it with the comment that their brothers "never walked down stairs in that house."

Occasionally, the chance to interview an Old-Timer took me away from the Fort and on Dec. 8, 1949, I drove some 45 miles to "Dutch Flats" near Mitchell, Neb. There I located and talked at length with one Jacob Gompert, 87 years young, and one of the original "Dutchmen" for whom the flats were named.

Jacob Gompert came to America in 1887 after having served for three years in a Westphalian Hussar Regiment of the Imperial German Army. After a few months in San Antonio, Texas, he came to Alliance, Neb., and found intermittent employment as a cowboy on the PF (Pratt & Ferris) Ranch which included most of the valley land north of the North Platte River from the site of Henry, Neb., to Torrington, Wyo., with an upper ranch or feed farm where Lingle, Wyo., now stands.

In the spring of 1890, Jacob Gompert and his brother, Gerhardt, who had followed him over from Germany, attended the sale of buildings at Ft. Laramie. They purchased one building for $75. There followed many trips to the Fort to remove lumber from this building and haul it, one wagonload at a time, over the 40 miles of sandy road to "Dutch Flats." There it was used to improve their dugout homes and for fuel. Mr. Gompert emphasized the great importance of fuel to the homesteaders of the North Platte Valley and the difficulty which they had in getting it prior to the coming of the railroad about 1900. Cowchips and wood hauled from the hills northwest of Lingle were their sole supplies for many years.

On one of the first trips with lumber from the Fort, a wardrobe from the house they were dismantling was placed on top of the load. In crossing Rawhide Creek where the banks were very steep, the wardrobe fell into the creek. Mr. Gompert being alone had to walk about a mile to the homestead shack of Tom Powers to get his aid in reloading it. I hauled that wardrobe back to Ft. Laramie in my pickup; a donation to the Fort from the Gompert family. The Tom Powers just mentioned was an oft quoted Old-Timer who had died before my years at Ft. Laramie. It developed that Mr. Gompert had worked with him on the PF and he told of having drawn the short straw during a card game with Powers and one Al Kelly and having to ride from the upper ranch to Ft. Laramie in the middle of the night after two bottles of whiskey.

During his many trips to the Fort in 1890 and 1891, Jacob Gompert became well acquainted with some other Germans. Joe Wilde, the ex-bullwhacker, road ranch operator and peerless rough and tumble fighter, had acquired the old Cavalry Barracks and converted it into a combination hotel, tavern and dance hall. There the Gompert brothers often stayed and ate during their lumber salvaging trips and there they met Miss Elizabeth Haubruk, a German girl who lived with the Wildes as a member of their family. In 1892 she became Mrs. Jacob Gompert.

The Gompert brothers hauled one load of heavy planks from Ft. Laramie to the river bank north of Gering, Neb. There they were used on a bridge over the North Platte built cooperatively to give the settlers north of the river access to Gering. Before that, difficulty in crossing the river had forced the homesteaders to trade at Alliance, Neb., a five-day round trip according to Mr. Gompert. He recalled that one outfit had tried to raft timbers from the Fort down the river to Gering, but had so much trouble that no one else tried it.

Mr. Gompert repeatedly mentioned that by fencing the bottom lands north of the river from near Lingle to the Nebraska line the PF Ranch had closed the old Mormon Trail and forced the road up onto the sandhills adding greatly to the difficulty of hauling their lumber from the Fort to "Dutch Flats."

On August 19, 1950, Mr. Gompert and several members of his family came to Ft. Laramie and toured the grounds with us. Mr. Gompert seemed confused by all the changes that had taken place since his early visits, but he was able to identify the building he had bought and dismantled as the ruin of Officer's Quarters "B", the former Commanding Officer's Quarters and one-time home of such notables as Bvt. Maj. Generals Wesley Merrit and John Gibbon. Mr. Gompert indicated that all fixtures, good doors, and window sash had been removed from the building before the auction at which he bought it for $75.

(Courtesy Fort Laramie Historical Association)

The Cavalry Barracks, built 1875-1876, restored, housed two 60-man companies. Below is iron bridge across the North Platte River built by the Army, 1875-1876, on the Cheyenne road, spurring stage and freight lines.

The long porches of the Cavalry Barracks caused him to recall walking over or around numerous drunken or sleeping cowboys in walking to Joe Wilde's hotel dining room at the north end of the building. He thought that Joe Wilde had a "gold mine" in his tavern operations in the 1890s in spite of having to act as his own bouncer.

Sometimes Old-Timers arrived in batches and a notable example was the visit to the Fort in September 1950 of George O. Reid of High River, Alta., and Jacob J. Tomamichel of Medora, N.D.

George Reid was known to us through his long letter of Dec. 20, 1945, to Merrill Mattes, published in *Annals of Wyoming* in July 1946. We will not repeat Reid's many interesting comments on Ft. Laramie in that letter but his credentials as an Old-Timer are impressive. He was born in 1872 at Ft. McPherson, Neb., where his father was corral boss. He lived at Ft. Laramie from 1875 to 1880, where his father was similarly employed until fired for knifing a gambler—self-defense according to George—and then on nearby ranches, notably that at Register Cliff, until 1892. The Reids then moved north to the Little Missouri River country near Medora, N.D. There George served as sheriff of Billings County for four years before moving to Canada. In Canada he served 23 years in the Royal North West Police [sic] and four years as Chief Guard at a Royal Canadian Air Force Base.

Jake Tomamichel we recognized as the son of Hospital Steward John Tomamichel who had served at Ft. Laramie from 1878 to 1899. Born in 1873, Jake had lived with his parents at the Fort only part of that time, leaving home to live with the Reids at Register Cliff and become a cowboy. He too moved to Medora with the Reids and acquired a small ranch. Later, we learned from several sources that Jake was known for many years as one of the best ropers on the Northern plains.

These two Old-Timers, both well past 75, led us on a merry chase around the Fort area. They were intent on seeing all their old haunts, and pointed out things they remembered and answered questions as we went.

They remembered the rifle range and its location north of the Fort, with eight target butts against the hills and firing points at distances up to 1,000 yards. This range is not shown on any of the old Army ground plans of the Fort. They also claimed that at one time the range officer had permitted them to pick up lead slugs and brass shells from the range to sell at 15 cents and 17 cents a pound.

George Reid remembered a big cottonwood tree full of Indian

burials across the river south of the old corral, but said it was cut down when he was very small, probably late in 1876. He also remembered seeing squaws scavenging in the Fort dump for condemned bacon, etc.

Jake Tomamichel remembered eating in the Cavalry Barracks with his future brother-in-law Sgt. William Kelley and that the soldiers were issued individual jars of oleomargarine at that time.

Both men remembered going to school in various buildings, and both left school at an early age to avoid rough treatment by soldier teachers who often got drunk trying to avoid teaching duty. They also remembered seeing the hay contractors' wagons stopping by the river to throw sand in the hay to increase the weight before checking in on the Quartermaster's scales.

Ordnance Sgt. Leodegar Snyder who served at Ft. Laramie from 1849 to 1886 was remembered by both men. Reid stated that in 1876, while most of the troops were in the field, Indians raided close to the Fort, and Snyder cleaned up and loaded some of the obsolete cannons. When Indians appeared on the hills near the Fort a few shells from those cannon scattered them. He also recalled that, at the time, civilians living near the Fort were encouraged to come in at night. The Reids did so one night, but when George and his brother found bedbugs in their bed their mother packed them all off home with the remark that she would rather fight Indians than bedbugs!

As noted earlier, not all our Old-Timers were men, and on Aug. 20, 1953, we were pleased to visit at length with Mrs. John Oliger of Denver who was brought to Ft. Laramie by a friend from Cheyenne. Mrs. Oliger first came to Ft. Laramie in 1887 as Ingrid Carlson, a domestic servant in the household of Col. Henry C. Merriam, Commanding Officer of Ft. Laramie and the Seventh Infantry. On Oct. 10, 1889, she was married to Pvt. John Oliger, H Company, Seventh Infantry. The wedding was held in the Rustic Hotel with B. A. Hart, Justice of the Peace, officiating. In this connection, Mrs. Oliger stated that during the years she was at Ft. Laramie there was no chapel or chaplain, but that occasionally Colonel Merriam had an Episcopalian minister from Cheyenne come up and conduct services in his home.

While looking at photographs from the 1880s, Mrs. Oliger was able to confirm many of the identifications made by Colonel Brechemin and others. On visiting the Fort buildings she could only provide new information in the case of the Commanding Officer's house. There she was the first person able to remember a reasonable ground plan of the missing kitchen wing. She confirmed statements by Maime Sanderock Robertson and others that the CO's house was the only one with inside plumbing, having a full bathroom upstairs and water piped into the kitchen. All others had only hydrants at the back doors. She questioned our identification of a small building behind this house as a stable. She stated that Colonel Merriam had a stable farther back in which he usually kept four personal horses. She felt that our "stable" was part of the chicken house, which was closer and frequently raided by skunks.

Mrs. Oliger described the colonel's household as usually consisting of Col. and Mrs. Merriam; their five children; Miss Kitty Boyd, the Colonel's niece; his cousin, Charles Merriam, a civilian engineer; a governess and four servants. Quite a houseful, even with seven bedrooms available!

She remembered most of the barracks as having bunks, not cots, and that the soldiers used straw ticks which they were required to refill monthly. A private's pay was $25 each two months, but with 50 cents deducted in Washington, her husband only got $12.25 a month. He retired from the Army in 1914 as a sergeant.

Our next Old-Timer had no connections with the military at Ft. Laramie but we had looked forward to interviewing him for a number of years. Louis Wilde was born in 1884 on a ranch eight miles up the Laramie River from the Fort. His father was the Joe Wilde remembered by Jacob Gompert, George Reid, and others as a bullwhacker, peerless rough-and-tumble fighter and one of the major bidders of the Army's sale of Fort buildings in 1890. At that sale he purchased the Cavalry Barracks and several other buildings. Moreover, he soon acquired at least 320 acres of the best land in the former military reservation. In addition to converting the barracks into a hotel, dance hall, and saloon, the Wildes also irrigated and farmed the bottom lands east of the Fort until about 1917. Hence, he was able to point out and explain changes made in the Cavalry Barracks and the Commissary Storehouse during those years. This information was very valuable in our on-going structural restoration program.

Louis Wilde advised us that a tornadic wind had destroyed about one-third of the barracks' veranda roof in about 1910, necessitating re-roofing and some structural changes we had deduced from photographs and physical evidence. He also stated that when purchased by his father, the barracks was without window sash, but that he had bought some back from the Army and obtained some from other buildings. This tends to confirm a statement made by Jacob Gompert about the condition of the building he purchased.

We asked Mr. Wilde about the missing "elevator" in the Commissary Storehouse and he stated that it had never been an elevator, just a hoist. He then described a large wooden wheel built up of boards with 2" x 6" spokes on an 8 to 10 inch shaft on which was wound the hoist rope with an iron hook on the end. An endless rope making a

(Fort Laramie National Historic Site Archives)

Louis Wilde, one "Old-Timer," had no military connection with Ft. Laramie, and was born in 1884 on a ranch eight miles up the Laramie River from the post.

Formal guard mount in 1885 was on parade ground in front of Officers Row.

full turn around the large wheel extended through the existing holes in the floor into the basement so the hoist could be operated from there or upstairs. We later reconstructed this hoist from his description and much to the surprise of some of our workmen, it functioned quite well.

Now the source of our last Ft. Laramie story can hardly be considered an Old-Timer since he had never been to the Fort before, but his story so impressed me at the time that I recorded it in detail.

On May 23, 1951 we were pleased to have a visit from Col. P.W. Allison, U.S. Army retired, of Salem, Ore. Colonel Allison's interest in Ft. Laramie stemmed from the fact that his father had been stationed here in 1872 as a Second Lieutenant of the Second Cavalry, soon after being graduated from West Point. Colonel Allison related a number of tales of Army life which his father had told him about Ft. Laramie. Here is one we found sufficiently different and interesting.

In June of 1872 Lt. James Nicholas Allison of K Company, Second U.S. Cavalry, arrived at Ft. Laramie equipped with a fine thoroughbred horse and a large hunting dog, part Russian Wolfhound.

Soon after his arrival he joined a small party of young officers on a wolf hunt along the hills east of the Fort. The dogs soon sighted a wolf and Allison being better mounted than his companions outdistanced and lost them in the ensuing chase.

Later, as he picked his way down from the hills toward the Oregon

Trail to return to the Fort, his horse went lame and he stopped, removed a stone from one of her shoes, and turning to remount he saw a lone horseman riding rapidly eastward on the trail. Allison's path intersected that of the lone rider who he took at first to be an Indian with a flapping blanket, but as he came nearer, he saw it was a young woman in an old-fashioned long riding habit and feathery hat. Thinking that she was a newly arrived visitor as the Fort, he sought to stop her to warn her against riding so far out alone, but she raised her quirt which glittered in the sun and whipped her great black horse to dash past him and out of sight over a rise of ground. Dashing in pursuit, Allison was amazed on topping the rise to find no one in sight, and his amazement grew as he examined the little used trail and found no tracks, while his wolfhound cowered against him in an unprecedented show of fear.

As he looked about in astonishment, a shout from a ridge to the south apprised him of the fact that one of his officer friends was at hand. Soon another lieutenant was beside him, first chaffing him about the lady who had given him the go-by, and then sharing his perplexity at the lack of any tracks or trace of her.

After returning to the Fort and dining with the assembled officers, their ladies, and guests, Allison assured himself that no lady present could have been the mysterious rider. Then fully aware that he might be made the butt of many jokes, he told the group of his queer adventure. Before any jocular comments could be made, the Commanding Officer (probably Bvt. Maj. Gen. John E. Smith, Fourteenth Infantry) spoke up with "Well Allison, you have just seen the 'Laramie Ghost'," and told the following story.

Back in the days when Ft. Laramie was a fur-trading post, a factor of the Post brought with him his beautiful daughter who had been educated in Eastern schools and was an accomplished horsewoman. The factor warned his daughter never to ride out alone and ordered his assistants to see that she did not leave the Fort alone at any time. However, there came a day when the factor was away and his daughter mounted her favorite horse, a beautiful black, and despite the protests of the people in the Fort rode eastward down the Oregon Trail and was never seen again. Her father returned and searched for her for weeks, but no trace was found. In later years a legend grew among the Indians and traders of the valley that every seven years the ghost of the factor's daughter would be seen riding down the old trail.

Still incredulous, Lieutenant Allison inquired until he found an old

Indian squaw who had been at the Fort when the factor's daughter rode out never to return. He asked the old squaw how the girl had been dressed and his amazement grew as she gave a description of a girl in a long dark green riding habit with a feathered hat and a jewel-handled quirt such as he had seen as the mysterious lady whipped her mount to dash away from him on the trail. Allison was convinced that he had seen the "Laramie Ghost" and buried the incident in his memory until years later. Then as he rode the train through Wyoming, he heard cowboys on a depot platform talking about how a rancher had just seen the "Laramie Ghost" but his train started up before he could question them for details of the incident.

Now you may not believe in ghosts and in our eleven years at the old Fort, we did not see the ghost just described. However, if any place in the West deserves a few ghosts, I am sure you will agree that it is Ft. Laramie.

Sources and References

Letter & Attachments, Brechemin to Herb, Jan. 23, 1951
Letter & Attachments, Brechemin to Herb, Feb. 15, 1951
Memorandum to the files, re Col. P.W. Allison, June 4, 1951
Memorandum to the files, re Col. Louis Brechemin, Aug. 12, 1948
Memorandum to the files, re Mr. Jacob Gompert, Dec. 20, 1949
Memorandum to the files, re Mr. Jacob Gompert, Aug. 21, 1950
Memorandum to the files, re Mrs. John Oliger, Aug. 24, 1953
Memorandum to the files, re George O. Reid & Jacob J. Tomamichel, Oct. 5, 1950
Memorandum to the files, re Mr. Louis Wilde, June 21, 1954
References to the contributions of the Sanderock Family are in part from a "Preliminary Report on the Rehabilitation of Officer's Quarters A during 1956 to 1958" by David L. Hieb, in Ft. Laramie NHS files, Aug. 20, 1958.
Some names and dates were obtained from stones in the Ft. Laramie Cemetery. Other names and dates, etc. were obtained or corrected by reference to the "Post Returns" and other Ft. Laramie records.

About the Author

David L. Hieb, a corresponding member of the Denver Western-ers, died of a heart attack at his Estes Park, Colo., home on Dec. 29, 1980. Denver Westerners will remember him as the speaker at the 1978 Summer Rendezvous. He told then about old-timers he had met and interviewed at Fort Laramie National Historic Site, Wyo., while he was Superintendent there from 1947 to 1958. These were men and women who had actually lived as children at Ft. Laramie prior to its abandonment as a military post in 1890, or descendants of officers and others who had served there during the Indian Wars.

Hieb was a legend in his own right, for as Fort Laramie Super-intendent he was responsible for most of the splendid restoration work accomplished there. He started his National Park Service career as a seasonal ranger at Rocky Mountain National Park in 1930, and later served as a ranger at Carlsbad Caverns National Park and Blue Ridge Parkway.

After Ft. Laramie he became Regional Chief of Boundary Stud-ies in Omaha, then Superintendent of George Washington Carver and Herbert Hoover birthplaces before retiring.

Merrill Mattes, longtime Denver Westerner, recalls, "For 50 years Dave was one of my best friends. We met on Longs Peak in 1929 when I was a guide for the Boulderfield Hotel concessionaire, and he was a guide for the YMCA Camp. We both had lengthy careers with the National Park Service, and as Regional Historian it was my privilege to work closely with him in the Ft. Laramie restora-tion program. Jim Bowers, Posse Member, worked for Dave as Ft. Laramie's first ranger."

"Navajo Trading Post" by *Delano*

C.N. Cotton and
His Navajo Blankets

By Dr. Lester L. Williams

*W*HEN C.N. COTTON DIED in 1936 in northwest New Mexico a newspaper as far away as Columbus, Ohio, marked the passing of the man "who gave the Navajo blanket its start on the way to world fame." He is of interest to me because he was my grandmother's oldest brother, and my family always regarded him as famous and wealthy and one member of the family who had made a success of his life. We visited him in Gallup, N.M., in 1930, and this visit had a profound influence on me and probably caused me to come West to live.

During his life in New Mexico and Arizona, Mr. Cotton's ideas and innovations influenced trade between Navajo and whites. He exerted pressure to improve size, pattern, color, and quality of Navajo blankets and he advertised far and wide to develop a demand for them. Being a shrewd trader, he knew that prosperous Indians would be good customers at his trading post. Despite his importance in the Indian trade, little is know of him generally.

Clinton Neal Cotton was born April 12, 1859, in central Ohio on a farm just west of Howard, nine miles east of Mt. Vernon. [His mother was Mary Neal Cotton and his father was Liberty Leslie Cotton. His father, famed for his prodigious memory, was well known as an educator and a lightning calculator who traveled around frontier Ohio giving demonstrations of how fast he could do various calculations—as fast as a modern-day calculator.] When he was just 11, in 1870, his father died and C.N. Cotton was forced to leave school and go to work to help support his mother and younger brothers and sisters. One job he held was apprentice telegraph operator.

At age 22, in 1881, he went west to Albuquerque. In later years he told of how on the trip west the train stopped in Las Vegas, N.M., and waited while all the passengers walked to the jail to look through the bars in the door to see Dave Rudabaugh chained to the floor. Dave was one of the more lethal members of Billie the Kid's gang and was in jail at Las Vegas charged with murder from Feb. 27 until Dec. 3, 1881, when he escaped via a hole chiseled through the wall.

In Albuquerque, Cotton looked for a job, and Henry Abel sent him to the A & P Railroad where he was hired as telegraph operator. In March 1880, the Atlantic and Pacific Railroad had begun building west from Albuquerque, on what became the main line of the Santa Fe. Early in 1881, Guam at milepost 138.8 west from Albuquerque was the end of track, where young Cotton worked as a telegrapher. In 1881 the A & P telegraph line was the only rapid communication in all of northwest New Mexico Territory. C.N. Cotton as operator was the only link with civilization and a very important person.

By Feb. 13, 1881, the end of track was 10 miles farther west at Wingate, station for Ft. Wingate, one of the largest and most important military posts in the Southwest. The new railroad had no buildings at Wingate, and a boxcar was set off beside the track to serve as station, telegraph office, and living quarters for Cotton. While this made living rather primitive, he thrived on it. A story appeared April 29, 1883, in the *Sunday Inter Ocean*, a Chicago newspaper, telling of an expedition into the Southwest to visit the Zuni Pueblo. The correspondent wrote of stopping at a station called Wingate where he found no town, only a station house and a water tank and a boy seated at a telegraphic instrument and a great Newfoundland dog sleeping at his side. The boy said he was from Mt. Vernon, Ohio, had been out there at the lonely mountain all winter, and liked it. The dog had been found by some trackbuilders a few months before, nearly starved, in a snowdrift beside a dead man, and the telegraph operator had adopted the dog.

C.N. Cotton must have written some enthusiastic letters home telling of the wonders of his new homeland, because in 1882 his younger brother Fred Cotton (1867-1926) came to Grants, N.M., to work as telegraph operator. Years later he returned to Mt. Vernon to build up a prosperous lumber business.

In 1882, C.N. Cotton returned to Ohio to wed Mary Alice "Allie" Crain, daughter of a college professor. She was a resident of Howard, Ohio. The ceremony was performed in the home of her parents, and the newlyweds left that afternoon for New Mexico. Their honeymoon cottage was the boxcar on the siding at Wingate, and their first child, Charles McGugin Cotton, was born there. During World War II, Charles, who had become very wealthy, needed to establish his place

(Author's Collection)

Clinton Neal Cotton was working as a telegrapher when this picture was taken in New Mexico in 1882.

of birth to prove he was an American citizen in order to operate his yacht in the Los Angeles harbor. Family attorney Herman W. Atkins of Gallup was able to find Chief Henry Dodge (Chee Dodge), frequently an interpreter in early negotiations between whites and Navajo. The chief had come into the boxcar right after the birth. He recalled the event, and his affidavit established the fact that C.N. Cotton's first son was indeed an American citizen.

The railroad reached Gallup on April 13, 1881. My mother told that when the Cottons wanted to go from Wingate to Gallup to shop, Uncle Clint would put Aunt Allie on a handcar and coast downhill to Gallup, but he had to work hard to pump the handcar uphill back to Wingate.

Cotton's restless energy and ambition wouldn't let him remain long as a telegraph operator, but all the rest of his life he had a mannerism of subconsciously tapping out messages in Morse with his right thumb and index finger as if using a telegraph key.

Sometime while at Guam or Wingate, Cotton made the acquaintance of Juan Lorenzo Hubbell. Hubbell Parker once told that at one time Cotton was going to teach Morse Code to Lorenzo Hubbell so the latter could get a job on the railroad, but instead they went into business together. They became fast friends and were associated in business ventures for the remainder of their lives.

Juan Lorenzo Hubbell was born in 1854 in Pajarito, N.M. In 1870 he traveled to Utah Territory and at a crossing of the Colorado now known as Lee's Ferry, he met John D. Lee, a Mormon trader. Next he went to Ft. Defiance, A.T., and established a friendship with Thomas Keams. Probably in 1872 he started in the Indian trade as an employee of a Mr. Coddington, who operated a trading post at Ft. Wingate. Hubbell was employed as issue clerk at Defiance Agency from July 1 to Oct. 1, 1876. McNitt, in his book *Indian Traders*, says Hubbell "next went to the vicinity of Ganado Lake, traded there for more than a year—probably in 1878—and bought the Leonard Post where he settled down." This became the Hubbell Trading Post, and it prospered. (It became a National Historic Site in 1967.)

Law enforcement was badly needed, and in 1882 Hubbell was elected sheriff of huge Apache County in northeast Arizona Territory. By his courage he was well qualified for this responsibility. Two years later when he ran for reelection, he realized he needed a reliable partner to operate the trading post while he was at St. Johns, the county seat, 96 miles distant. This led to the partnership of Hubbell and

Cotton, when on Sept. 23, 1884, Cotton bought a half interest in the trading post at Ganado. Hubbell was reelected sheriff of Apache County on Nov. 4, 1884.

In the Special Collections of the University of Arizona Library in Tucson are letter-press copies of letters written by C.N. Cotton at Ganado from 1884 through 1889. (A letter-press copy was the forerunner of carbon paper.) These copies provide documentary evidence, in Cotton's own handwriting, for his part-ownership of the trading post, and these letters provide much insight into the hardships and trials of everyday life there. Cotton, with his wife and infant son, moved to Ganado in September 1884, and letters in Cotton's handwriting provide a business record of the partnership. At the same time Hubbell moved to St. Johns to serve as sheriff, and became a partner in another business there.

Despite having left school at age 11 to work, Cotton wrote excellent business letters. Conducting business 50 miles from the nearest railroad and telegraph meant that all business was transacted by mail. Cotton wrote letters to wholesalers in Albuquerque; letters about mail carrier service they contracted to provide; letters about the huge quantities of hides and wool they shipped to Albuquerque; and letters to their teamster Ben Bill of Manuelito.

On Dec. 17, 1884, Cotton wrote to the collector for the Internal Revenue Service in Prescott, Ariz., stating that he now owned a half interest in the store at Ganado and requesting information about a license to sell tobacco. Two days later he asked for quotations for purchasing a carload of flour. On Jan. 7, 1885, he wrote again to the IRS collector in Prescott, sending a $2.40 check for tax and penalty.

On Jan. 10, 1885, he borrowed $1,200 from D.L. McGugin who had been a neighbor back in Ohio. He also borrowed $2,000 from his father-in-law. With this for capital he bought sheep which he grazed near the trading post. A year later he repaid the notes.

He wrote to Albuquerque for silk handkerchiefs of cheapest black silk a yard square with a narrow red stripe as border and fringe 1 inch long all around and indicated if these suited the Indians he could use a large quantity. He wrote to the Post Trader at the fort in Custer, Mont., for buffalo robes and mountain lion skins, and offered Navajo blankets at $3 to $5 each. On Aug. 8, 1885, he offered blankets 4 by 5 feet at $2.50 each.

As Laura Gilpin emphasized in her book, *The Enduring Navajo*, early traders had to be remarkable people, and pioneers in every sense.

They had to conduct business using a most difficult language. To exist, they had to be shrewd in their dealings. To the trading post the Navajo brought wool to sell at shearing time; in the fall they brought sheep and cattle. Year-round they brought for barter hides, piñon nuts, jewelry, and blankets. The trader was the Indians only contact with the outside world.

John Bowman, Indian agent for the Navajo Reservation, on Feb. 22, 1886, wrote a report to the Commissioner of Indian Affairs describing life and trading on the reservation. He noted that he was at a station very isolated and difficult of access. He reported that the Indians were very sharp traders—nomads with lots of valueless time who would ride many miles to strike a better deal. Traders along the railroad had an advantage over the licensed traders inside the reservation because they were spared the costs of freighting goods from the railroad. The traders might carry a stock worth from $500 to $5,000 consisting principally of flour, sugar, coffee, calico, leather, blankets, tobacco, and meats. In exchange, the Indians brought in sheep and goat pelts, wool, and Navajo-made blankets. They also made coin-silver buttons of various sizes and styles. When they wanted to buy something and had no wool or pelts to exchange, they simply cut off some buttons. June and July were the best months for trade, when wool was sheared and sold. The Indians were well aware of the value of the wool and if the offered price was not up to their expectations, they would seek another trader. All traders were expected to furnish free tobacco and to make numerous presents to influential Indians. Competition was so keen that sometimes traders paid as much for the wool as they could obtain on the Albuquerque market.

Bowman went on to describe the location of some of the trading posts. Tis-i-le where Messrs. Clark and Aldrich had a store, about 50 miles north of Bowman's post in a mountainous section, was inaccessible by wagon during the winter. He wrote:

> Manuelito's camp would be the best point for trade of any store were it not for the fact that the Indians who frequent that locality are of a very drunken disposition and no one has yet been found who was live enough to keep a store there any length of time, although several have tried it.

Bowman recommended the commissioner license anyone who was of good morals and desired to trade on the reservation. "If it were not profitable to the trader he could quit."

U.S. Indian Inspector Robert S. Gardner on Sept. 25, 1886, wrote a detailed report of his inspection of the Navajo Agency. The Navajo population included 3,322 males, 6,344 females, and children 7,692, a total of 17,358. The Moqui (Hopi) Pueblos had 704 males, 703 females, and 572 children, totaling 1,979.

The report stated:

> The Navajo have about 250,000 horses, 300 mules, 500 burros, 800,000 sheep, 300,000 goats and 1,050 head of horned cattle. Many of the horses are fine large ones, in good flesh and valuable. The sheep are small and of a poor grade producing but a pound or two of wool per sheep and that of poor quality and coarse. The sheep should be improved by the purchase of at least 1,000 good quarter-blood Merinos or Cotswold bucks. The Indians are true nomads and live more of a pastoral than an agricultural life, with average farms being only from 1/4 to 5 acres which are indifferently and poorly cultivated. Corn, wheat, pumpkins, melons, and beans are planted. Little hay is raised so if the winter is severe sheep and goats starve. It is estimated that half of the Navajo live on public land south of the reservation. During the last quarter, $930 worth of lumber for use by the Indians for windows and doors was delivered at Manuelito Railway Station but the Indians only picked up two-thirds of it.

Gardner noted that C.N. Cotton was trading without license at Ganado or Pueblo Colorado [red pueblo]. He stated: "Mr. Cotton is a good and responsible man and should he apply for license I see no reason why he should not get one." He also reported:

> Wm. A. Olmstead, Agency Physician, is a competent, faithful and efficient employee, he is active and energetic in the proper discharge of his duties and takes an interest in visiting the Indians and prescribing for their ills.

Finally, Gardner stated that "Henry Dodge, the Interpreter, is faithful and efficient and well earns his salary."

Life in Ganado in the 1880s was rugged, and Cotton's wife, Mary Alice Crain Cotton, must have come from fine pioneer stock. She is described as pretty, vivacious, sometimes quick-tempered, and always well-dressed, and a picture of her bears this out. They ordered for their 2-year-old son three pairs of size 4½ cashmere cardinal infant's stockings. A suit for Mr. Cotton had to be ordered from a tailor. He requested a sack suit and sent a sample of the cloth to be used. He specified the pants be of medium width, "not dude pants," not-so-awfully-large coat, padded heavy on the shoulders, and single-breasted. Shoes were a problem too, and he wrote to his old hometown, Mt. Vernon, Ohio, to Silas Parr to request a pair of his best French-calf button shoes with glove-kid top. He noted that Arizona was a sandy country and very hard on shoes and he exhorted him to please make the sole the best he could.

On June 22, 1885, Cotton bought the remaining half-interest in the trading post at Ganado and all interest in wool owned by the partnership. A series of letters in June 1885 informed various firms and the deputy collector of internal revenue in Prescott that Cotton had purchased Hubbell's interest in the trading post.

Records show that a license to trade at Pueblo Colorado—now Ganado—was issued to C.N. Cotton Nov. 22, 1887, and renewed regularly up to Oct. 4, 1900. In applications for license Cotton listed Juan Lorenzo Hubbell as his clerk.

Cotton failed in his attempt to establish a trading post at Chinle, at the mouth of Cañon de Chelly, a gathering place and natural fortress for the Navajo, making it an especially favorable place to trade. Many Navajo farmed fertile bottom lands in the cañon. Hubbell and Cotton discussed locating a trading post there and in June 1885, Cotton bought out Hubbell's interest in the proposed Chinle store. On Nov. 1, 1885, Cotton petitioned the Office of Indian Affairs for a license to operate a trading post at Che-ne-le Valley and provided a $10,000 bond. His bond named as the location Toh Lee Sheen, about one mile from Cañon de Chelly. John Bowman, Indian agent at Ft. Defiance, recommended the license be granted. Several solid citizens wrote letters extolling Cotton's character and supporting his request. No action was taken on the petition.

On July 28, 1886, Michael Donovan opened a trading post at Chinle with former Indian Agent John H. Bowman as his clerk. Why was the application of Cotton passed over and the license granted to Donovan? Policy required a trader to live at his post, and barred absentee ownership or multiple licenses. In 1886 the trading post at Ganado was not within the reservation so Cotton did not consider a license to be required. Nor was he requesting a second trader's license at Chinle. Cotton's trading post at Ganado and Thomas Keams' at Keams Cañon were considered to be off the reservation, so no license was required and they did not report receipts.

Competition for reservation trading was fierce, and politics played a big part in licensing. Perhaps the employment of former Indian Agent Bowman mitigated in favor of Donovan's license.

To give an idea of trading at Chinle, S.S. Patterson, U.S. Indian agent at Ft. Defiance, reported on March 1, 1887, the receipts of the four trading posts on the Navajo Reservation. He showed Donovan's gross receipts at Chinle as $16,360.50 from July 28, 1886 to March 1, 1887; gross receipts for a full year for Aldrich & Sweatland at Tse-a-lee, 50 miles north of Ft. Defiance, $10,947.47; Weidemeyer at Ft. Defiance grossed $4,602.80 during eight months; and S.G. Reeder at Ft. Defiance grossed $8,448 for a year.

The report indicated that Donovan may have been only a figure-head, and others may have invested in the goods sold. Patterson hoped the successor to Donovan, whose license was due to expire, "will be a person who will conduct an honorable business there on his own account and that no more annoyance will be heard from the quarter."

In December 1886, Cotton went to Washington, carrying letters from Sumner Howard, former chief justice of Arizona Territory, and introducing him to Senators Logan, Palmer, and Devuges. Cotton was characterized in these letters as one of the most reliable and substantial of Arizona's citizens. The letters requested the senators' help in securing Cotton an audience with the Commissioner of Indian Affairs. He also had a letter from Gen. George W. Morgan of Mt. Vernon, Ohio, introducing him to Senator Payne, stating: "He is a young man of intelligence and when residing among us had the reputation of being a person of integrity." Cotton's address in Washington was in care of William C. Cooper, member of Congress. When Cotton returned to Ganado he sent Mrs. W.C. Cooper of Mt. Vernon, Ohio, a pair of Navajo bracelets and some Moqui baskets. He wrote her:

> These baskets are much sought-after by Washington ladies to use as plaques. Drive a nail through the center and put up high on the wall to get good effect. Please accept with my compliments.

Cotton's audience with the commissioner, Dec. 10, 1886, ended in his being promised a license to trade at a point beyond Chinle Valley.

On Nov. 1, 1886, Congressman Frank Hiscock, a member of the House Ways and Means Committee, wrote to the Commissioner of Indian Affairs stating that Michael Donovan, who was licensed to trade with the Indians at Chin-Lee Valley, had left to attend to his business in the East, and that ex-Indian Agent John Bowman was managing the business. Donovan then requested the license be transferred to Bowman.

On May 8, 1887, Donovan died and Cotton bought his stock of goods with the understanding that the license would be transferred to him. For this he gave notes to John Bowman for $450 and $2,000, for the store building, and other considerations. Apparently he interpreted the promise of a license to trade at a point beyond Chinle Valley as about the same as at Chinle. July 1, 1887, Cotton began running the store.

On Sept. 22, 1887, Patterson, Ft. Defiance Indian agent, reported to the Commissioner of Indian Affairs that Cotton was operating Donovan's old store without a license but under a promise that one would be granted. Patterson received no reply from Washington, no license was forthcoming, and just prior to Nov. 26, 1887, the agent closed Cotton's store at Chinle "as being conducted contrary to law." John Bowman wrote Cotton: "Sorry you didn't get the license for Chinle. You better sell out for $300 or $400 or give the keys to the Indians." (Evidently Cotton and Bowman were close friends, for Cotton named his second son John Bowman Cotton.)

Again Cotton asked Senator Payne to intercede for him with the Commissioner of Indian Affairs, but without success. The loss of this trading post must have been a severe financial blow, but the store at Ganado prospered, and Cotton wrote to a friend from whom he had borrowed money that the store made him from $2,500 to $3,000 a year—big money for 1887. He also invested profitably in sheep.

Cotton's Indian customers sometimes posed problems. There was always danger on the reservation and he often went armed. I recall his gun, a Colt's Single-Action Army, commonly called the Peacemaker. All the bluing was worn off from being carried many miles in a holster. On Sept. 27, 1885, he sent the gun back to the Colt factory with a letter stating it was pretty badly used up. He asked them to put new sear notches in the hammer, or install a new one. In 1888 he sent his Marlin rifle, caliber .40-70, for repairs. That same year he wrote to the Indian agent at Ft. Defiance to complain that an Indian named Haa No Ne Be Ga had threatened to kill him, the same Indian who held up Hawthorn's store, 25 miles south of Ganado.

On Nov. 10, 1885, the son of Tymolti came in to the store and asked to see a silver belt he had left there in pawn. (He had lost the belt betting on the wrong horse.) When Cotton laid the belt on the counter, the brave grabbed it, ran out, mounted his horse, and raced away. Cotton asked the Indian agent to recover the belt.

When first established early in 1878, the trading post at Ganado was not on the Navajo Reservation. When the reservation was enlarged by Executive Order on Jan. 6, 1880, the southern boundary was moved six miles south, taking in the trading post. Juan Lorenzo Hubbell is said to have homesteaded 160 acres there and considered his land outside the reservation and he was therefore not required to have a trading license. However, Hubbell never filed his claim and only had squatter's rights. When Cotton purchased the trading post from Hubbell, he believed that, since the facility was not originally on the reservation, he did not need a license. This influenced his attempt to open the post at Chinle. After much wrangling with the Indian agent, finally Mr. Atkins, the Commissioner of Indian Affairs, compelled Cotton to take out a license, and on Nov. 22, 1887, he was granted the first license to trade at Pueblo Colorado. The license was renewed on Oct. 4 every year at least until Oct. 4, 1897, and each year J.L. Hubbell was listed as "clerk."

About 1890 pressure was put on Cotton, and indirectly on Hubbell, with a threat to revoke the license, tear down the buildings, and deny their claim to the property. At the time the improvements were valued at $12,000. Cotton considered it a great injustice, when the trading post had not been excluded from the extension of the Navajo reservation in 1880. He secured affidavits from numerous citizens who testified the trading post had been continuously occupied since 1878. Samuel E. Day testified he had surveyed the southern border of the reservation and personally knew the trading post was located there before the extension. Attempt was made to exempt the post from the Executive Order of Jan. 6, 1880, but it was concluded it would take an Act of Congress to accomplish this. Finally in January 1900, a bill was introduced in the House by Representative Smith from Arizona (H.R. 4001) to exclude settlers with bona fide prior claims of settlement from the Executive Order of Jan. 6, 1880, which extended the boundaries. This bill was passed by the House on March 5, 1900, and by the Senate on March 28, but was vetoed by the President. (The veto may have been the result of an amendment attached to the bill which opened to mining claims a portion of the Navajo Reservation. An identical bill without the objectional amendment was passed by Congress in 1902, and signed by President Theodore Roosevelt.)

Finally in 1907, J.L. Hubbell made formal application for a homestead claim. After furnishing proof of the use to which the land was put and correction in the exact location of the homestead, a patent was granted, then a deed was issued and recorded on Aug. 22, 1917. This was 39 years after Hubbell first occupied the ranch and must be close to the all-time record for delay in getting title to land.

When sale of the Hubbell Trading Post from C.N. Cotton back to Juan Lorenzo Hubbell was consummated is uncertain. The license issued to Cotton on Oct. 4, 1897, lists J.L. Hubbell as clerk. A letter from C.N. Cotton dated April 24, 1899, is on letterhead showing Cotton had a trading post at Ganado. This letter to Indian Agent Hassled states: "Mr. Hubbell's interest in the land and mine are the same, and if his claim is allowed it will be perfectly satisfactory with me." The last known letter on this same letterhead is dated April 25,

1901. Cotton probably could not legally have conveyed the ranch and trading post to Hubbell until the title was cleared in 1902.

During the time Hubbell and Cotton were partners, also when Cotton owned and ran the store alone, and later when Hubbell worked as Cotton's clerk, they did much to help the Navajo improve their products. C.N. Cotton, Hubbell's junior by five years, had no previous experience as a trader, but he had an unusual aptitude and a burning desire for success. He was a shrewd Yankee trader and advertised to other traders that they carried a full supply of indigo and yarn; he secured quotations on carload lots of flour in 22-pound sacks; he attempted to get better prices on hides and wool. He wrote endlessly all over the country for beads just the right size for the Indians to use.

Hubbell and Cotton made a good team. Hubbell was a gentleman, imitated the ways of the gracious Spanish don and was hospitable to a fault. All who came his way were welcome for a meal, for the night, or for many days. Cotton was also a gentleman, and honest, but in addition he was a sound businessman and insisted that every deal turn a profit. Acquaintances have described him as kindly, outgoing, good to young people, dedicated to business, and exciting to work for. He wanted things done right, was fair, and generous. His secretary for 20 years called him a "wonderful human being" and believed he actually did more to develop the Indian trade than Hubbell.

In February 1889, Cotton wrote to C.E. Vandever, Navajo Agency agent, at Monsha, that Chief Gana Monsha was seriously ill at his home near Cotton's store. The sick chieftain was one of the principal leaders of the tribe, and a great peacemaker. Cotton said an Indian council decided the trader should write and have the agent send the agency physician for a few days to attend their very ill chief. The agent complied, and even offered to provide a horse for the doctor, but the latter refused to go, saying it was impossible for him to go horseback as he had never had any practice in riding. The agent wrote that this refusal was a great disappointment to the Indians, and would lessen their confidence in the agent, and be a serious barrier in future efforts to induce them to seek the agency physician instead of their own medicine men.

On Aug. 7, 1889, Vandever wrote to the Commissioner of Indian Affairs in Washington:

> Of Mr. Cotton I can speak from personal observation. He resides upon the reservation and personally conducts his trading establishment as required by the regulations better than any Indian trader on the reservation. I know these to be facts because the store is located on the road between the agency

and Moqui where I hear from it every week.

Arthur W. Tinker, U.S. Indian inspector, wrote reports on all the trading posts on the reservation. On March 21, 1890, he reported on the Indian Trader Store of C.N. Cotton at Ganado:

> This is by far the best Indian trader store on this reservation. The buildings are large and well made, being built of stone. Mr. Cotton carries a large stock of goods and the prices charged are very reasonable. Nothing but cash is paid Indians for what they have to sell, and Indians pay cash for what they purchase. No credit is given. No silver bridles, belt buckles, or buttons, or any other articles are taken on pawn. Price lists in English are properly posted, but none in Navajo. Liquor of no kind is kept or sold. No breech loading arms, fixed ammunition or metallic cartridges are dealt in. No annuity goods are ever bought or sold. Mr. Cotton or his clerk are in no way interested in any herds of sheep, goats, cattle, or horses grazing on the reservation. This store is never open on Sundays. Gambling by dice, cards, or in any other manner not allowed.

Cotton and Hubbell began to demand higher quality in the blankets they purchased. During 1884 only 300 or 400 blankets were brought in for sale. Cotton prodded the weavers to produce more and better blankets. In October and November 1887, he sent many letters to dealers in the East, to Tiffany & Co. in New York, to San Francisco, and to Denver, extolling Navajo blankets.

Cotton noted the bright, aniline dyes brought in to Ft. Defiance by trader Ben Hyatt. Hubbell was particularly fond of the dark-red dye since called Ganado red, but objected to other chemical or artificial dyes. Cotton insisted, and a compromise was reached whereby the only aniline dyes they would sell would be red, blue, and black—colors the weavers found hard to produce from native vegetable or mineral dyes. Red seemed the most difficult color of all. The weavers found that black yarn, carded and spun from their black sheep, lacked uniform color and was various shades of gray. Thus a strong black dye was also needed. Cotton persuaded a dye manufacturer, Wells & Richardson of Burlington, Vt., to put up dyes in small packages, ready for use. These became the famous Diamond Dyes combining dye and mordant in one package which had only to be thrown into boiling water, envelope and all, and the wool boiled in the solution until the proper color was attained. There was no need to add vinegar or alum to set the color. These colors truly made the Navajo blanket.

Next, Cotton had a brilliant idea: sell the blankets as rugs. This change revolutionized the trade, and greatly increased the potential market for Navajo blankets. Hubbell then began to encourage weavers to produce blankets of very large dimensions, so big they could be used as rugs in very large rooms. One of these, woven about 1885, measured 12 by 18 ft. 2 in. This double-weave or two-faced rug was acquired by Cotton. In the brochure advertising the Hubbell Trading Post there is a picture taken by famous Indian photographer Ben Wittick in 1890, showing Hubbell in the foreground talking to a squaw. In the background to the right this blanket hangs on the line. In later years the rug was used in the dining room in the Cotton home in Gallup. After a table leg wore a hole in it, the rug was sent to trader friend Berton I. Staples in Coolidge for repair, but it never was returned. The rug is now in the Gladin Collection in the Museum of Northern Arizona at Flagstaff, and before 1962 the curator valued it at $40,000.

Often a Navajo woman would come in to the trading post and inquire how she could weave a better blanket for a higher price. Hubbell's solution was to provide room and board, and work place for a well-known painter, E.A. Burbank, to come and paint pictures of the better-quality blankets. The Indians were encouraged to imitate the paintings. These paintings hang in the Hubbell Trading Post today.

Dr. Joe Ben Wheat, University of Colorado professor emeritus of anthropology and retired CU Museum curator, indicates that Hubbell and Cotton and also a competitor, J.B. Moore, who had a trading post at Crystal, began to persuade the weavers to change their designs and to produce rugs copying Oriental patterns. Dr. Wheat states that Moore's 1903 catalog shows the old Navajo designs, but by 1911 the transition to Oriental rug design is quite evident.

In February 1888, Cotton wrote that he had more than 100 heavy, coarse Navajo blankets in stock for sale at 35 cents a pound. He also offered common saddle blankets at $10 to $12 a dozen; fancy blankets at $4 to $10 each; and large fancy blankets at $20 to $40 each. He shipped rolls of blankets to Albuquerque, San Francisco, El Paso, and to Tiffany & Co. of New York. One roll of blankets worth $2,660 went to Charles E. Aikens of Colorado Springs.

C.N. Cotton was also smitten with the commercial possibilities of the Navajo silverwork, although most of their jewelry at that time was rather crude and rough, and very heavy. (An example of it can be seen today on the statue of Manuelito in Gallup). Prior to 1900, most Navajo silverwork was made just for themselves. Cotton discussed it with Hubbell, then brought in from Cubero a Mexican silversmith, Naakaii Daadil (which means thick-lipped Mexican), and introduced him at Ganado in 1884. Mexican silversmiths started teaching

Photo taken about 1890 shows Juan Lorenzo Hubbell, C.N. Cotton's clerk at Ganado, seated on a stump, dealing with a Navajo. On line at far right is large Navajo blanket (12' by 18'2") later used as a rug for many years in Cotton dining room in Gallup home.

(Ben Wittick Photo, Collections in the Museum of New Mexico) the craft to Navajo men in Ganado. Cotton wrote later that in 1898 he shipped a mass of crude early Navajo silverware to the Denver Mint as bullion and received $800.

On several occasions Cotton wrote to the cashier of the First National Bank of Albuquerque requesting he be sent $250 or $1,000 in silver by the first express. Probably most of that silver found its way into Navajo jewelry.

Later Cotton was said to have supplied Navajo silversmiths $2,000 a month in Mexican silver dollars, preferred over silver bullion because it cost 10 cents less an ounce and was harder than pure silver, easier to forge, and wore better.

On March 22, 1889, he offered for sale "a few pieces of ancient pottery found in ruins at Cañon de Chelly at $1 to $5 per piece." This was not then illegal, and the Indians themselves brought in artifacts for sale.

Cotton's letters from Ganado indicate he was buying and storing large quantities of wool. He later ran into monumental problems in getting the wool to market, and he had a continuing and overwhelming stricture in his cash flow. He wrote letters to Albuquerque banks about his overdrafts, stated he had enough wool in his warehouse to pay all his obligations, and asked that his note be protected.

Because of difficulties with transportation, Cotton could never catch a favorable market for his wool. He had problems getting supplies for his family and goods for sale in the trading post. The nearest railroad was 50 miles away and the nearest bank was in Albuquerque. By 1888 he must have concluded the way to get ahead would be to develop a wholesale business, selling to traders but especially buying wool, blankets, and jewelry, and establish this business at a point favorably located for transportation. Where better than along the Atlantic & Pacific Railroad? At that time Gallup was the station on the railroad from which Cotton hauled his freight.

On Aug. 29, 1888, he wrote Biddle of the A & P requesting a lease on land at the Gallup siding where he could build an adobe warehouse. He indicated he wanted to get the building up that fall before winter set in.

He directed goods to be sent to him at Gallup, to his warehouse. The building was just north of the Santa Fe tracks extending west from Third Street, in the center of Gallup. (It still stands there today.)

In February 1889, he ordered letterheads printed for his business with the heading:

Office of
C.N. COTTON
INDIAN TRADER
Horses, Navajo Blankets, Moqui Pottery,
and Indian Curios a specialty.
Railroad Station
Gallup, New Mexico

As Cotton transferred his interests, he began building a home in Gallup. In his letter to the Commissioner of Indian Affairs March 30, 1889, he stated that his wife Alice and two children had been living in Gallup since November 1888, while he continued to run the trading post at Pueblo Colorado Ranch. (His second child, a daughter named Barbara for Juan Lorenzo Hubbell's daughter, had been born in Coolidge on July 31, 1887.)

Prior to 1890, Cotton and his wife acquired lots 14 through 20 of Block 42 of the Gallup townsite and began to build their home at the northeast corner of Coal and Fifth streets. On March 22, 1890, a deed of trust was recorded for the property. The earliest part of the home, about 35 by 45 feet, contained five rooms and later was the southeast part of the structure.

During his years at the Ganado Trading Post, deep in Indian country, Cotton developed a close friendship with Chief Manuelito. He later related that Manuelito, last and haughtiest of the Navajo war chiefs, had signed with all 12 chiefs the peace treaty with General Sherman in 1868, ending the long warfare with the United States. Cotton was believed to be the only white man ever to have penetrated the hard shell of the old war leader. Manuelito, born in 1819, died in 1894. Some say his death occurred in 1893 but advertising brochures of the C.N. Cotton Co. show Manuelito's date of death as 1894.

To further support the 1894 date there is also a letter in the Navajo Archives at Window Rock dated Feb. 2, 1894, about a quarrel between Manuelito and Chiquite which had been going on for some 18 years. First Lieutenant Plummer, acting Indian agent, wrote that he would speak to Manuelito when he next came in and advise him not to trouble the other man. Plummer's next letter on Feb. 26, 1894, talks of distribution of Manuelito's property, so apparently the chief died between Feb. 2 and 26, 1894.

Cotton commissioned his friend Herman McNeil, architect and sculptor of the Chicago World's Fair of 1893, to make a likeness of the chief. The figure was placed in the gabled front of Cotton's large wholesale building, and the sculptor is said to have received his fee in Indian blankets. Cotton also used a likeness of Manuelito on various business publications. The warehouse in Gallup now houses another business. A new brick front has been added on the east end of the building but Manuelito's statue is still visible through a special window.

The year 1888 was a propitious time for Cotton to move to Gallup, fast becoming a supply center for the Indian trade. Cotton's store was the first big wholesale house, and his pleasing personality and keen eye for business soon had him supplying every trader within 100 miles.

McNitt writes:

> His astuteness is illustrated by his obtaining exclusive regional control of two items basic to the Navajo trade: Arbuckle's coffee and Pendleton blankets. To most Navajo of that time, any coffee or blanket under another name was either counterfeit or an inferior substitute. The trader who was even dimly aware of his Navajo preferences—and most of them were keenly aware—naturally must stock his shelves from Cotton's warehouse. Charlie Newcomb, one of those traders, once said that Cotton paid the Arbuckle's distributor 7 cents a package, or $7 for a case of coffee. Newcomb would pay Cotton $8 for the case, and sell it at Hans Neumann's Guam post where he clerked, for $10. Pendleton blankets came in two grades, Newcomb recalled. "A fringe made the difference between a shawl and a robe. It used to cost us $7 for a robe and $8 for a shawl, and I suppose Cotton made a dollar profit either way. And he sold worlds of them—the Indians wouldn't buy anything else." His secretary in later years, Mrs. Florence Turner, recalled Cotton would order as many as 1,100 Pendleton robes and shawls at a time.

Gallup's young people enjoyed Cotton's generosity. He often bought long strings of theater tickets and passed them out on the street. Then Cotton would join the children to see the show. He sat in the back, puffing on his big black "El Araby" cigar, much to the dismay of the theater manager and in disregard of the "No Smoking" signs.

Although he loved his cigars, Cotton never drank and was violently opposed to alcohol. If he ever found a bottle of whiskey in his home, he would pour it out, then throw the bottle in the trash can. In his terminal illness he was given a toddy. He commented, "I have fought whiskey all my life, now I am down, sick, they make me take it."

In October 1913, C.N. Cotton served as foreman of a grand jury to consider 30 cases of persons accused of selling whiskey to the Indians. The jury concluded:

> In view of the conditions in the neighborhood of Gallup with reference to selling liquor to Navajo Indians and bootlegging, as shown by the evidence

before this jury. . . this jury earnestly recommends that some steps be taken by which a special deputy United States Marshal be located at Gallup.

On Feb. 15, 1915, the Gallup Town Council set annual license fees for saloons at $300, and for wholesale liquor dealers, $600. Cotton thought the fees should be much higher. In 1916, he ran on the Republican ticket and was elected mayor of Gallup for one term.

Six months after its establishment, Cotton became president of the first bank in the county, the McKinley County Bank. He operated it for 16 years before selling. In 1916 he entered the banking business again, opening the Merchant's Bank in the front room of the big Cotton wholesale house. Today the bank is a prosperous financial institution with total assets of more than $34 million.

In 1910, a Miss Koenig, a German immigrant, found employment in the Cotton home. Four years later she quit her job to marry. When visited in Gallup in 1975, she was Mrs. Gasparich, alive and well, bright, spry, and with a keen memory. She recalled the Cotton household well. She said Mrs. Cotton had warm brown eyes, was rather quick, and yet frail and sick. Mrs. Gasparich remembered that all the Cotton children were spoiled. Barbara, the second child, was nicknamed "Topsy."

Once William S. Hart, the cowboy star and hero of silent movie fame, came to Gallup. Over the years he had bought many blankets from Cotton. At the time there was a special blanket on display on the wall. It was an unusual design, of continuous hexagons, so shaded that sometimes they appeared to be convex and at other times concave. Hart asked the price of the blanket, and Cotton said it was one of a kind and not for sale. Hart said price was no object. Cotton told Hart not to leave town without checking with him again. Just before Hart left town, Cotton quoted him a price of $500. Hart thought the price was outrageous but grudgingly bought the blanket. The next time the weaver came to the store, Cotton gave her an extra $50 for the blanket he had sold to Hart.

The Cotton home at 406 W. Aztec St. in Gallup started out in 1888 as a five-room adobe house. Four additional rooms were built on the north in 1895.

The third addition to the home was an enormous parlor, extending west from the original structure. The fourth and last addition was the west wing built in 1908 which contained more bedrooms, and even a bowling alley. These additions made a U-shaped structure, 81 to 84 feet in each direction.

(Author's Collection)

Cottons started building this home after moving to Gallup in 1888. Girl on the wall is Cottons' daughter Barbara.

Mrs. Gasparich recalls that in 1912, Theodore Roosevelt made a trip to Gallup, stayed as a guest in the Cotton home and she was privileged to meet him. She also mentioned that Cotton's room, a combination bedroom and office, was in the southeast corner of the home, the original section. Cotton had a safe built into the wall. North of it was a slightly smaller bedroom called the Hubbell bedroom where Juan Lorenzo Hubbell stayed when he made a trip to Gallup.

A number of movies were made around Gallup, and Victor Fleming, often a director of these films, was a frequent guest in the Cotton home. I recall very vividly a movie of Billie the Kid directed by Fleming, which contained footage of Kit Carson's Cave near Gallup.

In July 1911, Florence Turner, age 19 and fresh out of business college in Albuquerque, went to work for Cotton for a month or two, to fill in for a secretary who was ill. After three months, Cotton asked her to stay on and she continued until he retired in 1930. She always

C.N. Cotton was a great supporter of the Gallup Fire Department. He is at the wheel of a new 1926 American LaFrance pumper.

said there were two important men in her life, her husband and Mr. Cotton.

Mrs. Turner remarked to me: "He is the only man in Gallup who can pick up any woman in town and drive to red rocks and back and not get talked about."

She also said that if an old-timer got down on his luck and sick, Cotton would put him in the hospital and pay the bill. She said Cotton launched trading careers for several men who had worked in his warehouse and demonstrated their honesty and ambition, lending them funds to stock their proposed trading posts.

In 1919 Mrs. Cotton went to the Mayo Clinic for her health, then returned home. She died Dec. 12, 1919.

Herman W. Atkins, an attorney, came to Gallup in 1923 and subsequently became Cotton's attorney. When visited in 1975, he had a portrait of C.N. Cotton on the wall of his office and described him as the finest man he had ever known. He said that while Cotton had a temper and occasionally would tell someone off, he was always a gen-

(Courtesy Mullarky Photo Shop; Author's Collection)
This portrait photo of C.N. Cotton was made in Gallup in
late 1920s.

tleman, was kind and considerate of his employees, and never made a
show of his wealth.

On May 19, 1928, Cotton wrote to H.J. Hagerman, governor of
New Mexico, to complain of bootleggers who were selling liquor to the
Indians. He stated: "I fear that the Indians are going to be in a very
deplorable condition in the next few years, and be charges on the
government." His letter was forwarded to the Secretary of the Interior
in Washington, and a reply was received from the Assistant Prohibition Commissioner that that bureau would cooperate in suppression
of the liquor traffic among the Indians generally, and with the Navajo.

In 1930, Cotton started his retirement. First he sold his large wholesale business to Gross-Kelly, and retired from the Merchant's Bank. The C.N. Cotton Co. was disincorporated in 1932. Cotton retained his blanket room in the basement of the front, or east end, of the C.N. Cotton Co. building. In that room, over the years, he kept what was generally considered the world's largest and finest inventory of Navajo blankets, and usually worth more than $100,000, way back then.

In April 1934, Cotton's health failed and he ceased all trading. In 1936 his condition became worse. He was seriously ill three months, then his condition became critical for a week and the newspaper carried daily bulletins telling of his health. He was cared for at his home by nurses and his personal physician, Dr. D.M. MacCornack. C.N. Cotton died at his home at 3:07 a.m., Sept. 20, 1936.

The list of honorary pallbearers included New Mexico Gov. Clyde Tingley and read like a "Who's Who" of Indian traders. The newspaper account of Cotton's death was the lead story in the *Gallup Independent.* In addition there were notices announcing the closing for his funeral of the Chamber of Commerce, Gallup city offices, McKinley County offices, and all places of business in Gallup.

On his death, Cotton's estate passed to his daughter, Barbara Cotton Seymour. She died in 1940, and her estate went to her son Clifton Cotton Seymour. He sold the house to the Catholic Diocese and the Bishop occupied it until 1978, when the house was sold to Downtown Inc., headed by Basilio DiGregorio. Ambitious plans were made to convert it to a multipurpose community center and historic museum, but the $400,000 cost for renovation was a stumbling block.

In 1982 fire, probably started by transients, caused some damage to the house. Another fire on June 22, 1983, left the house a shambles. Damage was so extensive the ruins were bulldozed away and the site became a used-car lot.

Sources and References

1. Interviews, telephone calls, letters, and tapes:

Atkins, Herman W. Gallup, N.M. Interview Oct. 2, 1975, and letter Dec. 17, 1975.

Bartlett, Mrs. Katherine, senior librarian, Museum of Northern Arizona, Flagstaff. Transcript of taped remembrances of C.N. Cotton by Florence Turner.

Brugge, David M., anthropologist, Chaco Center, Albuquerque. Letters Jan. 22, 1976, Feb. 6, 1976, and Nov. 8, 1977. (This reference marked the start on the trail to unearth the life of C.N. Cotton.)

Fellin, Octavia, librarian, Gallup Public Library. Numerous interviews and letters. Miss Fellin wrote a passage about Manuelito, appearing in *America's Indian Statues* by Marion E. Gridley.

Gasparich, Tom, and his mother, Mrs. Gasparich. Multiple interviews. Gallup.

Greenslade, Thomas B., archivist, Kenyon College, Gambier, Ohio. Letter Jan. 9, 1976.
Guest, John, chairman of the board, Merchants Bank, Gallup. Interview Oct. 2, 1975.
Noe, Mrs. Katie. Telephone interview Feb. 24, 1978.
Rouse, C.M. Interview on history of the Gallup Light and Water situation from 1899 to 1931 inclusive.
Stacher, Herbert C., Gallup. Correspondence about his father, S.F. Stacher, first Indian agent to the Navajo of the Eastern Navajo Jurisdiction.
Turner, Florence, Gallup. Interviews, multiple telephone calls, and letters.

2. Letters and Reports:

Archives of the Navajo Nation, Window Rock, Ariz.; and J. Lee Correll, archaeologist and supervisor, research section, Parks & Recreation Resource Management Branch, the Navajo Tribe. Letters and reports relating to C.N. Cotton.
Atchison, Topeka & Santa Fe Railway Co. Letters from W.S. Autrey, L.R. Thomas, C.R. Lake, and Bill Burk and *Santa Fe Magazine* for May 1924, and letters from Santa Fe Archives.
McNitt Collection, State Records Center & Archives, Santa Fe, N.M. Letters and reports relating to C.N. Cotton.
The National Archives, Washington, D.C. Letters and reports relating to C.N. Cotton.

3. Special Collections and Public Records:

Abeyta, Chief Alfred, Chief of Gallup Fire Department. Search of Gallup Fire Department records, Oct. 2, 1975.
Certificate of Death of Clinton N. Cotton, 1936.
Hubbell Trading Post, National Historic Site, Ganado, Ariz. Trading post files with help of Ailema Benaly and Tom Vaughn, superintendent.
Library of the Univ. of Arizona, Tucson. Special Collection. C.N. Cotton letter book and Clint Bolby Jr., librarian, Special Collections.
Probate Court File No. 558, McKinley County Court House, Gallup. Will of C.N. Cotton.

4. Books, Periodicals, and Theses:

Amsden, Charles Avery. *Navaho Weaving, Its Technique and History.* Glorieta, N.M.: Rio Grande Press, Inc., 1934, 1972.
Curto, J.J. "Indian and Post Trader Tokens: Our Frontier Coinage," published in the *Numismatist,* September 1951.
Gilpin, Laura. *The Enduring Navajo.* Univ. of Texas Press, 1968.
Hannett, Arthur Thomas. *Sagebrush Lawyer.* New York: Pageant Press, Inc., 1964.
James, George Wharton. *Indian Blankets and Their Makers,* copyright 1914, third printing, Glorieta, N.M.: Rio Grande Press, Inc., 1974.
Jeffers, Jo. "Hubbell Trading Post, National Historic Site." *Arizona Highways,* March 1975.
Marshall, James. *Santa Fe, the Railroad That Built an Empire.* New York: Random House, 1945.
McNitt, Frank. *The Indian Traders.* Univ. of Oklahoma Press, 1962.
New Mexico State Library, Santa Fe, Nov. 19, 1976, Virginia Jennings, reference librarian. *New Mexico Historical Review,* Vol. 18, 1943; Reeve, Frank D., *The Government and the Navajo, 1883-1888;* Twitchell, Ralph E., "Leading Facts of New Mexican History, McKinley County."
Newspapers: *Gallup Independent, McKinley County Republican, Gallup Herald, Columbus (Ohio) Dispatch* and *Sunday Inter Ocean,* Chicago.
Rodee, Marian E. *Old Navajo Rugs, Their Development from 1900 to 1940,* Univ. of New Mexico Press, 1981.
Wheat, Dr. Joe Ben. "Three Centuries of Navajo Weaving," *Arizona Highways,* July 1974, and interview March 16, 1977.
Wolfe, Barbara A. Master's thesis, Department of Architecture, Univ. of New Mexico, 1974. Subject: "The C.N. Cotton House, Gallup, New Mexico."
Woodward, "Navajo Silver," Bulletin No. 14, Northern Arizona Society of Science and Art, Flagstaff, December 1946.

About the Author

Dr. Lester L. Williams, author of "C.N. Cotton and His Navajo Blankets," states, "I have been told I was born Aug. 3, 1914, in Mt. Vernon, Ohio. After graduating from Mt. Vernon High School in 1932, I earned a B.S. Degree in 1936 and a M.D. in 1940, both at Western Reserve University in Cleveland."

Dr. Williams served as an Air Force Flight Surgeon in World War II, from 1942 to 1946, attaining the rank of captain, and was awarded a Bronze Star and the Air Medal. He has been in the private practice of medicine in Colorado Springs since 1946.

Now a Reserve Member, Dr. Williams has been a member of the Denver Posse of the Westerners since 1954, and was Sheriff in 1971.

"I helped organize the Pikes Peak Posse of the Westerners in 1976, and was its Sheriff," he recalls. He also helped organize the Historical Society of the Pikes Peak Region in 1974, and served as its president.

"I have given a number of papers at Posse Meetings, and they have appeared in previous *Brand Books*," he said.

Dr. Williams has written two books: *Fighting Fire in Colorado Springs* and *C.N. Cotton and His Navajo Blankets*. In the *Golden Anniversary Brand Book*, Dr. Williams is the author of the chapter on C.N. Cotton, as well as the article, "Old Mose, the Great Grizzly."

"The honor I cherish most was being named Honorary Chief of the Colorado Springs Fire Department, the only honorary chief in its history," he said. "Recently I was named an honorary member of the Pikes Peak Posse of Westerners, one of six in its 18-year history."

In 1984, Dr. Williams received the Vesta Bowden Award of the Colorado Health Care Association, its highest award, for "Service to Nursing Homes."

"Smoke Signal" by *Delano*

Gerard Curtis Delano —
Master Painter of the West

By Richard G. Bowman

O NE OF THE TRULY important Colorado and Western artists was Gerard Curtis Delano, who painted the West as he saw it and was world-famous for his paintings of the Navajo. The great Western artist, Charley Russell, once described the Navajo as being "picture-book people," and the work, inspiration, and total dedication of this unusual man, Delano, certainly proves this to be an understatement. Delano's works in both oils and watercolors have been awarded first prize in many national competitive exhibitions.

Jerry Delano—as he liked to be called—was a native of Marion, Mass., born April 14, 1890, the only child of Capt. Robert Graham Delano and Amanda Luce Delano. According to an unpublished autobiographical account, he was a direct descendant of the French Huguenot pilgrim Philippe de Lannoy, who landed at Plymouth in 1621 from the ship *Fortune*. At an early age, Jerry's talents and instincts were apparent to his parents, and they greatly encouraged his interest in drawing and painting. As a young man, Delano studied at the Art Student's League of New York under the excellent draftsman George Bridgeman, painters Vincent Dumond and Edward Dufner, and the famous artists N.C. Wyeth and Harvey Dunn. This important early training served him well in the years to come.

After serving in the Navy during World War I, he decided to travel to the West, arriving in Denver by train in June 1919. Spending several weeks in the city, he then traveled to Cheyenne to attend the famed Frontier Days rodeo, and there was able to sketch the action of the cowboy performers. "This is truly what I'd come for," he said.

In 1921 Delano homesteaded on Cataract Creek in Summit County between Dillon and Kremmling, in the heart of Colorado's Blue River Valley. Here he lived the life of a cowboy and homesteader, gathering experience for the authentic feel of Western life that complemented his illustrations.

Jerry Delano (by car hood), John A. McGuane (driver), and W.P. Gray left New York for Denver on July 9, 1920

A very delightful friend of mine, Mrs. Uda Harvey, then in her 80s and now deceased, lived on a ranch in the Blue River area, and told of how Delano had come from New York with another man whom they called Mack. They both stayed and worked on a cattle ranch nearby to pay their board and room. Jerry, as Mrs. Harvey called him, was a fine-looking young man, had finished art schools, and was really anxious to paint the West.

She said, "I myself loved to draw and paint as far back as I can remember, and we were really sort of kindred spirits, both having a great love for the beautiful mountains, the rushing streams, and everything that was a part of them. Jerry took up land for a homestead up Cataract Creek on the Blue River, and my husband helped him put up a log cabin which served both as a home and studio for him, and I understand the cabin is still standing. From time to time, I'd seen many of the paintings he was working on and always believed I was a help in making decisions on certain little details. I recall he was trying to figure a way to best show the snow in a blinding blizzard, and he finally figured out that the flip of a tooth brush doused in white paint resulted in a most realistic effect. The snows always seemed to come early and stay late. This gave a magnificent motivation to a person who so loved to paint the wilderness as Jerry did. We left the Blue River Country before Jerry, and never did see him again in person, but these beautiful memories always remained. During the many years since then, I've admired his beautiful paintings as they appeared in many newspapers and magazines, and felt blessed many times to have been personally acquainted with this great artist."

In the mid-1920s, Delano again returned to New York, and had a studio there for many years on East 57th Street. He painted covers for such magazines as *Colliers, Cosmopolitan, Western Story, True Stories, Ranch Romances*, and others. He also painted subjects for various calendar companies, and of prime importance was the Indian series he did for the Santa Fe Railway.

In between all this work, he still managed to study much with the great artists Wyeth and Dunn, which certainly extended his depth of knowledge and techniques as an artist. He was quite successful until the Depression set in, publishing houses started going broke, and the need for artists and illustrators indeed became very lean.

A long-time friend of mine, Gene Rakosnik, found for me a small rare book titled *Western Ballads*, with illustrations by Jerry Delano. Gene asked Jerry if he really did the drawings in this book, and received the blunt reply, "It was one of those projects that helped me put food on the table during the Depression." The many illustrations included in the book are quite humorous, and show some of the influences of both Wyeth and Dunn.

After struggling to make ends meet, Delano decided to head back to his homestead in Colorado. Borrowing $300 from a friend, he piled his belongings into his 1928 Buick and left New York for good.

In 1936 he signed a contract with Street and Smith Publishing to do a series of drawings and stories under the title of "Story of the West" for *Western Story*. These stories and illustrations were to appear weekly. The series was a chronological account of all the events which highlighted the entire development of the West, up until modern times. Because of the extensive research that was necessary, Delano established a studio in Denver where he spent the winter months, with fre-

Delano and neighbor put up a log cabin (still standing) on Cataract Creek in Summit County, Colo., where Jerry homesteaded in 1921. Interior view is of paintings, studio.

(Author's Collection)

quent trips to the library and in drawing the illustrations and writing the stories. The entire series ran for two years, and included 104 drawings with text. The series came to an end in 1940. This seemed to be the turning point in Delano's life, and at last he was able to start on his great desire to paint the West.

The sales of his paintings were steadily increasing, and in the fall of 1943 Delano first visited the vast and colorful state of Arizona and the Navajo reservation. Here he viewed with awe the magnificent red sandstone canyons. When he met the Navajo, Delano realized that they were the people he most wanted to know and paint. The Navajo reservation occupied nearly 9 million acres in Arizona alone, plus valuable acreage in southeastern Utah and northwestern New Mexico. Theirs is the largest Indian reservation in the United States, about 25,000 square miles, and is the largest in population—approximately 100,000.

Alexis McKinney, retired managing editor for *The Denver Post*, stated:

> First time I ever met Jerry Delano was shortly after Paul Gregg died—long-time artist of *The Denver Post*. Not very long after his death, various paint-ers from this part of the country would come up to *The Post* and talk to me about art, and while I don't think any of them came right out and said they hoped we would appoint them as *The Denver Post* artist, none really could take the place of Paul Gregg. At this time, I discussed with Palmer Hoyt, who had been publisher of *The Post* for about a year, the idea of encouraging Western artists to paint paintings we could use on the front cover of *The Post* roto on Sunday, and in other words, sort of spread the good work around. Among the very first to be invited was Gerard Curtis Delano, who was asked to bring in two or three of his paintings. He asked if he could show me some, and of course I think anyone in the world, whether he was an artist or an art critic or not, would be taken immediately by Delano's paintings. They were beautiful. The upshot of that was that I asked him if he would like to have one of his paintings on the cover of *The Denver Post* rotogravure section, and he said he would. It was quite a notable fact that immediately after his paint-ing appeared [May 11, 1947] he became recognized in this part of the coun-try. You couldn't have a painting on the front cover of *The Denver Post* roto section without having hundreds of thousands of people see it, and an artist's fame would spread accordingly. Another additional benefit that came out of this visit was that not very many months later, Delano brought in a Navajo Indian artist named Harrison Begay. Begay, who was a very modest, unas-suming Indian, had brought some sketches. Later he went to his hotel and in a few days brought down two paintings of a Navajo woman on horseback, one of which we used on the front cover of the roto. It wasn't much longer after that, that Harrison Begay was known as the most famous of all the Na-vajo artists, and I would credit Jerry Delano, if not having discovered him, at least to having recognized that this was an opportunity for him to get wide-spread recognition, and this he did help to achieve for Harrison Begay. There-

(Author's Collection)
Jerry Delano: He knew the West firsthand.

fore, not only was Delano interested in art as a whole but in other artists, and I think he was a very genuine and generous person in this regard."

Of all the West, Arizona interested Delano most. He stated:

There is a vastness, an immensity, and a peaceful hush of an enormous cathedral about Arizona's great canyons. Whoever has been within these walls, and has seen the flocks of sheep and goats grazing, heard the distant tinkle of the lead goat's bell, listened to the haunting song of the bright-skirted shepherdess, and who has seen in the distance an approaching rider, a tiny speck against the massive canyon walls, must yearn to perpetuate his impressions of those precious moments. That is why I paint the canyon and the Navajo. The Navajo people are a proud and beautiful race of great dignity. It is my idea to show them as I know them. There are few poorer people anywhere, yet it would be difficult to find a happier lot, and I wonder if there is not a lesson in this for all of us.

Delano became well acquainted with the Navajo language, an important asset for him during his many trips to the reservation.

What made Delano such an exceptional artist was his power in giving a vivid sense of the hidden qualities of nature. Delano called his

(Author's Collection)

In June 1968, Gerard Curtis Delano and his wife Blanche visited the National Cowboy Hall of Fame and Western Heritage Center in Oklahoma City, in the company of another artist, Olaf Wieghorst and wife Maybel. They are looking at a Delano painting, "The Canyon."

paintings "designed realism." He maintained that no pictorial rendering by man can equal nature, and said that the basis of good art is forceful composition, great simplicity, and accurate drawing. An artist must know his subject thoroughly and this must come from study, observation, and insight, with a strong emotional feeling. The last is more important than mere knowledge. Delano had the keen eye to see, the heart to understand, and the skill to place on canvas the color, solitude, and nobility of the life of the Navajo. He did this with a personal style that is original and imaginative. His authentic and sympathetic portrayal of the beauty and dignity of these colorful people is unsurpassed by the work of any other artist. Painting was not just a profession to Delano, it was his life.

Delano was a bachelor for many years, until he met Orah McCowan of Denver, and they were married in 1949. On her death in 1957, he married Blanche Ebert, from Opdyke, Ill., and they lived part-time in Denver. Delano and his wife Blanche maintained a home in Denver but spent most of the summer and fall at their home in Opdyke. Delano loved the peace and quiet of this small town, and he turned out many beautiful paintings there.

Delano was a deeply religious man in his own way. In November 1959 appeared an article in *Good Business*, titled "God's Hand on my Shoulder," by Gerard Curtis Delano. Here he stated:

> I began regularly in my nightly prayer, "God give me the power to paint pictures better than any I've done, paintings so fine and beautiful that people will love them and be inspired by them." I know now that I am but a channel for God's ideas. I know that his messages are constantly given to me, telling me what to do on each painting to make it beautiful. I know and acknowledge that all good comes only from God, that from him alone come all good ideas and all supply, and I know now the trust of Jesus's statement, "Seek ye first his kingdom and righteousness, and all these things shall be added to you." As my sales have increased, so have my gratitude and my tithing to Him from whom all blessings come. Visitors to my studio often ask whether I paint on order or speculation. My answer is, neither, I paint on faith. For I have faith that each finished painting will give real pleasure to most of those who see it, that someone will love it enough to buy it, and that God will supply me with all material needs. I love my work and am completely at peace in doing it. I am happy in knowing that one thing I do well, and in feeling, in fact, whatever I do, I am able to do because God's hand is on my shoulder.

In February of 1972, Delano wrote his good friend Danny Davey in Santa Ana, Calif., that his show in January at Park Floral "had the largest attendance we've ever had. Some of the artists say these are the finest paintings I've ever shown, and at the age of 81, [I am] painting better than ever, and I think so too."

In October of that same year, Gerard Curtis Delano died suddenly. One of my deepest regrets is that I never knew him personally, nor had the reward of his personal acquaintance. The collecting of his paintings, the study and research of his life, have given me real pleasure, and many times along the way I have the feeling that I've always been a long-time friend and acquaintance.

The following 16-page color section includes 24 paintings by Gerard Curtis Delano, from Richard G. Bowman's 1990 biography of the artist. Except for the Indian head on the opposite page, all the paintings bear the artist's titles, and identify present owners. We have sought to provide a representative selection of Delano's work. The pictures are arranged to start with modern subjects, then go back to earlier events, e.g., the Cherokee Trail of Tears (1838) and the Lewis and Clark Expedition (1804-1806). While Delano was often referred to as the "Master Painter of the Navajo"—and several of his Navajo pictures are included here—he painted with a broad brush the panorama of the West.

Delano at easel, working on oil, "IN BONNET AND PAINT," depicting three Sioux Scouts in full war paint. (*Courtesy Alexis McKinney*) All the color pictures in the following section are by Gerard Curtis Delano.

"SADDLING UP," watercolor.
(*From Private Collection*)

Above, "FALL RIDIN'" and below, "AUTUMN LEAVES," near Kremmling, Colorado. Both are oils. (*From Private Collections*)

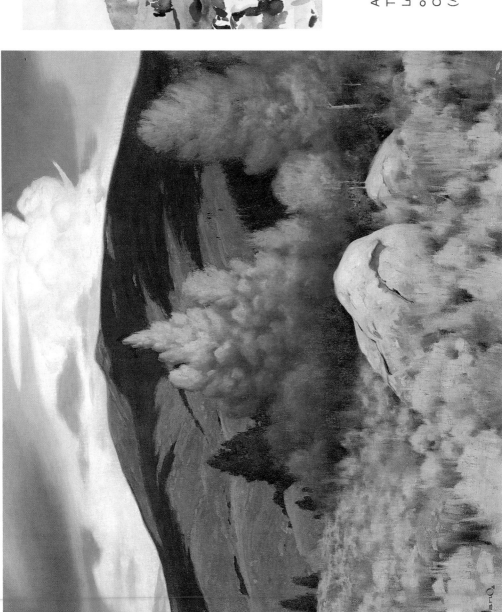

Above, "BRINGING HOME THE HERD," watercolor. Left, "ALONG THE BLUE," oil. Probably near Delano's Colorado homestead. *(From Private Collections)*

"PUEBLO CEREMONIAL DANCE," oil. (*Collection of Dr. Odey Johnson, Courtesy Thomas Gilcrease Institute of American History and Art*, Tulsa)

"LOCAL GOSSIP," oil. (*Gertrude Spratlen Collection*)

1966 Santa Fe Railroad calendar, one of several Delano produced for the company. At left, "NAVAJO BOY," oil. (*Dick and Mary Bowman Collection*)

"CANYON DEL MUERTO," watercolor. (*Dick and Mary Bowman Collection*)

"MONUMENT VALLEY," oil. (*Santa Fe Railroad Collection of Southwest Art*)

Above, "CUSTER ON THE WASHITA" (*Dick, Mary Bowman Collection*);
below, "THUNDERING HOOVES." (*Ted, Christine Mollring Collection*)

"SIOUX SCOUTS," oil. (*Courtesy of the May Gallery*)

"THE CHISOLM TRAIL," oil. (*Courtesy Texas Art Gallery*)

© Gerard Curtis Delano

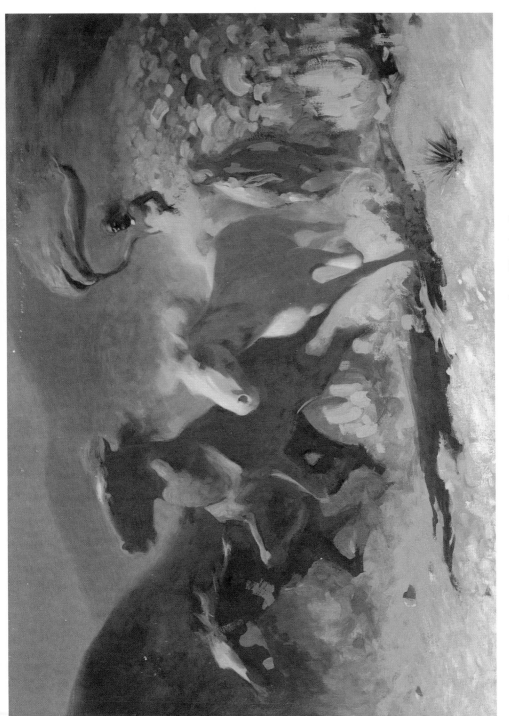

"MOONLIGHT STAMPEDE," oil. (*Collection of Ray Imel*)

"INDIAN TALK," oil. (*Bill and Dorothy Harmsen Collection*)

"WHERE THE GRASS GROWS HIGH," watercolor. (*Anschutz Collection*)

"TRAIL OF TEARS," oil. (*Gertrude Spratlen Collection*)

"MEDICINE BIRD," oil. *(Collection of Dick and Mary Bowman)* This colorful macaw has been traded up from Central America until it has come into the hands of this Sioux warrior, and he is very proud of his medicine bird.

Above, "SIOUX INDIANS WATCHING THE LEWIS AND CLARK EXPEDITION," oil.
(*Bob, Madeline Dickerman Collection*) Below, "IN THE CIRCLE OF DEATH," oil.
(*Private Collection*)

About the Author

Richard G. "Dick" Bowman in 1990 published his biography of Gerard Curtis Delano, *Walking with Beauty.* The beautiful volume included 121 full-color reproductions of Delano paintings. The Denver Westerners is indebted to Dick Bowman for the use of the Delano works—paintings and black-and-white sketches—used in this *Golden Anniversary Brand Book.*

Dick considers himself a native of Denver, where he has lived since he was 6 years old. He attended schools in Denver for the most part. During World War II, in 1942, he entered the Army Air Corps. He survived the rigors of Air Corps Cadet flight training, and participated in a tour of duty with the famed Eighth Air Force in the European Theater. While he was on his 12th mission as a pilot, his B-17 was shot down by German fighters, in a raid over Stuttgart.

Parachuting safely into enemy territory, he managed to survive two cold winters and 21 months of hospitalization and incarceration as a prisoner of war, including an 18-month term at POW Stalag Luft I, on the Baltic Sea. Bowman was finally liberated by the Russian Army in May 1945.

For the past 25 years, Dick has successfully engaged in real estate development in the Denver area and elsewhere.

In addition to his interest in collecting Western art and researching the artists, he is extremely interested in Western Americana, and the history of the early West. He has written numerous articles and presented several programs, among which can be mentioned: "The History of Wells Fargo," "Collecting and the Study of Mormon Money," and "Paper Money of Colorado and the Early West."

Dick resides in Denver with his wife Mary. A longtime member of the Denver Westerners, Dick was well known to fellow Posse Members for his long service as Keeper of the Possibles Bag.

"Instruments Were Primitive" by *Max Smith*

Colorado Hospitals
of the 1800s

By Kenneth L. Gaunt

*T*HE LAND THAT is now Colorado belonged to Spain in 1800, and the inhabitants were various Indian tribes. Medicine was being practiced in several ways, each village having its own medicine man who was both religious leader and physician. His tepee was usually the largest in the village and was covered by leather hides sewn together and was decorated with colorful paintings depicting the history of the village. Inside, the center was reserved for the ceremonial dances, the most important being the Sun Dance for "Good Medicine."

Opposite the east-facing door was the village medicine rack with the medicine arrows, war bonnets, lances, and shields. Hung from the tepee poles were various animal parts, plants, herbs, dolls, whistles, and other paraphernalia he used. Another "cure" was the use of ceremonial sand paintings: intricate pictures using different colors of sand. This ceremony took nine days to complete.

The medicine man was also very knowledgeable about various plants and herbs, and more than 200 plants which he used have been identified and many are still accepted drugs today. The pioneer physicians as they moved west also used these plants and herbs, and even utilized some of the other practices, such as the sweat lodge and sweat trench, built with much ceremony in each camp.

Another of the tepees served as an "obstetrical ward." When a woman's labor began, a rope was suspended from the top of the tepee and she would stand, grasping the rope, until the baby was expelled and caught by a midwife. If the baby was malformed it was put outside the camp and left to die.

In 1801, Spain retroceded the western land to France, and in 1803 President Thomas Jefferson bought the Louisiana Territory from Napoleon for $15 million.

In 1806, the United States sent Lt. Zebulon Pike to trace the Arkansas and Red rivers to their source. Accompanying Pike and his 18 troops was a civilian physician from Virginia, John H. Robinson. He was 29 years of age and had studied medicine in St. Louis for a little more than a year. Dr. Robinson was furnished with some medications and was to attend the sick in exchange for his accommodations. He was also to do a study of the plant life, animals, and geography. While we find no real practice of medicine, he undoubtedly did attend the frozen feet of the men who attempted to climb Pikes Peak in minus 18 degree weather in November 1806, clad only in summer uniforms. Dr. Robinson also probably saved some lives when, after four days without any food in camp, while crossing into the San Luis Valley in the dead of winter, he was able to kill a buffalo.

In 1820, Maj. Stephen A. Long's expedition entered Colorado from the north. The physician and historian with the group was Dr. Edwin James, a very learned man. Dr. James and two companions were the first white men to ascend Pikes Peak. Neither he nor Dr. Robinson had hospital supplies, but it is interesting to note that neither doctor lost a single patient, nor did Colonel Dodge in 1835, on his exploration. (Fremont later took the chance of not including a physician in his exploration company.)

The early trading posts made no provisions for either a physician or a hospital. A Dr. Hempsted is known to have been the resident physician at Bent's Fort. When Col. Stephen W. Kearney and Col. Sterling Price entered Colorado and camped near Bent's Fort in 1845, it is recorded that a field hospital was set up at their camp.

Military hospitals originated in 1818 when the Army appointed a Surgeon General and gave him direct authority over the Army medical officers. He began to formulate the regulations for field hospitals and on-post hospitals.

By 1820 military hospitals were sufficiently well organized to function efficiently and established chiefly for emergency purposes at Army posts along the frontier. The regulations advocated the use of a new building, preferably of wood construction. The importance of ventilation was stressed as well as the number of cubic feet of air space surrounding each bed. In Colorado, however, many hospitals were built of adobe and this often caused problems because of the incorrect making of the adobe and improper supports for roofs and walls. Buildings were to be placed on a large expanse of ground so that they might be widely separated from administrative buildings and barracks. The usual capacity was adequate for 25 to 60 men. The dispensary, storeroom, kitchen, mess hall, washrooms, and bathrooms were usual-

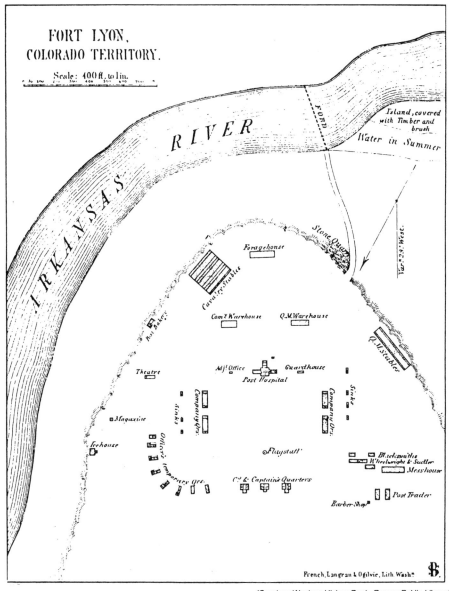

(Courtesy Western History Dept., Denver Public Library)

Ft. Lyon, C.T., was near present-day Las Animas.

ly inside or attached to the building, and latrines were some distance away. Some posts put their sinks over a canal or stream and thus disposed of waste. The medical orderly might live in the building, but more often was in a nearby tent or lean-to.

Hospital equipment was carried in the field in a hospital wagon loaded with litters, folding cots, tents, surgeon's drugs, equipment, and instruments. These instruments were stored in fitted wooden boxes, and by the time of the Civil War the sets were quite complete.

In the annual surgeon's reports of 1868-1869, it is interesting to note that the number of personnel who became ill was about 150 percent of garrison strength. The diseases reported were typhoid fever, malarial fever, diarrhea and dysentery, tonsillitis, epidemic catarrh, venereal disease, scurvy, rheumatism, and catarrhal affections. The last included laryngitis, bronchitis, pneumonia, and pleurisy. Deaths averaged one a year per post.

Colorado's first Army fort was Ft. Massachusetts, commissioned March 31, 1852. The fort was about six miles north of the present site of Ft. Garland (east of Alamosa), and intended to protect the settlers in the San Luis Valley. It was poorly situated defensively and poorly constructed, and was more than 200 miles from its supply sources. The men suffered from lack of clothing and supplies and during the winters of 1853 and 1856 most of the troops were moved south into New Mexico.

In 1856 construction was begun nearby on a new post, named Ft. Garland. A hospital, built of adobe, consisted of two six-bed wards, a dispensary, lavatory, and separate latrine. The adobe bricks were improperly dried before the walls were built, and the beams were too small and set too far apart. Soon the building began to settle, the beams broke, and the ceiling and walls had to be supported. The hospital building was abandoned in 1877, and Ft. Garland was shut down in 1883.

Ft. Wise, first named Ft. Fauntleroy, was commissioned on June 30, 1860, and was a short distance east of Bent's "New Fort of 1853." Major Sedgwick constructed this fort, which had a 26-bed hospital. In 1866 the Arkansas River overflowed its banks and the fort was flooded out. A new site was selected some 20 miles east near the town of Las Animas.

A new fort was constructed, and commissioned as Ft. Lyon on June 1, 1867. The first hospital consisted of one old hospital tent for a dispensary, a 15 ft. by 25 ft. canvas ward, and a canvas kitchen. Soon the hospital was installed in a fine sandstone building in the middle of the fort. This later became the post headquarters. A third hospital was established with an executive building and two wings. One wing

(Courtesy Western History Dept., Denver Public Library)

In 1873, Denver Hospitals and Sanatoriums erected first unit of what became Denver General Hospital.

contained the patients ward; the other wing housed the mess hall, kitchen, and attendants' room. Another patients ward was added a year later, each ward having one water closet and bathroom, 12 beds, a wardmaster's room and a linen room. (It was here that Kit Carson died on May 23, 1868. The house in which he lived is now a Memorial Chapel.)

This post was abandoned in October 1889, and remained vacant until October 15, 1906, when it was occupied and used as a U.S. Naval Hospital until 1922. It then became a tuberculosis sanatorium for the U. S. Health Service. In a few months it was transferred to the Veterans Administration as a tuberculosis, general medicine, and mental hospital. Since 1933 its principal function has been that of a mental institution. Thus the hospital at Ft. Lyon is the oldest existing hospital in Colorado, although its service was not continuous.

The Territory of Colorado was established on Feb. 28, 1861, and in September of that year, Camp Weld was established by Gov. William Gilpin. This small camp was on the banks of the South Platte River near Denver and housed the First Regiment of Colorado Volunteers. The hospital was a two-story building, 24 ft. by 40 ft., with a dispensary, large ward and mess hall on the first floor, and a 40-patient ward on the second floor. This camp experienced several periods of trouble, one being a money shortage when Governor Gilpin issued his own drafts on the U. S. Treasury for $375,000, which the government did not want to honor. Two devastating fires destroyed most of the camp buildings and the post was abandoned in 1865. (A marker on Eighth Avenue under the viaduct marks the site in Denver.)

Camp Rankin in the northeast corner of the state was built in 1863 to protect pioneer settlers, mail and passenger coaches, and freight wagons from the Indians. The original fort and almost all of the town of Julesburg were wiped out on Jan. 7, 1865, by the Indians who had been aroused by the Sand Creek Massacre. The fort was moved, rebuilt, reinforced and, in November 1865, was renamed Ft. Sedgwick.

The hospital at Ft. Sedgwick was an L-shaped adobe building measuring 28 ft. by 100 ft., with a wing 28 ft. by 32 ft. It contained 10 beds, a dispensary, stewards room, kitchen, dining room, storeroom, and surgeon's quarters. There was no bath, washroom, or water closet attached to the building. It was here that Michael Beshoar, an Army doctor, first practiced medicine in Colorado. After about a year, he left the Army, came to Denver, then went to Pueblo where he practiced medicine, started the *Pueblo Colorado Chieftain* newspaper (later the *Pueblo Chieftain*), and opened the first drugstore in the south part of the state. He later went to Trinidad, Colo.

Since Camp Weld had been closed for two years, the citizens of Denver requested that another post be established in Denver. Finally in 1886, after 20 years, the Army was convinced that Denver was the most logical place to locate a permanent military installation, and that several small outlying forts could be abandoned. General Sherman picked a site 10 miles from the center of the city, and 640 acres of land were selected for the reservation. The public lost no time in raising $33,000 for the purchase of the land. The Army moved in on Oct. 22, 1887. Construction required almost seven years. First known as Ft. Sheridan, it was officially named Ft. Logan on April 5, 1889, in memory of Gen. John A. Logan, an outstanding Union officer. The buildings were constructed of red brick and included a hospital with two 42-bed wards. Records show the hospital was constructed in 1888 at a cost of $19,865. Additions were made at various times until 1949 and it was torn down in the 1950s. A new hospital was constructed and in 1960, when the federal government transferred all of Ft. Logan to the

St. Joseph's erected in 1876 in Denver, is Colorado's oldest continually operating hospital.

State of Colorado, the hospital became part of the Fort Logan Mental Health Center.

Other military forts were at Ft. Collins, Ft. Junction, and Ft. Morgan. Each had a small hospital.

The first physician to practice in Denver was Dr. Levi Russell, in 1858, and by 1860 there was a fair complement of physicians in the Territory. In 1860 the Jefferson Medical Society was formed and one of its first acts was to adopt a code of ethics and establish a bill of rates.

History is vague, but there seem to have been two "City Hospitals." The first was organized in January 1860 by Dr. McDowell and was between 19th and 20th streets on Larimer Street. During the same year, Dr. J. F. Hamilton was appointed City Physician and opened a small hospital, also named City Hospital, in a house at 16th and Blake streets. It was closed in 1861.

County poorhouses were started and served as dispensaries and hospitals for periods of time. In 1862 Arapahoe County took over a 1½-story building on 11th Street as a poorhouse. In 1867 it was aban-

(From St. Luke's Hospital Historical Committee Papers)
St. Luke's Hospital was housed 1881-1891 in the Grand View Hotel, 17th
and Federal, in Denver.

doned and a large building at Ninth and Champa streets was procured
and used as a county hospital.

Early in 1873 the county bought three acres at the corner of Sixth
and Cherokee streets and built the first unit of what was to become
Denver General Hospital.

In 1870-1871 the Episcopalians organized Saint Luke's Hospital in
Central City.

In 1871, the Rev. Father Raverly, a pastor in Central City, asked
the Sisters of Leavenworth to start a hospital there. However, he was
transferred to Denver and plans were dropped. Father Machebeuf
became the Catholic Bishop and he requested that the Sisters open a
hospital in Denver. In 1873 Mother Xavier agreed that the Sisters
would rent a house and open a hospital on a small scale until the
magnificent building proposed by the Bishop could be built.

On Sunday morning, Sept. 14, 1873, Sister Theodora McDonald,
Sister Veronica O'Hara, and Sister Mary Clare Bergen arrived in
Denver to serve at the hospital. A small brick house containing six
rooms and a basement at Market Street between 25th and 26th streets

was rented. That this location was near the "red light" district did not concern the Sisters in the least. The next week they opened the institution first known as St. Vincent's. After one month, the building being inadequate, they were compelled to rent another smaller house and add four Sisters to the staff. After a year they moved to the former St. James Hotel at 22nd and Blake streets, where the rent was $80 a month. Meanwhile a foundation for a new hospital was begun by the Bishop, who was so infatuated with his plans that the Sisters called it the "Hotel Dieu." It was to be five stories high and contain 50 rooms. However, it had to be abandoned because it was too near some smelters, and the foundation was below grade. More than $10,000 was lost in this dream.

A subscription was taken up throughout the city and state for another hospital. Ex-Gov. John Evans gave a city lot, which was sold for $1,000 and Ex-Gov. Gilpin and his wife gave Fractional Block 12, Park Avenue Addition. So it was that at 18th and Franklin streets, St. Joseph's Hospital was erected in 1876. Thus St. Joseph's is the oldest continuously operating hospital in Colorado. Dr. F. J. Bancroft and Dr. Justus were the first physicians.

While traveling to Denver by train, the first Sisters of St. Joseph's Hospital met a young priest from Leadville, a Father Robinson, who later petitioned the Mother House to send three Sisters to open a hospital in Leadville. In December 1878, three Sisters arrived in Denver by train en route to Leadville. From Denver they boarded the train for the first 17 miles, then traveled by stage coach in 40-below weather. By the second day, they were nearly frozen. That night was spent at a ranch and the third day a wagon bed, with wheels replaced by sled runners, was used to travel the last six miles to Leadville. The people of Leadville donated funds, and Sister Mary Fischer, Francis Davy, and Bernard Pendergast selected the location for the hospital on lots donated by W. H. Stevens. A frame structure was begun immediately, and on March 1, 1879, a bitter-cold night, a patient was brought in and laid upon some shavings. A workman boarded up the windows, hung a door or two, and the Sisters tended their first patient. He was a prospector who had become frozen while crossing the Mosquito Range. The man died four days later, and Father Robinson administered the last rites. Soon other patients came in—27 measles cases at one time—and the rolls increased to 70 patients.

Several more Sisters were added to the staff, and in June 1879 the hospital had to be enlarged. Then $4,000 was raised for an addition,

(Pictures Courtesy Western History Dept., Denver Public Library)

Above, Glockner Sanatorium. Below, Union Printers Home. Both are in Colorado Springs.

to be "lathed, plastered, and painted." A chapel, 12 ft. by 29 ft., was included, as well as a laundry. The most common complaints of patients were plumbism or lead poisoning, injuries, typhoid, and frozen extremities.

In 1881 St. Luke's Hospital was founded in Denver. Surely it was

Mrs. Sarah Griswold Spalding who initiated and maintained the hospital, although, it was her husband, John Franklin Spalding, the Episcopal Bishop, who received the honor.

In June 1881 the Grand View Hotel at 20th Street and Federal Boulevard was purchased for $7,000, and a hospital was opened. Most of the funds were raised by the Ladies' Hospital Aid Society who also furnished many necessary items, such as dishes, bedding, food, furniture, and equipment.

In 1888 a city ordinance was passed prohibiting the building of a hospital inside the city limits, declaring such an institution to be a nuisance. This was directed at St. Luke's Hospital, which hoped to build a hospital at 19th and Pearl streets. Finally, in 1890, the court ruled that a hospital was not a nuisance and the cornerstone was laid on Sept. 20. During that night someone painted the cornerstone black and the paint remained in the lettering for many years. The new building was dedicated on Oct. 18, 1892.

Other hospitals would appear throughout the state as the need arose. A mining accident, an epidemic, or an uprising such as the Trinidad War of 1867, would result in small hospitals being opened for short periods of time.

The Union Pacific Railroad Hospital at 40th and Williams streets in Denver was opened in 1884.

The National Jewish Hospital for Consumptives was founded in 1890 at Spivak and completed in 1899.

The Denver Homeopathic Medical College and Hospital Association was founded in 1894 at 2348 Champa St.

St. Mary's Hospital was founded in Pueblo by the Sisters of Charity, who came in 1882 to nurse the sick. By 1883 the hospital at Quincy Street and Grant Avenue was a three-story facility.

In 1882 the Sisters moved from a store-front hospital in Conejos to Durango. In 1885 they built Mercy Hospital, a two-story sandstone, 25-bed facility.

The original Miner's Hospital in Breckenridge was turned over to the Benedictine Sisters in 1886 and renamed St. Joseph's. It was closed in 1890.

St. Joseph's Hospital was founded in Ouray in 1887 by Bishop Machebeuf and the Sisters of Mercy. It was brought out of debt in 1896 by Camp Bird Mine owner Tom Walsh and later purchased by the Idarado Mine but ceased operating as a hospital in 1958. The Ouray County Historical Society bought the building where it opened a museum in 1971.

St. Nicholas Hospital at Cripple Creek was founded in 1895 by the Sisters of Mercy. It was saved from the fire of 1896 and was replaced in 1898. Cripple Creek had about 10 hospitals during its big boom, most of them in private residences.

Victor had two hospitals in the 1890s. The Red Cross Hospital was where Jack Dempsey was treated after an accident in the Portland Mine.

Silverton started a hospital in 1883, but it was not opened until 1909.

Citizens Hospital was opened in Aspen in 1891, and was unaffiliated with any church.

The Miner's Hospital was opened in 1893 in Telluride. The impressive stone building is now a museum.

St. Joseph's Hospital, Georgetown, was opened in 1880, but the train tracks ran nearby and one night several houses and the hospital were burned down by a fire caused by sparks from the engine. The building was torn down and the brick used to build a new church.

Gunnison, Lake City, and Fairplay also had small hospitals.

The Institution for the Blind and Mute in Colorado Springs was authorized by the Territorial Legislature in 1874. By 1899 there were 100 pupils.

The State Asylum for the Insane was established in Pueblo on Feb. 8, 1879. One large building was built. In 1893 additional buildings were needed and the cottage plan was adopted. At the close of 1899 there were 316 males and 177 females in the institution.

There was yet another class of hospitals to be opened in Colorado which were to have a tremendous impact upon the state. These were the tuberculosis sanatoriums. The first Colorado settlers noticed the warmth of the winters and the moderate extremes of heat and cold.

Several physicians said that the pure, stimulating, and dry air had reduced capacity for conducting heat and electricity, and therefore helped cure pulmonary diseases.

During the first years, the sufferers were told to cross the plains slowly and halt for a week or two at various points in western Kansas to allow their lungs to adjust to the thin air. In 1883, a Denver physician, Charles Denison, joined in organizing the American Climatological Association. For two decades the association encouraged scientific discussions of the Colorado climate. Americans and foreigners, alike, flocked to Colorado. Every November the asthmatics and

Colorado Hospitals and Sanatoriums

NAME	LOCATION	FOUNDED
St. Joseph's	Denver	1876
Denver County	Denver	1879
Sisters'	Leadville	1879
Park County	Fairplay	1880
St. Joseph's	Georgetown	1880
Minnequa	Pueblo	1880
St. Luke's	Denver	1881
St. Mary's	Pueblo	1882
Denver Rio Grande RR	Salida	1883
St. Joseph's	Ouray	1884
Santa Fe Railroad	LaJunta	1884
Mercy	Durango	1884
Steele Memorial	Denver	1885
Fremont County	Canon City	1885
Cottage Home	Denver	1886
St. Francis	Colorado Springs	1887
St. Raphael's	Trinidad	1888
Glockner Sanatorium	Colorado Springs	1889
Telluride	Telluride	1890
Citizens'	Aspen	1890
Union Printers Home	Colorado Springs	1892
St. Anthony's	Denver	1892
Oakes Home	Denver	1894
St. Mary's	Grand Junction	1895
St Nicholas	Cripple Creek	1895
Larimer County	Fort Collins	1895
Boulder Tubercular	Boulder	1896
Woodcroft	Pueblo	1896
University of Colorado	Boulder	1898
Park Avenue	Denver	1898
Sutherland's	Loveland	1898
Montcalm Sanatorium	Manitou Springs	1900

consumptives fled the cold, dark winters of the East and filled Denver and Colorado Springs boarding houses. In the 1870s and 1880s, it was estimated that one-third of the population consisted of recovered invalids.

Physicians began to advise institutionalization, for tuberculosis was found to be contagious. Landlords then began rejecting newcomers' applications for rooms and employers slammed the doors in their faces. In 1889 Glockner Sanatorium was opened in Colorado Springs, followed in 1892 by the Union Printers Home. Soon there were many other tubercular hospitals, including Montcalm which opened in 1900 in Manitou Springs. By 1900 there were 32 hospitals and sanatoriums operating in Colorado.

Military Facilities

POST	COMMISSIONED	DECOMMISSIONED
Pike's Log Stockade	Feb. 1807	March 1807
The Old Spanish Fort	1819	Abandoned
Ft. Massachusetts	March 30, 1852	June 24, 1858
Ft. Garland	June 24, 1858	Oct. 2, 1883
Ft. Wise	June 30, 1860	July 22, 1884
Camp Weld	Sept. 1861	1865
Ft. Collins	Oct 23, 1864	July 16, 1872
Ft. Junction	Spring 1864	
Ft. Morgan	1864	1868
Ft. Sedgwick	Sept. 1864	July 22, 1884
Ft. Stevens	July 1866	Sept. 26, 1866
Ft. Reynolds	June 12, 1867	June 19, 1872
Ft. Lyon	June 1, 1867	Oct. 1889
Camp Custer	Aug. 1877	Three days only
Cantonment on White River	Oct 11, 1879	July 12, 1883
Ft. Crawford (Cantonment on the Uncompahgre)	May 31, 1880	July 22, 1884
Ft. Lewis	Feb 17, 1879	1891
Ft. Logan	Oct 26, 1887	To date
Camp Adams	May 1, 1889	May 17, 1889

Bibliography

Bannerman, Francis. Military Goods Catalogue, 1907. Glendale, N.Y.; reprinted by Benchmark Publishing Co., 1970.

Brandes, T. Donald. *Military Posts of Colorado.* Fort Collins, Colo.: Old Army Press, 1973.

Custer, Elizabeth. *Boots and Saddles.* Norman: Univ. of Oklahoma Press, 1961.

Daniels, Helen Sloan. *The Ute Indians of Southwestern Colorado.* Durango Public Library Project, 1941.

Denison, Charles, M.D. *Health Resorts of Colorado.* Boston: Houghton, Osgood, 1881.

Hafen, LeRoy R., Ph.D., Lit. D. *Colorado and Its People. Vol II.* New York: Lewis Historical Publishing Company, Inc., 1948.

Hafen, LeRoy R., Ph.D., Lit. D. *Our State: Colorado.* Old West Publishing Co., 1966.

Hart, Herbert M. *Pioneer Forts of the West.* Seattle: Superior Publishing Co., 1967.

Ingersoll, Ernest. *Knocking Around the Rockies.*

Laubin, Reginald. *The Indian Tipi.* Norman: Univ. of Oklahoma Press, 1957.

Lee, William Storrs. *Colorado.* New York: Funk and Wagnalls, 1970.

Rockwell, Wilson. *The Utes: A Forgotten People.* Denver: Sage Books, 1956.

Sethman, Harvey A. *Century of Colorado Medicine 1871-1971.*

Smiley, Jerome C. *History of Denver.* Denver Times-Sun Publishing Co., 1901.

Taylor, Ralph C. *A Guide to Historic Pueblo.*

About the Author

Ken Gaunt is one of the old-timers of the Denver Posse of the Westerners, having become a Corresponding Member in 1955. Now a Posse Member, he has been elected the organization's Deputy Sheriff for 1995. He presented his paper, "Colorado Hospitals of the 1800s," in 1974. He is also well remembered in the organization for his dramatized, costumed portrayal of early-day bunco artist, Soapy Smith in "Soapy Smith Returns to Denver."

Ken retired as chief pharmacist of St. Luke's Hospital in Denver, and has been licensed by the Colorado State Board of Pharmacy for more than 55 years. Born in Colorado Springs, he is a fourth-generation native of Colorado. His mother arrived in the Springs in 1895, and her family worked for Gen. William Jackson Palmer, pioneer entrepreneur and railroad builder. "There are two more generations of the family now in Colorado," Ken adds.

Gaunt is a World War II veteran, having served with the 168th Field Artillery Battalion of the Colorado National Guard. In addition to Western history, his many interests and hobbies include travel, photography, ancient coin-collecting, ice-dancing, and raising emus and llamas.

"Painless Parker drew big crowds," *Courtesy Denver Public Library.*

Early Colorado Tooth Tinkerers

(And the Fight Against Painless Parker)

By Dr. George W. Krieger

*T*HE FIRST RECORDED practicing dentist in Denver was Eugene A. Crocker. Little is known of him, except that his office was on Larimer Street between F and G (or today's 15th and 16th) streets. By 1868, Dr. Crocker had left Colorado Territory for parts unknown. The first published reference to dental care, however, was in the Dec. 14, 1859, *Rocky Mountain News.* J.W. Smith, M.D., was located one door east of the Apollo Hall (1425 Larimer St.). His ad stated that "Dr. Smith is prepared to perform any DENTAL operation desired." This points up the interchangeability of the various health resources, at that time. Physicians—or barbers—often extracted teeth, while some dentists took care of some injuries. In fact, Dr. Mallory Catlett, fresh out of dental college, found this out firsthand in Victor. Because of a lack of physicians, Dr. Catlett ended up treating many of the injured, and helped identify bodies following the 1904 Independence Mine Depot dynamiting. He did similar duty the following year, after an Independence Mine accident.

In truth, there were other dental practitioners in Colorado before Drs. Crocker and Smith. The Indians certainly must have required some sort of dental treatment, even if it simply consisted of the plucking out of a loose tooth. When a problem arose that was more major, the Indians consulted their medicine man for help. In 1855, the Rev. William Leah of Omaha, Neb., described a Pawnee medicine man's treatment of an aching wisdom tooth. "He danced around the patient in a semicircle, rattling a gourd . . . he took a small stone knife and cut an 'X' on Running Wolf's cheek, directly over the throbbing tooth. He sucked at the cut lightly . . . pretended to draw out the fang . . .

Some Indian Remedies

Cow Parsnip — raw root pieces inserted into tooth cavities to stop pain.

Indian Gum Plant — cottony fuzz from the base of the plant inserted into cavities.

Indian Tobacco — poultice of leaves placed along gum for toothache.

Little Rabbit Brush — finely mashed leaves inserted into cavities.

Locoweed — decoction of boiled root used for toothaches and granulated eyelids.

Penstemon — root portion chewed and inserted into cavity.

Prickly Ash (Toothache Tree) — mainly east of Mississippi — bark chewed for relief.

Prickly Poppy — root portion chewed and inserted into cavity.

Smokebush — stems chewed to relieve toothache.

Sweetroot — piece of raw root applied to aching tooth.

Utah Juniper — leaves pounded, moistened and tied in a cloth with a hot rock then held on jaw for swollen sore gums and toothache relief.

Willow — mashed roots applied to gums to relieve toothache.

Yarrow — green leaves could be chewed to relieve pain.

Yellow Prince's Plume — pulped root inserted into tooth cavities or along gums.

—From *Medicinal Uses of Plants by Indian Tribes of Nevada*, 1957, Train, Henrichs, and Archer.

---

then dashed it into the fire. 'The Evil Spirits cannot use it again,' he said triumphantly." On the off chance that this sort of treatment did not solve the problem, teeth were extracted by pounding them with a stone against a stick as a wedge. Another way to pull a tooth was to tie a buckskin thong to it, then fix the other end to some immobile object (such as a tree), jerking the sufferer's head away from it. In some tribes, a red-hot leather-working awl was poked into a cavity to reduce pain. Most anything that could be mashed up and pushed into the tooth, or chewed on, was tried to fight dental pain. One book about the tribes of Nevada lists 14 different plants used for toothache relief, such as yarrow, prickly poppy, locoweed, and penstemon. Other Indian dental customs included not throwing something on the fire that had been chewed, lest the fire chew one's teeth; and immediately spitting upon seeing a shooting star to prevent tooth loss.

The Sept. 24, 1861, issue of the *Rocky Mountain News* contains ads for Dr. W.W. Thompson and Dr. W.F. Griswold. By the Dec. 9 issue, only Dr. Griswold was listed, one door east of the Broadwell House at G (16th) and Larimer streets. Dr. Griswold came from Leavenworth, Kans., to Denver, then soon moved on to Montana in search of gold. Such was the transient nature of frontier dentistry, with many of the practitioners attracted to Colorado by gold mining, not by teeth. Eastern dental students would often put aside their studies for a year or two, and travel to the Rocky Mountain gold camps to seek their fortunes. When gold did not appear in every pan or shovelful, these argonauts often turned to street-corner dentistry to subsist, before returning to school.

That there were, indeed, dentists in mountain communities is evident from a Jan. 2, 1864, *Rocky Mountain News* ad for Dr. Isaac B. Brunel. Dr. Brunel's office was on Main Street in Central City, two doors down from the bakery. This same paper, by the way, carried an ad for a Dr. L.W. Frary, located near the corner of Larimer and F (15th) streets. The first city directory for Denver, published in 1866, listed two dentists: Eugene Crocker and Charles P. Moffett. Dr. Moffett had an office in the Medical Block of Larimer Street (between F and G streets), until his death in February 1884. The *First Annual Rocky Mountain Directory and Colorado Gazetteer* in 1871 listed five Denver dentists, serving 9,000 people. Their names were C.P. Moffett, R.C. Mowbray, J.H. Sutfin, B.W. Rogers, and William Smedley. The last two brought some true professional stability to Denver dentistry with their partnership in 1870.

Dr. B. Wesley Rogers came West to improve his health, as did so many other Colorado pioneers. He set up practice on May 25, 1867, in a 9-by-13-ft. room at G and Larimer streets. In November 1870 he went into partnership with Dr. William Smedley, an 1866 graduate of the University of Pennsylvania College of Dental Surgery. Dr. Smedley was a truly adventurous soul, having taken a wagon-train journey in 1862 from Council Bluffs, Iowa, to Oregon—just to try it. From the west fork of the Green River in Wyoming, he and his friend David W. Culp left their wagon train to go it alone—the train was too slow for them.

The wagon train was subsequently wiped out by Indians, while Culp and Smedley were able to make it to Salem, Ore. The 2,000-mile trip took five months, recorded by Smedley in a fascinating journal, *Across the Plains.* The Sept. 28, 1862, entry described travel through the Cascade Mountains:

Persons unacquainted with mountain roads could scarcely believe it possible for wagon and team to go down, without all being demolished together—and their passage can only be effected by removing all but one yoke of cattle, and rough-locking all four of the wheels, or by attaching a treetop behind the wagon to drag after and hold it back.

Dr. Smedley had a long and influential career in Denver. In 1887 he became the first president of the Colorado State Dental Association. His sons Will and Clyde also had distinguished dental careers, as have his grandsons Charles and John. Dr. John Smedley is a highly respected Denver dentist and teacher, while Charles Smedley is a Littleton practitioner immortalized as "Hardrock" Smedley, East Tincup's favorite dentist, on Pete Smythe's old Denver radio broadcasts.

While it is not recorded, perhaps it was Dr. William Smedley who took care of the famous toothache that led to the discovery of Marshall Pass in 1873. While commanding a party of the Wheeler Survey of the Rocky Mountains, William Louis Marshall was struck by "one of the worst toothaches that ever befell a mortal." The survey party was near present Silverton in the San Juan Mountains. They were some 30 miles from any Denver dentist who could relieve the pain, so

(From Author's Collection)

Dr. William Smedley, left, had a long and influential career in Denver. In 1887, he became the first president of the Colorado State Dental Association. Eugene A. Crocker is believed to have been the first practicing dentist in Colorado, and was listed in Denver's first City Directory in 1866.

severe that Marshall could not open his mouth or move his jaw.

The main party was to follow Cochetopa Pass, 60 miles northeast of Silverton, while Marshall sought a quicker route. He and packer Dave Mears set off on mules heading for a depression in the divide that Marshall had recalled seeing. Fighting bad weather and fallen timber for six days, they traveled 12 miles to the top. Ignoring the tooth pain, Marshall carefully charted the pass that would bear his name and be used eight years later by the Denver & Rio Grande Railway (17 miles southwest of Salida at 10,846 ft.).

Mears and Marshall then headed on to Denver, beating the rest of the party by four days and saving 125 miles.

Dr. Reuben B. Weiser came to Georgetown in 1872. At various times he served as a state senator, chief of the Georgetown Champion Volunteer Fire Department, and dean of the Denver Dental School. His May 24, 1877, ad in the *Georgetown Courier* stated:

> The care of the teeth is too often neglected. Filling is neglected till too late. Dr. R.B. Weiser, whose dentistry work in this town for the past five years has given universal satisfaction, is one who keeps up with the times, his work table being supplied with all the approved modern instruments. For sets of teeth, he has the celluloid base, a composition taking the place of other bases, and much cheaper. Chloroform and ether used when desired.

The ad of his competitor, Dr. G.W. Avery, stated simply, "Anaesthetics administered when practicable." At high altitudes, gaseous anesthetics were certainly less dependable. The first anesthetic would have been whiskey, administered in large doses. Later, chloroform on a cloth was used to knock out a patient for a few minutes. Another was ether, poured over a cone-shaped mask.

Nitrous oxide—laughing gas—was produced by heating ammonium nitrate, and the gas was then stored in tanks. The general anesthetic effect lasted for only 90 seconds and was dangerous, as it basically asphyxiated patients, causing them to turn blue. This was later made safer by the addition of oxygen, to reduce its effect.

Local anesthetics, injected to numb an area, came along in 1884 with the use of cocaine. The story is related of a South Platte mountain dentist who gave cocaine to a lady to extract her tooth. When the procedure was done, the patient felt weak, and the dentist had coffee brought to her. While easily accepting the use of cocaine for her teeth, the lady refused the coffee, stating that she never drank anything stronger than beer after breakfast.

Dr. John Grannis came to Colorado Springs in 1886 from Ohio, seeking a cure for his tuberculosis. This tall, self-effacing man would

Dr. John H. "Doc" Holliday of Atlanta, Ga., received a dental degree in 1872, and for a time was a faro dealer in Denver. He returned to Denver in 1882 and was later arrested. He died of tuberculosis in Glenwood Springs, Colo., in 1887.

(Courtesy Western History Dept., Denver Public Library)

be remembered today only as the second Colorado State Dental Association president, had not "Crazy Bob" Womack stopped in Grannis' office for a filling. Bob had found some float ore, and was convinced that gold had to exist in the Cripple Creek area.

Womack became a frequent visitor to Grannis' North Tejon house and on Dec. 2, 1889, gold fever grabbed him. Dr. Grannis, though far from being a rich man, was persuaded to borrow $500 at 7 percent interest to grubstake Bob, in exchange for one-half interest in anything found. In October 1890, Bob Womack discovered a 2-foot-wide shaft of rock on his Grand View claim, which later became the El Paso Lode. More money was needed to develop the vein, but little interest from mining men was forthcoming. In 1891, Womack again asked Dr. Grannis for money. The dentist reluctantly borrowed $600 more from the Exchange National Bank at 12 percent interest, using his dental equipment as collateral.

At the end of 1891, Grannis bought out Bob's half interest in the

El Paso Lode for $300, then sold a four-fifths stake to Claire Frisbee for $8,000 in early 1892. The Cripple Creek/Victor gold rush had finally hit, making Dr. Grannis a wealthy man. After losing all his El Paso Lode profits to bad mining ventures in Arizona and Mexico, Dr. Grannis returned to dentistry in Colorado Springs, where he died in 1911.

Dr. John H. "Doc" Holliday of Atlanta received his two-year dental degree in 1872 from the Pennsylvania Dental College in Philadelphia (one source says the Baltimore Dental College). Because of tuberculosis, this 5-foot-10 rail-thin man ventured West in search of improved health. By the time Doc Holliday arrived in Denver, using the assumed name Tom McKey, dentistry was no longer his chosen profession. The year was 1876, and as a faro dealer and killer, he hit the mining towns of Central City, Leadville, and Idaho Springs. After getting into legal trouble in Denver, Doc moved on to Deadwood, S.D.; Cheyenne, Wyo.; and Ft. Griffin, Texas, where in 1878 he met Wyatt Earp.

After notorious stops in Dodge City, Kans., and Tombstone, Ariz., Doc Holliday returned to Denver where he was arrested in 1882. Following release from jail in May of that year, Doc continued gambling and drinking in Denver and environs. He traveled by stage from Leadville to Glenwood Springs with Wyatt Earp, to mete out revenge to an old foe. Arriving in Glenwood Springs in May 1887, Doc Holliday died on Nov. 8. While his tombstone overlooks the town of Glenwood Springs, controversy exists as to the actual location of Holliday's remains.

On page 6 of the 1895 *Field & Farm* #475 F 16, is a short anecdote, "Frontier Dentistry." It states:

> Years ago a group of cowboys rode into Pueblo and, while cantering down Santa Fe Avenue, came to a sign "Painless Dentistry." They emptied their guns into it, and then one of the company dismounted and went in to get a sore tooth attended to. The dentist was a quiet-looking young man. "See here!" shouted the cowboy, as he advanced toward the chair, "I want a tooth fixed, and I don't want any high-toned prices charged, either." He threw himself into the chair, laid his gun across his lap, and told the dentist that if he hurt him he would shoot the top of his head off.
>
> "Very well," replied the dentist with a slight laugh, "then you must take gas, for this is a bad tooth and will give trouble." The cowboy swore, but finally yielded and presently was insensible. The man of the forceps pulled the tooth and then, before his customer regained consciousness, he securely tied him hand and foot to the chair. Then taking the bully's gun the dentist took up his position where the patient could see him when he came to. As the cowboy struggled back to consciousness, the first thing of which he was

sensible was the dentist pointing the revolver at him, and saying, in quiet tones: "Now, then, don't move. Just open your mouth as wide as possible, and I will shoot the bad tooth off. This is a painless process. No danger, sir, unless you happen to swallow the bullet. Are you ready? Then here goes! One, two, three." Bang went the gun, knocking a hole in the wall behind the chair, and the dentist rushed forward, holding out the tooth in his hand to show to the bully, who roared for mercy. The dentist cut his bonds on condition that he should restore the sign outside the office. After paying five dollars for the tooth, the cowboy departed, convinced that even a tenderfoot may have nerve.

Dr. R.J. Forhan told the story in the 1956 New York *Brand Book* of how he came to practice dentistry in Cripple Creek. In 1894 at the age of 27, he was a successful Denver dentist with a wife and an infant daughter.

One evening, Dr. Forhan was enjoying the view of his soon-to-be completed six-room dream house, when he was approached by a man wishing to buy it. Somewhat surprised, Dr. Forhan asked the outrageous price of $9,000 and was stunned when the stranger started peeling off $500 bills from a wad in his pocket. The buyer stated that he had made his fortune in Cripple Creek, buying and selling claims. With the intent of getting more easy money, Dr. Forhan moved his dental office to Cripple Creek, a town he described as "nothing more than a double row of shacks, two blocks long, lining a road blasted out of rock." With his office located over the Post Office, he could survey the "main recreational activities of Cripple Creek: mining, drinking and gambling."

Most of his dental work consisted of extracting teeth. This he found so difficult to do on the burly miners that he had a special set of forceps made with longer and stronger beaks.

Dr. Forhan found that the high altitude made the use of laughing gas unpredictable. Patients often stopped breathing, so he developed a technique of rhythmically stepping on the rubber gas bag to keep the patient alive. This once shocked a husband and wife who had brought their mother in for an extraction. When the patient started turning blue, the husband and wife fainted dead away on top of the dentist as he started stepping on the rubber bag.

Dr. Forhan had developed a toothpaste he wanted to market by mail, called Forhan's Pyorrhea Preparation. This, plus the fact that his wife and daughter had remained in Denver, led to his leaving Cripple Creek—though he had a busy practice. After moves to California and Texas, Dr. Forhan ended up in New York City where he sold his paste formula for $10 million.

A mountain dentist of a different style was Waltus Jewel Watkins. He is known by his letters, published in the fall 1967 *Colorado Magazine.*

Waltus was born in 1852 near Lawson, Mo. He did not find his calling to dentistry till the mid-1890s, after trying several other jobs. Bitten by the gold bug, in 1895 he and his wife Minnie headed to southwestern Colorado. Immediate wealth did not come their way, and this discouraged Minnie. She returned East with the promise from her husband that he would follow soon. W.J. did not keep his promise, however, and instead sold their household goods for $35. Minnie was never seen again, while Dr. Watkins took up life as an itinerant dentist for the next 30 years.

Armed with a questionable temporary license, Watkins went to Jimtown (near Creede) in December 1898. The following excerpted letters were addressed to his brothers in Missouri:

Dec. 18, 1898 — "I think I can do well here in the practice of dentistry. These miners get from $3 to $5 per day. . . . There is a dentist here. . . . Some of the people here won't let this dentist work for them. He gets drunk and raises Old Ned."

On March 9, 1899, Watkins wrote that he had two 32-candle power incandescent lights in front of his chair. The reason for the lights was that, like most other mining camp dentists, Dr. Watkins kept night hours to accommodate the miners. His Sept. 25, 1899, letter said:

I go prospecting every Sunday and Wednesday. I have a half-interest in two claims which I think will bring me some money next year. . . . I have to practice dentistry to make a living. . . . Dentistry is dull. . . . I think I will have to go to Denver in December and stand my examination. I don't think I can hoodoo the dental board any longer.

In December he did go to Denver and passed his examination to practice legally in Colorado. By early 1900, Dr. Watkins had given up mining as too dangerous. In September he moved his base of operations to Craig, while making side trips to Hotchkiss, Steamboat Springs, and Baggs, Wyo. On Jan. 4, 1902, he reported having a tooth problem of his own.

"I got my teeth mended in Denver, and the day I got to Craig, I broke one of the crowns off. No I didn't say a word, but if I had had hold of that dentist I would have walked his log."

The Sept. 21, 1904, entry indicated a run-in with a competitor: "Went to Hayden and found a dentist had been there for a month. . . . I looked him up and found he had no license to practice and told him he had better 'git' but he. . . just staid until I had him arrested."

By 1907, Dr. Watkins indicated an interest in Nevada mining claims, but revealed his feeling when he said: "I could make money in that country if I would stay there, but I would rather be a poor dentist in Colorado than be wealthy and have to live in that country."

To get an idea of the dental prices of the early days, it's interesting to look at Dr. G.W. Stone's Jan. 1, 1895, *Rocky Mountain News* ad. In his office at 17th and Curtis streets, he charged 50 cents to $1 for any filling except gold—gold was $1 and up. There was a difference in price, also, in extractions: with anesthetic 50 cents, and without, 25 cents. Gold and porcelain crowns were $5. The ad goes on to state that "by using our own local anesthetic we can and do fill or extract teeth without pain."

Dental equipment and materials were generally very different from that of today. The dental chairs required the practitioner to stand up, and could be basic or elaborate. It is said that one Meeker dentist had a saddle fitted as a chair to help his cowboy patients relax. A piece of equipment once very popular was the dental cuspidor (or spit-

(From A History of Dentistry in Colorado 1859-1959; Courtesy H.F. Hoffman
This nattily attired group is the Colorado State Dental Association, at their 14th Annual Meeting, assembled in 1900 on the steps of Bowen's Hotel in Boulder. William P. Smedley, second from the right, front row (full white beard), was CSDA's first president.

sink). The first fountain cuspidor in Colorado was owned by Dr. J.M. Downing, who sold it to Theodore Ashley, who sold it to Henry F. Hoffman on April 1, 1900.

Dental amalgam fillings came to the United States in 1833, and early Colorado dentists often took filings from silver coins to mix with mercury. The excess mercury was then squeezed out in a chamois skin, using pliers. This fact bothered Dr. Will Eames of Glenwood Springs, who in 1959 published a paper in the *Journal of the American Dental Association* on the one-to-one-amalgam ratio.

Because of the mineral wealth near many Colorado towns, it is said that dentists would use gold that they had panned themselves to fill teeth. Dental gold was also purchased from the mint.

Herman Blaurock, a Denver manufacturing jeweler, was a pioneer user of Colorado dental gold. By 1904, he was producing dental gold full-time. He was assisted by his son, the late Carl Blaurock, a former Denver Westerner. Carl took over the business in 1923, and retired in 1972.

Dental drills were foot-operated, slow-speed contraptions that heated up, and rattled the patient's tooth. Some hand instruments, such as extraction forceps, have changed very little over the years.

X-rays were discovered by William Roentgen in 1896, but it took 13 years before Dr. Arthur H. Ketchum, the first Colorado orthodontist, acquired Colorado's first X-ray machine. At first, X-rays were produced by revolving 8-by-10 in. glass plates that created static electricity. It took 5 to 15 minutes to expose a film, and 30 to 60 minutes to develop it.

One other important discovery was what Colorado Springs dentist Fredrick S. McKay dubbed "Colorado Brown Stain." Upon arriving in Colorado Springs in 1901, Dr. McKay soon noticed many people native to the area had permanently brown-mottled teeth. The "Father of American Dentistry," G.V. Black, at McKay's behest, visited Colorado in 1909 to investigate and report on the affliction. It was not until the early 1930s that Alcoa chemist H.V. Churchill determined some Colorado water contained high levels of fluoride. This was the cause of the stains, but it took a few years longer before it was determined that fluoride in the water inhibited dental decay. In 1951, public health dentist Dr. Robert Downes made Grand Junction the first city in Colorado to have artificially fluoridated water.

Organized dentistry came to Colorado on April 5, 1887, when 10 dentists met in Denver to charter the Colorado State Dental Associa-

(From A History of Dentistry in Colorado, 1859-1959; *Courtesy H.F. Hoffman)*
The Cripple Creek Short Line hauled this group between Colorado Springs
and Cripple Creek, for the Colorado State Dental Association's 1902 annual
picnic. (William Smedley is white-bearded gentleman atop engine's boiler.)

tion (State was later dropped from the title). Dr. William Smedley was
elected president. Yearly meetings have been held ever since. In 1910,
the National Dental Association (later called the American Dental
Association) met in Colorado.

In August 1887, the trustees of the University of Denver approved
the installation of the Denver Dental School in the Haish Building, at
the northeast corner of 14th and Arapahoe streets. The first class of
five was graduated in 1889. In April 1896, the University of Colorado
established a competing school at 18th and Stout streets. After the
University of Denver brought suit against this new school, the CU
school ceased operation. It was reestablished in 1897 as the Colorado
College of Dental Surgery at 18th and Larimer streets. In 1901, the
two schools merged, occupying the Haish Building as a home until
1911, when they moved one block west to 1320 Arapahoe St. The
University of Denver closed the school in 1932 as it was a money-loser
and Colorado was without a dental school until the University of
Colorado opened the present school in 1973. (The author was in the
third class.)

Legal protection from unprincipled dentists was provided by a state practice act as early as 1888. This action led to the fight against Painless Parker. Painless Parker was not truly a Colorado dentist, although he did stage a few tooth-extraction exhibitions in the state. However, it was in Colorado that he met his Waterloo, so to speak.

Edgar Randolph Parker was born in 1872 in Tynemouth Creek, New Brunswick, Canada. His powers of salesmanship manifested early when, at age 7, he sold the playground of one of the many schools he was ejected from to a fellow student for 25 cents. Another school expelled Edgar for drawing advanced and explicit pictures on the blackboard. At age 15, he was packed off to Acadia University in Nova Scotia to study for the ministry. A few weeks later, Edgar was returned home with a letter from the school stating that "An ordinary interest in young women is to be expected in healthy young men, but to say that Edgar Parker reaches the extraordinary in this respect is understatement of the grossest kind."

During the next few years, Edgar worked on a schooner, was ejected from another seminary (for spreading "worldly unrest"), and traveled the Canadian backwoods as a horse-and-wagon peddler. At age 17, Parker found his calling when he was admitted to the New York College of Dentistry. When he was caught practicing illegal door-to-door extractions (to keep the bills paid), he was expelled. This fact hadn't been reported to the Philadelphia Dental College, however, when they admitted him. He was graduated in 1892.

Returning to Canada as Dr. Parker, money did not immediately roll into his coffers. Thinking that pain was the problem, Edgar had a local druggist mix up cocaine and other painkillers (which he dubbed "hydrocain"). He tried it first on a dog, then on himself, with successful results. Then, ethical practice was thrown out the door.

Dr. Parker decided to adopt the style of the fire-and-brimstone, street-corner preachers:

> We found each other right there—those wonderful rubes and I. They needed dentistry worse than I needed money, if such a thing was possible. Without hesitation I let them have the sermon. I offered to pay $5, which I didn't have, to anybody who felt the slightest pain having a tooth removed, and pretty soon they were snapping at the bait like wildcats in a chophouse. Well, friend, I took in $8 that night with no refunds. Also I took 33 teeth out of 12 patients and nobody screamed. Why, I'll never know. I ran out of hydrocain on the seventh patient.

This style did not sit well with the local dentists, who had Parker arrested. Getting out of town seemed prudent, so Parker outfitted a red wagon with signs and headed for the Canadian wilderness.

His trademark top hat acquired the first of several bullet holes in one small town, when Parker made the mistake of telling the locals (gathered around his wagon) that the dental trust had driven him to this godforsaken town. Immediately, a pistol shot blasted Parker's hat off his head and a voice rang out: "I'm Parson J.B. Towers and I don't aim to hear this fair territory called godless by a little runt in the pay of Satan."

Over time, Parker built up a "Dental-Medicine Show" with Indian dancers, sword swallowers, bearded ladies, Irish tenors, and hootchy-kootchy dancers to liven up his street-corner tooth pulling.

In 1895, he moved to New York, resolving to try it as an ethical dentist. He married Frances Wolfe and once again found himself unable to pay the bills. On the sly from his new bride, he contacted William Beebe, a 300-pound former circus agent, who advised him to adopt the name PAINLESS Parker.

Dr. Parker added a brass band to the troop. While a confederate in the crowd would become the first to sit in Parker's chair and fake having a tooth pulled, real patients could not be counted on to not to scream and fuss. Because of this, Parker would stamp his foot when he was about to pull the tooth, and the band would launch into a rousing tune guaranteed to drown out any noise.

Within 10 months, Painless Parker had hired 14 more dentists to handle three chairs each, and revenues had risen to $5,000 a day. His signs could not be ignored, proclaiming such things as "Painless Parker—I Am Positively IT In Painless Dentistry" in huge letters. He hired tightrope walkers and human flies to shout his praises from the sides of his buildings. Parker had acrobats, dancing girls, thespians, jugglers, minstrels, choral groups, and a 15-piece brass band to draw attention. He would also fling coins out of a bucket to the crowds.

By 1904, Parker was a millionaire and a nervous wreck. He decided to take his troop on the road again, one day extracting 357 teeth which he had made into a necklace. This didn't solve the stress problem, and the following year he decided to retire to Los Angeles. At 33, he didn't stay retired for long, and soon acquired a new brass band, mind readers, jugglers, and acrobats.

By 1910, Painless had amassed a new fortune and new enemies, as evidenced by a scathing anti-Parker piece in the September 1910 issue of *Hampton's Magazine*, titled "Tooth Tinkerers."

With movies bringing down the curtain on many circuses, Painless

(From A History of Dentistry in Colorado, 1859-1959)
Parker's offices at 15th and Welton streets in Denver, from 1923 to 1926.

realized a dream in 1913 when he acquired his own Parker Dental Circus, for peanuts. In addition to the usual circus trappings, there were placards and banners adorned with Parker's crest—his Vandyke-bearded face superimposed on a molar. The bandstand was made to resemble a giant set of jaws ready to eat the musicians.

Between performances, Dr. Parker would dive into his sermon on the evils of dental disease and the Dental Trust (the ADA). He would urge the masses to follow him to his dental/medical tent before tooth miseries got the best of them. Said Parker, "When they did follow me, a disturbing question was settled in my mind. I knew that the folks we used to call rubes, the finest people this country has ever produced, were still abroad in our land."

Parker often performed for the press, fixing his circus animals' teeth (including placing a giant gold inlay in the tooth of a hippopotamus). He was a sad man when Mrs. Parker forced him to sell the circus.

After a 1915 move to San Francisco, Edgar Parker legally became Painless Parker to avoid the legal tangle created by operating under an assumed name. Painless lived 50 miles south of San Francisco, in the Santa Clara Valley on a 300-acre spread he named Valle Vista. He

"David and Goliath" ad ran in Nov. 2, 1926, *Denver Post.*

also bought a yacht which he dubbed *Idalia*. Painless dreamed of expanding his franchises into every corner of the United States, and in 1922 he rented a suite of rooms at 15th and Welton streets in Denver. The fight had begun.

Colorado law required dentists to be licensed in the state before they could practice, so Painless advertised and threw parties for seniors at the University of Denver Dental School in search of employees. This didn't work out so well, and it is said that when Painless Parker's office opened on Dec. 1, 1923, it was with dried-out alcoholic dentists. In 1926, Painless sought to change the law to allow any out-of-state dentist to practice in Colorado.

Parker threw his weight behind Amendment 6 to the tune of more than $100,000. He bought newspaper ads, and even had his own publication, *Dental Liberty.* He compared himself to David fighting the Goliath of the Dental Trust.

The story is told that as Parker spoke to Denver residents, Dr. A.H. Ketchum dropped a bag of water from his 12-story office building on Parker's head. Parker began loudly decrying the monopoly that would resort to such violence. *The Catholic Register* and *The Denver Post* came out against Parker and, in spite of parades led by Painless' red sedan, the people defeated the amendment by 50,000 votes. At the same time, the California State Board suspended Parker's license for five years, for aiding an unlicensed person to practice dentistry—the Painless Parker franchise.

Parker closed his Denver office and returned to California. "I was surprised they didn't raise my hair. They just took my canteen and turned me loose in the desert," he recalled.

While this ended his plans for total U.S. expansion, Painless needed no sympathy. His yearly gross was said at one time to be $3.5 million. After Parker sold Valle Vista and Mrs. Parker died (in 1945), he took up residence in his Market Street San Francisco office. He died there on Nov. 8, 1952, at age 80.

Acknowledgements

Carl Blaurock	Dr. Skip Neiberger
Dr. Jack Cooper	Thomas J. Noel
William A. Douglas	Dr. Charles Smedley
Dr. Robert Downes	Dr. John Smedley
Dr. Will Eames	Pete Smythe
Ted Krieger	Colorado Historical Society
Dot Krieger	Colorado Springs Pioneers Museum
Dr. Roy Lininger	Denver Public Library
Dr. Miles Markley	

Sources and References

"An Historical Review of Orthodontics in the Rocky Mountain Area." Rocky Mountain Society
    of Orthodontics, 1972.

Bancroft, Caroline. "Dentistry in Colorado." *Colorado and Its People*, Vol. 2, pp. 407-419, L.R.
    Hafen, ed., 1948.

Borneman, Walter. "Marshall Pass—Denver and Rio Grande Gateway to the Gunnison Coun-
    try." Colorado Springs: Century One Press, 1980.

Carter and Butterworth, *Dental Collectibles and Antiques*. New York: Ashcraft Inc., 1985.

Christen, Arden, DDS. "Edgar Randolph 'Painless' Parker (1872-1952) The 'P.T. Barnum'
    of Dentistry." *Journal of the Indiana Dental Association*, Vol. 65, No. 5, Sept./Oct. 1986.

Coquoz, Rene. "Doc Holliday in Leadville." Denver Westerner's *Roundup*, Vol. XXIII, No. 5,
    p. 9, May 1967.

Denver City Directory. D.O. Wilhelm, 1866.

Donavan and Whitney. "Painless Parker—Last of America's Tooth Plumbers." *Colliers*, Vol.
    129, Jan. 5, 12, 19, 1952.

Douglas, William A. *A History of Dentistry in Colorado 1859-1959*. Boulder, Colo.: Johnson
    Publishing, 1959.

First Annual Rocky Mountain Directory and Colorado Gazetteer. S.S. Wallihan & Co., 1871.

Forhan, R.J., DDS. "How Dentistry Came to Cripple Creek." *New York Brandbook*, Vol. 3,
    No. 4, p. 79, 1956.

"How a Pueblo Dentist Got Even with a Cowboy Bully." *Field and Farm*, No. 475 F16, p. 6,
    1895.

Jones and Forrest. *Denver, A Pictorial History*. Boulder, Colo.: Pruett Publishing, 1973.

Looper, Joseph W. "John Henry Holliday DDS: Georgia's Most Famous Dentist." *Journal of
    the American Dental Association*, Vol. 87, Aug. 1973.

McCardell. "Tooth Tinkerers." *Hamptons Magazine*, Vol. 25, pp. 305-314, Sept. 1910.

McGee, Ren Proctor. "Oral Hygiene." April 1922.

McKain, Neil. "Parker's Fast Pluck." *Westways*, Vol. 66, #13, pp. 40-42.

Noel, Thomas J. *Denver's Larimer Street*. Denver: Historic Denver Inc., 1981.

Ring, Malvin. *Dentistry: An Illustrated History*. New York: Harry Abrams Inc., 1985.

Rocky Mountain News, various dates.

Smedley, William. *Across the Plains: an 1862 Journey from Omaha to Oregon*. Boulder, Colo.:
    Johnson Books, 1994.

Sprague, Marshall. *Money Mountain—The Story of Cripple Creek Gold*. Boston: Little, Brown
    and Co., 1953.

The Denver Post, various dates.

Train, Percy; Henrichs, James R.; Archer, W. Andrew. "Medicinal Uses of Plants by Indian
    Tribes of Nevada." Lawrence, Mass.: Quarterman Publishing, 1957.

"Waltus Jewel Watkins, Frontier Dentist." *Colorado Magazine*, Vol. 44, No. 4, p. 9, Fall 1967.

About the Author

No more appropriate author could be found for "Early Colorado Tooth Tinkerers and the Fight Against Painless Parker" than Dr. George W. Krieger, Elizabeth, Colo., dentist.

It was the second paper prepared for the Denver Westerners by Dr. Krieger. He previously presented an article on the life of George W. Kelly, early Colorado horticulturist.

Dr. Krieger, who resides in Parker, Colo., is a Posse Member, and is the son of Theodore Krieger, 1995 Sheriff of the Denver Posse, and Dorothy Krieger, the third Posse Member in the family.

George Krieger was born in Valley Forge, Pa., in 1953. The Krieger family moved to Littleton, Colo., in 1959, and to Broomfield, Colo., in 1961. George was graduated from Broomfield High School and in 1974 received a degree in environmental biology from the University of Colorado. He received his D.D.S. Degree in 1979 from the CU School of Dentistry. He practiced dentistry in Brush, Colo., for four years, then moved back to the Denver area in 1983. In addition to his practice at Elizabeth, he served as a faculty member at the CU School of Dentistry, 1983-1989.

George and his wife Aimee have two daughters, Brenna and Hilary.

"Vigilantes at work" by *Delano*

The Colorado Bench and Bar:

Refined or Rustic Lawyers?

By John Milton Hutchins

*A*N OLD-TIME ATTORNEY, Horace Hawkins, when addressing the Colorado Bar Association in 1938, asserted, "Historians have failed to record the name of the lawyer who first invaded the land of mountain and plain now known as Colorado."[1] Mr. Hawkins, like many an advocate, overstated his case. Jerome Smiley, in his monumental work on the history of Denver, unequivocally stated that the first lawyer and jurist in the Cherry Creek region was Judge George Hicks Sr., one of the Cherokee Indians in the William Green Russell gold party of 1858.[2] But the first attorney who came to the diggings to work in his profession was David C. Collier. Also arriving in 1858, the religious Mr. Collier had started the first Sunday School in the region by the time other lawyers came to the area in 1859.[3]

As is common in any boom area, there soon were lawyers in abundance. The Colorado diggings by the end of 1859 had a ratio of lawyers to the general population that was higher than the norm in settled regions.[4] Five law firms found it necessary to advertise for clients in the Dec. 28, 1859 issue of the *Rocky Mountain News.*[5] In Central City and Black Hawk, it was said probably with some exaggeration, that lawyers outnumbered miners two to one.[6]

But early Colorado hardly was a utopia for the bench and bar, especially during the years 1858 to 1861. Prior to the establishment of Federal territorial authority in mid-1861, Colorado was a nightmare as a legal system.

The first miners and settlers at the confluence of the South Platte River and Cherry Creek in the fall of 1858 called a meeting "to establish security and to prevent and punish crime."[7] They established themselves as Arapahoe County, Kansas Territory and voted on a representative to sit in the Kansas Legislature. A territorial delegate to Congress was also elected, although that seemingly contradicted the formation of Arapahoe County, K.T. In March 1859, there was an election for Kansas County officials.

But another mass meeting, in Auraria in April 1859, backed statehood status for the as-yet totally unorganized region. This meeting resulted in a constitutional convention and a proposed state constitution which was defeated in September 1859, by a vote of 2007 to 649.

Then came the so-called Territory of Jefferson. In October, another election was held in which another representative was elected to the Kansas Legislature and another delegate was elected to Congress to represent a new entity called Jefferson Territory. Follow-up elections later that month produced a legislature for the impromptu territory, and that body adopted full civil and criminal codes.[8]

Jefferson Territory was divided into nine counties and provisional Gov. R. W. Steele appointed a probate judge for each county, to be replaced later by elected judges. Justice of the Peace Courts and a Supreme Court were also established. The courtroom procedure adopted, like the name of Jefferson Territory itself, showed the influence of southern Democrats—no blacks, mulattoes, or Indians could testify.[9]

Meanwhile, Arapahoe County, K.T., elected officials found they had no real power or authority. Likewise, when Jefferson Territory attempted to impose taxes, its legitimacy was rejected by many citizens, especially in the mountains.

In the absence of real government, various localities took steps to establish some semblance of law and order. In the mining communities Miners' Courts sprang up. First, a meeting of all occupants of a proposed district would be held. At this meeting, the miners would set district limits, adopt a miners' code, create offices, and elect officers. These officials constituted a Miners' Court to settle all claims and punish offenses in the district. Appeals from the courts would be made at a mass meeting, from which there was no further appeal. Some miners' districts might also elect a judge to conduct the Miners' Court.[10] An early resident described the source from which the Miners' Court drew their authority:

> I was intensely interested in watching [the miners] as they came from up and down the river to these miners meeting, walking with vigorous step, independence of personal character, evidencing freedom from oppressive taxation and the tyranny of unrighteous laws; each man with a revolver dangling from his belt, rifle over his shoulders, and for a finishing appendage, a knife in his scabbard, thus embodying a walking arsenal, constituting a moving legislature, thus prepared to legislate and enforce law with undelayed or untrammeled facility.[11]

In Denver and some other locales, only the so-called People's Courts were established. These were *ad hoc* meetings of citizens, who convened on call when some felony, including murder, occurred. These extralegal tribunals were anything but lynch mobs, and they were conducted with basic forms of due process and procedure. Mountain man, trader, and merchant Uncle Dick Wootton described the events surrounding Denver's first hanging after murder of one of its citizens.

> A court was organized and a jury of 12 men empaneled. The prisoner was defended by an able lawyer, but according to the custom in those days his confession was admitted as evidence and the verdict of the jury was that he should be hanged at two o'clock in the afternoon of the day of tribunal. . . . It was as neat and orderly an execution as ever took place anywhere. . . .[12]

In addition to the courts mentioned thus far, there were also claims clubs, municipal courts, courts for Arapahoe County, and court for another provisional territory called Idaho Territory. Forum-shopping litigants and defendant thus had a field day.[13] It was in this background of a jurisdictional and legal morass that the early Colorado bench and bar had to operate.

In Denver, much of the legal work stemmed from the wild and violent tendencies of the community and the attempts of law-abiding citizens to enforce some order. Many People's Courts were convened in 1860. As an example, following a fatal shooting in a saloon, a trial was held in Denver Hall, another saloon, before a thousand spectators. The judge had the sheriff empanel a jury of 24 men, who took an oath to do justice. The prosecutor, David C. Collier, made an opening statement, followed by an opening by the defense attorney. Witnesses were called and examined and cross-examined. Both lawyers then made closing statements. The jury retired and came back with a unanimous guilty verdict. The sentence was submitted to the crowd and all called out to hang the defendant. The whole trial lasted three hours.[14]

It should not be presumed that the use of defense counsel at People's Courts was an empty and ineffectual gesture. When Carroll Wood, one of Denver's notorious gang of "bummers," was tried before a People's Court in 1860, he was defended by several lawyers, including the eloquent A. C. Ford. One of the 12 jurors balked at hanging Wood, and Wood was instead banished from Denver.[15] Lawyer Ford had earlier successfully defended in a People's Court John Scudder for the murder of Peleg Bassett.[16]

But lawyer Ford paid a heavy penalty for his oratory and supposed criminal connections. On Sept. 5, 1860, Ford was taken from a coach outside of Denver and shot by persons unknown.[17]

The number of attorneys appearing at the People's Courts tends to show both that parties were not underrepresented and that lawyers were not overworked. In September 1860, the murder trial of James Gordon was conducted under the cottonwoods by Wazee Street. The presiding judge was A. C. Hunt, later a territorial governor. Defendant Gordon was represented by five attorneys. There were three prosecutors, including Hiram P. Bennet, later a territorial delegate to Congress. The trial occupied three days, held before a 12-man jury. Gordon was convicted and executed.[18]

The People's Courts, themselves, produced a temporary need for legal talent. But the resulting hangings tended to quiet things down so much that there was an adverse economic impact on the legal community. In the summer of 1860, an advertisement appeared in the *Rocky Mountain Herald* over the names of eight members of the local bar:

> We, the undersigned attorney Counselors at law, convinced by a long experience here without Courts, either of Kansas Territory or some other government which certainly does not now exist, the practice is worse than useless both for ourselves and the public—announce by this notice our determination to close our law offices . . . until such time as regular and constitutional tribunals of justice are established in our midst.[19]

There was similar surplus of legal talent in the southern part of the region. Attorney Irving Stanton, in addressing the Colorado Bar Association in 1913, recalled how it was:

> George A. Hinsdale and Wilbur F. Stone in February 1861, when I first met them, were practicing law in Cañon City before a People's Court, presided over by a lawyer named John Howard. There were other lawyers in the town at the time, but the gentleman named had the lion's share of the legal business, and they were not overworked.[20]

One problem affecting the bar was that there were no real requirements for admission. Virtually anyone with a modicum of education and an alleged good moral character could attempt to practice.[21] Cyrus Carpenter, later to become a governor of Iowa, was one who joined the gold rush to the Pikes Peak mines. Although he had not been affluent enough to study law, he practiced in the Denver courts in the winter of 1860-1861, with the help of some law books sent by his brother in California.[22]

The Miners' Courts, which held primarily civil, as opposed to criminal, proceedings, likewise admitted anyone to practice before them without any sort of restriction, testing, or proof of qualification. For example, a young lawyer from Missouri named Aleck arrived at the Gregory Diggings penniless, friendless, and dressed as a tramp. Almost immediately, he was engaged to handle a mining claim in a court being held in a log cabin. Aleck "cut loose, assumed to know all the law and some to spare . . . pounded the table, scattered the papers, sawed the air and pawed the dirt floor like a lassoed steer in a Texas corral."[23] Fortunately for Aleck he won the case and was paid a surprising $50 in gold dust.

Just as there were no requirements for admission, neither were there continuing standards to practice. Ethical problems were bound to occur. John D. Young, a miner from Illinois, explained one occasion that arose when a gold seeker got a court judgment against a rancher for lost or stolen mules.

> [B]ut the poor fellow could not remain [in Denver] that long under expenses so he entrusted its collection to a lawyer of good standing in the city. . . . His lawyer was to send the price of his mules in a month but he never got a cent of it nor received a bit of information from his lawyer. There is no doubt but what the latter got the money and appropriated it to his own use. A honest man is a rare thing to be found in any place but I think it impossible to find one at all in a gold producing country.[24]

Barney Ford, an early black emigrant to Colorado, also met up with a cheating attorney in 1860 Denver. The lawyer advised his client to file any mining claim of Ford's in the lawyer's name, in order to better protect it. The lawyer, for his legal services, would charge Ford 20 percent of the mineral's proceeds. Ford did make a strike near Breckenridge, filed the claim in the lawyer's name, and awaited the contract the lawyer promised him. A month later, the Denver lawyer began ejectment proceedings against Ford.[25]

It is probably no surprise that the miners in at least one newly organized district adopted a rule that allowed no lawyer to practice or even reside within the district. This supposedly contributed to the truth-seeking process.[26]

Problems of quality were not restricted solely to the bar. The jurists of this unorganized period also created substantial problems, both in, and out of the courtroom.

Lawyer William P. McClure, a James Buchanan appointee as Denver postmaster and the Chief Justice of the Supreme Court of one of the extralegal governmental entities, became offended at a newspaper article written by O. J. Goldrick. At the point of his revolver, the honorable Judge McClure forced a written retraction from Goldrick. McClure was haled before Denver Municipal Judge Jacob Downing, who ordered the posting of a peace bond. McClure denounced Downing's authority and it was only when armed force backed up the coura-

(Author's Collection: From Hall's History of Colorado, 1889)
Maj. Jacob Downing, Denver municipal judge.

geous Downing that McClure submitted to the Municipal Court order.
When the Civil War broke out, McClure left Denver to join the Rebel
cause.[27]

Another troublesome judge of southern extraction was Dr. James
Stone, who was judge of the Miners' Court in the Mountain City
District. Stone, who also was a Jefferson territorial legislator, challenged territorial secretary Lou Bliss to a duel in March 1860. Although some thought Bliss, being a Northerner, would not fight, he
did and the judge ended up Stone-cold and dead.[28]

John Sherman, who was elected as judge of a provisional Denver
"People's Government" in 1861, was an alcoholic Ohioan whose drinking had reduced him to poverty. The voters believed that the election

was the best way to give him a second chance at life.[29]

Such elections were possible, for there were no formal requirements for judges during this period. When an uneducated nonlawyer rancher was elected probate judge in Pueblo County, in 1859 or 1860, he defeated Judge John Howard. When Howard's friend, Judge Wilbur Stone, asked Howard if the successful candidate had yet qualified for office, Howard replied, "Well, he has filed his bond and taken the oath, but all hell wouldn't qualify him!"[30] In fairness to the unnamed rancher jurist, it should be noted that Judge Howard was the one who, when his wife deserted him, divorced her by filing a quit-claim deed as to any interest in her.[31]

The lawyers of the region tended to support any movement for organized government. In the 1858-1861 courts of Colorado, it was not even safe to practice. Cyrus Carpenter wrote his wife in Iowa:

> Less than a week ago, a man was shot down in the Courtroom where I was speaking and I have become so habitated to such ruffianism that when he was picked up and carried out I went right on with my speech, not stopping five minutes.[32]

Without an organized territorial government there could be no standards, for attorney or judges, no quality or quantity control, no appellate system, no finality of judgments, no judicial immunity when imposing sentences.

While the bench and bar appear to have worked with and within the provisional legal system of this early period, they yearned for a formal Federal territorial judicial system and were not satisfied with the temporary expedients. One citizen commented in the *Rocky Mountain News* in 1860 on the attitude of the Denver bar toward a proposed city government:

> This appears to be a very acceptable plan of government to the committee who framed it, as well as to all the business and laboring men of that meeting. The only ones made any objection to it were the lawyers—they took sides for and against the plan and consumed the whole evening gassing over it. Now sir, as a laboring man and a mechanic, I protest against having our time consumed at all our public meetings by any such notoriously gassing fraternity as the Lawyers.[33]

Finally, early in 1861, Congress, with the absence of most of the Southern delegations who had opposed both the admission of Kansas as a state and the creation of Colorado as a territory, established both of those entities. Although Colorado was formed as a territory on Feb. 26, it was not until May 1861 that Gov. William Gilpin arrived in Denver. The territory now had a three-member Supreme Court, and each of these assigned the justices to their districts on July 10.

The Supreme Court appointed four lawyers to a committee to review qualifications of attorneys, and 31 applicants were admitted to practice before the court on the second day of the session. Among them were Governor Gilpin, Moses Hallett, and Henry M. Teller.[34]

With a territorial government, and a Territorial Supreme Court, there was organized a territorial law library. In preterritorial days, the bench and bar primarily relied only on those basic law books that they individually owned. These volumes included, for example, *Blackstone's Commentaries* and *Greenleaf on Evidence*.[35]

Apparently, the law library was part of the general territorial library until 1872, when it was placed under the control of the Supreme Court. Volumes were marked with special Territorial Supreme Court bookplates. Although it is difficult to say exactly when certain volumes became part of the territorial law library, it is certain that the pre-1876 library was extensive. There were state reporters from at least the following jurisdictions: Alabama, Arkansas, Georgia, Illinois, Iowa, Maryland, Massachusetts, Minnesota, Missouri, Nebraska, Nevada, New Hampshire, New Jersey, New York, North Carolina, Pennsylvania, Rhode Island, South Carolina, Vermont, and Wisconsin. The statutory and treatise volumes included items from such jurisdictions as the Federal Government and California, Kansas, Michigan, Montana Territory, and Ohio. It is quite clear, then, that attorneys, at least in Denver, had access to a first class law library for that era.[36]

President Lincoln's appointments to the Colorado Supreme Court were Benjamin Hall of New York as chief justice and S. Newton Pettis of Pennsylvania, and Charles Lee Armour of Maryland as associate justices. It did not take long for trouble to develop on the court.

Pettis, after receiving a favorable reception in Colorado, decided that he "would never marry the territory."[37] He resigned shortly thereafter without ever holding a single session of court in Colorado.

Chief Justice Hall would last but two years on Colorado Territory's high court. His early efforts were directed at attempting to get the judicial machinery moving and also in aiding in the suppression of disloyalty in the territory. These efforts on behalf of the Union were at first praised, and later condemned, by Coloradans. His reports to President Lincoln reflected poorly on the territory by overestimating Southern sympathies.[38]

Armour, however, was by far the worst of the original appointees. The members of the bar considered him a talented but cranky tyrant. According to Wilbur F. Stone, a later Supreme Court justice, Armour "required everyone taking an oath to swear on an old, musty Bible and kiss the begrimed book, regardless of the labial transfusion of prehistoric microbes."[39] In September 1863, lawyer James M. Cavanaugh was so upset at one of the judge's decisions, that he published a handbill that accused Armour as "infamously tyrannical," of being a "judicial vagabond" who pretends to be a "judge" and of being "a liar and a coward."[40] Armour was so generally unpopular that, unable to secure his removal, the territorial legislature redistricted him to Conejos and Costilla counties. "But," according to Judge Stone, "with sublime defiance he refused to visit [his district] or resign his office, but smilingly smoked his imported cigars . . . sipped his toddies . . . [and] drew his salary. . . ."[41]

Stephen S. Harding of Indiana, was Colorado's second chief justice. A contemporary observer summed him up:

> This Judge Harding is from Indiana, and was sent by Mr. Lincoln to be Governor of Utah, but becoming offensive and ineffective there, he was recalled, and given this judgeship to break his fall. But besides a broken character as a public officer, he brought hither such scandalous, Mormon ways of living, as to shock all shades of public opinion, which is now uniting to drive him out of the territory.[42]

Harding allegedly had brought a mistress along from Utah. Judge Stone related that Harding's "venality and general unfitness became so odious that finally the bar organized what now would be termed a boycott against him."[43] Harding never did resign. He simply left for Indiana one day and never came back.

Colorado's other justices during the territorial period were Moses Hallett, Allan A. Bradford, Charles F. Holly, William H. Gale, William Gorsline, Christian Eyster, James Belford, Ebenezer T. Wells, and Amherst W. Stone. They were an eclectic group.

The appointment of unpopular "carpetbag" justices did tend to strengthen the political forces in the territory that favored statehood, or at least those that encouraged the use of local legal talent on the federal bench. It was felt that a truly Colorado judiciary would be "both more intelligent and independent than that furnished by the Washington authorities."[44] Territorial judges, also, were subject to the whims of presidential politics. When two of the three Supreme Court justices suddenly were replaced by President Grant in 1874, the rumor was that it was the result of a poker game on the Potomac.[45]

Beginning in 1866, the Territorial Supreme Court had a majority of justices who were either from Colorado or who were generally approved.[46] Justice Holly, however, found that his Colorado credentials did not prevent trouble for himself of a legal nature. He was indicted in his own judicial district in Central City for committing adultery with a doctor's wife. Although he was acquitted for lack of proof, his judicial career was ruined.[47]

Justice Eyster was more fortunate. An observer in Colorado in 1867 remarked, "He is the most popular official in the Territory. . . . It will be gratifying to his many friends in the East to know that he is deservedly esteemed here both as a citizen and as a judge."[48] But he was considered soft on crime.

By far the most outstanding high court jurist was Chief Justice Moses Hallett. Hallett's Colorado legal career spanned a half century, and his story is largely that of the Colorado legal system. A boyhood friend reviewed Hallett's career by saying, "His wise and able decisions, especially in litigation growing out of mining claims, have been accepted by the bench in other states as sound. Judge Hallett has a judicial mind, cold blood judgment, and is unpartial [sic] and conscientious."[49] What is more important, while on the Colorado Territorial Supreme Court, Hallett wrote a landmark decision which put the Western water law of prior appropriation on a solid footing, something for which present water law lawyers—apparently half of whom are in Colorado—ought to be grateful.[50] Hallett also collected and digested the first Colorado Supreme Court reports.

Colorado's lower-level trial judges had a broad range of outlook and experience. For example, Juan N. Gutierrez Sr. of Trinidad was elected probate judge of Las Animas County in 1867.[51] In mentioning another judge, an 1872 visitor to Georgetown commented:

> The judge of probate, elected by an unprecedented majority, is a young man of twenty-four. Colorado is the paradise of young men; but they must be young men of talent, energy, tact, pluck, and of a fiery yet chivalrous spirit.[52]

Youth and endurance could be necessary requirements for trial judges in the Western territories. An 1860s visitor to Montana, A. K. McClure, told what he saw when viewing proceedings:

> I have recently given four day's attendance to our Western court, where justice is judicially administered with variations of which Blackstone never dreamed in his philosophy. . . . Of the facts the jurors are the sole judges, without judicial explanation or any suggestions whatever from the court, and cases go hap-hazard [sic] to the juries, and are kicked from post to pillar by windy advocates. . . . If I had been judge the four days I attended court, I'm sure half the bar would have been in jail the first day, and probably the residue would have been stricken from the roll before I had got through. . . . I have found the same loose system of the administration of justice prevailing in Colorado, Utah and Idaho.[53]

(From Fred and Jo Mazzulla Collection)

Georgetown's extensive legal fraternity was well represented in this 1874 photo, taken in front of John H. McMurdy's law office, and Georgetown's first Post Office. (This later became the law office of Edward O. Wolcott.) Numbered in the picture are 1. Robert S. Morrison, 2. L.F. Yates, 3. Frank Pope, 4. Frank Delamar, 5. McMurdy, 6. Charles C. Post, 7. Wolcott, 8. John A. Coulter, 9. unknown, and 10. William R. Kennedy.

One factor that probably did not contribute to the dignity and orderliness of court proceedings was the trial settings. For example, trials in both territorial Larimer and Weld counties were held in courthouses that were residential log cabins.[54] Larimer County Judge John Washburn and his family had to endure heavy cigar smoke as they attempted to sleep upstairs in their cabin above deliberating jurors one night in 1864.[55] The sessions of the Third Judicial District of the Territorial Court, Moses Hallett presiding, were held in "an old adobe building with a dirt floor."[56] Young lawyer Charles H. Toll practiced in this "doby" courtroom and he noted the "strange scene" occasioned by the tallow candlelight.[57]

Even a murder trial held in the old Langrishe Theater in Central

City in the 1860s suffered from inadequate courtroom facilities. Halfway through the defense argument it was discovered that the floor of the packed house was giving way. Over strenuous defense objection, Judge Bradford cleared the building before disaster struck.[58]

Unfortunately, there was also some proof that the territorial judges still were operating under violent frontier conditions. Probate Judge Elias F. Dyer of Lake County became involved in one of those bloody local disputes such as occurred in Grand Lake, Colo., in 1883; Tombstone, Arizona Territory, in 1881; and Lincoln County, N.M., in 1878. Whether the judge's side was more right than the opposition's probably will never be known,[59] but the courage of Judge Dyer cannot be questioned. Having been threatened by a vigilante group and forced temporarily to flee Lake County, Dyer returned to his courthouse in Granite to preside over an attempt to bring some of his opponents to trial. The judge's last letter to his father [the Rev. John L. Dyer], on July 3, 1875, demonstrated the risk he knew he was taking:

> Dear Father, I don't know that the sun will ever rise and set for me again, but I trust in God and his mercy. At eight o'clock I sit in court. The mob have me under guard. . . . There is no cowardice in me, father. I am worthy of you in this respect. . . . [L]ike him who died for all; I die, if die I must, for law, order, and principle; and too, I stand alone.[60]

The judge was shot through the head in his courtroom. His murderers never were officially identified. Although Judge Dyer may have been something of a wastrel, his death was that of a true hero.

Sometimes lawyers, too, had to operate within the more violent frontier emotions lurking just below the veneer of supposedly organized society. In 1865 after President Lincoln's assassination, an emotional People's Court in Central City was convened to deal with a loudmouthed troublesome Southerner. The rightful authorities, unable to avoid the general course of events, sought to guide the trial to a nontragic ending. Attorney Charles Post, later a Colorado Attorney General, helped manipulate the mob in deciding not to hang the defendant, but instead to send him to Denver for lesser punishment.[61]

Similarly, in 1869 in the town of Evans, there was an unprovoked murder of a townsman by a railroad worker. Instead of relying on the legitimate territorial justice system to take its course, a People's Court was organized. This trial was less like a mob than the 1865 affair in Central City. Nevertheless, the young attorney appointed by the judge could not save the murderer from the resulting "suspended" sentence.[62] Such People's Courts (and there were some in Denver) at this time in Colorado history were certainly wrong and probably unnecessary, not to mention lost fees for those practicing in the appellate arena.

The lawyers who made up the bar in federal territorial times were, like the judges, a mixed and sometime colorful lot. Only a handful need be mentioned to demonstrate this point.

Some proved their patriotism during the War of the Rebellion. John P. Slough, a Denver attorney originally from Ohio, became colonel of the First Colorado Infantry that defeated Confederates in New Mexico in 1862. Slough left Colorado, however, and eventually became chief justice of New Mexico Territory. He was killed by a lawyer named Ryerson in 1867.[63] Maj. Jacob Downing was another Denver lawyer who served with the First Colorado in New Mexico, as well as participating in the Indian Wars of 1864 and 1868. He also was the first to introduce alfalfa into the territory.[64] S. W. Waggoner, a judge in preterritorial Denver, was a captain in the Second Colorado Cavalry. He was killed in a hotly contested battle with Todd's Missouri guerrillas in 1864. He rests, surrounded by the brave men killed with him, in Woodlawn Cemetery at Independence, Mo.[65]

The bar of Colorado Territory also had a distinction rare for the entire nation: a black attorney. For a few weeks in 1862, a "mulatto" held the appointive office of assistant district attorney for Arapahoe County. He accounted for his dark skin by claiming to be part Indian. He resigned his office to join the gold rush to Montana.[66]

Of course, attorneys in Territorial Colorado sometimes suffered from an affliction that traditionally afflicts members of the bar. Gen. L. Bowen of Denver and Pueblo was a sound lawyer who unfortunately had a "strong propensity for getting drunk, generally at the time he was most needed . . . . [M]any and varied were the plans adopted for sobering him."[67]

However, with rules of admission, it also was possible to police the bar. At least by 1871, the Territorial Supreme Court issued frameable certificates of admission to practice.[68] The high court took these certificates of practice seriously. In 1871, the Supreme Court determined that Marmaduke Green, duly elected to the office of district attorney of Pueblo County, could not serve, since he was not a licensed attorney.[69] And, in 1874, the high court disbarred Samuel E. Browne, who had been Colorado's first United States Attorney, for failing to pay money over to a client.[70]

Generally, however, the bar of Colorado before statehood apparently was ethical, competent, and rich in background. Justice Stone recalled some members in a 1908 bar address. There was George W.

Purkins, a Virginian, "a cultured lawyer of the old school, classical and the most graceful and eloquent speaker we ever had;" William S. Rockwell, a former Wisconsin judge; Robert S. Morrison, author of a standard textbook on mining law; George F. Crocker, a former city attorney of Chicago; Thomas Macon of Cañon City, "one of the best criminal lawyers of the West;" and many others.[71]

Samuel E. Browne, disbarred in 1874.

There also were attorneys to look after the interests of Colorado Territory's Hispanic population. Mariano Larragoite was a native New Mexican who emigrated to Trinidad in 1869, and served in the territorial legislatures of 1872 and 1874.[72] One General Baird, also of Trinidad, was a former attorney general of the Republic of Texas. He was able to represent the Spanish Americans of Trinidad because of his perfect fluency in Spanish.[73]

Apparently, there were no regularly admitted women attorneys in Colorado before statehood. It is likely that Colorado men generally felt the same as their Montana counterparts: "A woman is queen in her own home; but we neither want her as a blacksmith, a plough woman, a soldier, a lawyer, a doctor, nor in any such profession or handicraft."[74] Fortunately, things have substantially changed.

The bench and the bar of territorial Colorado were thus a varied lot. Some were undoubtedly rascals. Some would have been competent in any state in the Union. But they tended to have a spirit that made them realize they were serving in a rather rude but freer transitory period. A group of attorneys, in that last full territorial summer of 1875, traveled the circuit on the West Slope with presiding Judge Hallett. Between trials, they fished together, they dined together, they sang together, and they lodged together. In one case, a man named Palmer employed attorney George Q. Richmond to replevin a jackass that a poor Mexican claimed was his. The jury declined to award the burro to Palmer and the *pro se* (unrepresented by counsel) Mexican rode off on the animal. Judge Hallett, aided by the district attorney, then penned a poem. Following are portions:

> The leading case in court this term
> Presents a question rare;
> 'Tis not of human rights or wrongs,
> Or flagrant crime laid bare;
>
> 'Tis not of lands and tenements,
> Nor yet of grain nor grass;
> But whether a horseshoe brand was stamped
> Upon old Palmer's — burro.[75]

On Aug. 8, 1876, a week after Colorado's admission to the Union, Jonathan W. Webster, clerk of the Colorado Supreme Court and librarian of the law library, received Vol. 4 of the Nebraska Reports. A printed bookplate, proclaiming the volume to be the property of the Supreme Court of Colorado Territory, was duly pasted in the front of the book. Then, an unknown hand wrote above the bookplate, "Colorado State Library." The hand then took pen in hand and underlined, for emphasis, the word "State."[76] The days of the Colorado Territorial Bench and Bar were over.

Endnotes

1. Hawkins, "Old-Time Lawyers and Judges of Colorado," *Colorado Bar Association Proceedings* (Denver: 1938), p. 94.
2. Smiley, *History of Denver* (Denver: 1901), p. 675.
3. *Ibid.*
4. *Ibid.*
5. Marshall, "Early Denver History as Told by Contemporary Newspaper Advertisements," *Colorado Magazine*, Vol. 8, Sept. 1931, p. 169.
6. Hawkins, *loc. cit.*
7. Stone, *History of Colorado*, Vol. 1 (Chicago: 1918), pp. 168-169.
8. *Ibid.*, p. 171.
9. Hawkins, *op. cit.*, p. 96.
10. See, e.g., Mumey, *History and Laws of Nevadaville* (Boulder, Colo.: 1962), p. 40.
11. Lamb, *Past Memories and Future Thoughts* (Denver: 1905), p. 41.
12. Conrad, *Uncle Dick Wootton* (Chicago: 1957), pp. 363-364.
13. Hafen (ed.), *Colorado and Its People*, Vol. II (New York: 1948), pp. 371-372.
14. Smith (ed.). *John D. Young and the Colorado Gold Rush* (Chicago: 1969), pp. 48-54.
15. Raine, *et al.*, *Denver Murders* (New York: 1946), p. 23.
16. Zamonski and Keller, *The Fifty-Niners* (Denver: 1961), p. 101.
17. Dorset, *The New Eldorado* (New York: 1970), p. 126.
18. Raine, *op. cit.*, pp. 27-30.
19. Zamonski and Keller, *op. cit.*, p. 146.
20. Stanton, *Sixty Years in Colorado* (Denver: 1922), p. 170.
21. See Hawkins, *op. cit.*, p. 97.
22. Thorne, *Cyrus Clay Carpenter and Iowa Politics, 1854-1898* (Iowa City: 1974), pp. 54-55.
23. Stone, *op. cit.*, p. 241.
24. Smith, *op. cit.*, p. 144.
25. Parkhill, *Mister Barney Ford* (Denver: 1963), pp. 101-103. Another biography of Ford, however, does not contain this story, so it may be an invention.
26. See Hawkins, *op. cit.*, p. 94; Fritz, "The Constitution and Laws of Early Mining Districts in Boulder County, Colorado," *University of Colorado Studies* Vol. 21, March 1934, p. 134; Hall, *History of the State of Colorado*, Vol. I (Chicago: 1889), p. 220.
27. Richardson, *Beyond the Mississippi* (New York: 1867), pp. 305-306; Zamonski

and Keller, *op. cit.*, pp. 174-183.
28. Hill, *Tales of the Colorado Pioneers* (Denver: 1884), pp. 50-54.
29. Hafen, *Reports from Colorado: The Wildman Letters, 1859-1865* (Glendale, Calif.: 1961), p. 290.
30. Baskin, *History of the Arkansas Valley* (Chicago: 1881), p. 769.
31. Stanton, *op. cit.*, pp. 170-171.
32. Thorne, *op. cit.*, p. 56.
33. Smiley, *op. cit.*, p. 694.
34. Hall, *op. cit.*, p. 268.
35. Stone, *op. cit.*, p. 745.
36. In about 1982-1985, most of the sets of territorial law books listed here were ordered removed from the Colorado Supreme Court Library, for lack-of-space reasons. Many were sold to various out-of-state law schools and lawyers, but many ended up in Dempsey-dumpsters and were scrapped. A few were rescued from the dumpsters and purchased by the author, who fortunately already had done a very sketchy survey of the books that can never be repeated.
37. Guice, "Colorado's Territorial Courts," *Colorado Magazine*, Vol. 45, Summer 1968, pp. 218-219; Hafen, *op. cit.*, p. 373.
38. Guice, *The Rocky Mountain Bench* (New Haven: 1972), pp. 27-33.
39. Stone, *op. cit.*, p. 734.
40. Parkhill, *The Law Goes West* (Denver: 1956), pp. 21-22.
41. Stone, *loc. cit.*
42. Bowles, *Across the Continent* (Springfield, Mass.: 1866), p. 61.
43. Stone, *op. cit.*, p. 735.
44. Bowles, *op. cit.*, p. 60.
45. "Senator Charles S. Thomas' Old Timers Speech," *The Denver Bar Association Record*, Vol. I, No. 13, Dec. 1924, p. 4. Thomas, however, was a Democrat originally from the South, so the rumor is suspect.
46. Stone, *loc. cit.*
47. Guice, *op. cit. (The Rocky Mountain Bench)*, pp. 65-66.
48. McClure, *Three Thousand Miles Through the Rocky Mountains* (Philadelphia: 1869), p. 106.
49. Chetlain, *Recollections of Seventy Years* (Galena: 1899), pp. 40-41.
50. See *Yunker v. Nichols*, 1 Colo. 551 (1872).
51. Taylor, *Trinidad, Colorado Territory* (Pueblo: 1966), p. 56.
52. Greenwood, *New Life in New Lands* (New York: 1873), p. 105.
53. McClure, *op. cit.*, pp. 332-335.
54. Watrous, *History of Larimer County, Colorado* (Fort Collins: 1911), p. 148; Geffs, *Under Ten Flags: A History of Weld County,*

Colorado (Greeley: 1938), pp. 93-94.
55. Watrous, *op. cit.*, p. 113.
56. "Extracts From Address Delivered by George Q. Richmond at Old Timers Day," *The Denver Bar Association Record*, Vol. I, No. 9. August 1924, p. 7.
57. Dr. Henry W. Toll, "Letters of a Young Lawyer," The Denver Westerners *Roundup*, Vol. 51, No. 1 (Jan.-Feb. 1995) pp. 12-13.
58. Stone, *op. cit.*, p. 745.
59. See Opus, "The Lake County War, 1874-75," *Colorado Magazine*, Vol 47, Spring 1970.
60. Dyer, *Snow-Shoe Itinerant* (Cincinnati: 1890), pp. 313-314.
61. Hill, *op. cit.*, pp. 106-110.
62. Townshend, *A Tenderfoot in Colorado* (New York: 1923), pp. 110-130.
63. Poldervaart, *Black-Robed Justice* (Santa Fe: 1948), pp. 67-71.
64. Steinel, *History of Agriculture in Colorado* (Fort Collins: 1926), pp. 411-414; F. D. Coburn, *The Book of Alfalfa* (New York: 1906), pp. 243-245.
65. Stanton, *op. cit.*, pp. 110, 159. Such is the local fame of Waggoner and his men that the groundskeepers at the large Woodlawn Cemetery readily will direct one inquiring of the "Colorado soldiers" to the flagpole and worn monuments marking their resting places. Ironically, George Todd lies buried about 150 yards away, killed in a fight with other Coloradans later that year.
66. Parkhill, *op. cit.*, p. 125.
67. Baskin, *op. cit.*, p. 771.
68. "Senator Charles S. Thomas' Old Timers Speech." *The Denver Bar Association Record*, Vol. I, No. 11, Oct. 1924, p. 4; Sweet, *A Princeton Cowboy* (Colorado Springs: 1967), p. iv.
69. People v. Hallett, 1 Colo. 352 (1871).
70. Matter of Samuel E. Browne, 2 Colo. 552 (1875).
71. Stone, *op. cit.*, p. 743.
72. Corbett, *The Legislative Manual of the State of Colorado* (Denver: 1877), p. 341.
73. Stone, *op. cit.*, p. 744. However, Baird must have been a deputy or assistant attorney general in Texas, for he is not listed in Speer, *Texas Jurists, 1836-1936* (Austin: 1936).
74. Dimsdale, *The Vigilantes of Montana.* (Helena: 1915), p. 61.
75. Stone, *op. cit.*, pp. 746-747. Judge Stone did not indicate if this published version was "sanitized" from the original.
76. See endnote 36. This was the volume found by the author to be the first received by the library after statehood. The portion of the volume containing this notation is in the possession of the author.

About the Author

John M. Hutchins is the author of two chapters in the *Golden Anniversary Brand Book*. The first one, "Colorado's Territorial Bench and Bar," was presented for the Denver Posse of the Westerns in September 1985. (You'll find John's second article, "The Life and Times of Frank Canton," toward the back of this book.) A dedicated Westerner, John was Sheriff of the Denver Posse in 1994.

A native Virginian, John and his family moved to Colorado in 1950. He was graduated in 1969 from Northglenn High School, then attended the University of Colorado, winning a B.A. degree, Phi Beta Kappa. He earned his law degree from CU in 1976.

John became assistant U.S. Attorney in Denver in 1990, after having served eight years as assistant and, later, first assistant Colorado Attorney General. In 1981, he had his own law practice in Meeker, Colo., and subsequently was assistant city attorney in El Paso, Texas.

A major in the U.S. Army Reserve, John was assistant staff Judge Advocate and defense counsel, First Cavalry Division, Ft. Hood, Texas, 1977-1981.

John was an elected member of the Northglenn Charter Commission in 1975, and later was a Northglenn city councilman, 1976-1977. He and his wife Dale have a son, Adam Edward.

"The villain still pursues her . . ." by *Max Smith*

Theatre in Denver, 1859 - 1881

By James Osborn

*T*HE TENTS, LOG CABINS, and dirt streets that were to become Denver offered little entertainment in 1859, besides the usual Taos Lightning and a game of chance dealt on the head of a barrel. This state of affairs prompted Gen. William Larimer to write to his wife in the winter of 1858-1859, "Tell Col. Thorne that Charley Blake is building a new house, 90 feet by 60 feet. He says it will make a good theater building. . . ."[1]

The building was constructed in the spring of 1859 to be used as a hotel, but soon became a gambling hall and saloon. This palace for tenderfoot gold seekers ended up being 100 feet long and 40 feet wide, with a dirt floor and canvas roof and windows. The first entertainments in the hall were bands and theater shows that were equally as crude as the surroundings. This building, known as Denver Hall, was on present-day Blake Street between 14th and 15th. It was sold and became the famous stable and livery called the Elephant. On May 23, 1862, the name was changed to the Elephant Corral. One of its many incarnations exists today as an office building.[2]

As the town grew, so did competition for Denver Hall. A gambling place called Cibola Hall was built at the corner of Ferry and 4th streets in Auraria. However, civilization had arrived when Barney and Company constructed the Apollo Hotel, the first hostelry with wood floors. It served as a combination restaurant, gambling hall, and saloon. The second floor, known as Apollo Hall, was the site for the first truly professional theater performances. General Larimer's wife did contact Col. Charles R. Thorne as the letter instructed. Colonel Thorne managed a Chicago theater at this time and had been involved in theater in New York since the 1820s, including the National Theater in 1854. Lured by the gilt of gold-laden, theater-starved patrons, Thorne arrived in Denver in 1859. Arrangements were made with the Apollo Hall owner Libeus Barney, and a temporary stage was set up at one end of the hall. The following is a review from the Oct. 6, 1859, issue of the *Rocky Mountain News*.

> Thorne's theater opened on Monday evening last night with the "Cross of Gold," followed by a popular song by Miss Wakely; a favorite dance by M'lle Haydee; concluding with the farce of the "Two Gregories." The whole performance was excellent and unexceptional. Colonel Thorne can hardly be excelled in any country, and he is most ably supported by his company of stars. Miss Wakely's singing is excellent, and M'lle Haydee, as a danseuse, has no superior. There was an overflowing house, and frequent loud applause. Upon being called out, Col. T. assured his audience it was his design to spend the winter here, and erect a commodious and elegant theater in the spring. On Tuesday evening was played the "Old Guard," dancing, singing, and the "Swiss Cottage" in conclusion. There was a good house and rapturous applause. Last evening was given the "Idiot Witness" and the farce of a "Kiss in the Dark" with like good success. Our people are most fortunate in the establishment of a theater at this time—and that theater Thorne's—to help the long winter months to pass pleasantly. We hope that they see to it that he receives the patronage he deserves.[3]

Obviously, the performances by the Thorne Star Company were a big success. Libeus Barney wrote this account:

> Last night was ushered in an event of paramount importance to Pikes Peakers. Mr. Charles Thorne, the far-famed itinerant theatrical showman, with a company of 11 performers, six males and five females, made their debut at "Apollo Hall" before a large though not remarkably select, audience. Admittance, one dollar; comfortable accommodations for 350; receipts $400, which tells well for the patronage, if not for the appreciation, of art in this semi-barbarous region.[4]

Barney doesn't seem to appreciate his clientele's level of refinement even though they were happy to part with some "dust" for almost any diversion. In fact, gold dust was the common form of currency and scales were in use at the ticket office. Mr. Barney claimed that one day, in need of a beaver hat, he swept the dirt from the ticket office floor into a gold pan and collected $13.56 in weight. Theater performances at Apollo Hall above the saloon and casino were not a genteel affair. Clinking glasses, the crack of billiard balls, wild songs and laughter from below, interrupted performances. At this time candles lit the stage. So during love scenes, if patrons were not distracted by stagehands who blew out candles and relit them to create moody lighting, they may have been by the occasional gunshot. Sometimes the distractions were in the theater, as reported by the *Rocky Mountain News*.

> We are sorry to say that the audience was somewhat disturbed on Tuesday evening last, by the pranks of a drunken man, who is hereby notified that a rigid police is established, and he and all such will be summarily ejected if good order is not kept.

Apollo Hall or Theater was white frame building with balcony.

Apparently Colonel Thorne had enough of this sort of audience and left Denver for good after only two weeks. His troupe remained active in Denver under Mademoiselle Haydee. The next local sensation was comedy actor Mike J. Dougherty, an Eastern actor who came to the region to mine. Mining wasn't working out so he went on stage at the Apollo Hall in the play, "Perfection," as well as another, "The Omnibus." Dougherty was a huge hit, especially while performing the comic song, "Paddy's Wedding," which brought down the house. Apparently, he excelled as an Irish drunk or as an old gentleman. Dougherty stayed on the Denver stage scene until his death in 1865. During this time he received many benefits.

A benefit was a common practice in the 1800s to financially reward popular actors and actresses. The theater manager paid the expenses for a performance. The actor receiving the benefit would perform his favorite roles and keep the gate receipts. Some benefits were held for two or three minor actors at one time. Benefits were always well publicized in newspapers as good public relations for the theater.

Another popular entertainment of this era was minstrel shows. These were black-face white singers with banjos and mostly rowdy

(Author's Collection)

Irish actor John Langrishe, 1829-1895.

songs, but were very popular, more popular than theater performances. In 1860 the most renowned of the minstrel acts were the Cibola Minstrels and the Converse and Petrie Ethiopian Minstrels.

The most popular showman arrived next—in fact a man known as the father of Denver theater. He was John S. Langrishe, born in Ireland in 1829. He came to America in 1845, and his first U.S. performance was "The Irish Attorney" at the Cheatam Theater in New York City. Langrishe was from a theatrical family and Langrishe was probably not his real name.

While in the East he married the great-granddaughter of Ethan Allen, Jeanette Allen. Organizing a theater troupe in 1859, Langrishe toured Western military posts. Arriving in September 1860, he gave his first performance. The short plays that night were "His Last Legs" and "Fifteen Years of Labour Lost," which was probably a temperance play. (Temperance plays were very common at that time. One of my favorite titles is "The Youth Who Never Saw a Woman." I wouldn't want to guess as to its subject matter.)

Langrishe's troupe was a great success and a six-night stand became permanent. He took over the Apollo Hall in 1860, replacing the candles on stage with oil lamps, a major technological advance. John and Jeanette Langrishe were the most celebrated performers in Denver theater until 1876, when he became editor of the *Black Hills Daily Pioneer.* He occasionally returned to Denver

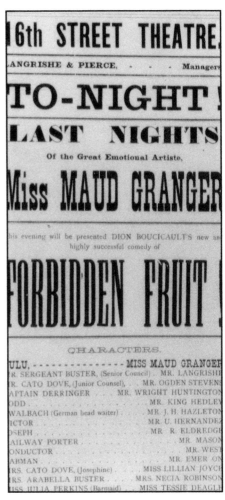

(Author's Collection)
16th Street Theatre poster of 1881 featured Langrishe production.

(Author's Collection)

Harry Richmond, Denver actor in 1860s, 1870s.

for theater purposes, and signed the Colorado Pioneer Society register in 1882. Langrishe retired to Wardner, Idaho. He died in 1895.

Another theater that deserves mention was the Platte Valley Theater at the corner of 16th and Lawrence. It was 90 x 50 feet with a 30-foot stage, and seating for 1500. The *Rocky Mountain News* praised its decor with this statement: "The finish throughout corresponds with the magnitude of the building. The walls and ceiling are plastered with a glittering hard finish, and the wood shines in paint and gildings."[5] The building was later renamed the Denver Theater. With new professional facilities and eastern theater troupes came more civilization and organization. As in most theaters there was a "green room," or actors lounge, next to the stage. Theater managers posted rules for their actors in the green room. The following are a few of the most interesting of them:

Green Room Rules

1. Any member of the company unable, from the effects of stimulants to perform, or appear, at rehearsal shall forfeit a week's salary, or be liable to be discharged.
2. For making the stage wait—three dollars.
3. Performer rehearsing from a book or part after proper time has been allowed for study shall forfeit five dollars.
4. A performer introducing his own language or improper jests not in the author, or swearing in his part, shall forfeit five dollars.
5. Performer who makes alteration in dress without consent of the manager or refuses to wear the costume selected shall forfeit three dollars.
6. Performer restoring what has been cut by the manager will forfeit five dollars.
7. No actor to address the audience without consent of the manager.

Also, here are some theater salaries of the 1870s:

Actors, walking, gentleman or lady	$20/week
Old man or woman	$24-40/week
Low grade talent	$10-25/week
Extras off the street	$3-4/week
Stage carpenters/scene shifters	$10-50/week
Ballet girls	$8-10/week
Ushers and dressers	$5-6/week

Besides Langrishe and others who put together legitimate theater, "variety halls" were very popular. Variety halls combined gambling, drinks, girly shows and theatrical performances. The earliest of these was the Criterion Concert Hall, in 1861. There were many others, but newspapers wouldn't accept advertising from most of these "Dens of Iniquity." However, this is a description published by the *Denver Tribune*:

> In crossing to the opposite side of Blake Street, or on the south side, west of F (15th), we are attracted by the blare of instruments and glare of lights, to another extensive establishment, known as the "Cricket." Besides a large hall and stage and bar room, the "Cricket" has an extensive room devoted to all the games of chance that were ever invented, and back of the hall a sort of hypothetical "Green Room" concentrated to purposes which we leave to our readers to imagine.
>
> The "Cricket" is a half-way "standard" place of amusement. There is no ostensible price of admittance, but anyone who indulges in the so-called "games of chance" is certain to pay very dearly for indulging in the experiment. "The Cricket" is an "all night" resort, and is generally thronged with a strange admixture of people.[6]

We find very few facts about the performers or performance at variety halls, but this description is from *The Denver Post*:

> Monday afternoon there would be a conference and at night the show, without rehearsal or script. This training taught actors to recognize possibilities, and they improve the part of their act which seemed to get the most response. Women had to "work" boxes and get the men to order expensive drinks. At this time vaudeville acts got sixty dollars a team for a week's work.[7]

In the 1870s many people were trying to get rid of vice in the growing city of Denver. Gambling was finally outlawed in Denver in 1873, which dealt a blow to variety halls. One of the main crusaders of the time was William N. Byers, publisher of the *Rocky Mountain News*. It is not clear if this was because of his puritan zeal or his zeal to sell papers. In any case, the following is an example of the kind of article he was fond of publishing to support the anti-vice campaign:

> A row occurred at the Cricket Hall last night, which resulted in a well-known sport named Barnum getting pretty badly hurt. He was endeavoring to get up a row between a couple of the girls employed in the hall, and upon being ordered to quit by officer Stout, made an attempt to draw his revolver, but the officer was too quick for him and brought him to terms by striking him two or three ugly blows over the head. The girl put in an appearance and was fined $40 and costs. Barnum was unable to appear. He occasions our officers a great deal of trouble and they would feel greatly obliged if he would make himself scarce hereabouts.[8]

Another of the famous variety halls was the Occidental. Here is its description:

> A few steps farther westward brings us to the "Occidental Hall" at the north-west corner of Blake and G (16th) streets. Going up a single flight of

stairs we enter a large hall blazing with light and flashy ornamentation. Here we find another commodious "bar" and a stage. Placards of "Beer 10¢" appear among the gaslights, and the numerous "Beer Girls" promenade the halls as waiters. About the walls are hung bulletin boards in flaring colors with the following advertisement: "More talent, Miss So and So, the great Prima Donna, late of Winter Garden, serio-comic singer danseuse, will appear every evening.[9]

Other tamer types of entertainment were available, as well. Previously mentioned blackface comedy minstrels, magicians, and lecturers entertained early Denverites. Even P.T. Barnum made an appearance at the Denver Theater on June 18, 1870,[10] presenting his popular lecture, "How to Be Healthy, Happy, and Rich." History doesn't record whether anyone in the audience actually became healthy, happy, or rich, but everyone was thoroughly entertained.

(Author's Collection)
Governor's Guard Hall, 15th and Curtis streets, was built in 1873.

Byers' campaign for upstanding entertainment ended in February 1873 in a new opera house called the Governor's Guard Hall. The new $26,000 building was at 15th and Curtis streets. This was a magnificent structure which served as an armory as well as opera house. The armory was for a group called the Governor's Guards, who raised the money for the building. These people were a sort of pre-statehood National Guard.

The Guard's opera house was a financial disaster. The management suffered with a lack of experience and the bad economy of the 1870s. In 1876 the opera house got a new lease on life, when Nate Forrester, a renowned actor and theater manager, leased the Guard's opera house and renamed it Forrester's Opera House. He put together the finest casts available. Forrester was the top impresario of the 1870s. That is, until H.A.W. Tabor, who in 1879 built the Tabor Opera House in Leadville, arrived in Denver.

Tabor proceeded to build the finest theater anywhere for the times. On Sep. 6, 1881, the Tabor Grand Opera House opened with Emma Abbott and her company appearing in "Maritana." The Tabor Grand was the talk of theater circles nationwide and as a result drew the best actors and actresses of the day, from Sarah Bernhardt to Fanny's Female Minstrels. The lavish decor boasted cherry wood furnishings, red damask hangings, and soft lighting. This tribute to theatrical luxury marked the end of pioneer theater in Denver.

Endnotes

1. Herman S. Davis, *Reminiscences of Gen. William Larimer*, page 168.
2. Melvin Schoberlin, *From Candles to Footlights* Old West Publishing Co., 1941, pp. 17-19.
3. The *Rocky Mountain News*, Oct. 6, 1859.
4. Libeus Barney, *Early Day Letters from Auraria*, page 39.
5. The *Rocky Mountain News*, Oct. 26, 1861.
6. *Denver Tribune*, Aug. 10, 1872, page 4.
7. *The Denver Post*, Aug. 15, 1870, page 5.
8. The *Rocky Mountain News*, May 18, 1870, page 4.
9. *Denver Tribune*, Aug. 10, 1872, page 4.
10. Schoberlin, *op. cit.*

About the Author

James W. Osborn, a Posse Member of the Denver Westerners, is an Iowa native. He was graduated from Des Moines Valley High School, and Iowa State University, where he had majors in psychology and journalism. Jim and his wife Lorraine moved to Denver in 1981, where he formed his own television production company, Rockywood Productions Inc. As a director and cinematographer, Jim has worked on several films and produced many television commercials. He has won seven Alfies—the equivalent of an "Emmy" or "Oscar" in the commercial film world—and a Grand Alfie for his film.

History has been a passion for Jim from an early age, culminating over the years in a Western and U.S. Cavalry artifact collection and militaria—anything stamped with "U.S." Jim says both he and his collection are dusted off and kept in order by his saintly wife Lorraine.

Original Father Dyer church in Breckenridge by *Max Smith*

The Rev. John L. Dyer,

The Snowshoe Itinerant

By Robert L. Brown

*T*HE REV. JOHN L. DYER was the best known and easily the most beloved of Colorado's nineteenth century circuit-riding clergymen. By association he came to be identified with the foundation of Methodism in the new territory of Colorado. He traveled on foot, by muleback, on snowshoes, and once in an emergency he fastened a pack saddle on a cow to attend his circuit. He was called Father Dyer although the title was not used in the Episcopal or Catholic context. The origins of this appellation are obscure. One early source implied that the term was used because Dyer was regarded as a father to his flock, or that he was nearly a surrogate parent to the far-from-home miner. Rev. Mark Feister feels that the people of Breckenridge lovingly bestowed the name on Father Dyer. But there is another possibility. In the last century it was common practice to refer to all older persons as mother or father. Carry Nation, who began her anti-saloon crusades when she was in her 60s, was called Mother Nation, even by her enemies. John Dyer was well along in years when he first entered Colorado.

Dyer was a native of rural Ohio, born on March 16, 1812, near the town of Chillicothe. At the tender age of 6 he was already employed as a farm hand. His employer paid him in whiskey. "I was born with a love for whiskey," he recalled, "but after getting stone drunk in a flax field at the age of 10, I swore off for the next 80 years." He joined the Methodist Church at the age of 20 in 1832. But he came to know God in the bottom of a lead mine at Potosi, Wis., in 1849. He never fully recovered from exposure to lead poisoning, and impaired eyesight plagued him for the remainder of his life.

John Dyer married for the first time in 1833. His bride, a native of Maine, was Harriet Foster, and she had been living on a nearby farm. During their 14 years of life together she bore him five children, three sons and two daughters. Harriet passed away in 1847. Because his young children desperately needed a mother, Dyer remarried too hastily. It soon developed that his new wife was still married to her second husband. Disillusioned, Dyer obtained an annulment. More that two decades would pass before he married again.

In 1853, at age 41, Dyer was admitted to the Methodist Conference at Fillmore, Minn. A contemporary account that appears in the history of Fillmore County describes him as being "harsh, crude and uncouth." Three years later he founded the small town of Lenora, Minn., and started a Methodist church there. Although it was formerly believed that Dyer was a lay preacher, the product of a camp meeting conversion, Dr. Martin Rist found a record that he was ordained by the West Wisconsin Conference of the Methodist Church in 1855.

At this point in his life Rev. Dyer recalled, "I made up my mind to see Pikes Peak." He was now 49 years old and nearly blind. With only $14.75 in his pocket he set out for the West with full trust that the Lord would provide. He left Lenora on May 9, 1861, on foot. Except for a short lift with a stranger, he walked most of the 700 miles from Omaha to Cherry Creek of Denver. The ordeal cut his weight from 192 to 163 pounds by the time he trudged into Denver on June 20. His son Elias had been there since 1860. Dyer's first assignment was to serve the raw new camp of Buckskin Joe in South Park. Following a reunion with his son, Dyer traded his watch for $20 worth of flour, side bacon, dried apples, sugar, salt, coffee, and a few cans of fruit.

Father Dyer remained in Denver for only one day. He left on June 21 and walked the nearly 100 miles to Buckskin Joe. The following February he traveled on foot to Denver in 2½ days to hear the Rev. John M. Chivington preach. Chivington spotted him in the congregation and yielded the pulpit to Dyer. [Chivington, presiding elder of the Rocky Mountain District of the Methodist Episcopal Church, was later made a major with the First Colorado Volunteer Infantry, in the Battle of Glorieta Pass.] In the following four months, Dyer traveled some 400 miles on foot, preaching three times weekly and receiving a total of $43 from collections. Both his hat and his boots were patched. He often walked the entire distance from Fairplay to Denver to save the 75 cents coach fare. He thought nothing of hiking from Denver to Central City or Breckenridge, with only a few hours of sleep. Aside from walking, Reverend Dyer traveled another 10,000 miles by horse or mule in his first two years of serving Colorado settlements. On one occasion he shoveled snow for 3½ days to go three miles.

During the South Park assignment he preached regularly at Buck-

Buckskin Joe was Father Dyer's first assignment in South Park. Photographer George Wakely took this view in 1860s.

skin Joe, Dudley, Fairplay, Alma, Hamilton, Tarryall, London Junction, Mosquito, Montgomery and Quartzville. Lacking a church or appropriate building, he preached in tents, on street corners, in private homes, in gambling halls, and even in saloons, or wherever he could gather a crowd. Once in a Fairplay barroom he requested that the owner remove a sign advertising "Good Whiskey." The bartender replied that he would be glad to cooperate since they were out of that brand, anyway.

The following story came from Fred Mazzulla [Denver attorney and one of the founders of the Denver Posse of the Westerners] and although I have been unable to confirm it from any other source, it is too good to overlook. At nearby Dudley, Dyer usually conducted services in a tent. On one occasion he was preaching from Isaiah and had planned to serve communion. A quantity of bread lay on a plate atop a makeshift altar behind the pulpit. Suddenly the tiny congregation burst forth in gales of laughter, an uncommon reaction to a text from Isaiah. With impaired vision, Dyer could observe no basis for levity until he chanced to turn around. Behind him a mule had pushed its head in between the rear tent flaps and was devouring the bread.

Father Dyer's sermons often followed patriotic themes, particularly between 1861 and 1865 when they were influenced by the Civil War. Although he possessed a deep compassion for human frailties, according to a contemporary he "preached the Word burning hot, emphasiz-

Sketch depicts Father Dyer preaching in saloon. He preached wherever there was an audience.

(Courtesy Western History Dept., Denver Public Library)

ing the wrath as well as the love of God." Following a series of sermons entitled, "The Five Great Sins of Breckenridge," he was able to secure a Sunday closing of the town's many saloons. On Monday the local paper lamented, "Twas a dry one, no place to go except to church." The four other sins were card-playing, dancing, indifference, and sabbath desecration. Dyer preached Hellfire and Damnation. He could use his fists too, and on one occasion he half choked a somewhat reluctant convert for not praying loudly enough.

John Dyer accepted the first of two assignments to Summit County's circuit in July 1863. His regular preaching stations were Park City, American Gulch, Delaware Flats, Galena Gulch, Lincoln City,

Fairplay's location made it one of Father Dyer's most important stations on his South Park circuit.

Father Dyer regularly preached at old salt works in South Park.

Mayo Gulch, Presto, and Breckenridge. He made the rounds regularly each two weeks. Later that same year he walked more than 100 miles to attend the Methodist Rocky Mountain Conference in Denver. Before leaving he was assigned to serve the new Lake County in addition to continuing in Park County. In Lake County his circuit included both Oro Cities, Cache Creek, Leadville and most of the satellite towns, including Robinson and Kokomo.

By the end of December 1863, Dyer was nearly out of money. The pittance he was paid by the church and poor returns from collections were inadequate to sustain his active schedule. So he sought the mail-carrying contract, carrying letters, packages, and gold dust from Buckskin Joe across 13,000-foot Mosquito Pass to Cache Creek and Oro City. Twice each week he made the 37-mile trek. He was literally a one-man pack mule. The pay was $18 weekly. In winter he made the trip on snowshoes. Once while making his circuit he was shot at from ambush for having been a witness to murder. Dyer always felt that God would protect him. The fact that the bullet missed him strengthened his conviction. Somehow he still found time to preach three times each week.

Dyer's snowshoes were of the Norwegian type, or skis. He made them himself, 4 inches wide and 9 to 11 feet in length. Sensibly, he usually traveled at night to avoid snowslides. He was caught once and buried in 6 to 8 feet of snow. He

(From Collection of Evelyn and Robert L. Brown)

In the Breckenridge Methodist Church, stained-glass panel depicts Father Dyer on skis.

prayed first, then dug himself out and proceeded to deliver the mail. His career as a postman lasted from 1863 through 1864, earning him the title of Snowshoe Itinerant.

Dyer's fierce determination and unusual mode of travel brought him national recognition earlier in this century. In its issue of Jan. 13, 1936, *Time Magazine* noted that Rev. John Dyer, a Methodist clergyman, had carried the mail to his parishioners on skis in the early 1850s, thus introducing skiing to the nation. Typically for *Time*, the article was in the sports section. Furthermore, Dyer wasn't even in Colorado in the 1850s. He was still in Minnesota. Obviously he didn't introduce skiing to the nation, or even to Colorado. But he seems to have been the first skier known to us by name.

In March 1865, Father Dyer was assigned to a circuit in northern New Mexico, where he held the first Protestant service on the Maxwell Grant. Although he was infringing on the territory of Father Machebeuf, Dyer converted hundreds of former Catholics to Methodism. Among them were soldiers, farmers, miners, gamblers, and, he claimed proudly, "One Romish priest." Dyer held Father Machebeuf in high esteem, calling him "A great worker." "But," said Dyer, "I have the advantage of a good wife to help me." It might be appropriate to note here that Father Dyer had remained a widower for more than two decades. In November 1870 he married Lucinda Ranking of Douglas County. Church duties in New Mexico were concluded in 1874 when he was recalled to accept charge of the new Erie-Plattville-Fort Lupton circuit.

On July 4, 1875, the Dyers were enjoying a well-deserved rest in Spring Valley, near the present Air Force Academy. Unfortunately, that very day Dyer's son, Elias, now a 39-year-old Lake County judge, was brutally murdered in his own courtroom at Granite. Judge Dyer had the misfortune to be assigned to adjudicate a dispute between two area ranchers over water rights. Both had threatened to kill him if the decision went against their side. Surprisingly, his killers granted him a last wish that he be permitted to write a final letter to his father. It said in part:

> Dear Father, I don't know that the sun will ever rise and set for me again, but I trust in God and his mercy. At eight o'clock I sit in court. The mob have me under guard. God comfort you and keep you always. . . . I die, if die I must, for law, order and principle; and too, I stand alone.
>
> Your loving and true, and I hope in some respects, worthy son, Elias Dyer

Father Dyer's assignment was short-lived in northern Colorado. He returned to South Park in July 1876 where he continued to serve

(From Collection of Evelyn and Robert L. Brown)

In Montgomery, Father Dyer used this crude log building as a chapel. (It may now be seen at Fairplay.)

until 1879 when he was sent over to Breckenridge for a second time. During his South Park tenure he often climbed 14,172-foot-high Mt. Bross and 14,286-foot Mt. Lincoln, to preach for the workers at the Moose Mine. He was 66 years old at the time. From the base of the mountain to the first shaft was a distance of five miles. The last structures were just 300 feet below the summit.

The following year Dyer was again given charge of the Breckenridge district. Despite his years he still covered most of his circuit on snowshoes. He regularly crossed both French and Georgia passes to reach his preaching stations. At age 68 he built his first church. The year was 1880 and it still stands in Breckenridge. Because it had no bell, in 1886 Dyer began ringing the fire alarm for church purposes, until the town trustees revoked the privilege. So he rang it again the next Sunday anyway. A steeple with its own bell was added to the little church in 1890. But in 1891 the bell was destroyed by vandals. Another now hangs in its place.

Dyer concluded the Summit County assignment when he was in his 73rd year, but he continued to preach there occasionally until he was

(From Dyer, 1890; artist, Folger)
The Rev. John L. Dyer, 1812-1901.

76 as they had no regular pastor. During this latter period he was constantly troubled by the "lower elements" who kept stealing the church organ for dancing. Dyer called it their "bacchanals." As a devout nineteenth century Methodist he regarded dancing as an instrument of the devil and a sure road to damnation.

While living in Breckenridge Father Dyer tried his hand at mining. He either discovered or acquired a mine called the Warrior's Mark. The year was 1881. It was modestly successful and he once had 50 men working there. A small community called Dyersville grew up along a creek just below the mine. County records showed 10 Republicans and 7 Democrats registered at Dyersville for the election of 1882. In common with most mines, the Warrior's Mark failed and Dyer lost his investment. He said later that wire gold working, whiskey, cards, mismanagement, and fast women ruined the average mining property. The remains of Dyersville can still be seen below Boreas Pass, near the foot of Indiana Gulch.

After leaving Breckenridge Dyer retired to Denver. He lived on Glenarm Place for a time, then he moved to University Park. During his active career he had preached in more new towns than any other Colorado clergyman. Colorado's State Senate appointed him their chaplain in 1885 and his stained glass likeness now appears in the Capitol dome. Three years later his wife passed away. Father Dyer made a last nostalgic visit to the Breckenridge church in 1899, two years before his death. To John L. Dyer the Deity was always very real, and on June 17, 1901, he went home to his Maker. One of his last utterances asked forgiveness for those who had slain his son. He was in his 90th year at the time of his passing.

At Breckenridge the original 1880 church has been moved and expanded, but is still used. In summer the ladies bring wild flowers to place behind the altar. Services are held early so that the minister may leave for Leadville to preach the 11 o'clock sermon. Near Fairplay, 13,855-foot-high Mt. Dyer also honors his name. Both Colorado and Methodism are better for the fact that this remarkable, humble, and dedicated man passed our way.

Bibliography

Collins, Dabney Otis. "Preacher on Snowshoes." Colorado Outdoors Magazine, February, 1981

Draper, Wanetta, and Hunt, Inez. *To Colorado's Restless Ghosts.* Denver: Sage Books, 1960.

Dyer, John L. *The Snowshoe Itinerant.* Cincinnati: Cranston and Stowe, 1890.

Feister, Mark, Rev. *Blasted Beloved Breckenridge.* Boulder, Colo.: Pruett Press, 1973.

Ferril, Thomas Hornsby. "Circuit Rider of the Frontier." *The Rocky Mountain News,* Denver. (no date).

Fleming, Naomi. "Father John L. Dyer, The Snowshoe Itinerant." *Colorado Legends,* Breckenridge, Colo.: 1983.

Rist, Martin. "Rev. Father John L. Dyer, Pioneer Colorado Preacher and Skier." The Iliff Review, Vol. XXXIII, #3, Fall, 1975.

Spring, Agner Wright. "Elias Dyer, Judge in Breckenridge." True West, Sept.-Oct., 1967.

Zilch, John H. "Memorial to 'Father' John L. Dyer." Denver: The Colorado Magazine, July, 1963.

About the Author

Robert L. Brown is a retired teacher whose career includes the University of Denver, Denver Public Schools, and the University of Colorado. His teaching areas have been the history of Colorado and Western history.

He has written 11 books, one of which is in a 14th printing. Three are concerned with ghost towns, two others are involved with hiking and mountain climbing. The rest are regional histories.

An active speaker on Western subjects, Bob presented 11 lectures in the Museum of Natural History's Imax Theater during 1988 and 1989. He also made 21 hour-long guest appearances on Peter Boyle's radio programs. Since becoming a member of the Denver Posse of the Westerners Brown has presented 16 papers. With his wife Evelyn, three other presentations have been made at the Posse's Summer Rendezvous and Christmas parties.

Robert Brown served as the Denver Posse's Sheriff in 1969. In 1989 he became the second Westerner to receive their coveted Lifetime Achievement Award. The paper on the Rev. John L. "Father" Dyer was originally given before the Denver Posse on May 28, 1986.

Robert and Evelyn McCall Brown recently celebrated their 50th year together. They have two children and two grandchildren.

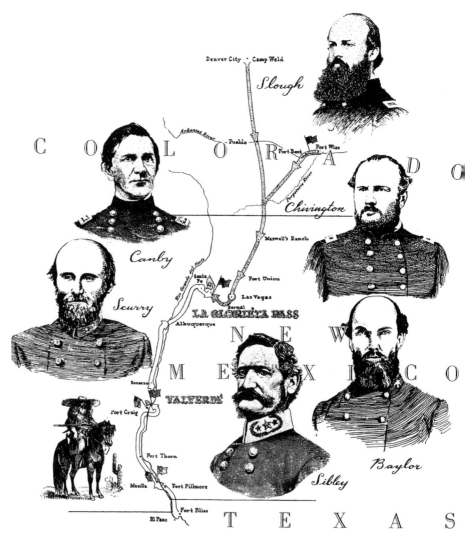

"Glorieta Theater" by *William J. Barker*, 1948 Brand Book

The Battle of Glorieta Pass

By Kenneth Pitman

*W*AS THE CIVIL WAR battle fought at Glorieta Pass in northern New Mexico on March 26-28, 1862, the "Gettysburg of the West?" What impact did the battles and skirmishes fought in the West have on the outcome of the Civil War?

According to many early Western publications, the First Colorado Regiment kept the West in the Union. In fact, according to *The Golden Jubilee* of April 23, 1909, "Although outnumbered three-to-one, in hard-fought battles, they drove back the invaders under Maj. [Gen.] Henry H. Sibley into Texas."

According to this report, had the Confederates succeeded in sweeping through Colorado to the north, they would have been able to hold the Rocky Mountain Region after the "Great Rebellion" was over. They would have split the West from the East, and the conflict would have been between the North and the South and West.

Would this have happened? Or do these observations merely reflect regional feelings of self-aggrandizement? A discussion of the reasons for the conflict at La Glorieta Pass and of the results of that conflict may further sharpen the focus on those questions.

At the time of the outbreak of hostilities during the Civil War, the West was in political and emotional upheaval over what course to follow. Many persons from the South had come to the Colorado goldfields to seek their fortunes. Would those who supported the Union cause prevail?

Jefferson Davis, president of the Confederacy, on Feb. 14, 1862, issued a proclamation declaring the New Mexico region to be organized as the Territory of Arizona. He appointed Col. John Baylor to be the military governor and commander of the Confederate force for that region.

Major Sibley, an officer in the United States Army, was stationed in New Mexico Territory at the start of the Civil War. He resigned his U.S. Army commission on May 13, 1861, and immediately entered the service of the Confederacy. Sibley, a citizen of Louisiana and a West Point graduate, had fought against the Seminole Indians; engaged in

Leaders in the Battle of Glorieta Pass were Union Col. Edward R.S. Canby (left); and Gen. Henry H. Sibley, Confederate commander of the Army of New Mexico.

the military occupation of Texas; fought in the Mexican War; and had quelled Mormon disturbances in Utah. He also had overseen the construction in New Mexico of Ft. Union, north of Las Vegas, a major depot with arsenal and storage buildings.

On Dec. 14, 1861, Sibley assumed command of those Confederate troops whom he had enlisted. He named his forces the Army of New Mexico—more affectionately dubbed Baylor's Babes and Sibley's Brigade. The brigade consisted of approximately 3,510 men, described as

Notable in turning back Confederate invasion were William Gilpin, Colorado Territorial governor (left); and Maj. John Chivington, First Colorado Volunteer Infantry.

most hardy, courageous, and efficient. Union troops referred to these men as Texans. A *Harper's Weekly* cartoon of one of Sibley's soldiers portrayed a "Texan" on horseback, armed with a sword, a tomahawk, rifle, pistols, and a bottle of whiskey.

Sibley's Brigade was assigned to drive the federal forces from New Mexico. One of Sibley's officers, Lt. Col. William R. Scurry, was made commander of the Fourth Texas Volunteers. He was a widely respected veteran of the Mexican War, a lawyer, and a politician from Clinton, Texas. A.B. Peticolas, who served under Scurry, wrote in his diary that Scurry was "the best officer, most polished gentleman and most popular Colonel in the whole outfit."

During this same period, Col. Edward Canby assumed command of U.S. troops in New Mexico, with orders to get ready to resist any invasion by Confederate forces from Texas. Canby, born in Kentucky, was a West Point graduate. He had fought in the Seminole and Mexican wars, and was considered both cautious and conservative in military operations.

William Gilpin, first governor of the Colorado Territory, was reputed to be an intelligent, courageous, and patriotic leader. He realized the need to defend the Western territories and proceeded to organize the First Colorado Volunteer Infantry. Gilpin's authority to finance such an undertaking was questioned in later years. But, aided by such leaders as Charles Cook, Jep Sears, Dave Moffat, and Joe Chaffee, the governor acquired the necessary funds for the action.

John Slough, a prominent lawyer of Denver City, was made a colonel in the regiment. He had originally come from Cincinnati, where he had been a member of the Ohio Legislature. While not an ideal military leader, he was considered capable. The men did not particularly care for him as he did not communicate well with them. They said he had "an Eastern swagger about him."

The Rev. John Chivington, presiding elder of the Rocky Mountain District of the Methodist Episcopal Church, was offered the chaplaincy of the regiment, but he insisted upon a fighting post, and was made a major.

Chivington was born in Lebanon, Ohio, of Scottish and Irish descent. His father remarked that he was a born fighter. In addition, he was a staunch foe of human slavery. His men came to have the highest regard for his ability, bravery, and stature. It should be noted that John's brother, Lewis Chivington, became a Confederate colonel and was killed at the battle of Wilson's Creek in 1861.

General Sibley proposed to Confederate President Jefferson Davis a military campaign to conquer the New Mexico Territory. A force, raised in Texas, would invade New Mexico, defeat the small and weak Union forces there and capture their supplies. Sibley thought he could enlist large numbers of New Mexicans to augment his Texas army. After defeating the Union forces in New Mexico and capturing Ft. Union, the major U.S. supply center, Sibley would continue north to seize the mining districts around Denver City. Upon obtaining that wealth for the Confederacy, he planned to take the Texans west to Utah where he expected a welcome by the Mormons, who felt alienated from the United States. With Mormon support, Sibley envisioned invading California. There he would seize the mines and warm-water ports of the Pacific.

In January 1862, the Texans moved northward from Ft. Bliss. They encamped for some time at Ft. Thorn, about 40 miles farther up the Rio Grande. On Feb. 7, Sibley set out with about 3,000 men and a large supply train on his expedition to the north. The next major fort encountered was Ft. Craig, south of Albuquerque, under the command of Union Colonel Canby.

Sibley stopped within a mile of the fort and "invited" Canby to leave the protection of the fort and to fight outside. Canby refused. Sibley decided to bypass the fort and move on to Ft. Union, prized as a major supply depot.

(It is a myth that Canby and Sibley were brothers-in-law, although both had attended West Point and fought together in conflicts preceding the Civil War. Some of the troops may have believed the tale, but it was false.)

Canby, realizing what Sibley intended, challenged the Confederates at a ford a few miles upstream near the little town of Valverde. The fighting was furious, and at first it appeared Union forces would win, but the Texans eventually took better strategic positions. Finally, Union forces backed away and returned to Ft. Craig. The Texans continued their march, taking Albuquerque and Santa Fe without resistance.

Colorado Territorial Governor Gilpin had begun organizing a militia. The men were rough and unruly, and many came from the mines outside of Denver City. For example, a Sam Cook organized a mounted company of men from the South Clear Creek Mining District. These troops were initially stationed at Camp Weld, two miles south of what was then Denver City.

Most of the men were eager to fight, and were bored with camp life. On occasion they stole chickens, vegetables, bacon, and whiskey from the citizenry. There was almost universal disgust with their behavior. In late February 1862, the "Pikes Peakers," as they were called, marched for New Mexico.

On March 7, 1862, near what is now Trinidad, Colo., Colonel Slough formed the Colorado Regiment into two columns for the final march to Ft. Union. To the west were the Sangre de Cristo peaks. The columns stayed on the Santa Fe Trail and climbed the Raton Range. On March 8, as they prepared to make camp at the southern end of the Sangre de Cristo spur, a courier appeared from Col. Gabriel Paul, then in command at Ft. Union. Paul sent word of Sibley's successful advance to Santa Fe, and of the impending Confederate attack on Ft. Union.

The already exhausted Coloradans discarded everything but guns, ammunition, and blankets, and resumed the march through extreme cold and snow. They hiked 92 miles in 36 hours and arrived at Ft. Union on March 9. In spite of their heroic feat, the volunteers were not warmly welcomed by the well-trained and disciplined Regular Army troops at Ft. Union, and the Coloradans had to camp on the outskirts of the post. Nor did Colonel Slough help the morale of the Colorado troops with his haughty and distant demeanor.

Colonel Canby was in Las Vegas, New Mexico Territory, at this time. He had left ambiguous orders on protecting the fort. Slough, in his cold way, called attention to his seniority, and boldly assumed command. Slough and Paul disagreed on Canby's orders. Colonel Paul wanted to wait as long as possible at the fort, then destroy it before it was captured. Slough wanted to meet the Texans and harass them without waiting for an attack.

Slough drilled the Pikes Peakers for 12 days at Ft. Union, and on March 22 the regiment marched south toward Santa Fe. Of the 1,342 men, there were three detachments of cavalry, and the rest of the troops were afoot. Their artillery consisted of eight small cannons.

Even though Paul vigorously objected to Colonel Slough's plan, Slough asserted that the best way to defend the West was to leave Ft. Union and to meet the Texans head-on. He further directed that all of his troops be involved. In fact, he took many of the Regular Army troops with him. A few regulars and volunteers were left behind to guard Ft. Union.

On March 25, Slough sent Chivington and an advance force of 418

(Courtesy Colorado Historical Society)
Adobe structure was main building of Kozlowski's Ranch.

men toward Santa Fe. Late that night this detachment encamped near Kozlowski's Ranch.

The ranch had served as a rest area for travelers on the Santa Fe Trail before the war. Nearby were the ruins of the Pecos Mission where the early Franciscan friars had introduced Christianity to Pueblo Indians.

Martin Kozlowski, the owner, was born in Warsaw, Poland, in 1827. He married in England and came to America, then in 1853 enlisted in the First Dragoons of the U.S. Army. He served five years in New Mexico Territory fighting Indians, then left the Army in 1858 and settled on the 600-acre ranch.

Chivington decided to use Kozlowski's Ranch as a staging area. A large spring near the ranch provided ample water, and the troops camped on a nearby bluff. They named the spot Camp Lewis after one of the officers in the regiment.

Kozlowski was very supportive of the Union, and complimented the men for not stealing anything from the ranch.

Chivington learned that Confederate scouts had been at the ranch earlier in the evening, inquiring whether any Yankees had been about. A contingent of 20 men from Captain Cook's company was sent to intercept the Texas scouts, and captured them at Pigeon's Ranch, farther up the trail toward Santa Fe. The Confederates were caught before daybreak, with no shots fired.

One captured officer, Lieutenant McIntyre, was a deserter from Colonel Canby's staff, and had fought on the side of the Union at the battle of Valverde. Captain Hall, another Confederate, was a widely known citizen of Denver City. Chivington learned from these men that advance troops from Sibley's force were at the western end of La Glorieta Pass and would be moving toward Ft. Union.

On the morning of March 26, 1862, Major Chivington left Camp Lewis with a detachment of troops to scout in the direction of Santa Fe. Soon they passed Pigeon's Ranch, a hostelry on the Santa Fe Trail. The ranch was named after its owner, Alexander Vallé, a Frenchman. Vallé had a peculiar, birdlike one-two-three-glide style of dancing that observers said was pigeon-like. Vallé proved to be a friendly, amenable, and entertaining host. The ranch had many rooms where the occupants could eat and sleep in private. It had secure areas for animals and wagons, and an adobe-walled yard.

Chivington's detachment continued toward the pass and was near the summit of the divide about one and one-half miles beyond Pigeon's Ranch around 2 o'clock. As they started to descend the trail through a narrow gulch, they encountered a scouting party from Sibley's lead column, commanded by Confederate Maj. Charles Pyron. Chivington pressed forward, anxious to strike the main body of troops. Battle cries rang out. "We've got 'em this time! Give 'em hell boys! Hurrah for the Pikes Peakers!"

The trail was narrow for another three-fourths mile, until it angled to the right and opened into the long, wide reaches of Apache Canyon. As the Coloradans moved into the canyon, they could see the Texans coming in at the opposite end.

Major Pyron had some 600 men on foot. The Confederates had left their horses resting at the west end of the canyon, and were investigating a report that there were about 200 Mexicans and 200 U.S. Army troops in the vicinity. They had expected an easy victory.

The Coloradans quickly took cover and began firing. The Texans, surprised but unruffled replied with their two howitzers. Chivington, strong-voiced and impressive in the saddle, took complete control and vigorously exhorted his men to spread out and continue the fight. He ordered Capt. George W. Howland to take his small cavalry unit to the rear, and to charge the Texans at the slightest indication of their retreat.

Captains Wynkoop, Anthony, and Walker were sent with their companies to the left along the slope of the canyon, to lay down a

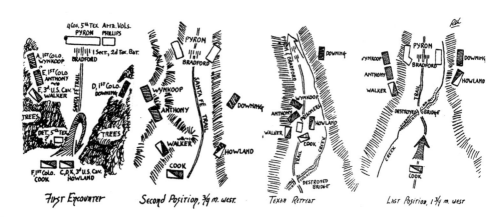

(Battle maps courtesy Westernlore Press)

Battle of Apache Canyon, left: first clash of Union, Confederate forces; second position, ¾ mi. west; last position, 1¾ mi. west; far right, Texans' retreat.

flanking fire from above the Texans. Captain Downing's men were sent to the mountainous area on the right. The Texans had been completely outmaneuvered, and the intense gunfire from both sides on their positions forced them to retreat.

An arroyo, in most places 20 to 25 feet deep, cuts through the upper part of the Apache Canyon. At one point, a 16-foot bridge spanned the arroyo. The Texans crossed the bridge, then destroyed it. They set up the two howitzers on their side of the arroyo, and took stations on each side, on the mountain slopes. It seemed to be a strong strategic position.

Chivington's troops, in hot pursuit, were under heavy fire from the Texans' rifles and artillery. Chivington started issuing orders. According to soldiers who served under him, he had a pistol in each hand, and one or two more belted in reserve. He gave his orders with great energy. One of the captured Confederate officers said he emptied his revolver three times at the Colorado major and ordered his company to fire a volley at him. Vallé said of Chivington, "E poot iz 'ead down and foight like a mad bull."

Chivington was angered by Howland's failure to follow orders and to attack the Texans as they retreated. He dismounted the Captain's troops and sent them up the canyon's right slope, along with Downing's men. By now, the Texans were becoming impressed with the ability of the Colorado troops.

The rest of the Coloradans were spread out in front, with Captain

Cook's cavalry sent to the rear. Soon Chivington ordered Cook to charge. The captain raised his saber in the late afternoon sun, and started the charge with 103 men, mainly those from the south Clear Creek area. They rode faster as they galloped along the well-worn trail. Increasing enemy fire came from both sides of the canyon. The horses jumped the arroyo at its narrowest point. Only one horse failed to make the leap, and horse and rider died at the bottom of the ravine.

The rest of Cook's Clear Creekers went hell-bent through the Texans' line up to the mouth of the canyon. Cook yelled, "We're going back!" and rode through the Confederate lines, crossing back and forth three times.

The Texans were almost routed but managed to save their howitzers.

Dusk was approaching, and the hurt and exhausted Confederates abandoned their positions. Both sides had many casualties, and more than 70 Texans were taken as prisoners. Chivington set up a hospital at Pigeon's Ranch.

The Confederates asked for a truce late in the evening, to bury their dead and to care for their wounded. A truce was agreed upon until 8 a.m. the next day.

Both sides started to prepare for a major battle. Pyron's Texans had been reinforced by Colonel Scurry at Johnson's Ranch, at the western end of the pass. Scurry had made an all-night march from Galisteo, and brought along a large wagon train of supplies.

Chivington was joined by Slough's forces. Neither side broke the truce the next day, March 27. They nervously scouted each other and planned strategy. Scurry, confident of his Texans' abilities, and knowing how they had succeeded at Valverde, decided to attack the Union forces on his own terms.

Early on March 28, Scurry marched eastward with about 1,100 men and three cannons. At about the same time, Chivington set out with some 400 troops on a route to the south to scout the Confederate rear in the area of Johnson's Ranch. It was hoped that the Confederates could be forced to retreat, and Chivington's troops could ambush them.

Colonel Slough was left with about 700 men to face Scurry's Texans. Slough's men were fatigued after a forced march of 35 miles to support Chivington.

It should be noted that the men under Slough had little confidence in his abilities. Some even questioned his loyalty, although this was

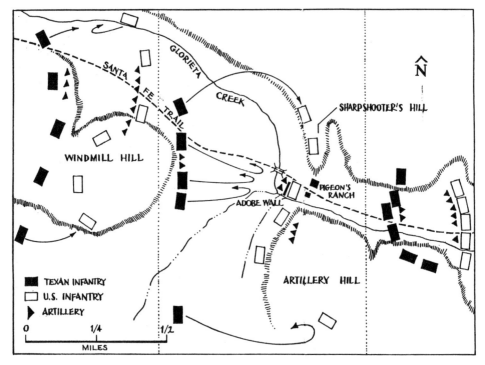

Positions of troops during daylong battle around Pigeon's Ranch at Glorieta Pass.

unjustified.

One of his captains in later years stated that he had watched the colonel carefully to detect any action favorable to the enemy. If he had, he said he would have shot Slough on the spot.

Around 10 a.m., Slough's troops reached Pigeon's Ranch. The troops broke ranks to rest and obtain water, and to visit the wounded left there after the fight in Apache Canyon. They were almost completely surprised when pickets rushed back, exclaiming that the Texans were only 800 yards away.

The battle opened in a gulch about one-half mile west of Pigeon's Ranch. Scurry deployed his Texans on a ridge west of Windmill Hill. Slough positioned his Union troops on the west slope of Windmill Hill.

The ensuing battle lasted about three hours. Union troops under the command of Captain Kerbler tried to follow an irrigation ditch to outflank the Texans on the right, but Scurry repulsed their attack.

Confederate Major Pyron attacked Captain Downing's company

(Courtesy Colorado Historical Society)
Pigeon's Ranch, Santa Fe Trail hostelry, was built by Alexander Vallé.

on the opposite flank, and pushed them back toward Pigeon's Ranch. The federal troops were under heavy fire and outnumbered. Expecting an immediate charge on their position, they retreated 800 yards. They formed a line along the ledge of rocks to the north (Sharpshooter's Hill) and below the Vallé house, across the arroyo and to the wooded bluff to the south (Artillery Hill).

Scurry directed the Texans from the east slope of Windmill Hill, ordering a series of attacks on the Union center. These moves were repulsed, as was an attack against Artillery Hill. However, a Confederate flanking attack against Sharpshooter's Hill succeeded, the Texans took the ridge, and the Union center collapsed. Union forces on Artillery Hill were almost captured.

About 4:30 p.m., Slough set up his final battleline one-half mile east of Pigeon's Ranch. The Union troops wanted to continue the fight, but Slough insisted that they had fulfilled their mission of harassing the enemy.

About that time an ambulance bearing a flag of truce came from the Texas lines. Maj. Alexander M. Jackson, an assistant adjutant and

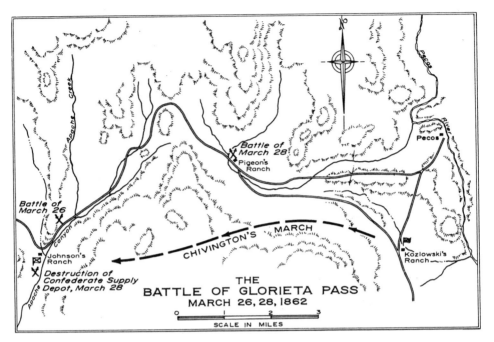

Three battle sites plus Chivington's march on Confederate supply train.

one of the leaders for the whole expedition, asked for a suspension of hostilities until noon the following day to care for the dead and wounded. Morale of the Union troops sank. They thought the Texans would resupply and continue the attack after the truce ended.

While this fighting had gone on, Major Chivington had taken four companies on a southern route to the rear of Scurry's forces. Charles Gardiner, a member of Company A of the First Colorado Infantry, affectionately called the "Pet Lambs of Colorado," recalled what happened during this maneuver. He said that Chivington's plan was to go around the enemy and head the Confederates off and make them surrender, or slaughter them as they came through. The Union troops were unsuccessful as the Texans "wouldn't drive worth a cent."

Lt. Col. Manuel Chavis of the New Mexico Volunteers was selected to guide Chivington and his men. Chavis was reputed to be a brave, intelligent, and skillful officer. He led the column to a trail that was south of Pigeon's Ranch. While following this trail for eight miles, the troops could hear the fighting at Pigeon's Ranch.

A mounted company was sent forward to scout, at first in the direction of the fighting, then toward Johnson's Ranch. The scouts captured a sentry on the crest of the mountain overlooking the Confederate wagon-train encampment about 1 o'clock in the afternoon.

According to Gardiner, the Union troops silently approached a bench of the mountain about 1,500 feet high and directly above the supply wagons.

"Then we sat and rested near an hour, watching the unconscious Texans, jumping, running footraces, etc.," Gardiner recalled.

Colonel Scurry's supply train consisted of 80 wagons, 500 horses and mules, and one fieldpiece.

Chivington's troops started down the mountain silently. About two-thirds of the way down, one of the officers yelled, "Who are you below there?" One of the Confederate officers replied, "Texans, goddamn you!"

"We want you!" replied the Union officer. The Texan retorted, "Come and get us if you can!"

The Union troops heard the command, "Go for 'em!" and they slid down the steep incline "like wild Indians." The Texans fired two volleys, then broke ranks. Most of them were captured.

The Union soldiers were allowed to ransack the wagons, but because they had to return over the steep mountain, all of the wagons and most of the supplies had to be destroyed.

The sad task of bayoneting the 500 or 600 horses and mules was carried out so that Scurry's troops could not recapture them.

Couriers informed Chivington that he and his troops should return without delay to help Slough. They were cautioned to take a different route back to avoid the Texans. They were guided by a French priest who supposedly knew the trails of the region. His knowledge was questioned by many of the men, but they arrived safely in the Union camp about 2 o'clock the next morning.

Chivington's troops had inflicted a stunning blow at Johnson's Ranch. The Texans had few options without supplies, and retreated to Santa Fe, leaving their wounded to be cared for by the Union forces.

There are varied reports on casualties, but the best estimates are that Slough lost one-fourth of his men, and the Confederates probably the same.

Canby's troops dogged Sibley's column as the Confederates continued their retreat to Texas. At least on one other occasion the federal forces thought they could defeat Sibley, but Canby refused to continue the fight, stating he didn't want the cost and burden of taking care of

Sibley's men.

The overly cautious Canby ordered the Coloradans back to Ft. Union. The men were incensed, and Slough was so disgusted that he resigned his commission. (He was later appointed brigadier general in charge of the military district of Alexandria, Va.).

What was the impact of this conflict on the outcome of the Civil War? With only a few thousand troops engaged, it can be argued that the battle was insignificant. But if Sibley had taken Ft. Union and then marched into Denver City, would large numbers of Union troops have been diverted to the West? Would foreign interests have entered the conflict on the side of the South? These questions cannot be answered, but the significance of the battle should not be underestimated.

Why was General Sibley so frequently absent at critical times of decision? His troops felt that alcohol was a major factor in his behavior. Sibley—inventor of the Sibley tent, the Sibley howitzer, and the Sibley stove—years later went to Egypt and became a general of artillery.

Dr. Don Alberts, author of *Rebels on the Rio Grande*, is involved with the Glorieta Battlefield preservation effort. He said much of the area is under the protection of the U.S. Park Service. Dr. Alberts, a member of the Westerners in Albuquerque, noted that Pigeon's Ranch is near a paved highway and subject to vandalism. However, the road may be closed to help save the battle site. Kozlowski's Ranch is now a part of property owned by Mrs. Greer Garson Fogelson, and part of the protected area.

Sources and References

Alberts, Don E. *Rebels on the Rio Grande*. Univ. of New Mexico Press, Albuquerque, 1984.

Barker, William J. "Apache Canyon Showdown." Empire Magazine, *The Denver Post*, November 13, 1949.

Buchanan, John W . "Denver Saved at the Battle of Glorieta Pass." Empire Magazine, *The Denver Post*, March 25, 1962.

Gardiner, Charles. "The Pet Lambs at Glorieta Pass." *Civil War Times Illustrated*, November 1976. Pp. 30-37.

Hollister, Ovando J. *Boldly They Rode*. Golden Press, Lakewood, Colo., 1949.

Kerby, Robert Lee. *The Confederate Invasion of New Mexico and Arizona, 1861-1862*. Westernlore Press, Los Angeles, 1958.

McCoy, Raymond. "The Battle of Glorieta Pass." *New Mexico Magazine*. Bureau of Publications, State of New Mexico, Albuquerque, August 1951.

Whitford, William C. *The Colorado Volunteers in the Civil War*. Rio Grande Press, Inc., Glorieta, N.M., 1971. (Reprint of original 1906 edition, Colorado State Historical and Natural History Society, Historical Series No. 1.)

About the Author

Kenneth Pitman, a member of the Denver Westerners for five years, is the author of "The Battle of Glorieta Pass."

Pitman is well versed in military matters, having served as an officer in the U.S. Army, stationed in Panama with the Fourth Battalion, Tenth Infantry Division. He left the service with the rank of captain.

Ken was born in a small farming community in central New Hampshire—"a village that's beside Peyton Place." He was graduated from the University of New Hampshire in 1964, with a major in life sciences.

He received his master's degree from the University of Northern Colorado, where he was also an instructor in biology. For the past 25 years, he has taught science in Littleton School District Six, primarily at Heritage High School. He has also taught evening courses at Arapahoe Community College.

Ken stresses he is an "amateur history enthusiast," but the Westerners are indebted to him for his excellent account of the battle of La Glorieta and Apache Pass.

"Attack on the Overland Stage" by *Delano*

The Julesburg Indian Attacks

January 7 and February 2, 1865

By Mark E. Hutchins

I N THE EARLY MORNING hours of Nov. 29, 1864, Chief Black Kettle's Cheyenne and Arapaho village on Sand Creek in southeastern Colorado was attacked by troops of the Third Colorado Cavalry under the command of Col. John M. Chivington. The "Hundred Day Service" regiment had hardly returned to Ft. Lyon when Indian fugitives from the battlefield were already moving northward. After a hard journey for many of them, they joined the Cheyenne camp at the head of the Smoky Hill River.

A council was held and it was decided that a war pipe would be sent to the Sioux and Northern Arapahos. An invitation was sent to these two tribes to join the Cheyennes in a war against the whites. It was at this time that Black Kettle had been temporarily replaced by his people. His place was taken by two other Cheyennes, one of whose father had been killed at Sand Creek.

The first to receive the pipe bearers were Pawnee Killer's Oglala and Spotted Tail's Brulé Sioux camps on the Solomon Fork. Next were the Northern Arapahos on the Republican. The chiefs of both these groups welcomed the opportunity to smoke the pipe. The Northern Arapahos had come south from their land north of the Platte River to visit the Southern Arapahos. When they learned that tribe was wintering south of the Arkansas River, the northern group went into camp on the Republican. Among the many warriors who joined these various camps was a young Oglala named Crazy Horse. One local historian mentions in her account of the Julesburg attacks that Sitting Bull was present, as well.

In the first weeks of December the three tribes met on Beaver Creek where between 800 and 900 lodges were assembled. This massive village consisted of Southern Cheyennes, Northern Arapahos, Oglalas,

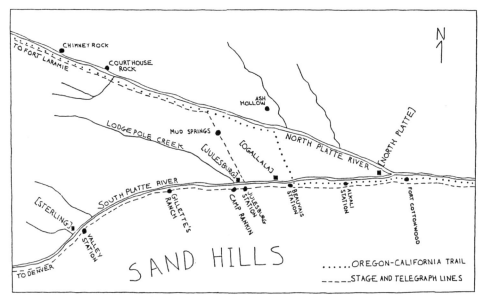

(Map by Author)

Julesburg area map showing Camp Rankin.

and Brulé Sioux. The village possibly contained about 150 lodges of Oglalas, 250 of Brulés, and 80 of Northern Arapahos. Southern Cheyennes made up the remainder. At the end of December the Indians moved to Cherry Creek, a tributary of the Republican River. It was here that George Bent arrived, joining his brother, Charley, who was already in the village.

George and Charley were the sons of William Bent, one of the co-founders of Bent's Fort on the Arkansas River. Since their father had married into the Cheyenne tribe the two young men had spent a considerable amount of time with these people.

At the beginning of the new year an important council was held. A decision was made to attack the stage and telegraph station at Julesburg on the South Platte River. Julesburg was chosen for two reasons: the first and most important, the Indians were badly in need of food. The second reason was to seek revenge for the Sand Creek attack. About 1,000 warriors prepared to march. Women and ponies would be used to carry away the plunder. Both of the Bent brothers planned to join the massive Indian force.

Black Kettle had not joined the movement northward. Many of the Cheyennes had become angry with him after the Sand Creek battle.

They held him responsible for having had faith in the promises the white men gave, but his people dropped the matter after a few days. Saying goodbye to his friends and relatives, Black Kettle with a small band of followers chose to go south below the Arkansas.

About Jan. 5, 1865, the Indian procession left Cherry Creek. Since it was the Sioux chiefs who had accepted the offer of the war pipe from the Cheyennes, they led the march with the warriors following in orderly columns. The men of the soldier societies protected the front, rear, and flanks. This particular formation was not used for protection against attacks but to keep any rash young warriors from slipping away and by premature activity giving advance warning to those whites in the vicinity of their intended target. Once more the Indians went into camp, this time some place on Whiteman's Fork, a branch of the Republican. Not far from here was another spot which would become well known in a few years—Summit Springs. At the camp on Whiteman's Fork the final preparations were made for the Julesburg attack.

Julesburg, or Old Julesburg as some have referred to it since the present town lies some distance from the first location, was on the south side of the South Platte near the mouth of Lodgepole Creek, in the extreme northeast corner of Colorado about 200 miles from Denver. During the 1850s much of the westward movement on the Oregon and California trail forded the Platte at this place giving it the names Upper Crossing or California Crossing of the South Platte. A stage station was established by the Overland Stage Company next to the trading store run by Jules Beni or Reni.

Julesburg was situated in a level valley some distance from the river. The valley was several miles wide with sand hills both to the north and south not too far distant. George Bent gave a good description of what the Platte was like at this time. He mentioned it as being "about 2,000 feet wide, dotted with small islands covered with bushes and other vegetation. The banks are low and there is very little water in the river, often less than a foot, and in the highest stages of the river, about three or four feet." No trees lined the river here so timber had to be hauled from Cottonwood Canyon many miles away near Camp Cottonwood, later Ft. McPherson, Neb.

By 1865 Julesburg was a vital link on the stage line. The Overland Company had built a large station house along with an eating house, stable, blacksmith and repair shop, granary, and storehouse. The buildings were all enclosed at the rear by a large sod corral. Besides the property owned by the stage company, there was a large mercantile store which sold all types of goods to people on the trail. Last, but not least, was the telegraph office. Almost all the buildings were constructed of cedar.

After the beginning of the Indian troubles the previous summer, a small post had been built not far from the group of buildings just across the mouth of Lodgepole Creek. The post was named Camp Rankin, but after September 1865, it became officially Ft. Sedgwick. It measured only 360 by 240 feet. The interior consisted of a stable, barracks, headquarters, and quartermaster depot made of cottonwood and cedar logs brought from Cottonwood Canyon. The walls surrounding these buildings were of sod and had rectangular lookout towers at the southeast and northwest corners. At the time, the fort was garrisoned by troopers of Company F, Seventh Iowa Volunteer Cavalry commanded by Capt. Nicholas J. O'Brien and assisted by 2nd Lt. Eugene F. Ware. O'Brien and Ware proved to be a good team; they were about the same age and both experienced officers.

Nicholas J. O'Brien, a native of Ireland, was 25 when he received his appointment as captain Jan. 17, 1863. He also had an older brother, George M. O'Brien who was a major in the same regiment. Eugene Fitch Ware was born in Hartford, Conn., in 1841. Before joining the Seventh Iowa on Feb. 14, 1863, he had already done extensive campaigning in both infantry and cavalry.

O'Brien and Ware felt the best location for building the fort was where Samuel Bancroft had his ranch. At this time, Bancroft was serving as postmaster of Julesburg. After receiving permission from headquarters at Ft. Kearny and concluding a successful agreement with Bancroft, the troops took over the ownership of the completed buildings and proceeded to enlarge and strengthen the quarters. While the fort was being completed, the men cut large quantities of hay for storage and stacked it in the northwest corner of the fort.

The Seventh Iowa men were uniformed much like all the mounted regiments then serving under the Union. More than likely they wore in the field a dark blue plain "sack" coat (fatigue jacket) with a falling collar, or the shell jacket with stiff upright collar. A forage cap or broad-brimmed hat and light blue trousers completed the uniform. They were armed with the Gallagher single shot carbine, 1860 Army Colt's revolver, and a heavy dragoon saber. If the officers and men could afford them, they would substitute for the inferior Gallagher a repeating firearm such as the Henry or Spencer carbine.

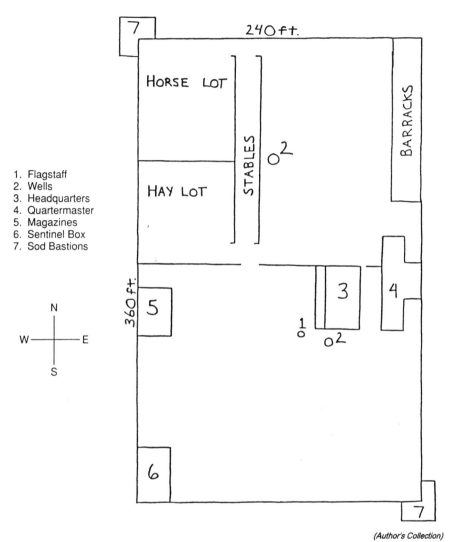

(Author's Collection)

Fortification at Camp Rankin, from a plan by Eugene Ware.

At daylight on Jan. 7, 1865, the Indian camp began to make its final preparations for the advance on Julesburg. As the warriors applied war paint and donned feather war bonnets, the women prepared the pack ponies to move into the settlement as soon as resistance had ceased. The war chiefs knew that the soldiers would stay behind the fort's walls if they were aware of the size of the force arrayed against them. It was decided that if a small picked group of warriors could lure the soldiers out into the open and lead them into the sand-hills, the main body of hidden warriors could cut them off and kill them all. In keeping with this plan of attack, Big Crow, leader of the Cheyenne Crooked Lance Society, was chosen to lead the decoy party. He took 10 picked warriors with him. They hid in a large ravine which extended from the sandhill bluffs down to the river bank. This ravine was called Devil's Dive, a stretch of ground that was so rough that it took travelers most of one day to cross.

The decoy party had hardly entered the ravine when a stagecoach approached from the east. The opportunity for attack was too much to resist for some of the young warriors. As the coach sped close by the ravine opening, a number of arrows were shot in its direction, and Big Crow and his decoys gave chase. However, when the stage reached the station, Big Crow gave up the chase and led his group toward two Denver-bound trains a short distance away. They circled the wagons and taunted the men with shouts and more arrows.

When the *Rocky Mountain News* interviewed O'Brien for its Nov. 26, 1915, edition, he stated that the first warning was when the stage dashed up to the station and the driver had arrows sticking in the heavy buffalo coat he wore, but he was more scared than hurt. When

(Collection of John M. Hutchins)

"The whole troop is hurriedly saddling."

the Indians began molesting the wagon trains, this galvanized the garrison at Rankin into action. Within a short time Captain O'Brien and 38 troopers rode out to give assistance to the trains. As to the number of O'Brien's force, sources differ. Some accounts say O'Brien had 38 men; Lieutenant Ware gives the number of men as 60. Lieutenant Ware was not present as he was on detached duty at Ft. Kearny.

Also joining them was Col. Samuel W. Summers, commander of the Seventh Iowa who was visiting the post, and a number of civilians. As the column began to pursue Big Crow's warriors toward the hills, the teamsters of the besieged wagons withdrew to a nearby ranch with several casualties. When O'Brien and his men were near the hills, the main body of the Indians poured down on them.

It did not take long to see that the soldiers would be overwhelmed. Colonel Summers quickly ordered a retreat, shouting to Captain O'Brien to take some of his men back to the post and man the howitzer. He and several others would cover their withdrawal. Some of the men were on foot as their horses had been killed. Fourteen men had been killed and a number were wounded. Because of the desperate situation, the dead were left on the field while the remainder of the troops barely made it back to the fort. While this was going on, the employees of the station had made a dash for the fort.

With the soldiers no longer a threat, the Indians began their pillaging. After mutilating the bodies of the dead soldiers and teamsters, the greater number of Indians moved on to the main purpose of their attack. They started packing up as many supplies as they could, carrying them away from the now-deserted buildings of Julesburg. What the warriors and women did not take with them, they destroyed. Windows and furniture were broken, bolts of cloth from the store were thrown out on the ground, and some of the colored cloth was tied to horses' tails. Even money from the abandoned stagecoach was chopped up and the thrown to the winds. Several times the women loaded the ponies and took them to the hills and returned for more loot. The warriors wanted to set fire to the buildings, but they were deterred from doing so by the chiefs, who said they would probably return again after the warehouses were restocked. The damage at Julesburg had been limited to broken windows, furniture, and other items that could be replaced.

When the Indians withdrew into the sandhills, Captain O'Brien and his men took stock of the damage done and the casualties inflicted on his force as well as those of the Indians. Of the 38 soldiers who rode

Drawing by a modern artist depicts the looting of Julesburg after an Indian attack.

out of Rankin, 14 were killed, among them one sergeant and two corporals, and as many men were wounded. O'Brien said that as many as 30 to 46 Indians were killed, some by the fort's brand-new Parrott fieldpiece. George Bent mentions that no Indians were killed.

Again the sources differ as to the number of casualties. Ware says that one sergeant, three corporals, and 10 privates were killed. Still further, a newspaper reported shortly after the fight that a number of citizens joined the soldiers in the fight and that 14 troopers and four citizens were killed, making a total of 18. These figures coincide with the number of fresh graves George Bent remembers seeing outside the stockade during the second attack a few weeks later.

The majority of the Indian force returned to their camp on Cherry Creek. It took them three days to make the trip because the ponies were loaded with so much loot. After a couple of days of celebration and feasting, a council decided that they would all move north of the Platte to join the northern tribes on the Powder River. During the next weeks while numerous bands of warriors raided east and west of Julesburg, the Indian village crossed the ice-covered Platte 23 miles west of that place and made camp. Besides stage stations, ranches and stores felt their sting, as well.

One of the places subjected to repeated attack was the ranch of Holon Godfrey. His ranch was strongly fortified with sod and adobe. He also dug tunnels and built a hiding place for his family. Godfrey went so far as to put up a sign with "Fort Wicked" painted on it. When asked the reason for such a name, he replied, "The Cheyennes and Sioux know well enough, I guess."

Not just the large Indian village, but the smaller ones as well, were quickly stocked with the belongings taken from the whites. George Bent said he never saw so much plunder in an Indian village as there was in the one along the river. There was lots of fresh beef, wagon-loads of bacon, hams, big bags of flour, sugar, rice, cornmeal, shelled corn, tins and hogsheads of molasses, canned meats and fruits, cloth-ing, dress goods and silks, and hardware. A good many of these things the Indians had never seen before. Several wagon trains containing mining equipment and whiskey bound for the Colorado gold miners had been taken. By the end of January the Indians felt it was time to move on, but first they would pay Julesburg another visit.

On Jan. 28, at Camp Cottonwood, Captain O'Brien received a tele-gram from Rankin. The message said that Indians were plundering everywhere. The stage stations between Julesburg and Valley Station 50 miles west were burned and destroyed. All travel was stopped, and many people were killed. He was ordered to return to his post at once with Lieutenant Ware, a squad of 10 men, and a howitzer. Captain O'Brien and his small party quickly headed west. At Alkali stage station when they arrived on Jan. 30, O'Brien found a company of Seventh Iowa cavalry along with a west-bound stage that was being held there for safety. The captain in charge lent O'Brien an additional 10 men, and two stage company officials also wanted to go along. These officials were Andrew Hughes and an assistant superintendent identified only as a Mr. Clift.

On the last day of the month O'Brien's group, including the stage, passed Beauvais Station, about 20 miles east of Julesburg. Since it was so poorly defended, six soldiers were left at the station. On reaching Dick Van Cleve's ranch, four more men were dropped off, and it was decided to take Mrs. Van Cleve in the coach which would supposedly be out of danger. After leaving Van Cleve's, the party overtook a train of 19 wagons which increased their numbers.

At about 2 p.m., Feb. 2, the party reached the Devil's Dive where smoke was observed billowing over Julesburg. The following para-graphs are taken from the Nov. 26, 1915, *Rocky Mountain News* recollections of Captain O'Brien.

From concealment the captain could see that Indians covered the area in all directions, circling their horses around the station and other burning buildings at close range. They were around the fort but at a longer range, remembering the howitzer was there. O'Brien estimated that about 1,000 warriors were taking part in the attack. Going back to his group, he told them the situation they faced. Rather than going back the way they had come, their only chance was to make a dash for Rankin. The Indians were unaware that they were nearby. They were obscured because the wind was blowing the smoke from the burning buildings in their direction, and the weather was somewhat hazy.

Ordering the howitzer loaded with canister, O'Brien had a soldier carry a friction primer so he could fire the gun from horseback. Before they started, he made final preparations for the others in the group. Lieutenant Ware was to ride in the front followed by four troopers. Then came the captain and the gun squad. Last was the stagecoach with the driver in the front box accompanied by the two company officials on top and Mrs. Van Cleve inside for a total of 15. Surprisingly, in his book, *The Indian War of 1864,* Lieutenant Ware does not mention Mrs. Van Cleve. O'Brien commented that Mrs. Van Cleve was the bravest woman he ever saw. To this, she replied, "Captain, I want you to give me a revolver. I am going to take part in the fight." O'Brien said, "I handed her one and I must say she made the best use of it, firing first out of one window, then out of the other after the dash was on its way." Giving Hughes last-minute instructions, O'Brien said, "Andy, we probably won't live through this, but I want to sell our lives as dearly as possible," to which Hughes replied, "Go ahead, Captain, I'm ready to sell."

Once everything was ready, they proceeded. At first the group moved at a slow rate until they came into full view of the warriors near the settlement. They apparently took the Indians by surprise with their appearance for the red men acted confused at first. Drawing closer to the fort, the howitzer was fired at Indians gathering ahead of them. Still a mile from safety with hostiles on both sides, O'Brien ordered the men to draw sabers as they pushed on. With Indians determined to bar the way to the fort, the officer in charge of Rankin rushed out his fieldpiece and fired until the way was clear for O'Brien. With their arrival, there was great rejoicing within the fort for the Indians had been in the area most of the day.

In her book, *Destination: Denver City,* Doris Monahan tells that this dramatic entrance into Julesburg did not actually happen. She states that when O'Brien and his command first saw the smoke rising from the burning buildings, the 19 wagons circled for defense at a safe distance from the Indians. The fort's artillery piece kept the Indians at bay while O'Brien and his party entered the fort with no interference from the Indians.

The ransacking of the buildings and warehouses was eventually finished, and the Indians left them in smoldering ruins. However, the Indians did not immediately leave for they proceeded to make camp a short distance away near the present site of Ovid, Colo., and spent the night dancing and shouting wildly. As had been done during the Jan. 7 attack, it was wisely decided not to send a force out to drive off the Indians. Instead, the occupants would make the best possible defense with what they had at hand. There were about 100 soldiers and 50 citizens crowded into the small fort.

Captain O'Brien placed both soldiers and civilians in strategic locations to guard the walls. One of the howitzers was placed on the roof of the stables. The highest point within the fort to observe the activities of the Indians was the top of the 80-ton haystack in the northwest corner. To protect themselves from the cold weather, O'Brien and Ware dug down into the top of the haystack and kept watch through field glasses. To prevent attack from fire arrows, kettles of water were placed along the top of the sod walls.

While the two men were closely following the celebration outside the walls, a fire arrow arched into the sky and landed in the hay nearby. Within an instant, Trooper Jimmie O'Brien (apparently no relation to the captain) put out the flames with a well directed cup of water. For the rest of the night everyone kept on extreme alert.

The Indians had cut down telegraph poles for several miles on either side of Julesburg. These poles were used for a large bonfire that was kept burning for most of the night.

In the morning Lieutenant Ware went to the spot after the Indians departed before daylight, and he found the cause for the late night celebration. The Indians had consumed much of the whiskey they had captured, and the bottles were left scattered on the prairie. Captain O'Brien's dog, Kearny, was discovered hanging from a telegraph pole with its throat slashed.

The reason for the Indian's departure up Lodgepole Creek was soon apparent. Just after dark Col. Robert R. Livingston arrived with about 400 troops made up of Seventh Iowa and First Nebraska veteran volunteer cavalrymen. According to Lieutenant Ware, there was much rejoicing by the civilians in the fort, who by means of concealed supplies, got "gloriously drunk and had to be put in the guardhouse."

So ended perhaps the most exciting days of Julesburg's history. Later in June Brig. Gen. Patrick E. Connor, who had succeeded Gen. Robert Mitchell as military district commander, led an expedition of 1,000 troops to punish the Indians who had attacked Julesburg. Connor's force encountered the Indians 15 miles from the present-day location of Sheridan, Wyo. The Indians were severely beaten and scattered. Their encampment and large quantities of equipment and food were destroyed.

In 1866 Capt. Nicholas J. O'Brien resigned from the Army and married in Iowa the same year. He returned to Julesburg where he opened a general store and became mayor of the town. Later he moved to Wyoming and was on the commission that approved the building of the state capitol. He also was the first Republican sheriff of Laramie County. In 1897 he became a permanent resident of Denver.

Lt. Eugene F. Ware left the Army shortly after these events with the rank of captain. He eventually became a historian and a U.S. pension commissioner. He died in 1911. It is interesting to note that Ware, like a lot of Westerners of his time, did not have a very high opinion of Indians. His thoughts probably did not change any when in 1883 he received word that Federal Judge H. C. McComas and Mrs. McComas were killed by Apaches 20 miles north of Lordsburg, N.M. Mrs. McComas was Eugene Ware's sister.

As for George Bent, after raiding several years with his mother's people, he returned to help his father, William Bent, work for peace. He died in 1918.

Bibliography

Ambrose, Stephen E. *Crazy Horse and Custer.* Doubleday & Company, Inc., Garden City, 1975.
Berthrong, Donald J. *The Southern Cheyennes* . Univ. of Oklahoma Press, Norman, 1963.
Dunn, Ruth. *Indian Vengeance at Julesburg.* Privately published by Ruth Dunn, 1972.
Dunn, Ruth. *The Burning of Julesburg.* Privately published by Ruth Dunn, 1973.
Grinnell, George Bird. *The Fighting Cheyennes.* Univ. of Oklahoma Press, Norman, 1915.
Holmes, Louis A. *Fort McPherson, Nebraska.* Johnsen Publishing Co., Lincoln, 1963.
Hyde, George E. *Life of George Bent.* Univ. of Oklahoma Press, Norman 1966.
Hyde, George E. *Red Cloud's Folk: A History of the Oglala Sioux Indians.* Univ. of Oklahoma Press, Norman, 1937.
Hyde, George E. *Spotted Tail's Folk.* Univ. of Oklahoma Press, Norman, 1961.
Monahan, Doris. *Destination: Denver City.* Swallow Press (Ohio Univ. Press), Athens, 1985.
Rocky Mountain News, Nov. 26, 1915. Files of the Colorado State Historical Society Library, Denver.
Stuart, Capt. A. A. *Iowa Colonels and Regiments.* Mills & Co., Des Moines, 1865.
Ware, Capt. Eugene F. *The Indian War of 1864.* Univ. of Nebraska Press, Lincoln, 1960. (Originally published by Crane & Company, 1911.)

About the Author

Mark E. Hutchins, a Posse Member of the Denver Westerners, has had an interest in history for as long as he can remember. He was born in Washington, D.C., and lived his first eight years in nearby Virginia. As a small boy he was drawn to the adult history section of the local library in Falls Church. He and his brothers were exposed to local history during weekend family excursions to nearby museums, battlefields, and other historic spots. Summer vacations were often taken at more distant sites in Virginia, Maryland, and Pennsylvania. When the author and his family moved to Colorado in 1961, his interest in history continued.

After being graduated from Northglenn High School in 1972, he attended Community College in Denver, North Campus, and received his associate degree with a major in history. He has a B.A. degree in history from Metropolitan State College, Denver. He has also completed several courses on the architecture and preservation of old buildings and additional classes in history. Mark worked for five and one-half years at the Adams County Public Library in Northglenn, and later was employed in the AT&T Computer Center in Westminster.

The author has worked as a volunteer at the Colorado State Historical Society. In 1989 he spent two weeks in Washington, D.C., working at the Smithsonian's National Air and Space Museum archival department. As a result of this experience, Mark's interest in aviation has been intensified, and he is now interested in the future of Denver's upcoming aviation museum, at the old Lowry Air Force Base.

"The Buffalo Hunt" by *Delano*

Colorado's Odd Couple

The 1872 Visit of Grand Duke Alexis and Gen. George A. Custer to the Mile High City

By Robert G. "Bob" Palmer

*T*HE FLEDGLING CITY had never been so thrilled. Denverites were atwitter in December of 1871 with news that the Grand Duke Alexis, third son of the Russian Czar, would visit their fast-growing little city on Cherry Creek as part of his royal tour of America. The visit would be all the more welcome because winter had brought early cold and snow. A January social event of such magnitude would warm the citizens' spirits and "put Denver on the map."

Along Larimer Street, plans were laid for a dazzling Ducal Ball to honor the 22-year-old son of Czar Alexander II. Though just a youngster—a "sprig of nobility," according to the *Rocky Mountain News*—Alexis would easily rank as the most distinguished visitor in Denver's dozen years of existence.

And not only that, Alexis would be accompanied by an entourage that included a Russian ambassador, an admiral of the Czar's navy, 12 distinguished aides to the Royal Court, and prominent American military figures, including Gen. Philip Sheridan and "Boy General" George Armstrong Custer of the famed Seventh Cavalry. Here was a chance for the "Queen City of the Plains," as Denver was already calling itself, to pull out all the stops.

Time was short, however. The Grand Duke was already touring the big cities of the Eastern United States, having been sent by his father on a round-the-world expedition. Ostensibly, the global tour was to widen the young man's horizons before he assumed serious responsibilities at home. In truth, the handsome prince had been entangled in a messy love affair with a beautiful commoner. His father thought a two-year junket to foreign lands would be an excellent

In January 1872 Lt. Col. George A. Custer (left) and Grand Duke Alexis posed for this picture in Denver following buffalo hunt south of North Platte, Neb. Custer holds buffalo tail trophy in his right hand. *(Original photo by "Scholter," courtesy Custer Battlefield National Monument and Western History Department, Denver Public Library.)*

"cooling off" period.

Alexis had arrived in New York City Nov. 20, 1871, on the Russian frigate *Svetlana*. U.S. warships in the harbor gave him a 21-gun salute. Once ashore, the towering prince was greeted by huge crowds.

New Yorkers cheered and waved U.S. and Russian flags as Alexis proclaimed, in heavily accented English, ". . . the friendship between

America and Russia is as strong as it will be lasting, and nothing can disturb it."

Part of the excitement surrounding his visit stemmed from rumors that the mutton-chopped prince had come to America seeking a bride. As a result, the crowds he encountered included an unusually large percentage of the city's most lovely, eligible maidens. During the parade up Broadway, young women were seen fainting on the sidewalks. A newspaper reporter spoke of the adulation of the crowds and described what he called "the waving stream of shining bayonets, gorgeous uniforms, and emblazoned banners" that accompanied the gilded carriage bearing Alexis and the New York mayor along the thoroughfare. "And from every housetop," the reporter wrote, "fair hands waved flags and handkerchiefs and cheered the young duke in his triumphant progress."

The parade was the kickoff to a whirlwind of tours, receptions and elegant social events that delighted New Yorkers. The prince's days were spent on tours of the city and in meetings with business and political figures, but at night the figures he found most interesting were clad in evening gowns, vying for every dance.

From New York City, Alexis and his 14-man entourage of nobles, aides, and diplomats journeyed to Washington, D.C., and more receptions. President and Mrs. Grant greeted the prince at the White House, and led the royal party inside for a meeting with assembled Cabinet members, legislative leaders and their wives, and guests. In the Red Parlor, Alexis fixed on Mrs. Grant. With boyish enthusiasm he confessed his fascination with America and told her something of his family's fairy-tale life in St. Petersburg. He flattered the President with his knowledge of the Civil War and Grant's great battles with Robert E. Lee. Finally, he told the President of his burning desire to see something of the American Frontier and, if possible, go buffalo hunting. Grant told him it would be arranged.

As usual, however, the Grand Duke's broadest smiles were reserved for the pretty daughters of the dignitaries, who flocked about him like doves. Occasionally, when his attentions to a particular girl grew too eager, an aide would tactfully intervene. Usually, such duties fell to the aristocrat in charge of the tour, Admiral P.H. Possiet, who had been Alexis' social and political mentor for many years. On other occasions it was the Duke's English-born tutor, W.F. Machin, who separated His Highness from some moon-struck damsel. (Machin was also designated Russian Councillor of State.) Usually, both aides had their work cut out for them.

From Washington, the Ducal Tour swept through Philadelphia, Boston, Montreal, Ottawa, Toronto, Buffalo, Cleveland, St. Louis, Milwaukee, and Chicago. In the latter city, a newspaper writer said, "Chicago lay in ruins at his feet." The good-looking, young royalist seemed determined, in the writer's words, "to shake the hand of every male in the country and dance with every pretty girl." Whether Alexis ever eluded his chaperons long enough to lure a lady to his chambers no one knows, but he did get his wish to go buffalo hunting.

Soon after the Grand Duke's departure from the White House, orders had gone to first the State Department and, from there, to the War Department. Everything was to be done to arrange a safe and successful buffalo hunt for the son of the Czar. The President wanted red-carpet treatment for the young man whose father, only a few years earlier, had sold the United States a parcel of land called "Alaska" for $7,200,000. Grant was eager to strengthen ties with a ruler who could part with so much for so little.

In St. Louis, Lt. Gen. Philip Sheridan, whose soldiers policed 2½ million square miles of the frontier, was instructed to arrange a lavish, Western boondoggle for the Russian prince. Cost was no object. Here was a chance, Sheridan thought, to have a little fun, himself. From his headquarters, Sheridan set the telegraph lines to humming. There would be a buffalo hunt. The hunt would be staged near North Platte in Nebraska. Sheridan, himself, would accompany the Ducal Party, along with his popular brother, Col. Mike Sheridan, as aide-de-camp. Although the Plains were largely peaceful at the time, Sheridan also ordered two companies of the Second Cavalry, under Brig. Gen. Innis Palmer, to provide security by setting up camp in advance near North Platte, where they would be joined by the others on Jan. 18.

Since plans also called for the dignitaries to visit Denver following the hunt, the party would include a man Coloradans knew and admired, Lt. Col. George "Sandy" Forsyth. Four years earlier, Forsyth and a detachment of 51 civilian scouts had fought off more than 500 Sioux and Cheyenne warriors in eastern Colorado at Beecher Island, with heavy losses on both sides.

Finally, Sheridan determined to trot out two of the most renowned young men the West could offer: The "Boy General," George Armstrong Custer, and the famed Buffalo Bill. William F. Cody was scouting with the Fifth Cavalry when he got Sheridan's wire to drop everything and hightail it for Ft. McPherson, Neb., where he would be taken aboard the Ducal Train.

If Bill Cody was pleased, Custer was ecstatic over the "out of nowhere" invitation. This, because for five months the restless cavalryman had been stuck in the sleepy, Southern hamlet of Elizabethtown, Ky. His Seventh Cavalry Regiment had been pulled out of Ft. Hays, Kans., and broken up for garrison duty at half-a-dozen posts in Kentucky and South Carolina, where their primary duties consisted of suppressing the Ku Klux Klan and running down moonshiners. Within hours, Custer's beautiful wife Elizabeth was helping her "Autie" pack his bags. They made plans for Elizabeth, or "Libbie," to join the Ducal Party after it left Denver and headed back East, if Custer could talk General Sheridan into letting him stay with the Russians until they left the country.

It was a genuinely happy man who threw his buckskins, guns, and baggage aboard a train and headed for Omaha to join Sheridan and the Grand Duke for an elegant adventure at government expense.

The Russians, meanwhile, were winding up their tour of Chicago, which had been left in ruins by the Great Fire of only two months before. As soon as possible, they made their way to St. Louis and on to Omaha for the gathering of the buffalo hunters.

The train, on the St. Joseph Road, was made up of five Pullman cars, two sleeping carriages, two parlor carriages, one diner, and several baggage cars. Sheridan and his staff of half a dozen came aboard in Omaha, as did Custer. The next day they stopped at Ft. McPherson to pick up Buffalo Bill and a fellow scout, John B. Omohundro Jr., better known as "Texas Jack." At midday Jan. 13, 1872, the rollicking trainload of hunters reached North Platte. There, in comparatively mild weather, they clambered into wagons for the 50-mile ride to a camp on Red Willow Creek, which was christened "Camp Alexis." Waiting for them were some 140 men of the Second Cavalry and, across the creek, 100 or more Sioux Indians, led by Brulé Chief Spotted Tail, one of Custer's old adversaries.

Buffalo Bill had enticed Spotted Tail and his people to join the camp so Alexis could see real, live Indians. For their part, the Sioux were interested in adding to their stores of buffalo meat.

A photograph of the scene at Camp Alexis—though none was taken—would have shown an amazing congregation. Here, in the middle of winter, in a remote corner of the West was a gathering of Russian aristocrats and royalty, American Indians, U.S. military leaders, and legendary civilians: Red Men, White Men, and European bluebloods. Yet, by all accounts, they got along fabulously.

The encamped cavalry detachment greeted the new arrivals with a lavish dinner, served in field tents strung together to form a dining hall. At dark, the scene was lit by a great bonfire and, beneath the stars, the Russians joined the soldiers in song. Spotted Tail and chosen warriors joined the firelit brotherhood, examining the party's guns and equipment, while conversing in sign language with Custer and Buffalo Bill. The Russians, fascinated with the Indians' paraphernalia, began trading clothing, food, and ammunition for feathered headdresses, and bows and arrows. It was a good start to what became a storybook outing in the Old West.

Jan. 14 dawned clear and cold. Buffalo Bill and Texas Jack were up early, scouting the distant hills. By 8 a.m. they were back with word of a small herd of buffalo 10 miles off. "Accordingly," said a biographer, "the hunters were soon in their saddles, armed to the teeth. Custer, to whom was assigned the duty of initiating his Imperial Highness into the mysteries of buffalo hunting, [was] the most dashing cavalry officer in the service . . . next to General Sheridan."

The two-day hunt was a big success. How many buffalo were taken was not recorded, but enough, apparently, to satisfy everyone involved. Alexis turned out to be an excellent and fearless horseman. "Nearly as good a rider as I am," Custer later told his wife. Using Buffalo Bill's famous horse, "Buckskin Joe," the Grand Duke took three buffalo tongues and tails, plus the head of the largest animal, which later adorned a wall in his royal quarters at St. Petersburg. Alexis also watched in awe as Spotted Tail's braves rode through the herd bringing down buffalo with bows and arrows.

The final night, nearly all the Indians joined in a raucous celebration, highlighted by the promised Sioux war dance.

Together with the prince, Sheridan, Custer, and Buffalo Bill were the centers of attention, creating what amounted to a reception line—shaking hands, exchanging compliments and laughter, enjoying the rare sense of good will that infected Indians and White Men alike.

And even here, Alexis found a girl to ogle. Along with others, he was vying for the attentions of Spotted Tail's teenage daughter, who was both beautiful and flirtatious. A written account of the evening described her:

> She is a modest maiden of some 16 summers, and that she is comely, is clear from the fact that some of the members of our party were evidently more interested in her than in the sanguinary stories of the warriors who were shouting and stamping in a circle.

A band of Chief Spotted Tail's Brulé Sioux joined in the buffalo hunt.

Custer drew attention by presenting her with a set of earrings which enabled him to spend considerable time fastening them on her ears, a chore that drew envy on all sides. It was noted that Miss Spotted Tail left the White Man's camp with a blanket full of gifts, clothing, food, and trinkets, provided by lovestruck Americans and Russians.

Both days of the hunt, Custer and the Grand Duke rode side by side. In the evenings, Custer explained Indian customs and sign language, and thrilled the young Romanov with accounts of Indian battles. Custer was probably the most interesting American Alexis had met. It was apparent the blacksmith's son from Ohio and the Czar's progeny of St. Petersburg were kindred spirits. Each was fascinated by guns, horses, and beautiful women. And they shared a reckless enthusiasm for danger. It is probable that before meeting Custer, Alexis expected to encounter a prancing, arrogant Prussian of the sort that filled his father's court. Instead, he found a frank, fun-loving cavalier, as full of mischief as himself. On the other hand, Custer admired the Duke's geniality and zest for adventure. Repeatedly Alexis made Custer promise he would someday visit Russia, where they would tackle wild boars and hunt European bison (aurochs) in the Caucasus.

Breakfast came early, Jan. 16. As the soldiers ate, they watched the Sioux village moving off to the east. By 9 a.m., the White Men, too, had struck camp. The wagon train, with Buffalo Bill and the cavalry out front, headed for North Platte.

Stories were later told of a happening on the way to the railhead when Buffalo Bill gave the Grand Duke a demonstration of his skills as a wagon driver. With Alexis, Custer, Forsyth, and several others as passengers, Cody whipped his horses into a run and took off over a rutted trail at top speed with everyone hanging on for his life. The Russians, entrusted with the Duke's safety, must have been aghast as the wagon careened over the countryside, the horses at a dead runaway.

"Every once in a while," said Cody, "the hind wheels would strike a rut and take a bound and not touch the ground for 15 or 20 feet." Proving his skills, however, Cody stayed with it, and after the most hair-raising ride anyone had ever experienced, brought the wagon to a halt. He later estimated he had covered six miles in about three minutes. If true, the wagon would have been going 120 miles an hour, a fairly typical exaggeration, it is said, for Buffalo Bill. He also quoted Grand Duke Alexis as saying that he, Alexis, would rather return to Russia by way of Alaska and swim the Bering Sea, than repeat his ride with William F. Cody.

Whatever the case, the hunting party reached North Platte by midafternoon to find the Pullman cars waiting. Sheridan wired his old friend in Denver, former Territorial Gov. John Evans, that they were bound for Cheyenne and would be in Denver the next afternoon. Evans, who had built the line from Denver to Cheyenne a few years earlier, dispatched one of his Denver Pacific locomotives to Cheyenne to meet them and bring them on to the Mile High City.

Custer also sent a telegraph from North Platte to his wife in Kentucky:

> . . . hunt a splendid success. Grand Duke killed three buffalo. I killed my horse. Gen. Sheridan and staff and myself invited to accompany him to Denver and the mountains. Return via Kansas Pacific. We leave tonight. Will telegraph from Denver.

The reference to killing his horse was a joke. Years earlier, while hunting buffalo in Kansas, Custer had accidentally shot his wife's favorite horse, Custis Lee. He was riding the horse in pursuit of a buffalo, but as he leveled his pistol to fire, the horse suddenly threw his head and took the slug right between the ears. Custer was catapulted 20 or 30 feet through the air, hit the ground dazed but not seriously hurt, and had to walk miles back to camp. Ever after, Libbie teased him about killing Custis Lee.

At North Platte there were goodbyes to be said. The cavalry detachment was headed back to Ft. McPherson, as were Buffalo Bill and Texas Jack. Before leaving, Cody accepted a "priceless" fur coat from Alexis, plus a gold-and-diamond stickpin.

Rolling west toward Cheyenne, the Russians and their now-bonded Yankee friends strolled from car to car exchanging jokes, drinks, and laughter. The Grand Duke was soon bellowing what had become his favorite American tune, Lydia Thompson's "If Ever I Cease to Love," which, according to Elizabeth Custer, who heard him singing it later in Kentucky, came out: "Eef eveh I zeese to luff."

The stopover in Cheyenne the morning of Jan. 17 was supposed to be brief, for the Duke was expected in Denver the same afternoon. But an accident which could have been serious created delays. As the train was backing in the Cheyenne rail yards, two of the Pullman cars derailed. The rear truck on the car occupied by the Russians came off the tracks, jolting the occupants. General Sheridan's car, however, nearly turned on its side. Sheridan and a dozen others were sent sprawling, but no one was seriously hurt.

As described in the newspapers, "The Duke's car was soon got up-

William F. "Buffalo Bill" Cody was scouting for the Fifth Cavalry when he was ordered to join the Grand Duke's hunting party in Nebraska. Photograph was taken in 1872.

(Courtesy Western History Dept., Denver Public Library)

on the track again; but General Sheridan's was in worse condition and not got upon the rails for several hours. The general insisted the Duke continue on to Denver, promising to follow as soon as his car was in condition to move."

Unaware of delays in Cheyenne, some 4,000 people had gathered at the Denver Depot for the Duke's expected arrival at 5 p.m. The crowd represented nearly half the town's population. Denverites realized nothing could equal the opulent celebrations accorded the Duke on his Eastern tour, but as the *Rocky Mountain News* put it, at least Denver's welcome would be sincere:

> Our Western people are plain and matter-of-fact. They know their worth and are always ready to show it the regard it merits. It may be done in a humble way, but the recipient knows that the honors are heartfelt and that they spring from a sincere nature.

Unfortunately, most of Denver's "sincere and humble" folk grew tired of waiting after three hours in the cold and went home. Only about 1,500 remained when, at 8:30 p.m., the train finally arrived.

Minutes later, the most exotic visitor the city had ever seen stood before them on the gaslit platform, an event grandiloquently described by *Rocky Mountain News* editor William Byers:

> The Grand Duke put a finishing touch upon his pearl-colored glove, buttoned his great coat, lit a cigarette and stepped upon the platform, followed by Admiral Possiet, Governor (Edward) McCook and the Hon. John Evans. The Duke advanced with a military air, gazing neither right nor left, apparently oblivious of the fact that he had stepped into the edge of a crowd of staring Westerners.

The Westerners not only stared, they cheered, screamed, and clapped enthusiastically, some singing "For He's a Jolly Good Fellow." Governor McCook shouted a welcome while the "sprig of nobility" smiled and waved to the crowd, uttering words of appreciation that were lost in the uproar.

To Alexis, crowds were crowds, yet there was no mistaking the enthusiasm of Denverites who surged alongside the carriage that bore him into the center of town. A grinning Tom Smith, who owned the clarence [carriage] in which the Duke was riding, guided a set of matched grays through the throngs of welcomers whooping and hollering on both sides of the street. To the Russians, their first look at a Western boom town had to have been impressive.

Indeed, Denver in 1872 was in a marvelous period of growth and prosperity. In his book, *A Gallery of Dudes*, author Marshall Sprague described the community that greeted Alexis:

> If the Grand Duke expected a shack town of pistol-packing men and hurdy-gurdy women he must have been surprised. [The city] bloomed with mining prosperity which had tripled its population and wealth in two years. Elements of Denver's modernity were everywhere—a new horse-drawn streetcar line, public schools, Charpiot's fine French restaurant, a roller-skating rink, circulating library, the John Evans Colorado Seminary, and large frame and brick houses; steam-heated and gaslit.

The cheering that echoed along the Duke's route came to a crescendo as Tom Smith drew the grays up to the boardwalk in front of the 4-year-old American House Hotel at 16th and Blake streets, the best the city could offer. Police cleared the entrance as the Duke's carriage and three others in the procession deposited the delegation at the door. Escorted by State Treasurer George Clark, the visitors trooped to the second floor and vanished into their rooms.

It was nearly midnight when the forgotten second train arrived, bearing the military contingent. Only a few hundred hangers-on met the party at the depot and dutifully applauded as they were welcomed by Mayor Joseph E. Bates. The Grand Duke's entourage had taken all 13 available rooms at the American House, so General Sheridan, his brother Mike, Colonel Forsyth, Custer, and the others were booked into the smaller Sargent's Hotel nearby.

This was Custer's first (and last) visit to Denver. He had led the Seventh Cavalry over hundreds of miles of the Plains, guarding the roads and stage stops that made it possible for Denver to exist in the 1860s. One wonders what his thoughts must have been as a carriage drew him through the city he had risked his life to protect. He rode in the rear of a three-carriage procession through the darkened streets, hardly recognized. Perhaps he wondered how many of the roistering Denverites he could see in the saloons were former members of the Seventh Cavalry. Desertion rates had been high in those days. Custer had even been court-martialed for having some deserters shot. But hundreds of "snow bunnies"—men who enlisted with the first frost and vanished in the spring—managed to escape the Army and join the gold-seekers in Denver.

Sargent's Hotel, at 18th and Larimer streets, was clean and comfortable. Just across the street was the home of the city's first Episcopal minister, the Rev. John H. Kehler, whose son Jack had been sheriff of both Jefferson and Arapahoe counties. When built in 1859, the Kehler house was the first brick home in Denver, although now there were many. The house would later be razed to make way for a famous hostelry: the Windsor Hotel.

After checking in, the bandy-legged Sheridan led his distinguished friends into Sargent's dining room where, before an admiring crowd, they were served the best the house had to offer. Fielding questions from onlookers, Custer found himself overshadowed by the illustrious Sheridan and his popular brother, both of whom were fawned over by newspaper reporters and Denver dignitaries. In the papers next morning the Sheridans were generously quoted, while Custer was scarcely mentioned. The *Rocky Mountain News* even got his name wrong, identifying him as Gen. George W. Custer, instead of George A., for Armstrong. At the same time, the newspaper had this to say about Phil Sheridan:

> Gen. Sheridan is too well known in the West to need any comment from us. His bravery and dash, his enviable record, his high position and his being "Little Phil" alone warrant him the utmost respect and warm feelings of Western people.

Ignored by the media, Custer was nevertheless up bright and early the morning of Jan 18. Finishing breakfast, he set out along Larimer Street looking for a telegraph office. Finding one, he wired Libbie:

"Ball tonight. To Golden City and mountains tomorrow. Start in the evening for Kit Carson. Then to Topeka. All well."

Of the Grand Duke Alexis, nothing was seen until shortly after noon when he opened his suite to greet a delegation from the Territorial Legislature, led by Governor McCook. With the ever-present Admiral Possiet, the Duke greeted each man pleasantly, intoning "Nize to zee you. . . sank you. . . da, nize to zee you."

Among the lawmakers were several men of Mexican descent, the first Hispanics Alexis had ever seen. The Duke quizzed Governor McCook about these dark and handsome, Spanish-speaking men: Where did they come from? What kind of people were they?

By this time, editor Byers had seen enough of the Grand Duke to favor his readers with the lowdown on the prince's personality:

> Alexis is a young man of stately mien, courtly bearing, intellectual demeanor and apparently little given to the frivolities of life, but rather of an investigative and practical turn of mind. He cares more for a clear insight into our customs, resources and manufacturing interests than for all the fuss made over him.

If they read Byers' personality profile on the Duke, Admiral Possiet and the Duke's other "handlers" must have chuckled at the description of their fun-loving, skirt-chasing charge.

Custer's wife Elizabeth had a much more accurate impression when she wrote, in later years, "Alexis' favorite diversions were wine, women and song, and especially women. The only scientific topic that interested him was anatomy . . . that of pretty girls."

Fortunately, a lot of pretty girls were expected at the Ducal Ball that evening. But first, Alexis—who must have groaned at the thought—had to take another city tour. Denver had made great strides and city fathers were eager to show it off. The population was pushing 10,000 (it would be 35,000 in eight years), and there were even predictions that someday more people would live in Denver than in the mining towns to the west. Several trains a day rolled into the city, filled with merchandise and new inhabitants. Most of the arrivals were men, some with families, looking for work in the mines and mills. But with them came a colorful assortment of farmers, gamblers, businessmen, and whores. Anything was possible, it was said, for someone with grit and a willingness to work.

For investors, opportunities were especially attractive. What was lacking in the territories was capital. The interest on money lent was 3 percent *a month*! Depending upon the terms, a $1,000 loan could return up to $300 a year.

For a time on the morning of Jan. 18, it looked as though the Duke's city tour might be snowed out. But there was no such luck for Alexis. By early afternoon the snow had ended and there was nothing for it but to bundle up and act princely.

Mayor Bates, who led the tour, rode with Alexis and Admiral Possiet in the first carriage of a five-vehicle procession. First came a stop to see the Legislature in session, followed by a visit to the Denver Branch of the U.S. Mint. Denverites cheered and shouted words of welcome as the carriages wound through the streets. Housewives stood outside frame houses holding children in the air for a look at the wondrous prince from far-away Russia.

Mayor Bates included in the tour a stop at his new brewery, the Denver Ale Co. Alexis quaffed a glass and pronounced it quite good. At the city waterworks, he also sampled the product, called "Adam's Ale," and praised it, as well. Since arriving in the United States, Alexis had been on endless city tours and this had to rate as one of the least entertaining, yet to the mayor and others, he seemed rested and in excellent spirits. One suspects he was sustained by the promise of the evening's festivities.

Custer was waiting for Alexis at a photography studio later that afternoon. There the two friends had a picture taken in their hunting garb. Custer, wearing a fur cap given him by the Duke, held his .50-70 caliber modified "trapdoor" Springfield in one hand, and a buffalo tail in the other. The Duke wore his green hunting costume, enhanced by a bone-handled revolver at his belt. An hour later, they were in the duke's suite at the hotel enjoying a dinner of buffalo steak and wine.

Years were to pass before Denverites experienced anything approaching the glamour of the Ducal Ball that night at the American House. It was the grandest social event in city history. For weeks, seamstresses had been plying needle and thread to costly fabrics. Some of the city's matrons had sent to St. Louis or beyond for suitable gowns and furs. The Russians were aglitter in courtly, military, or formal attire—gold-draped tunics with brass buttons and scarlet sashes—while the American officers broke out dress uniforms and swords.

In charge of arrangements was the city's Pioneer Club, made up of Denver's social gentry. By 8 p.m., nearly 300 people filled the dining hall, which had been cleared of tables and decorated with gay banners and flags. Breathlessly, the *Rocky Mountain News* reported: "Everything of the past must be wiped out entirely and the leaders of fashion will take a fresh start upon the pathway of joyous dissipation."

(Courtesy Western History Dept., Denver Public Library)
The Ducal Ball took place at Denver's American House, occupied by Alexis' entourage.

Beneath the gas lights of chandeliers, the Duke, tall and handsome as ever, entered the room escorting the governor's wife, who exhibited a daring off-the-shoulder, low-cut gown that raised the eyebrows of an applauding crowd. Behind them, sweeping into the ballroom came Governor McCook, himself, escorting Mrs. Shaffenburg, wife of the U.S. Marshal. General Sheridan was with Mrs. Phelps [probably the wife of prominent Denver attorney A.C. Phelps], and on the arm of Admiral Possiet was Mrs. George Randolph of Central City. The dignitaries led the entire swooning throng in an opening quadrille.

In the words of one beholder, "It was an instant fairy-tale of merriment," all the more wonderful in a small frontier community starved for culture and elegance. Once shed of Mrs. McCook, Alexis delighted everyone by turning himself over "in charming submission" to the lovely damsels of Denver.

According to editor Byers, the girls came from every direction:

> To be sure, there was a rush and a crush, a jam and push, but all had a chance to meet the lion of the evening and hold him in pretty close but rather pleasing quarters.

After each dance, the *Rocky Mountain News* reported, Alexis found himself surrounded by breathless young ladies who "happened to wander by" in hopes they might be selected for the next dance. Few were disappointed, said author Marshall Sprague:

> Before the ball ended, long after midnight, [the Duke] was dancing passably if not nimbly. He was even flirting a little with a Miss Monk, aged 15, and Miss Fleury of Golden, whom he declared to be the prettiest girl at the ball.

Remarkably, Custer wasn't there that night. At least he wasn't mentioned in any of the accounts of the evening. His absence is interesting because Custer was a key figure in the Duke's entourage, loved the company of women, and welcomed opportunities to mix with rich and influential civilians. The likeliest explanation is that Autie didn't bring a dress uniform. Unlike Sheridan, whose staff provided for his needs, Custer was traveling alone and apparently traveling light. Perhaps Custer and some of the others simply spent the night on the town.

The dancing at the American House went on until nearly 2 a.m., when the Duke finally wilted, offered his thanks and apologies, and retired to his rooms. It had been a marvelous night for the little city on the Platte. Editor Byers observed:

> For we have had a Ducal Ball; we have had a live duke; the ladies have danced with him and tried to talk to him; and men have shaken his hand and gazed with wonder upon his imperial form.

Most of the city slept late the following morning, Jan. 19, but the visitors set out early by train for Golden City, the prosperous mining center in the foothills 17 miles to the west. Golden City was the gateway to the fabled Gregory Diggings in Clear Creek Canyon. Gold had been found there in 1858, setting off the Pikes Peak Gold Rush of '59. Custer was more than curious. A few years earlier, he'd bought some Colorado mining stock and was eager to see what was being done with his money.

The day was bitterly cold. Arriving in Golden City, the travelers were taken from the train and put in carriages and buggies for the trip up Clear Creek on the rocky roadbed of the Colorado Central Railroad. A light snow was falling and steam blossomed from the nostrils of the laboring horses. The freezing tourists, their faces buried in scarves and blankets, must have wondered at the wisdom of January sight-seeing in the Rockies.

"The ride . . . was somewhat cold and unpleasant," said the *Rocky Mountain News*, "but the visitors were charmed with the gorgeous scenery. Alexis commented he wouldn't like to ride down the canyon in a narrow-gauge car."

Eight or ten miles later, they were afoot in the snow, exploring the entrance to a mine where, ". . . the wonderful fertility of the gold, silver, and coal mines was described to the observing Russian tourist." But a few minutes of watching ore cars being dragged from the adit was all anyone could take. Quickly the freezing group was hustled off to Huntsman's Rancho to warm up. A popular "truck stop" of the times, Huntsman's boasted good food, strong drink, and a furnace-like blaze in the fireplace. Soon Sheridan's staff was entertaining the Russians with old Army songs. Alexis, familiar with the winters of St. Petersburg, proclaimed Colorado weather rather balmy. In the words of a participant, ". . . there were loud praises of Colorado, and, with frostbitten ears, [we] insisted the day was one of the most charming of the season."

Still, it was deemed wise to head back before nightfall. On the way, the caravan stopped to view two distant peaks which were thereupon christened "Peak Alexis" and "Sheridan's Peak," names that unfortunately lasted only until the mountains were out of sight.

The steam-heated train offered a warm sanctuary as the party trooped aboard at 4:30 that afternoon to head back to Denver. Little time remained to prepare for their final departure at 10 o'clock that night for the little town of Kit Carson on the eastern Plains.

For Custer, the trip was turning out beautifully. Next to soldiering, his favorite pursuits were hunting and socializing with the elite. Now he was not only the best friend the Grand Duke had in America, but Alexis had talked General Sheridan into letting Custer accompany the Duke all the way back to New Orleans. Custer could hardly wait to wire Libbie that she would join the tour in Louisville. Even more exciting, Custer had won assurances from Sheridan that, as soon as possible, the Seventh Cavalry would be sprung from peace-keeping duties in the South and reassigned to the Missouri River frontier. Sheridan confirmed that trouble with the Sioux was inevitable in the gold-rich Black Hills. The general said a new fort was planned near Bismarck, on the Missouri River. Custer was assured that his regiment would be the first to occupy the new post—Ft. Abraham Lincoln. If the Sioux went on the warpath, Custer would be needed.

It was a genial group of officers who gathered in Sargent's dining room that night for their last meal in Denver. Relaxing at the table, they were toasted by Denver dignitaries who told them how much their visit had meant to the city. For their part, the soldiers proclaimed Denver to be the emerging jewel of the West, and pledged to return.

In the lobby and outside the hotel, lesser folks milled about, stealing a final look at the famous men who'd paid them a call.

As they dined, the visitors talked of the buffalo hunt scheduled the next morning. Custer, it seems, had run into a cowboy-musician after the Ducal Ball named Chalkley "Chalk" Beeson, who lived in Kit Carson. He told Custer the area was teeming with buffalo drifting southward toward the Arkansas River. In return for a ride home on the Ducal Train, Beeson offered to guide the party to the buffalo. It was an offer the hunters couldn't refuse.

Before the group left for Golden City that morning, Sheridan had wired Col. Floyd Jones at Ft. Wallace, Kans., telling him to meet the train in Kit Carson with 75 horses, 10 wagons, and whatever else was required. They were going to have a buffalo hunt.

Soon after 10 p.m., Jan. 19, couplings clanked, rails rattled and, in a miasma of smoke and steam, the train with its famed passengers drew slowly away from the Denver Depot. In his bunk, the rhythmic clatter of the rails in his ears, Custer was assuredly asleep within minutes. He was famous in the Army for being able to sleep anywhere, anytime, and under any conditions. Custer was scarcely 32 years old. At an age when most Army officers were just getting a good start, he had already served as a major general; had led thousands of men in great battles; had never been defeated; and was a national hero. But Custer believed the best was yet to come.

To his wife and other intimates, he confessed a belief that all his achievements were preordained. It was, he said, as if the gods had chosen him for immortality, for some purpose beyond his ken. All he could be sure of, he said, was that he would never be forgotten.

All was excitement the next morning in the tiny settlement of Kit Carson, 150 miles southeast of Denver. The train arrived about 4 a.m. and by first light, breakfast was being served in the dining car to a boisterous crowd of fur-clad hunters. The larder of the train had yielded a breakfast of champagne, caviar, and buffalo steaks—an epicurean beginning for what became one of the wildest, most reckless melees ever staged on the Plains.

Colonel Jones had arrived the night before with the wagons and horses. By 7 a.m., all was ready. More than 100 men were on horseback, while others—including railroaders, townsfolk, and soldiers from Ft. Wallace—jammed the wagons which soon bristled with guns. Custer, in buckskins, rode about exhorting the crowd and showing off his horsemanship. Finally, with the Grand Duke at his side, Custer fired his pistol in the air and galloped off to the southwest. The others struck out in a din of clattering wagons, shots, and hoofbeats.

Chalk Beeson, who was supposed to be the guide, had lent his horse to Custer and found himself in one of the wagons, drawn by two slow-footed mules. The dust, he recalled, was so dense, wagons nearly collided with one another, and with men on horseback.

Intuitively Custer led the horde straight to the quarry. On the brow of a hill seven or eight miles from town, he called a halt. In the distance were thousands of buffalo in several vast herds. Beeson likened it to watching a black tide of water flowing to the sea. Few had seen anything like it. Waiting for the others, Custer finally turned to Alexis. The Duke was seen to nod his head. With another pistol shot, they were off on a breathtaking, disorganized charge down the hill and out on the flats. Men were screaming at the top of their lungs.

A good account of the hunt was later provided by the editor of *The Grand Duke Alexis in the U.S.A,* William W. Tucker, who wrote in 1872 that the Kit Carson hunt made Alexis' earlier experiences in Nebraska look pretty tame:

> . . . the horses (being ridden by Custer and Alexis) were accustomed to the chase and seemed inspired with as much enthusiasm as their riders. They fairly flew through the air . . . at length it became apparent that both the Duke and the experienced Custer had lost all control of them. General Sheridan soon became an active participant and the trio poured a shower of bullets into the ranks and flanks of the stampeding animals. The experiences were becoming unusually exciting, even for such veteran sportsmen as Sheridan and Custer.

The terrified buffalo broke in all directions, one group turning directly toward the men coming up in wagons. They were met with a fusillade of fire.

Beeson's wagon was late getting into the fray. "When we arrived," he later recalled, "we saw two or three wounded buffalo trying to get away. We started to get a shot at them, and just then the whole crowd of hunters came charging over the hill."

The Grand Duke had singled out a massive bull. Tearing alongside the animal, he emptied his .45 into its flanks with no apparent effect. Tucker told what happened next:

> [The shots] only seemed to enrage the old fellow, as he did not appear to be injured in the slightest, but evidently cherished an ill feeling toward the disappointed Russian. He looked him full in the face, pawed the earth for a moment and then made a furious charge for his Imperial Highness. Alexis' superior horsemanship was very useful and barely saved him from a fate that an amateur would have likely suffered.

At one point, Chalk Beeson recalled, Sheridan and his companions came under a hail of fire from men on the side of a far ridge. "They jumped from their horses, seeking cover," Beeson said, "but Sheridan was too short in the legs to run, and threw himself in the buffalo grass. When he got to his feet, he was the maddest man I ever saw."

As the buffalo scattered, so did their pursuers. It became a contest of endurance. When the riders stopped to rest, the buffalo did the same. After a few minutes, the men resumed the chase and the exhausted bison once more began running. Custer and the Grand Duke engaged in three long chases after the initial attack. The Duke claimed at least a dozen animals before his horse and all the others gave out.

The hunt had lasted more than six hours and covered perhaps 50 square miles. Thousands of rounds of ammunition had been fired, and by various accounts, upwards of 200 buffalo were slain. By some miracle, no one had been hurt. Everyone agreed it was the biggest,

(Courtesy Kansas State Historical Society and Western History Dept., Denver Public Library)

The Imperial hunting party stopped in Topeka, where Lee Knight took this photo. From left, back row: Frank Thompson, Dr. Vladimir Kadrin, Lt. Col. George "Sandy" Forsyth, Count Olsonfieff, Army Surgeon Morris Asch, Maj. Nelson Sweitzer, Russian naval Lt. Tudor [Tudeer]; middle row: Russian New York Consul General Waldemar Bodisco, Russian Councillor of State W.F. Machin, Lt. Gen. Philip H. Sheridan, Grand Duke Alexis, Vice Admiral P.H. Possiet, Lt. Col. George A. Custer; front row: Lt. Col. James Forsyth, Russian naval Lt. Sterlegoff, Lt. Col. Michael Sheridan.

craziest buffalo hunt he'd ever seen or heard about. What no one realized was that it was possibly the last great buffalo slaughter on the Colorado Plains. Historical accounts of the years following 1872 carry no mention of buffalo herds in such numbers as those that greeted the Grand Duke. Three days after the Duke's train had pulled out of Kit Carson and crossed into Kansas, men in wagons were still harvesting tongues and hides on the hunting grounds.

The carnage at Kit Carson marked an end to the visit of the Grand Duke and Custer to Colorado. Neither would return. For another month, with Custer now the ranking American escort (Sheridan and his staff left the tour at Topeka), the Russians traveled east and southeast, taking in the sights through Kansas, Missouri, Kentucky, Louisiana, and finally, Florida. On Feb. 21, 1872, Alexis, a lieutenant in his father's navy, returned to the frigate *Svetlana* at Pensacola and set sail the following day for Havana. He assured Custer his days in Nebraska and Colorado had been the highlights of his American experience.

Elizabeth Custer joined the group in Louisville, serving as hostess of a steamboat ride down the Mississippi to New Orleans. Her primary responsibility, she wrote, was to supply "girls, girls and more girls" to keep his Royal Highness entertained.

From New Orleans the Custers returned to the hated Elizabethtown, Ky., where they waited nearly a year for Sheridan's promised orders sending the Seventh Cavalry back to the frontier. They enjoyed two happy years at Ft. Abraham Lincoln before Custer left for the Little Big Horn in the spring of 1876. There in Montana he found that "preordained fate" which, indeed, assured his lasting fame.

Alexis, third son of the Czar, lived until 1908, distinguishing himself only as one of the great European playboys of his era. Although there were rumors of a wife and son he was forbidden to acknowledge, he never officially married, but spent most of his life in Paris and other European capitals, courting beautiful and aristocratic women.

Custer had been dead five years when Alexis was appointed by his father to be High Admiral of the Russian Navy, a largely ceremonial post but one giving him entrée to the courts of Europe. It was one of the Czar's last appointments before his death. That same year, 1881, Czar Alexander II was assassinated. The new Czar was Alexis' brother, Alexander III, who died 13 years later. Ascending the throne in 1894 was Alexis' nephew, the ill-fated Nicholas II, the last of the Russian kings.

Through all this, Alexis remained High Admiral. He was in Paris in 1905 when word reached him of the destruction of Russia's Baltic Fleet off Japan during the Russo-Japanese War. Although the dissolute Alexis had had no part in the planning or execution of the disaster, he resigned as High Admiral.

As Europe drifted toward World War One and Russia slid inexorably toward revolution, the Grand Duke lingered in the parlors, ballrooms, and boudoirs of Paris. On Nov. 11, 1908, he died of pneumonia at his apartment, in the arms of a French actress, Madame Balista. He was buried in the Romanov Mausoleum at St. Petersburg.

Col. Mike Sheridan, who had been with General Custer in Denver, led a body-recovery party to the Little Big Horn in July 1877, 13 months after the battle that enshrined Custer and doomed the victorious Indians. There, on a bleak knoll above the river, Sheridan's men exhumed some bones and putrefied remains, believed to be those of Custer, and shipped them back to West Point for burial.

William F. Cody, of course, is presumably at peace under several tons of concrete atop Lookout Mountain west of Denver, where he died in poverty in 1917.

But once upon a time, during a brief moment in history, Cody, Custer, and Alexis rode together in the West, alive and beautiful. Until her death in 1933, Elizabeth Custer remembered the description of the trio as they appeared in 1872.

> The officers, though accustomed to fine physical development, told me that it was something to remember to have seen the three youthful, powerful, well proportioned men leading the cavalcade. The general, about 32, weighing possibly 167 pounds (and) Buffalo Bill, 25, and over six feet tall, were both in buckskins. The Grand Duke, 22, had a green belted riding costume. . . a Smith and Wesson pistol with the arms of Russia and America entwined on the handle, and a boar knife in his belt.

It was Elizabeth's cherished memory of a unique page in the history of the American West.

Bibliography

Beeson, Chalkley M. *Transactions of the Kansas State Historical Society.* Topeka, 1907-1908. Account of Beeson's role in arranging the Colorado buffalo hunt. Mimeographed copy.

Custer, Elizabeth B. *Custer, Cody and The Grand Duke Alexis.* Research Review Magazine, Vol. 4, No. 1, Jan. 1990. By Little Big Horn Associates.

Frost, Lawrence A. *General Custer's Libbie.* Superior Publishing Co., Seattle, Wash., 1976.

Merrington, Marguerite. *The Custer Story.* The Devin-Adair Co., New York, 1950.

Rocky Mountain News. Editions of Jan. 18, 19, 20, 1872, Denver. Colorado Historical Society.

Sprague, Marshall. *A Gallery of Dudes.* Mimeograph furnished by Colorado Historical Society, 1967.

Tucker, William W. *The Grand Duke Alexis in The U.S.A.* Interland Publishing Inc., New York. 1972 reprint of 1872 account taken from newspapers and periodicals.

About the Author

Robert G. "Bob" Palmer, widely known Denver television newsman, and a Corresponding Member of the Denver Westerners, is a lifelong student of "Custeriana." Palmer is a member of the Little Big Horn Associates and the Battlefield Historical Society. He has written numerous articles on Custer and the Indian Wars. He presented a paper on Custer and Grand Duke Alexis at the 1993 Winter Rendezvous of the Denver Westerners.

A Denver native, Palmer attended Denver West and Lafayette high schools, and earned a B.A. in journalism from the University of Colorado. Loretto Heights College awarded him an honorary doctorate in humanities in 1968.

Bob has the distinction of having delivered newscasts every weekday evening in Colorado since 1963. He began his career at KOA-TV (now KCNC-TV) in 1957 as a reporter, advancing to acting news director and chief anchorman. In 1968, he joined KMGH-TV Channel 7 as senior editor and anchorman, then returned to Channel 4 in 1982. He currently co-anchors the station's 5 p.m. news.

Palmer's honors are extensive. Most recently, he won the 1994 Governor's Award from the Colorado Chapter of the National Academy of Television Arts and Sciences. The Colorado Broadcasters Association named him "Broadcaster of the Year" in 1986. In 1985, he received CU's Norlin Award. In 1983, Sigma Delta Chi, honorary journalism society, cited him as "Colorado's Top Commentator." And in 1982, he won an Emmy Award for best regional news writing.

He has also taught journalism at CU and Colorado State University, and is on the advisory board of the CU School of Journalism and Mass Communications. He is a past-president of the Denver Press Club.

A four-year Navy veteran, Palmer served aboard the aircraft carrier USS *Lexington.*

Bob and his wife Gloria have three children and four grandchildren.

"The menacing Sioux" by *Delano*

War Club and Parasol

Frontier Army Officers' Wives

By Merrill J. Mattes

O NE OF THE SIDE EFFECTS of the women's liberation movement has been a flood of books about women on the Western frontier, the cutting edge of civilization against the wilderness. Fiction writers try to glamorize their roles, but historians have discovered that the mere facts of their hazardous existence are sufficiently intriguing to capture an audience.

We have always had books about *famous* women, such as Sacajawea of the Lewis and Clark Expedition; Narcissa Whitman, missionary to Oregon, the first white woman to cross the continent; little Annie Oakley of Buffalo Bill's Wild West Show; and Calamity Jane, a woman of somewhat different mold, saloon keeper, stage driver, and paramour of Wild Bill Hickok. The new wave of literature deals with *ordinary* women who, by our standards, lived *extraordinary* lives, a lethal mixture of drudgery and danger. They have been joyfully discovered, mainly by women historians in the forefront of the campaign for women's rights, rights unheard of in the male-dominated 19th century. As a result we have a proliferation of books and articles about the wives of fur traders, missionaries, gold miners, emigrants, homesteaders, and soldiers.

Before tackling the subject of officers' wives, a glance at some of the other categories of frontier females will help to put things in perspective.

The Rocky Mountain fur trappers who spearheaded the westward movement were not deprived of female companionship. Without ceremony they cohabited, of course, with Indian women by whom they frequently had offspring but from whom nevertheless they often separated, also without ceremony. This was true of the rank and file of American trappers, but sometimes their *bourgeois*, the man in charge of a trading post, would formally marry an Indian woman if a priest or pastor happened by. In Canada, formal marriages between traders and squaws seemed more the rule, but sometimes the traders brought white women into the wilderness. That fascinating story, including rivalries between women of two races, is revealed in a book by Sylvia van Kirk, *Many Tender Ties* (Norman, Okla., 1983).

The First White Women Across the Continent—the title of a classic three-volume work by Clifford M. Drury (Glendale, 1963-1968)—were the wives of missionaries who reached Oregon in 1836-1838. Of the eight men involved, seven brought wives and all but one of these were new brides, all of whom kept diaries which reflect little romance and much hardship and peril—storms, river crossings, illness, and unchristian quarrels. At the mountain rendezvous all were frightened by drunken revelries of Indian braves and whiskery mountaineers. Narcissa Whitman died in 1847, 11 years after her crossing, in a general massacre by Cayuse Indians.

Most 19th-century women lived a hard life. When John Faragher wanted to write a book about the unfair treatment of women in that century he found little in the way of personal records until someone tipped him off about the diaries of female covered-wagon emigrants. So he wrote a book entitled *Women and Men on the Overland Trail* (New Haven, 1979), and from this made a case purporting to demonstrate that a great many of these women were much abused. Now I have read more than 200 of these female emigrant diaries, and frankly I think the author distorted the evidence. He ignores the fact that the bulk of the population then was made up of rural people, poor by today's standards, and everyone, male and female, shared the resultant hardships and frustrations. In the case of emigrants, the picture I get is one of strong traditional family bonds, in which the husband yokes and drives the cattle, hunts game, and fights Indians, while the wife does what in the nineteenth century was the standard thing: she cooks, bakes, washes, sews and darns, cares for the children, and occasionally also manages the oxen when the old man is laid low by cholera or Indian arrow. The terms "sex discrimination" and "civil rights" had not yet crept into our vocabulary. The only unquestioned "right" was the effort of free men and women to survive.

Although men heavily outnumbered women during the covered-wagon migrations, especially during the California Gold Rush, the bulk of the graves that are still identifiable today are those of women, victims of disease compounded by exhaustion. Some emigrant women *were* brutally treated but, except in rare cases, it was by Indians, not by their husbands. Among the horror stories of the frontier are the kidnapings, rapes, and beatings of women like Fanny Kelly, Nancy Morton, Sarah Morris, and Mrs. Eubanks by Sioux and Cheyenne Indians in the 1860s. In the Mormon Church Library I discovered the diary of the husband of a Danish woman, bound of course for Salt Lake, who was lagging behind the wagon train when Cheyennes swooped down, threw her over a horse, and galloped over the horizon. She was never seen again, alive or dead.

One of these days I'd like to write a book about emigrant women, beginning with Nancy Kelsey, the first white woman to reach California, in 1841. This would be a story, not about the abuse of their civil rights, but about their quiet heroism in the face of unspeakable hazards and hardships. Meanwhile, there are some good books in print about emigrant women which are not tainted by Faragher's propaganda against 19th century males. Examples include Sandra Myre's *Ho for California* (San Marino, Calif., 1980) and Kenneth Holmes' *Covered Wagon Women* (Glendale, 1983, *et seq.*).

The published record of frontier Army wives is not as voluminous as those of emigrant women, but this category probably ranks second in the number of written accounts. These ladies also rival their emigrant sisters in the matter of stoic suffering and occasional heroism. I am confining myself to the wives of officers rather than enlisted men for the simple reason that enlisted men, as a rule, didn't have wives with them. Also, officers' wives were above average in education, so we have a quite comprehensive body of knowledge from their reports about their experience.

I got into the subject of Army wives in 1956 when retired Gen. Reynolds Burt, of Washington, D.C., contacted me, on the advice of a mutual friend, to see if I would write a book about his mother, Elizabeth, wife of Andrew Sheridan Burt, captain of Ohio volunteer infantry in the Civil War. Burt became a full general in the Spanish-American War, and spent the intervening years at Western Frontier posts. The memoirs of Elizabeth Burt in the Library of Congress became the backbone of my book, *Indians, Infants and Infantry*, published in 1960 by Fred Rosenstock.

Burt was attached to the Eighteenth U.S. Regiment of Infantry under Col. Henry Carrington, the first Regular Army troops to be sent to the Northern Plains to pacify Indians, following the Civil War. They assembled at Ft. Leavenworth and headed west up the Oregon-California Trail, 2,000 strong, via Ft. Kearny to Ft. Sedgwick, near present Julesburg. Here Carrington and the bulk of his command crossed the South Platte River and turned northwestward to Ft. Laramie and outposts in Powder River country, east of the Big Horn Mountains. Meanwhile, Burt and his company continued straight west along the line of the future Union Pacific Railroad, to be stationed at Ft. Bridger. Subsequently, he and his family went to Ft. Sanders at present Laramie, Wyo., and from thence up the Bozeman trail to Ft. C.F. Smith in Montana. Thereafter, along with successive promotions, he saw service at Ft. Omaha, Ft. Robinson, Ft. D.A. Russell, and twice at Ft. Laramie where, in the late 1880s, he was second in command. Today at Ft. Laramie National Historic Site his residence is known as "the Burt House," with many furnishings supplied by the son, Reynolds Burt, the sponsor of my book.

Elizabeth Burt was with Andrew every step of the way, her first infant son being with her when they started west in 1866. Her second child, Edith, was born in the blockhouse of new Ft. Sanders, and the youngest—this same Reynolds—was born in 1874 at Ft. Omaha. He lived to age 96, long enough to see my book published.

Elizabeth Burt's story is really one of epic proportions, bona fide historical melodrama with all the ingredients—a volunteer nurse on the

(Courtesy Fort Laramie National Historic Site)

Elizabeth Burt in 1902, well after her frontier adventures, and Col. Andrew S. Burt (about 1888), while he was in command of Ft. Laramie.

Civil War battlefront, meeting Andrew when he was recuperating from battle wounds; crossing the frozen Mississippi River on foot with her baby boy to reach Jefferson Barracks at St. Louis; riding out of historic Ft. Kearny with Carrington's grand Army to engage the Sioux; crossing the flooded South Platte at Julesburg and the rampaging North Platte on the Laramie Plains where several soldiers drowned; getting lost in a blizzard between Salt Lake City and Ft. Bridger; taking her little boy and her baby girl up the dangerous Bozeman Trail where their company was attacked by Indians at Crazy Woman's Fork; and later under siege at Ft. C.F. Smith in the Montana wilderness. Red Cloud and Crazy Horse were her enemies, but she was on friendly terms with the Shoshones under Chief Washakie and the Crows, led by Iron Bull. She was on speaking terms with Generals Crook and Sherman and many, if not most, of the ranking officers of the Indian-fighting Army and their wives.

Elizabeth Burt was a participant in so many episodes of frontier history that I deluded myself into thinking that some Hollywood producer would want to make a movie out of it, and my agreement with the publisher would have cut me in on the lucrative screen rights. Unfortunately, though it was well received by academics and history buffs, my book did not shape up as a best seller, which made the movie idea a pipe dream.

In preparing *Indians, Infants and Infantry* I dug up several old books about *other* Army officers' wives, so conceived the idea of writing *another* book about *all* of them. I drafted several chapters and even had a title in mind. It was to be called *War Club and Parasol.* Then my official duties with the National Park Service, including transfer from Omaha to San Francisco in 1966, and extensive travels, prevented my going through with the project until my retirement in 1975. But meanwhile a young lady named Patricia Stallard came out with a book entitled *Glittering Miser: Dependents of the Indian Fighting Army* (Fort Collins, 1978). About the same time Oliver Knight published his book, *Life and Manners in the Frontier Army* (Norman, 1978), based largely on data from the voluminous novels of Gen. Charles King about what he calls "an elite if exiled group," officers and their wives and sweethearts during the period 1865-1890. No point now in my writing about Army women as originally planned, and by now, books about frontier women—all kinds of them—are getting to be a drug on the market.

However, here are some excerpts from my aborted manuscript:

There are at least 12 wives of Army officers on the Western Frontier who have bequeathed their testimony. Besides Elizabeth Burt,
these are Mrs. Orsemus Boyd, Elsa Biddle, Elizabeth Custer, Margaret
Carrington, Frances Grummond, Sarah Canfield, Catherine Collins,
Cynthia Capron, Katherine Fougera, Mary Heistand, and Frances
Roe. (Since this was first written, accounts of eight more officers'
wives have been discovered and published, but I will have my hands
full with these original 12.)

The 12 husbands involved were evenly divided between cavalry and
infantry and during the period of historic interest ranked variously
from second lieutenant to full colonel. All had Civil War records. All
but one were Regular Army, and several were West Pointers. Four of
the men died in action, three killed by Indians, and one succumbing to
campaign hardships. Of the remaining eight, four achieved high military rank before retirement.

Somewhat alone among the wives is Catherine Wever Collins. She
was the mother of cavalry Lt. Caspar Collins who was killed in the
famous Platte Bridge fight of 1865 and for whom Casper [sic], Wyo.,
was named, and the wife of Col. William O. Collins, commander of
the Eleventh Ohio Cavalry stationed at Ft. Laramie during the early
1860s and founder of Camp Collins, now Fort Collins, Colo. She
arrived the earliest of our 12 Army wives on the Great Plains theater
of action and stayed there for the shortest period—less than one year.
All of the wives but she, at the time of their baptism into frontier
service, were young women, in their late teens or early twenties. Mrs.
Collins had been married for 20 years when she left Hillsboro, Ohio,
in the autumn of 1863 to join her husband.

Traveling by train, steamboat, and stagecoach up the Platte route,
she reached Ft. Laramie in November.   During that winter she en-
deared herself to the garrison by her interest in the welfare of those
afflicted by illness and accident, and earned the gratitude of historians
by her intimate descriptions of that famous post, the vicissitudes of the
mail train, and peaceful Indian visitors. Early in 1864 Indian alarms
were rampant along the Upper Platte, and it was not until late summer
that she was able to leave the fort in safety via the mule ambulance of
Gen. Robert B. Mitchell, commander of the district. She was escorted
by soldiers to Ft. Kearny, via Plum Creek Station, recent scene of an
Indian massacre of emigrants. She almost suffocated in the closely
packed stage to Omaha, and proceeded from thence home by steamboat. (Agnes Wright Spring, ed., "An Army Wife Comes West: the

Col. William O. Collins, commander of Ft. Laramie in the early 1860s, and founder of Camp Collins—now Fort Collins, Colo.; and Catherine Wever Collins, as she appeared in later years.

letters of Catherine Wever Collins," *Colorado Magazine*, October 1954).

Sarah E. Canfield, wife of Lt. Andrew Canfield, Co. D, Thirteenth Infantry, was a "short-termer" like Mrs. Collins, being on the frontier only a little more than a year, but she was a bona fide contemporary of Elizabeth Burt. While the latter was being marooned by Sioux and Cheyenne at Ft. C.F. Smith in 1867-68, Sarah was having a similar experience with Sioux and Crow at Camp Cooke, another infantry post in Montana, equally isolated and equally temporary at the junction of the Missouri and Judith rivers. Sarah is the only one of our 12 who ascended the length of the Missouri by steamboat, and left impressions of the chain of military posts which protected that important line of communication in the 1860s, notably Forts Rice, Randall, and Berthold.

Even more contemporary with Elizabeth Burt, both actors in the epic scenes of the Bozeman Trail or Red Cloud's War, were the two successive wives of Colonel Carrington of the Eighteenth Regiment of Infantry. When this big outfit left Ft. Kearny on May 19, 1866, for its march to Ft. Laramie, Elizabeth Burt and Margaret Carrington were acquaintances traveling in the same cavalcade. Beyond the crossing of the South Platte they parted, as noted before, the Burts heading for Ft. Bridger, and Margaret going with her husband, crossing the North Platte "Rubicon" into hostile Sioux territory to construct forts along the Bozeman Trail. With her were three other officers' wives, Mesdames Brown, Horton, and Bisbee. They arrived at the site that would become the Ft. Phil Kearny stockade on July 13. In August, Lieutenant Wands brought his wife in, her nerves jumpy from an Indian attack on the party at Crazy Woman's Fork. In November the circle was reinforced by the wife of Lieutenant Grummond.

The Grummonds came on from Ft. Leavenworth as far as the new Kansas Pacific Railroad had been constructed, then traveled by ambulance to Ft. Kearny, by government mail escort to Ft. Laramie and, after a brief pause there, to Ft. Phil Kearny. Lieutenant Grummond was among the 80 men killed in the Fetterman disaster late December 1866, engineered by Red Cloud and Crazy Horse. When Carrington, in momentary disgrace, was commanded to withdraw at once to Ft. Casper, widow Grummond accompanied Mrs. Carrington and children in a government wagon, suffering terribly from grief as well as from sub-zero weather. At Ft. McPherson Mrs. Grummond was met and escorted home by her brother. Years later, after the death of Margaret Carrington, Frances Grummond became Mrs. Carrington No. Two, to their mutual joy, no doubt, but to the eternal confusion of historians.

When Elizabeth Burt followed the perilous Bozeman Trail northward in November 1867, there was a new set of faces at Ft. Phil Kearny. The Carringtons, both numbers one and two, had fled the scene of Indian terror, and each would one day write a book about their common harrowing experience, Margaret Carrington's *Ab-Sa-Ra-Ka, Land of Massacre*, is one of the classics of Western literature, rich in historical detail and literary grace. It appeared in 1878 and thus became the first *published* account of an experience of an officer's wife on the Plains. Frances Grummond Carrington's *My Army Life*, published in 1911, dovetails accurately into the narrative. It includes a postscript account of a celebration at Sheridan, Wyo., in 1908 in memory of old Ft. Phil Kearny. Colonel Carrington and Frances were guests of honor.

The most famous of our 12 lady "reporters" is Elizabeth Custer, spirited young wife of George Armstrong Custer, the fair-haired "boy general" who achieved (a dubious) immortality by getting himself and

(Courtesy National Park Service, Historic Sites and Buildings)

Elizabeth "Libbie" Bacon wed Lt. Col. (Bvt. Maj. Gen.) George Armstrong Custer in 1865. (Print is from cracked glass-plate negative.)

others annihilated at the Little Big Horn in 1876. It took three books to get Mrs. Custer's story told—*Boots and Saddles, Tenting on the Plains*, and *Following the Guidon*—all time-honored classics of frontier literature. Elizabeth Custer is the only one of the 12 who has had appreciable recognition by modern historical writers. She outlived her controversial husband by more than 60 years. Her priceless collection of Custer's uniforms, arms, and memorabilia, is now exhibited at Custer Battlefield National Monument.

The Custers were married at Monroe, Mich., when George was on

Army leave in 1865. The honeymoon was quickly interrupted by a telegram from Washington, D.C., imploring the precocious cavalry commander to get on with the Civil War. Elizabeth, whose love for George had about it a Homeric quality, followed him right back to the scenes of hostilities. "The result," she writes, "was that I found myself in a few hours on the extreme right wing of the Army of the Potomac, in an isolated Virginia farmhouse, finishing my honeymoon alone." During the 12 years that followed, she says, "I hardly remember a time when I was not in fear of some immediate peril," referring to Indians who replaced Confederate soldiers as the chief menace.

There is a striking parallel between the Custer and Burt romances. They both blossomed in the middle of the Civil War. Both marriages occurred during leaves resulting from battle wounds. Both honeymoons were unsettled by alarms of war, and both wives joined their husbands at Union Army encampments. Following the war, both followed their husbands out upon the hostile Indian frontier.

In the autumn of 1866, about the time Elizabeth Burt was lost in a blizzard near Ft. Bridger, the Custers arrived at Ft. Riley, Kans., headquarters of the Seventh Cavalry, where the brevet-general (with the actual rank of lieutenant-colonel) assumed command of the garrison, and was soon launched on a series of well-publicized campaigns on the Kansas frontier. Elizabeth always followed her husband as closely as regulations and logistics would permit. Sometimes her determination endangered her life. Being left at Ft. Riley while George was out chasing Indians she could endure separation no longer and prevailed upon General Sherman to let her accompany him to Ft. Harker at the Kansas Pacific "end of track." Then she proceeded by government wagon to Ft. Hays, arriving in the crude tent camp at the height of the rainy season. But all discomforts were as nothing at this reunion: "Nothing dampened my ardor; no amount of soakings could make me think that camping-ground was not an Elysian field."

However, after enduring flood and pestilence at Ft. Hays, she fled back to Ft. Riley. Now it was George's turn to play the romantic theme, "Love Conquers All." Learning that the dread cholera was rife at Ft. Riley and imagining his dear "Libbie" prostrate with the disease, he flatly abandoned his command at Ft. Wallace and dashed the whole length of the Smoky Hill Trail, losing two troopers to Indians en route, to be at his wife's side. Army regulations take no cognizance of love. For this flagrant violation of orders, Custer was court-martialed and discharged. It was only through the intervention of his Civil War

In 1875 this group of Ft. Abraham Lincoln officers and wives—including the "Custer Clan"—went on a hunting trip. Eight persons on the outing died the following year at the Battle of the Little Big Horn. Libbie Custer (in black hat) is seated at center; George (in white jacket) stands at her left.

pal, Gen. Phil Sheridan, that Custer was later restored to rank and service.

After a two-year stint among Kentucky moonshiners, Custer was ordered to proceed with the Seventh Cavalry to Dakota Territory, setting up headquarters at Ft. Abraham Lincoln on the Missouri River opposite hell-roaring Bismarck. Libbie died a thousand deaths when her gallant one rode out at the head of a column in 1873 to protect Northern Pacific Railroad surveyors from the infuriated Sioux; in 1874 to invade the Black Hills in violation of Sioux treaty rights, and announce the presence of gold there; and in 1876 to punish the Sioux for raising objections to the Black Hills Gold Rush. This third expedition, to the Little Big Horn, proved fatal and the childless Libbie would cherish forever, and forever defend, the bright memory of a slain hero.

Katherine Gibson Fougera, whose reminiscences appeared in 1942 under the title, *With Custer's Cavalry*, was a friend of Libbie at Ft. Abraham Lincoln. She was, to begin with, Katherine Garrett, the unattached but highly eligible sister of Mollie, wife of Lt. Donald McIntosh, when she arrived at the fort in 1874 and was plunged into the color and excitement of a garrison of higher voltage, socially, than most others. When troops from neighboring Ft. Rice came upriver to join the Black Hills Expedition, Katherine got jolted by Lieutenant Gibson who displayed "a quality of life and movement that was electric." He was "straight as a Norway pine. His campaign hat was worn at a rakish angle and his clear olive skin abutted a moustache atop a mouth filled with flawless teeth. He was big, strong, and magnificent, and I was small and young and blue-eyed." The laws of physics are immutable. "It might have been lunar madness, but when we finally joined the others I had signed up for a permanent enlistment with the Seventh Cavalry."

Duly married with flourishes, upon the return of the expedition, Mrs. Gibson accompanied her husband on an assignment to New Orleans in 1875, but returned shortly to Ft. Rice. When he was offered a transfer to Custer's command, she prevailed on him to decline, having a premonition of disaster. Being with Colonel Benteen's command in June 1876, Gibson survived the massacre at the Little Big Horn.

Mrs. Boyd (*Cavalry Life in Tent and Field*, New York, 1894) and Elsa Biddle (*Reminiscences of a Soldier's Wife*, Philadelphia, 1907) spent most of their careers in the Southwest, so we will not dwell on their innumerable vicissitudes—scorching heat, tarantulas, bloodthirsty Apaches—but only stress the one factor that kept them sane, their deep affection and support for their husbands whose field assignments took a heavy toll of their health. Cynthia Capron, wife of a lieutenant stationed at Ft. Laramie, lost him to typhoid fever, a common killer at Western forts with poor sanitary conditions. He was buried at Ft. Russell (now Ft. Francis E. Warren, at Cheyenne) and she returned to her Illinois home with her children.

Marital fidelity to the end was the norm. Frances Roe, who tells her story in *Army Letters to an Officer's Wife* (New York, 1909) is my sentimental favorite. She showed bravery, constancy, and a resolute light-heartedness in the face of discouragements and dangers to herself and her gallant Captain Faye. Plagued by malaria and snakes dropping from the ceiling of her miserable hovel at Camp Supply, Indian Territory, she takes the view that "at dreadful places like this

(Courtesy Western History Dept., Denver Public Library)
Col. Faye Roe and Frances M.A. Roe. Dates of portraits are unknown.

is where the plucky Army wife is most needed." On one occasion Faye was given a doubly dangerous assignment at Cimarron Redoubt, halfway between Ft. Dodge and Ft. Supply, "surrounded by any number of villages of hostile Indians." She went along, despite protests of Faye and his superiors, to make some kind of home in the dugout fortification.

As a general rule, Army wives of either officers or enlisted men did not accompany their husbands on Indian campaigns or other missions where their personal safety was clearly in jeopardy. Mrs. Roe's deliberate invasion of hostile ground was a marginal case. Other exceptions have been noted among "camp followers," a term covering female help, whether unmarried, or married to enlisted men or noncoms. One female cook who accompanied the Seventh Cavalry on the Washita campaign, is described by Libbie Custer as "tanned, toughened," and indifferent to the whine of Indian bullets.

My unpublished manuscript has 20 chapters, with topics like Army Regulations, Change of Station, Transportation, Quarters Rotation, the Servant Problem, Food, Clothing, Public Health, and the Education of Army Brats. To close this account, I will offer a few random quotations—let's call them verbal gems doomed to remain underground—or shall we call them "desert flowers destined to bloom unseen."

ARMY REGULATIONS

Officers' wives might be veritable queens in the eyes of their husbands, and great deference might be shown them by enlisted men, but officially they did not exist! Every detail of Army life was governed by Regulations except the detail of matrimony. It cannot be said that the War Department frowned on the idea of love, marriage, and wilderness honeymoons. On the contrary, according to Mrs. Grummond, "General Sherman in 1866 urged all Army wives to accompany their husbands." It was Mrs. Boyd's understanding that the presence of wives "alone prevents demoralization, and officers are always encouraged to marry for that reason." Once married, however, the bride was adrift in a sea of regulations that applied only to her husband. Libbie Custer complained that "Regulations enter into minute detail on everything, even giving the number of hours that beans should boil, but not even a paragraph is wasted on the conduct of officers' wives."

Actually, it was only families of *officers* who were left out of account. Female servants and company laundresses, sometimes married to enlisted men, were included. The rule book said that each company was entitled to three or four laundresses and that a soldier had to get permission to marry and must await a vacancy in the laundresses' ranks before he could bring his sudsy princess into the garrison. Rations and the services of the post surgeon were available to these retainers, including female servants of officers.

SERVANTS

The word "servant" is disappearing from the American language, and we are getting accustomed to a world in which women of all social strata do their own housekeeping. Before 1900, however, one or more servants were an essential element of every well-regulated household. They were in plentiful supply, thanks to unlimited immigration from Europe, and to be without one was a confession of poverty. This was true everywhere with the exception of households on the Western Frontier. Army wives, whose need for servants was truly desperate, were victims of the only scarce labor market in America.

Women of whatever race, age, or degree of repulsiveness were exceedingly rare on the frontier. If imported, they were soon in big demand by soldiers as matrimonial partners, even those as homely and shapeless as a mud fence.

Mrs. Biddle's Bridget was so transcendentally homely that she went eight years before receiving a proposal. But when she finally was propositioned by a quartermaster sergeant at Camp Halleck she went overboard, becoming engaged and lending the fellow her life savings, around $300. As soon as he had supplemented this with funds taken from the company safe, he deserted and headed for Elko, Nev. He was caught and killed and the money recovered, but Bridget was disconsolate. Complains Mrs. Biddle: "I think she grieved after the rascally sergeant much more than she did for her money!"

Elizabeth Burt was experienced in all the vicissitudes of the problem. An Irish woman with the inevitable name of Bridget stayed with her just long enough to get "welded" to a blacksmith at Ft. Kearny. A black girl, Maggie, stood up under every trial until the Burts started up the Bozeman Trail. Stories of Indian atrocities, only too well-founded, prompted her to resign at Ft. Fetterman. The black servant Mrs. Burt then imported from Omaha developed an acute and incurable case of inertia, and the substitute Mormon girl was simply not bright enough to catch on to the simplest instructions. Mrs. Burt finally found her most dependable help among the off-duty enlisted men, called "strikers," who were glad to volunteer for the extra pay.

Frances Roe endured the trials and tribulations of finding a satisfactory cook in Montana Territory. Finally, she had to make do with a series of Chinese servants, all named Charlie, and all with exasperating peculiarities. The first Charlie refused to scrub the laundry before boiling. When rebuked, he tipped the tub and its contents on the kitchen floor and left the military reservation. The next one stalked out in high dudgeon when Mrs. Roe wanted the use of the kitchen, which he regarded as his sacred preserve. A third Charlie was constantly feuding with the striker over whose privilege it was to fire up the parlor stove. Each time the soldier would put on wood, Charlie would put on more, with the result that Mrs. Roe was almost baked alive and the house nearly reduced to ashes. Yet another of these strange silk-coated Orientals killed himself with a derringer when accused by soldiers of cheating at cards. The last one, distinguished by the name of Charlie Hang, elected to return to China, having accumulated a fortune of $1,200 by mining gold dust in his spare time. Despite her misadventures with them, she believed the Chinese made marvelous servants "if once you win their confidence and their affection then they are your slaves."

CHANGE OF STATION

Of all the tests of courage and forbearance to which Army wives were subjected, perhaps the sternest was "change of station." From the domestic viewpoint, these tended to be frequent, sudden, occurring at the most inconvenient time, distressingly expensive, and quite without rational explanation.

The Burts' experience was not untypical. From 1865 when the Captain launched his Western career at Jefferson Barracks until 1898 when he left Ft. Missoula he had 20 changes of assignment to post. Duration of these varied from only a few weeks at Ogallala Station to six years at Ft. Missoula. One- and two-year stints were the rule.

Some officers were shifted around with far greater frequency than the Burts. Lieutenant McIntosh of the Seventh Cavalry and his wife Mollie were sent packing to nine different Army posts in 11 months. Major Biddle and family were barely settled at Ft. Riley after an exhausting move from Ft. Bidwell, Calif., when he was ordered to Ft. Leavenworth. He was gratefully settling down once more when General Pope decided he should assume command at Ft. Lyon, Colorado Territory. At Departmental Headquarters, field officers were pawns on a chessboard. Fatigue of family and extra expenses resulting from these dislocations were, as Mrs. Biddle put it, "things not counted."

"Proceed without delay" was the usual phrase appended to orders, and this was to be taken literally. Large furniture, heavy draperies, and huge trunks filled with finery played no part in military life. Strikers could shove the entire contents of an officer's quarters into a government wagon and be on the march in less than two hours.

Sometimes these moves would simply involve shifting the household to the next outpost over the horizon, only a day or two distant. Often they were continental in scope. Katherine Fougera said that the process of "dashing back and forth across the continent" soon lost its novelty. When orders came for her husband to transfer from New Orleans to North Dakota, she assures us that she "displayed no Spartan qualities" but just sat down and bawled. There was a limit to the patience of a woman whose nest was forever taking wings.

About the Author

A biographical sketch of Merrill J. Mattes appears earlier in this book, at the end of the chapter entitled, "Seeing the Elephant." The accompanying article, "War Club and Parasol: Frontier Army Officers' Wives," was presented before the Denver Westerners in December 1984.

Mattes is a co-founder and present director emeritus of the Oregon-California Trails Association, headquartered in Independence, Mo., which actively promotes trail preservation, and publishes the quarterly *Overland Journal.*

"I will fight no more forever. . ." by *Max Smith*

The Nez Percé War
of 1877

By Richard A. Cook

*T*HE PURPOSE OF THIS narrative is to examine the Nez Percé War of 1877, and to summarize its highlights. In addition, you will see how one Army detachment after another, led by Civil War and Indian Campaign veterans, floundered in battle as the Nez Percé conducted a great fighting retreat which almost succeeded. As this treatise is only a summary, the reasons for the war and its background will not be discussed.

I. PRELUDE

"Tell General Howard I know his heart. What he told me before I have in my heart. I am tired of fighting. Our chiefs are killed. Looking Glass is dead. The old men are all killed. It is the young men who say yes or no. He who led the young men is dead. It is cold and we have no blankets. The little children are freezing to death. My people, some of them have run away to the hills and have no blankets, no food, no one knows where they are, perhaps freezing to death. I want time to look for my children and see how many of them I can find. Maybe I shall find them among the dead. Hear me my chiefs, I am tired, my heart is sick and sad. From where the sun now stands, I will fight no more forever."

With these poignant words, Chief Joseph of the Nez Percé Indians surrendered his little band to Brig. Gen. Oliver O. Howard and Col. Nelson A. Miles in the Bear Paw Mountains of Montana Territory on Oct. 5, 1877. Within a period of 11 weeks, this band of Nez Percé had moved approximately 1,300 miles and had engaged nine separate commands in 13 different battles and skirmishes. In nearly every case, although taking serious losses of fighting men, equipment and livestock, the Nez Percé fought their opponents to a standstill, and in some instances inflicted defeat. Gen. William Tecumseh Sherman, the Army's Commanding General, termed the struggle as ". . . one of the most extraordinary Indian wars of which there is any record."

II. THE BATTLE OF WHITE BIRD CANYON

By June 16, 1877, all of the Nez Percé bands who had not participated in the treaty of 1863 (which gave up specific Indian rights to the land of their ancestors) were required to move onto the reservation with the other bands who previously had agreed to the terms of the treaty. A few days before the deadline, several young warriors, inflamed by alcohol and taunted by an older member of the tribe for not avenging the death of one of their fathers at the hands of a white man, stole away from camp and killed four white men living along the Salmon River. Another white was wounded, and all were known to have been hostile to Indians. News of the raid reached Ft. Lapwai by Indian messenger who reported that the raid was one of private revenge and not a declaration of war by the non-treaty bands. General Howard, Commanding General of the Department of the Columbia at Ft. Vancouver, just happened to be at Ft. Lapwai on an inspection trip at that time. He believed this news as the truth until correspondence was received from one L.P. Brown, a hotel keeper at Mount Idaho. In effect, Brown indicated that the non-treaty bands had been gathering at one place and had become insolent and threatening to settlers moving to the security of Mount Idaho, a tiny settlement in the Idaho Panhandle. Since the local citizens of Mount Idaho had not heard about the slayings on the Salmon River, it is quite possible that Brown was trying to drum up justification for the forcible removal of the Indians from his locale in order to quiet the populace.

However, on June 15 a pair of whiskey freighters abandoned their load when attacked by Indians who, after consuming some of the captured booty, attacked a refugee party. Some whites were killed and others wounded. Meanwhile, hearing reports of the Salmon River killings, Brown sent a second message to Howard. In this communication he stated that the situation was desperate and he pleaded for help in the form of soldiers, arms, and ammunition. A third and final message came from Brown an hour later and it repeated the urgent call for assistance. Based upon the unsupported statement of this one man, it seemed apparent that the country was involved in an Indian uprising. General Howard quickly assembled his available forces and prepared for an attack upon the Indian encampment at the base of White Bird Canyon. This armed force was commanded by Capt. David Perry, and initially consisted of 93 men of Companies F and H, First U.S. Cavalry, and two other companies brought from the Wallowa Valley by Captain Whipple. Infantry troops were to come later from Walla Walla, and additional soldiers and supplies were requisitioned from Ft. Vancouver, near the mouth of the Columbia River. Captain Perry had been promised a large force of volunteers at Grangeville if he attacked at once, but when he was ready to depart, only 11 volunteers had joined his command. A little after midnight on June 17 the command, now approximately 117 men including 12 treaty-band scouts, reached the ridge above White Bird Creek. Here they waited for first light to guide them down the canyon to the Indian village. Alert Indian sentries previously had warned the village of their approach. The route the soldiers would have to follow wound along a treeless, rolling land with ridges and hills on either side. The village itself lay behind two buttes at the bottom of the slope. The total fighting strength of the encampment was approximately 150, but many warriors were unable to fight because of drunkenness. Others had no weapons or were too old, too sick, or too frightened to use them. Altogether, there were not more than 60 or 70 warriors with bows and arrows, shotguns, muskets, and a few modern rifles. The chiefs were uncertain whether to resist, but reaching a decision, they organized a truce team to try to arrange a meeting. Being cautious, however, the old men, women, and children were directed to drive the livestock to safety while the warriors prepared for the worst, concealing themselves along each side of the draw.

Before 3 a.m. the troops were again in motion and within an hour emerged from the draw. At that time, a group of six Indians under a flag of truce was observed directly to their front.

There had been no hint of an ambush or a surprise attack but the fighting began with two wild shots fired by a civilian volunteer by the name of Ad Chapman. Sergeant McCarthy stated in retrospect that, "some wild firing was done by our people from horseback, a rather shortsighted thing to do; for we had only an average of 50 rounds in the whole command."

The nature of the terrain, with many hiding places for ambush, should have put the troops on their guard, but since they were anticipating a surprise charge into the village, they ignored their surroundings. Other Nez Percé warriors waited behind the truce committee to see what would happen. As previously stated, the "volunteers" opened fire without waiting for Perry's command and it was returned by the warriors in the rear of the truce committee. In this exchange Trumpeter Jones, one of the two buglers, was killed. As the Indians started firing, Perry hastily deployed his troops across the draw and placed the volunteers to his left on a high knoll. The men in the center were dismounted while the ones on the right flank remained mounted. The battle was fought without any plan and the Nez Percé seized the initiative by charging the volunteers on the left flank, which sent them reeling to the rear in panic. This action exposed Perry's left flank while at the same time a charge led by Ollokot, Chief Joseph's brother, on the right flank of the line frightened the horses of the mounted troopers.

The troops in the center, seeing their flanks exposed and nothing but confusion all around, gave way and rushed for their horses. In a matter of a few moments, the whole command had been cut into small groups fighting desperately for their lives. Nineteen men with Lieutenant Theller tried to make a stand but were cut down against a rocky cliff. The remainder of the command fled the battlefield in panic leaving 34 dead. The Nez Percé gave chase as the Army fought a token rear-guard action in the direction of Mount Idaho where the Indians gave up the pursuit and returned to the village. The Nez Percé casualties were light with only two wounded and none dead. The most important result of this impromptu battle, besides spreading the alarm of an impending Indians war, was the fact that 63 rifles, a number of handguns and a considerable amount of ammunition were captured by the Indians.

OLLOKOT

Perry's forces were not outnumbered, nor had the Indians been better armed. In fact some of the warriors who participated in the battle acquired their weapons from fallen soldiers. Historically, the Battle of White Bird Canyon has been classed with the Battle of the Little Big Horn as an overwhelming defeat. Actually the two are similar only in respect to a lack of military caution and accessible reserves. Manpower was equally balanced but Indian maneuvering and marksmanship were decisive. It is also apparent that mediocre Army leadership and poorly trained troops contributed to this defeat. The loss of both trumpeters at the outset, leaving Perry with no means of control, also might have been highly significant. In addition, the command was worn out by 36 hours of marching and two nights of sleep. However, many people were ready to believe that the Nez Percé were supermen led by military geniuses. As a note of interest, Captain Perry later faced a court of inquiry regarding his leadership in the battle but was exonerated.

III. THE BATTLE OF THE CLEARWATER

The Battle of White Bird Canyon not only alarmed the settlements of the Northwest, but angered the rest of the nation whose memory of the Custer disaster of the year before was still vivid. As a result, and because it was apparent that the victory might encourage other Northwest tribes to rebel, General Howard sent for reinforcements throughout the West. Some were to come from as far away as Georgia and Alaska. Howard soon realized, however, that there were no real signs of a general Indian uprising, and he felt that a strategic emplacement of regulars would be all that was required. Howard also believed that a posture of watchfulness by the settlers and their volunteer militia would aid in preventing the danger of an all-out war in the area.

Within a week, General Howard took to the field with a force of 227 troops, 20 civilians and a large group of packers and guides. He marched directly to the Indian village, only to find that the original band had been joined by another group returning from hunting buffalo in Montana, and that they had moved the entire village to the south side of the Salmon River. Howard commented:

> No general could have chosen another position, or one that would be more likely to puzzle or obstruct a pursuing foe. If we present a weak force, he [Joseph] can turn upon it. If we make direct pursuit, he can go southward toward Boise for at least 30 miles, and then turn our left. He can go straight to his rear and cross the Snake at Pittsburgh Landing. He can go on down the Salmon and cross in several places, and then turn either to the left, for his old haunts in the Wallowa Valley, or to his right, and pass our flank, threatening our line of supply, while he has at the same time, a wonderful natural barrier between him and us in the Salmon. . . .

While the troops were planning to cross the river, information was received that Looking Glass, a famous tribal war chief, was planning to leave the reservation and join the hostile band. Accepting this as fact, Howard divided his forces and sent Captain Whipple with two troops of cavalry to intercept Looking Glass. As Whipple departed, Howard received boats and started his crossing of the Salmon River only to see the Indians disappear into the wilderness.

During the time Howard was wearily pursuing his enemy, Captain Whipple located Looking Glass' peaceful village. After an attempt to talk to Looking Glass with no success, Whipple without warning launched a vicious attack on the encampment. The Indians fled from the village to the other side of the river where they were rallied by their outraged chief. Looking Glass previously had desired peace, but as a result of the attack was left homeless. Consequently it is not surprising that the members of this band with few exceptions hastened to join the hostile force as the latter reached the Clearwater River.

About that time, Whipple received word that the main hostile band had evaded General Howard and had crossed back to the north bank of the Salmon River. Howard had tried to follow the hostiles, but couldn't cross to the north bank without retracing his steps to where he had left the boats. This is exactly what happened, and Howard's prey gained valuable time. For the time being, Looking Glass was forgotten and Whipple dispatched Lt. S.M. Rains with 10 men to reconnoiter his rear as the hostile Nez Percé were now in the vicinity. He dug in to await results which were not long in coming. In attempting to find the enemy, Rains and his men were annihilated and another group of scouts and civilian volunteers was mauled.

Yellow Wolf, when queried years later as to the hasty return of the belligerents back across the Salmon River, replied:

> It was from the first so fixed. We intended turning back if soldiers followed us south. That was how the war was to be carried out. The chiefs wanted the soldiers out of the way.

The Nez Percé then bypassed Whipple's force and the barricaded towns of Cottonwood and Grangeville to head for a hiding place on the South Fork of the Clearwater River. Here they were joined by the people of Looking Glass' band. This addition provided another 40 warriors, but also raised the total of women and children to approximately 450.

General Howard assumed that Joseph was the one responsible for the masterly way in which the Nez Percé had achieved success and for conducting the war with "white men's rules" as well. There had been no scalping and body mutilation by the hostiles, and noncombatants, including women, were treated with humanity and friendliness. The truth was that the Nez Percé had succeeded from a combination of overconfidence and mistakes on the part of the whites, and Indian courage coupled with the advantage of a rugged terrain. Also, it was a fact that Joseph sat in council but since he had never been a war chief, men like his brother Ollokot, Five Wounds, Toohoolhoolzote, Rainbow, and White Bird were the actual combat leaders.

On July 11, Howard, now with 400 troops and 180 scouts, packers, and teamsters, took up the pursuit once more. The hostile camp was spotted on the opposite side of the Clearwater, and the troops opened fire with a 4-inch howitzer and two Gatling guns in preparation for an attack. Taken by surprise, but not hesitating, Toohoolhoolzote, with two dozen warriors crossed the river, scaled a bluff to the same level of the soldiers and engaged them with accurate and deadly fire. This allowed time for more Indians to get into the fight with the intent of encircling their foe. Howard, surmising this, formed his troops in a square and ordered them to dig in. The fighting continued all day and to the next morning. The Nez Percé, outnumbered almost six to one, and occasionally under artillery fire, kept the command pinned down and on the defensive with expert marksmanship. Several hand-to-hand fights broke out and at one point the supply train was almost captured.

Additionally, the Nez Percé controlled the only spring in the area. This further discouraged the troops, already suffering from thirst under a merciless sun. By noon of the second day, the chiefs agreed there had been enough fighting without a decision and decided to withdraw. Joseph was given enough time to move the village and livestock. One by one the Indians ceased fighting and withdrew from the battlefield, and Howard's troops followed across the river to an abandoned camp. The Army lost 13 killed and 27 wounded, of whom two died later, while the Indians suffered four dead and six wounded. They had escaped from Howard once again.

Although the Indians had not been defeated, the troops had survived a battle and the Indians were driven from the field. Howard's failure to pursue his enemy rapidly was probably his most serious mistake of the entire campaign. The Indians themselves called Howard "General Day-After-Tomorrow" because of his policy of giving them a two-day lead. General Howard, instead of hounding the Nez Percé, who most likely would have dispersed their shattered bands and ceased their resistance, postponed pursuit until the following day.

(Courtesy western History Dept., Denver Public Library)

Brig. Gen. Oliver O. Howard

By that time it was too late, and the opportunity to end the uprising was gone.

From the beginning, Howard had underestimated his opponents even when his knowledge was based upon accurate information.

IV. FORT FIZZLE

The Nez Percé crossed the Clearwater north of Howard's location and paused to determine their next move. They reluctantly decided to leave Idaho, thinking that if that were the case General Howard would leave them alone. Looking Glass was of the opinion that once in Montana, with which he was familiar, the band could join the Crows and hunt the plains in peace. It was a difficult decision to make because it meant leaving their homeland behind. Looking Glass was declared supreme chief for the trek to Montana and subsequently the homeless band started over the difficult Lolo Trail through the Bitterroot Mountains. Howard took up the pursuit which was as difficult for the pursuers, as for the pursued.

In all fairness to the Army, it should be pointed out here that part of Howard's force was infantry and that he was attempting to capture an elusive and cunning mounted foe. A few days later in Montana, at the eastern exit to the trail, a force of 35 soldiers of the Seventh Infantry and 200 citizen volunteers under the command of Capt. C.M. Rawn, attempted to establish a log barricade in order to halt the Nez Percé retreat.

By July 25, after nine days in the mountains with 2,000 horses in addition to noncombatants, the Nez Percé appeared above the log fort. Joseph, Looking Glass, and White Bird went forward to persuade their opponents to allow their passage, stating that they were on their way to the Crows and would move peacefully through the valley, respecting the rights of the settlers and paying for what they needed. This satisfied the volunteers who, not wanting an Indian fight, departed for home leaving Rawn and his troops to defend the fort. Fortunately for Captain Rawn, whose orders were to resist, the Nez Percé conducted a feint at his position and bypassed it completely on another mountain trail. The log fort was soon dubbed "Fort Fizzle" and Rawn could do nothing more than withdraw to the settlement at Missoula.

V. THE BATTLE OF BIG HOLE

Keeping their promise, the Nez Percé refugees committed no hostile acts and bought what they needed from the settlers. This friendly attitude was reciprocated by the people of the Bitterroot Valley, but did nothing more than give the band a false sense of security. Consequently, they leisurely continued on their way south to the Big Hole Valley, where they made camp to rest awhile.

At this time, General Howard was struggling along the Lolo Trail across the Bitterroot Mountains in pursuit. Unknown to the Indians at Big Hole, a new element now entered the picture. A force of 163 regulars and 35 volunteers under the command of Col. John Gibbon had set out from Ft. Shaw, Mont., to intercept the Nez Percé.

On the night of Aug. 8, Gibbon's command arrived at a hill overlooking the unsuspecting Indian village, and at dawn he attacked the sleeping encampment in complete surprise. The soldiers charged, firing as they moved, and forded the shallow steam running in front of the lodges. As they swept into the village, shooting and clubbing men, women, and children, some of the victims were able to seize weapons and ammunition while fleeing to the far side of the encampment and the nearby forest. This group was rallied by White Bird, and standing their ground, fought back desperately against a suddenly faltering line of troops. The commander of the left flank had been killed in the charge,

GIBBON

and it was this portion of the line that began to give way under the surprise resistance from the village.

The soldiers gave ground to the right, confusing others on the right flank who were trying to set fire to the lodges. At that moment, White Bird struck on the right flank causing further confusion and panic among the troops. Gibbon, seeing the panic and having received a leg wound, ordered the command to withdraw to a position across the stream. As the withdrawal took place Gibbon found himself on the defensive as the Nez Percé swarmed after him. Moments later the little command was encircled and fighting for survival.

As the village was abandoned by the soldiers, Joseph rallied the survivors, picked up the dead and wounded, struck lodges, and driving the livestock in front, moved off to the south.

Meanwhile, Gibbon's position had become desperate, as the troops had run out of water. The Indians also captured the howitzer which immediately was run over a steep cliff. The command also lost a valuable pack load of ammunition during the retreat. By 11 that night, and after insuring the safety of the village, the remaining Indian combatants broke contact and performed a rear-guard action as they slowly followed Joseph and their village southward.

Gibbon's command, bloody and battered, was in no condition to follow. They had 33 soldiers dead and 38 others wounded. Of the 17 officers, 14 were casualties, and Howard coming upon them the following day found them in a dazed state, trying to take care of the wounded and burying the dead.

The Indians had also suffered, losing between 60 and 90 people, among whom were Rainbow and Five Wounds. Many of their casualties were women and children.

During the battle, the Nez Percé had set fire to the grass. At the last possible moment the fire changed direction and this was called by those who survived "an act of God," as it saved them all from certain death. Had the Nez Percé war chiefs been able to train their warriors in the use of a howitzer as well as they were trained in infantry and cavalry tactics, the battle might have become a miniature "Little Big Horn."

Coincidentally, Gibbon, upon seeing Howard's advance guard, must have known how Major Reno felt that fateful day on the Little Big Horn, 13½ months before, when Gibbon himself played the role of rescuer.

In retrospect, regarding the Battle of Big Hole, there were a few more Indians than soldiers but only a score or so were battle-experienced. Gibbon had within his command 16 experienced officers and numerous trained men who had the advantage of surprise and momentum. Yet the Nez Percé managed to throw off their attackers once again and in the process almost annihilate them. As a result of this fight, the Nez Percé suffered a serious setback but were able to recover to the point of continuing their flight for another 1,000 miles. Yellow Wolf later stated:

> No Nez Percé were there after those good-bye morning shots. We were not there to see the new soldiers you say came. They must have arrived after we followed the camp. In all the war, General Howard never came where we could see him.

VI. THE BATTLE OF CAMAS CREEK

The Nez Percé fled farther to the southeast and, in desperation, only one way seemed open to them. That was to turn north to Canada where Sitting Bull and the Sioux had fled before them. Looking Glass was blamed for the disaster at Big Hole, and Lean Elk succeeded him as primary war chief.

Howard missed an opportunity to get ahead of the fugitives because of civilian pressure for soldier presence to the south, but in an effort to cut them off before they reached Yellowstone Park he sent a token force under Lieutenant Bacon to Targhee Pass. When Bacon arrived at his destination there was no evidence of Indians, and after waiting several days he vacated the pass. When Howard finally arrived at the pass after the Battle of Camas Creek, he realized that Bacon had failed by being impatient, and the Nez Percé had evaded him again.

As the Nez Percé headed toward Targhee Pass and Yellowstone Park where they intended turning north to Canada, word was brought that Howard was not far behind.

On the night of Aug. 20, Ollokot and three other chiefs, leading approximately 28 warriors, rode into Howard's camp in a column of fours. They were mistaken for Bacon's detachment by the pickets, and before anything could be done, the Indians stampeded the pack mules out of camp. Soon the soldiers were in hot pursuit, but not close enough to prevent a trap being set. This was the Battle of Camas Creek. The soldiers finally managed to extricate themselves from the ambush, but one troop under the command of Captain Norwood was almost annihilated. Only Howard's timely rescue with more troops prevented another disaster. The night had saved them from the Indians' superb marksmanship.

General Howard now had to stop and procure more mules in the local settlements; thus, he lost his chance to overtake his prey as they crossed the Continental Divide and moved into Yellowstone Park.

VII. THE BATTLE OF CANYON CREEK

In Yellowstone Park, the Nez Percé managed to capture several groups of campers including a number of women. They narrowly missed capturing a party of vacationers among whom was Gen. William T. Sherman, the Army's Commanding General. The chiefs would not permit inhumane treatment of their captives, and allowed them to escape as the band made its way across the park.

Having been alerted to the fugitives' whereabouts, the Seventh U.S. Cavalry under the command of Col. Samuel Sturgis attempted to set a trap for the fleeing band in the upper Yellowstone Valley. The Nez Percé bypassed the ambush by going through a mountain wilderness that Sturgis thought was impenetrable, especially to an Indian band driving 2,000 head of horses. When the Nez Percé emerged in their rear, the surprised Seventh Cavalry gave chase with 300 men toward the present-day city of Billings, Mont.

When they were hardest pressed, the Nez Percé scouts for once failed, as they reported a strong force of troops across the shortest and best route north. In reality, it was only a small detachment of cavalry under Lt. Hugh Scott. This information caused the fugitive band to take a long and difficult detour.

STURGIS

Actually, the Nez Percé were assisted by Colonel Sturgis who, after taking a blocking position at the mouth of Clark's Fork, was persuaded to move. Like Bacon at Targhee Pass, Sturgis was several days early and abandoned his watchful waiting after he received reports that the fugitives were moving toward the Shoshone River. He didn't pause to think the they might double back, which they did. These maneuvers by the Nez Percé once again proved that their scouting and deception were excellent.

At Canyon Creek, the band turned north once more and on Sept. 13 the 7th Cavalry overtook them. A desperate fight took place as the Indian rear guard, hiding in gullies and behind rocks, held off the troopers while the women and children with livestock headed for the protection of a narrow canyon. During the fight Sturgis dismounted his men, which proved to be a costly error as this allowed the Nez Percé to escape into the canyon where they were able to build obstacles with boulders and brush, thus preventing the cavalry from following too closely. At dark, with the men tired and running low of ammunition and rations, Sturgis gave up pursuit. He had lost three killed and 11 wounded. The Nez Percé had lost only three, but the long flight was beginning to take its toll. Besides being weary, they were losing horses which, when lame, had to be abandoned. Others were being lost in the hurry to keep moving.

VIII. THE BATTLE OF COW ISLAND

Harassed and fearful of enemies, the Nez Percé intercepted and killed three couriers between Howard's and Sturgis's forces. They next discovered the Crow camp in the Judith Basin, destroyed it, and recaptured some of their horses which had been stolen from them by the Crow.

At Cow Island, the band ran off a frightened sergeant and 12 men at a supply dump located there. After plundering supplies and fighting off a minor attack by a small military force from Ft. Benton, the fugitives headed toward the badlands and rolling prairie, getting ever closer to Canada, the Bear Paw Mountains, and destiny.

IX. THE BATTLE OF BEAR PAW MOUNTAINS.

While the Nez Percé hurried north from Yellowstone Park, Howard sent a message via telegraph to Col. Nelson Miles at Ft. Keogh, Montana Territory (near present-day Miles City) suggesting that they attempt to head off the Nez Percé somewhere south of the Canadian border.

As for the Nez Percé, Yellow Wolf afterwards said, "We knew General Howard was more than two suns back on our trail. It was nothing hard to keep ahead of him."

On Sept. 24, the Nez Percé made an unfortunate change in leadership, which eventually was to lead them to defeat. Whereas Lean Elk was for hurriedly moving and crossing the Canadian border, Looking Glass was again appointed primary chief by the council. He knew Sturgis and Howard were far behind and was for a slower pace.

Upon reaching the Bear Paw Mountains, about 30 miles from the Canadian border, the small band paused to rest, confident the they had outdistanced their pursuers. Unfortunately they had underestimated the modern Army with its telegraph. Colonel Miles, with a force of 600 men, which included portions of the Second and Seventh Cavalry, the mounted Fifth U.S. Infantry, and a body of Cheyenne "warriors," hurried across Montana from Ft. Keogh in the east, to intercept the Nez Percé band.

On the morning of Sept. 30, Cheyenne scouts spotted the Nez Percé camp, and Miles ordered an immediate attack. The Seventh Cavalry, supported by the Fifth Infantry, charged the village, while the Second Cavalry was sent to encircle the camp to cut off escape.

The assault caught the Nez Percé in three groups. The group on the far side of the encampment was able to flee to the north. Some became lost, some were to die of hunger and exposure, and some eventually were to reach Canada in small, wretched groups. The second group, including Joseph, was trapped with the livestock. The third group was in the village which was protected behind a low ridge. This third group commenced firing at their attackers immediately, inflicting heavy casualties among the troops and halting the charge just short of the village. There were 2 officers and 22 soldiers killed in the assault, while 4 more officers and 38 troopers were wounded.

The encircling Second Cavalry had a better time of it as they were able to stampede the livestock, causing the Indians of the second group

MILES

to be split into small elements. A few got away, but most fought back in hand-to-hand combat or sought cover. After dark some of these were to reach the main body defending the village. One-third of their horses had been run off and several of the fighting chiefs had been killed. Among them were Ollokot and Toohoolhoolzote.

Because Colonel Miles had taken heavy casualties in the initial attack, he decided to lay siege to the village rather than risk another assault. In addition, he attempted to cut off the village water supply from the river, but troops detailed for this task reeled back from heavy Indian resistance. As the siege got under way both sides settled down and dug in. It was about this time that the weather turned bitterly cold and on Oct. 1 five inches of snow covered the ground. This added to the suffering of the Indian encampment as they fought for survival.

As the siege continued, Colonel Miles became concerned with a ru-

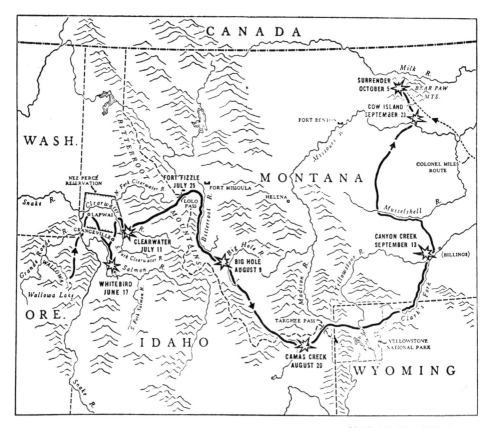

(Map from American Heritage)

The Nez Percé retreat covered 1,300 miles in about four months. Nelson Miles cut them off from Canada and safety.

mor that Sitting Bull and the Sioux were coming to the rescue of the Nez Percé. Hoping to hasten a surrender, under a flag of truce he lured Joseph to the Army camp. Joseph came, as he desired an honorable surrender, but he was seized instead and made a prisoner. The same day, however, one of Miles' officers was captured by the Nez Percé. An exchange was arranged, and Joseph was returned to his people.

On Oct. 4 General Howard and his command arrived at the battlefield. Upon seeing this, and getting promises from Miles that they would be honorably treated and sent back to Idaho, the chiefs held a final council. White Bird and Looking Glass still opposed surrender, but Joseph, pointing to the extreme suffering of the starving women and children, declared he was going to surrender in order to care for his people. As the council broke up, a stray bullet killed Looking Glass, whereupon Joseph mounted a horse and rode toward the Army's position, where the surrender took place.

After dark and while the surrender arrangements were being made, White Bird and a band of unyielding warriors escaped on foot in small groups toward the Canadian border. On the second day they managed to reach their goal and on the following day ran into mounted Indians—Sioux from Sitting Bull's village—who immediately took the fugitives under their care.

It was later discovered that a large Sioux war party, after some differences of opinion as to the location of the Nez Percé, actually had started south to aid the main body of fugitives. They were too late as other fugitives brought news of Joseph's surrender, and the Sioux turned back. It is interesting to speculate what might have happened to Colonel Miles (U.S. Army Commanding General-to-be) and his troops if the Sioux warriors had arrived in time to assist their brothers.

Surrendering with Joseph were 87 warriors—46 of them wounded—and 331 women and children.

Later, Miles wrote to his wife: "The fight was the most fierce of any Indian engagement I have ever been in."

X. CONCLUSION

In all, nine separate commands had participated in the Nez Percé War of 1877. They were the: First, Second, Third, and Seventh Cavalry; the Fifth, Seventh, Eighth, and Twenty-First Infantry; and the Fourth Artillery. Four Civil War generals had also been involved; Generals Howard, Gibbon, Sturgis, and Miles. Altogether there were approximately 500 casualties, which were equally distributed between the warring factions. The total warrior strength of the hostiles had been fewer than 200. However, if women and children are included, the total tribal population at any one time was approximately 700.

The Nez Percé had opposed approximately 5,000 soldiers, of which 2,000 were met in battle. There had been hundreds of civilians involved, and of the total number of whites, about 266 had been killed or wounded. The fugitives had lost 239 in casualties while they had marched almost 2,000 miles without a supply train and carrying a preponderance of noncombatants. They had come within 30 miles of complete success!

General Sherman, as has been already reported, called this war one

(Courtesy Western History Dept., Denver Public Library)
Nez Percé Chief Joseph

of the most extraordinary of which there was any record. He praised the Nez Percé skill in using advance and rear guards, skirmish lines, and field fortifications, and after the uprising in refraining from scalping, mutilating, and wanton slaying of civilians.

In attempts to throw Howard off the trail, the Nez Percé had made several detours. The key point in their strategy had been defense and mobility. The major battles were fought from fixed positions, but mobility had been exercised from within. At White Bird and Clearwater they were ready, as the Army's element of surprise failed. At Big

Hole and Bear Paw, surprise was the key element, but in the former the pause to burn lodges was the Army's undoing. Their reconnoitering and deceptive tactics were superb, while their marksmanship and use of terrain were outstanding. Finally, a combination of physical elements—together with the telegraph—enabled Colonel Miles to achieve victory over a proud and noble Indian nation. This was not the most glamorous chapter in the history of the U.S. Army as it emphasized the fact that the "Indian-Fighting Army" was poor and uninspired. Great numbers of warriors had been used as an excuse to explain the disastrous defeats at Ft. Phil Kearny and the Little Big Horn, but the small Nez Percé band held their own even when the odds were against them. More often than not, the Army's "victories" came from attacks on unsuspecting villages where surprise and overwhelming firepower made the difference.

After Joseph's surrender, the Seventh Cavalry stayed in the field to watch the Sioux and capture as many runaway Nez Percé as possible. The feelings of these men, as well as others in the Department of Dakota, were described in an officer's report: Maj. James S. Brisbin stated that, "Many of the older soldiers say the year of 1877 was the hardest they ever experienced, and if I may be allowed to judge, I will say, I never saw, even during the Civil War, harder or more dangerous service."

XI. EPILOGUE

Joseph's surrender speech was published, and touched the hearts of the American public. Overnight, he became the heroic symbol of his people and their cause. The U.S. government did not, however, return the Nez Percé to the Lapwai Reservation. Instead, they were sent by flatboat and boxcar first to Kansas, then to Indian Territory, where many became sick and died. Nevertheless, public sentiment finally forced the government to return the survivors to the Northwest. In 1885, eight years later, Bear Paw, Joseph and the remnant of his band were sent to the Colville, Wash., reservation. Many attempts were made to resettle them in their beloved Wallowa Valley, but all failed.

In 1904, at the age of 64, Joseph died on the Colville Reservation. Some people say he died of a broken heart. Perhaps he did, as suggested by the following quote from him, date unknown:

> The earth was created by the assistance of the sun, and it should be left as was. . . . The country was made without lines of demarcation and it is no man's business to divide it. . . . The earth and myself are of one main. The

measure of the land and the measure of our bodies are the same. . . . Do not misunderstand me, but understand me fully with reference to my affection for the land. I never said the land was mine to do with as I chose. The one who has the right to dispose of it is the one who created it. I claim the right to live on my land and accord you the privilege to live on yours.

Thus an era passed from the face of the land.

Bibliography

All photos used in chapter courtesy Western History Dept., Denver Public Library.

Beal, Merrill O. *I Will Fight No More, Forever, Chief Joseph and the Nez Percé Wars.* Univ. of Washington Press, Seattle, 1963.

Brown, Dee. *Bury My Heart at Wounded Knee.* Holt, Rinehart and Winston, New York, Chicago, San Francisco, 1970.

Brown, Mark Herbert. *The Flight of the Nez Percé.* Putnam, New York, 1967.

Downey, Fairfax. *Indian-Fighting Army.* Old Army Press, Fort Collins, 1971 (Reprint edition, originally published in 1941).

Gregory, Col. V.J., USAF, Ret. "Sunset on the Lolo Trail." *Military Review,* Vol. XLI, April 1961, No. 4.

Haines, Francis. *The Nez Percés.* First Edition. Univ. of Oklahoma Press, Norman, 1955.

Josephy, Alvin M. Jr. *Chief Joseph's People and Their War.* Yellowstone Library and Museum Association, 1964.

Josephy, Alvin M. Jr. *The Nez Percé and the Opening of the Northwest.* Putnam, N.Y., 1965.

McWhorter, Lucullus Virgil. *Yellow Wolf, Nez Percé Warrior 1865-1935.* The Caxton Printers Ltd., Caldwell, Idaho, 1940.

Wellman, Paul J. *The Indian Wars of the West.* Doubleday and Co., Garden City, New York, (originally published as *Death on Horseback,* 1947).

About the Author

Richard A. Cook retired from the U.S. Army in 1977 with the rank of lieutenant colonel after a distinguished 21-year career which comprised service in Europe; the Far East, including two tours in Vietnam; and the continental United States. He completed his undergraduate work in business administration at New Mexico Military Institute and the University of Idaho, and was graduated in 1956. In 1977, he was awarded an M.A. Degree in American History from Old Dominion University at Norfolk, Va. He is also a 1972 graduate of the U.S. Army Command and General Staff College at Ft. Leavenworth, Kans.

Dick joined the Denver Westerners in 1978 as a Corresponding Member; was elected a Posse Member in 1981, and became Sheriff in 1983. Membership in other organizations includes the Boulder Westerners, the Western Outlaw Lawman Association, the Order of the Indian Wars, the Colorado Horseman's Council, the U.S. Army Ranger Association, the Association of the U.S. Army, and the Retired Officers Association.

Until January 1995, he was Director of Emergency Preparedness for Jefferson County, but is now retired and resides with his wife in Westminster, Colo. He is interested in horses, Indian Wars history, and the great ocean liners of the twentieth century.

"Mountain Railroading" by *Max Smith*

How and Why the Railroads Came to Colorado

By Robert A. LeMassena

I T IS RELATIVELY EASY to determine which railroads came to Colorado, when they did, and where they laid their track. Just how they accomplished their missions is closely associated with why they did what they did. And the reasons are numerous, divergent among railroad companies, as well as within individual companies as the years unfolded. A vast range of human characteristics can be discerned: from generosity to greed, from chicanery to magnanimity, confidence to fear, brilliance to fatuity, from external duress to internal necessity, personal ambition to company politics.

Some railroads were well-considered investments; others were outright promotions. Moreover, more than just private persons were involved. Cities, counties, states and the federal government shared in decisions, as did great banks in Europe and the United States. There were violent encounters among locating crews, track layers, and operating personnel, and verbal battles in courtrooms, local New England offices, and foreign exchange rooms. What was obviously necessary was not always accomplished, and what was accomplished was not always obviously necessary.

At this remote time one would be bold, indeed, to assess the true reasons for how Colorado's earliest railroads developed as they did, even though we have the advantage of hindsight and a knowledge unrestrained by then contemporary limitations. At best, with the available evidence, we can make some reasonable assessments, with the important qualification that they are based on incomplete information.

One of Colorado's most influential railroads, the Denver & Rio Grande, has been intentionally omitted. It didn't come to Colorado, as did the others which form the nucleus of this survey. However, it is mentioned wherever its presence or actions influenced other railroads. It may be mentioned in passing, though, that originally the D&RG was but one of 25 corporations administered by the same group of men, and the whole corporate structure initially possessed more the appearances of a land-promotion scheme than that of a public transport facility.

In the various accounts, the author has deliberately substituted the names of familiar railroads for their unfamiliar subsidiaries, all in the interest of a better understanding. For example: Chicago, Rock Island & Pacific replaces Chicago, Kansas & Nebraska, and Colorado Springs replaces nearby Colorado City. (For those who desire a more exact nomenclature two sources are recommended: *Colorado Railroads — Chronological Development,* by T. E. Wilkins; and *Colorado's Mountain Railroads,* by R. A. LeMassena.) Also, for individual railroads, there exist adequate accounts of their construction, though most are out of print. The reader is cautioned to keep in mind the point of view of the various authors, who range from public relations men to hate-invoking officials on the public payroll.

ATCHISON, TOPEKA & SANTA FE

Initiated as a local railroad, the Atchison & Topeka saw visions of expansion to Santa Fe, N.M., after an infusion of capital funds from Eastern bankers, to capture freight traffic moving along this route. Yet a decade was to pass before the renamed railroad (AT&SF) reached the Colorado-Kansas boundary in 1873. Meanwhile, its immediate objectives had been altered, and instead of building toward Santa Fe through a region of sparse traffic, AT&SF redirected its rails to Pueblo, Colo., where they terminated in 1876. Traffic could be interchanged there with the Denver & Rio Grande, which operated a narrow-gauge line to Denver, and Pueblo was the gateway for a water-grade route into the heart of Colorado's precious metal-mining areas.

Still aware of its original objective, the AT&SF built next a main line from La Junta through Trinidad, and reached the Colorado-New Mexico line atop Raton Pass at the end of 1878. In the interim it had clashed with the D&RG's surveyors on the pass and in the Grand Canyon of the Arkansas River [Royal Gorge] west of Cañon City. In an attempt to eliminate further annoyance, it leased the D&RG in 1878, leaving itself free to build up the Arkansas to Leadville. During 1879 track was laid through the canyon between Cañon City and Texas Creek, and considerable grading was accomplished beyond. But

(From Collection of Jackson C. Thode)

This handsome 10-wheeled passenger locomotive was placed in service by the Atchison, Topeka & Santa Fe in 1892, and no doubt saw use on the Colorado lines of AT&SF between La Junta-Pueblo-Denver. (Locomotive was built in 1892 at Dunkirk, N.Y., and retired in 1923.)

domination of the D&RG was short-lived. By 1880 the smaller company had extricated itself from the lease, and in the ensuing settlement had purchased the AT&SF track and grade west of Cañon City. Thus, unable to penetrate Colorado's mineral kingdom, the AT&SF extended its intended Pueblo-Cañon City link only to Clelland, thence to a coal mine at Rockvale.

The AT&SF saved itself the trouble of building a line to Denver by inducing the D&RG to add a standard-gauge third rail to its track, and to acquire a few standard-gauge locomotives to haul AT&SF freight and passenger trains between the two cities. This arrangement lasted until 1887, when the AT&SF abrogated the terms of the agreement and entered Denver over its own rails. In the next year, the AT&SF reached coal mines at Kenwood beyond Rockvale, and some others at Cañon City.

Traffic on the line to Denver had not met expectations; hence in 1890 when the AT&SF found that the Colorado Midland was for sale, it bought the trans-mountain carrier. In effect, this acquisition put the AT&SF into the mining centers of Leadville and Aspen, and linked it with the highly independent Rio Grande Western at Grand Junction, where cars could roll through to Salt Lake City and Ogden, Utah, served by the Union Pacific's system. Whatever advantage was derived from this extension of influence was nullified by the financial panic of 1893, causing the failure of the AT&SF and the CM. The AT&SF was reorganized in 1895, but when the CM underwent a similar rearrangement of its obligations two years later, the AT&SF's equity was found to be without value.

Agriculture appeared to offer greater rewards than mining, a premise which induced the AT&SF to construct a secondary line along the northern side of the Arkansas River between Holly and Rocky Ford, Colo., completing it in 1908. Similar considerations in 1927 brought a long branch across the Colorado-Kansas boundary to Pritchett in southeastern Colorado. A decade later the AT&SF built a connection from Las Animas toward Amarillo, Texas. This line, crossing Oklahoma's Panhandle, was the last major railroad project in Colorado.

CHICAGO, BURLINGTON & QUINCY

The Chicago, Burlington & Quincy as a matter of corporate policy believed in agriculture to generate traffic for its manifold lines on the Great Plains. However, its otherwise conservative management felt impelled to extend a line westward to Denver. By so doing, it hoped to participate in the enormous long-haul traffic resulting from the silver-mining boom in Colorado's mountains. Accordingly, track crossed the Colorado-Nebraska line in 1881, and in the following year the rails reached Denver, the last spike being driven at Barr City. In 1882, the CB&Q also acquired the Denver, Golden & Salt Lake Railroad, which provided a bypass around Denver's new Union Station to a connection with railroads entering Denver from the south.

In 1887 the CB&Q obtained control of the narrow gauge Denver, Utah & Pacific, which hauled coal from mines along its line to Longmont, and building stone from quarries around Lyons. Outwardly there was nothing unusual in this acquisition, but the DU&P possessed a partially completed grade along the base of the mountains and into South Boulder Creek Canyon. Some additional work had been done farther up the canyon, at Yankee Doodle Lake, and several locations along the Colorado River, and surveys had been made as far as Glenwood Springs, much of this financed by the CB&Q through the DU&P's corporate structure. Lyons, also, was considered as an entry for a trans-mountain route leading eventually to Salt Lake City. Nothing came of either venture, but that part of the DU&P between

Utah Junction and Longmont was relocated and the entire railroad converted to standard gauge in 1889.

While its surveyors were exploring Colorado's mountains, its track gangs were building still another western outlet during 1887. Located between the CB&Q's route to Denver and the Union Pacific's main line, the new track crossed the Colorado Central at Sterling and terminated in Cheyenne, Wyo. This allowed the CB&Q to compete for transcontinental business, a supposition which was more imaginative than factual, because of the UP's logical unwillingness to short-haul itself without acceptable remuneration.

A corporate reorganization of the UP in 1890 yielded, among other things, the Union Pacific, Denver & Gulf railroad, an amalgamation of UP properties stretching from Wyoming through Colorado, New Mexico, and Texas to Fort Worth. This system had been severed from the UP in 1898 at the end of UP's receivership, and had been joined with the Denver, Leadville & Gunnison and some other companies to form an independent north-south trunk line of strategic importance, the Colorado & Southern. To protect itself the CB&Q built a connection from Alliance, Neb., crossing the UP at Sidney, Neb., and into Colorado to Sterling. UP track was used for several miles to Union, when a short segment was built to Brush on the CB&Q's main line into Denver. Completed in 1900, this was the CB&Q's last principal new trackage in Colorado.

Two giants, the Great Northern, and Northern Pacific railroads now entered Colorado, by the back door, so to speak. In 1901 they acquired the CB&Q, giving them access to Chicago, St. Louis, Kansas City, and Omaha, as well as Denver. They were intrigued by the C&S, which would give them a route from Billings, Mont., to Houston, Texas, on the Gulf of Mexico, and in 1908 they arranged for the CB&Q to acquire the C&S. Indirectly, this put the CB&Q in unexpected locations: Vasquez, N.M.; Baldwin, Leadville, and Graymont, Colo., all on C&S trackage, and in Grand Junction (half interest in the Colorado Midland), and Cripple Creek (ownership of the Colorado Springs & Cripple Creek District). Two wholly owned subsidiaries of the C&S were the 2-foot gauge Gilpin tramway in the Blackhawk-Central City district, and the Denver & Interurban electric interurban line between Denver and Boulder. This acquisition of the C&S system by the CB&Q put the latter railroad in second place behind the Denver & Rio Grande for route mileage in Colorado.

CHICAGO, ROCK ISLAND & PACIFIC

Last of the "trunkline" railroads to cross the prairie and enter Colorado was the Chicago, Rock Island & Pacific, which arrived too late to attain any of its corporate objectives. With six routes belonging to four powerful railroad companies penetrating its eastern boundary, Colorado lacked neither competition nor capacity to handle the state's inbound and outbound traffic. Every practical path through the Rocky Mountains was already occupied by a satellite of the Union Pacific, the Denver & Rio Grande, or the Colorado Midland, an independent railroad having its eastern terminus at Colorado Springs.

Apparently believing that it could purchase the CM, the CRI&P sent its track layers westward from the Colorado-Kansas line to Colorado Springs in 1888, just as the CM was being completed to Aspen and New Castle.

(From Collection of Jackson C. Thode)

The Chicago, Rock Island & Pacific displayed its "Silver Engine" at the Columbian Exposition in 1893. It is a splendid example of early locomotive design and construction, but it is doubtful this machine ever graced the Colorado prairies with its presence.

Immediately upon arrival at Colorado Springs, the CRI&P arranged to operate its trains to Denver and Pueblo over the D&RG, and in 1889, began to run them into Denver over the UP from their junction at Limon. A year later, when the Atchison, Topeka & Santa Fe added the CM to its system, the CRI&P's westward expansion through Colorado was forever halted. Eventually, it joined with the Southern Pacific in New Mexico, and thus was able to participate in transcontinental traffic.

COLORADO CENTRAL

It would not be stretching a point to state that the Colorado Central originated within Colorado's boundaries, and came into the state as well. Its beginnings can be traced back to 1865, when plans embraced a route connecting gold mines in upper Clear Creek Canyon, coal mines north of Golden, and farms southeast of Denver. Very quickly, however, the company's incorporators felt that their plans were too modest to be worthwhile. The farm branch was projected into Kansas; the coal line should connect with the Union Pacific's main line at Julesburg; and the Clear Creek track should surmount Berthoud Pass and terminate somewhere in Utah. Being a subsidiary of the Union Pacific put a damper on such unbounded enthusiasm, and nothing was accomplished until 1870 after the Denver Pacific had completed its track from Cheyenne to Denver. Promptly thereafter the CC was allowed to build a connecting line from Denver to Golden.

In 1872 a narrow-gauge railroad was built from Golden through Clear Creek Canyon to the gold-mining community of Black Hawk. A supply of coal was made available by adding a narrow-gauge third rail to the standard-gauge track from Golden to Arapahoe, then adding a narrow-gauge spur to the mine. In the following year a standard-gauge third rail was added to the spur, and standard-gauge track was laid to Longmont, presumably as the initial part of a line to Julesburg.

This arrangement of trackage soon proved to be unsatisfactory to shippers and passengers, the latter having been obliged to change trains in Golden. Coal, coming from points on the Denver & Rio Grande's narrow-gauge line, was transferred to standard-gauge cars at Denver, then retransferred at Golden, as was the coal which had come from the Denver & Boulder Valley's track east of Boulder. But the UP and CC were indisposed to alleviate the inconveniences until 1877,

(Courtesy Western History Dept., Denver Public Library)

The early Colorado Central, despite its primitive equipment, was a vital lifeline for Golden, Black Hawk, Central City, Idaho Springs, and Georgetown. Photographer Charles Weitfle captured these views in Clear Creek Canyon about 1880. (Top photo is a "mixed train." In bottom picture, buggy with three passengers must have been an early-day "piggyback shipment.")

when Golden was provided with a direct connection to the UP's main-line by means of a link between Hazard, Wyo., and Longmont. By the end of 1878 the narrow-gauge rails had reached Georgetown and Central City, and the three-rail track east of Golden was moved to the north, thus making Golden a through (instead of a sub) station. It was not until 1879 that the narrow-gauge third rail was added to the track all the way to Denver. In the meantime, the Golden City & South Platte had been organized to provide a bypass around Denver from Golden to Acequia on the D&RG. Considerable grading had been done, but when the narrow-gauge third rail was added to the track to Denver, the GC&SP was redundant; only a couple of miles of track to a clay pit south of Golden, laid in 1879, was its total accomplishment.

Golden was understandably jubilant in 1880 when the CC began to lay rails west from Julesburg along the South Platte River, but this changed to dismay in 1881, the junction having been made at La Salle on the UP's (formerly Denver Pacific) Denver-Cheyenne track. In 1884 there appeared to be some hope that the CC was on its way to Utah when track was built beyond Georgetown toward Loveland Pass; but, it terminated forever at Graymont.

Because the UP had acquired the Denver Pacific's line between Denver and Cheyenne in 1880, there was little need for the paralleling CC route. Some track at the southern end was removed in 1888, and in 1889 that portion north of Fort Collins was removed. Then, in 1890, the CC was combined with several other railroads in the UP domain to form a north-south trunk-line, the Union Pacific Denver & Gulf.

Closely associated with the CC were three subsidiary railroads. The earliest and largest was the Greeley, Salt Lake & Pacific, whose rails (despite the grandiose implications of its name) barely penetrated the foothills north of Denver. Its first line connected a stone quarry at Stout with Fort Collins in 1881, and in 1882 it completed a line from there to Greeley on the UP. In the following year its (narrow-gauge) rails ascended a steep canyon west of Boulder to reach precious metal mines at Sunset. In 1887 a branch was added to another quarry at Atkins, northwest of Loveland. The Denver & Middle Park brought coal from Glencoe to Golden in 1884, and in that year the Georgetown, Breckenridge & Leadville, presumably heading for the rich gold and silver mining country beyond Loveland Pass, extended track west of Georgetown to Graymont, where it terminated permanently.

DENVER PACIFIC, KANSAS ROUTE

The deliberate bypassing of Denver by the Union Pacific, for what was considered justifiable cause, resulted in the formation of a local company which intended to construct the Denver Pacific, a railroad linking Denver and Cheyenne, Wyo., on the UP's main line. Grading of the roadbed commenced at Denver in 1868, but it was not until 1869 when track was laid, beginning at Cheyenne and ending at Denver in 1870. This was Colorado's second railroad, the first having been the Union Pacific, which in 1867 dipped into the territory's northeastern corner.

Those who promoted and financed the Denver Pacific did so more from considerations of municipal necessity and economic survival than from any fervent desire to indulge in the business of railroad transportation. This may have been the reason why the owners of the DP leased the railroad to the Kansas Pacific, upon its completion.

Almost simultaneously, the KP began to build its main line from the Colorado-Kansas boundary toward Denver. Originally, the intent was for it to connect with the UP at the 100th meridian, but its promoters saw little profit in such a venture, and delayed construction until they received congressional approval to the make the connection west of Denver's meridian.

(From Collection of Jackson C. Thode)

Denver & Rio Grande's 3-foot-gauge "Shou wa no," with six driving wheels, was the first freight locomotive on the railroad. Picture was taken at the Baldwin Locomotive Works in Philadelphia, where it was built in June 1871.

KP track gangs met those of the DP, building eastward from Denver, at Strasburg on Aug. 15, 1870, thereby completing the first ocean-to-ocean rail route, an event which was somewhat of an anti-climax to the completion of the Pacific Railway (Union Pacific-Central Pacific) in Utah in 1869.

The DP had been wise enough to build a branch through the coal fields between Brighton and Boulder, where, coincidentally in 1873, a junction was made with the newly constructed Colorado Central line from Golden to Longmont. The KP was not nearly so successful with its southwestward extension from Kit Carson to Las Animas in 1873, and beyond to Swink in 1875. It quickly became obvious to the KP that it could not afford to compete with the Atchison, Topeka & Santa Fe in that territory, and the tracks were taken up in 1877.

Though the DP and KP were beneficial to Denver and its rival, Golden, the traffic handled by those two railroads was not sufficiently remunerative to keep them viable, and both failed financially. This situation gave financier and railroad speculator Jay Gould an opportunity to make a financial killing. He purchased the securities of the DP and KP at give-away prices, then threatened the UP with a rate-war east of Denver and a trans-mountain extension westward to Ogden. The UP's management, for some inexplicable reason, accepted Gould's bluff at face value, and purchased from him the KP and DP securities at par value. In 1880 the UP absorbed the two companies, giving it a monopoly of transportation between Denver and the East.

MISSOURI PACIFIC

A railroad, whose board of directors included such financial giants and manipulators as Russell Sage, Jay Gould, Samuel Sloan, Sidney Dillon, and Fred Ames, could not possibly be in business for any other purpose than the making of as much money as possible for its owners, who, for the most part, were those same individuals. Expansion, acquisitions, traffic, and competition were all secondary considerations in the quest for profits, which eventually reposed in the Missouri Pacific's treasury prior to distribution to the unholy alliance of ambitious financiers. Their specialty was the exploitation of troubled railroads, one of which was the Denver & Rio Grande, a narrow-gauge system in Colorado operating a three-rail track between Pueblo and Denver, primarily for the benefit of the Atchison, Topeka & Santa Fe.

The D&RG had just emerged from its first financial reorganization, and it was encompassed by standard-gauge competitors who could siphon off every bit of its freight traffic, except that of local nature in the mountains of Colorado. Without a friendly connection to the East the D&RG would remain in a precarious financial position, a situation which the MP's directors perceived. Consequently, they authorized the construction of a long line across Kansas and into Colorado, connecting with the D&RG at Pueblo, and completed in 1887. This corporate gesture gave the MP a route into Denver (just vacated by the AT&SF) and a possible outlet at Salt Lake City and Ogden, Utah, for westward expansion. The new line may not have been sufficiently profitable as an operating railroad, but its value in corporate manipulations was beyond calculation.

By 1890 standard-gauge trains were running into Grand Junction; by 1900 the MP was in complete control of the D&RG, and by 1910 the MP's system stretched all the way to the Pacific Ocean. It is interesting to note that the MP owned 50 percent of the D&RGW between 1924, having bought it from the Western Pacific Railroad Corp., until 1947 when the D&RGW was reorganized.

UNION PACIFIC

Union Pacific's management—those men directing the railroad's location, construction and financing—avoided Colorado as an element of policy, and accepted a few miles of track passing through the state's northeastern corner in 1867 as a matter of expediency. At that time the UP was building westward in great haste, in a massive effort to complete its portion of the Pacific Railway, joining Omaha, Neb., on the Missouri River with Sacramento, Calif., on the Sacramento River.

The route had followed the Platte River, and it could have continued to follow the South Platte right into Denver, a source of revenue traffic. However, the UP's main line turned back into Nebraska and passed through Cheyenne, Wyo., an event which made several Denver citizens so dubious of their city's future that they moved to Cheyenne.

Regardless of the fundamental factors which influenced its decision, the UP was faced with a choice between a traffic-less but relatively easy line across southern Wyoming to Ogden, Utah, or one which yielded some financial return, but which meant the route would have to surmount either Berthoud or Jones Pass. Either pass would have entailed exceedingly difficult construction and expensive operation, consuming far more time, money, and man-hours than the UP's managers felt they could allocate from an ever-meager treasury. (See note at the end.)

Jay Gould, who had acquired control of the UP in 1873, was responsible for the building of the Colorado Central line between Cheyenne and Denver, paralleling that of the Denver Pacific. This, plus his financial manipulations in DP and Kansas Pacific securities, enabled Gould to engineer the failure of the DP and Kansas Pacific securities, and their acquisition by the UP in 1880, at a substantial personal profit to himself.

These two railroads, the second and third to enter Colorado, gave the Union Pacific a near-monopoly of rail transportation to and from the state.

Other Gould-conceived machinations resulted in a lease of the CC in 1879, and the purchase of the Denver, South Park & Pacific (narrow gauge) railroad, plus a few other small companies, in 1880.

During the 1880s decade the UP spread its system throughout Colorado's north-central sector by means of wholly owned or controlled subsidiaries, the principal ones having been the Denver, Leadville & Gunnison (reorganized Denver, South Park & Pacific), and the Union Pacific, Denver & Gulf, a north-south artery extending from Wyoming to Texas (See separate account of UPD&G.)

The financial panic of 1893 caused the collapse of the UP system in that same year, and five years later, when the UP was reorganized, the railroad trackage in Colorado consisted primarily of the former DP and KP, plus the CC line between La Salle and Julesburg. Subsequently, the UP added only short branches, principally in agriculture country, to its lines in Colorado—to Briggsdale and Purcell in 1910 and Buckeye in 1924.

In 1936 the Union Pacific acquired the Laramie, North Park & Western railroad running from Laramie, Wyo., to coal mines at Coalmont, Colo., and absorbed it into the UP's corporate edifice in 1951.

Even before the Union Pacific was completed there were charges that fantastic profits were being made from its construction, and that the federal government was the victim of financial sleight-of-hand. Precisely the opposite was claimed by others. It would seem that anyone who wished to grind a personal axe could do so, using the Union Pacific as the whetstone, and a century later the opinions and analyses still continued.

It is the author's opinion that all of these investigations excepting one were based on incomplete information or inaccurate analysis, and were therefore faulty in their conclusions.

The one exception was the investigation by Robert W. Fogel, published by Johns Hopkins Press in 1960 as *The Union Pacific Railroad:
A Case of Premature Enterprise.* Fogel omitted nothing, and his
analysis followed the modern-day accounting technique of simulta-
neous present-worth comparison to determine optimum financial
strategy.

He concluded that no one involved in the construction, financing,
and investing in the UP really knew what they were doing at the time.
Yet they all received reasonable returns on their investments or contributions, just as though the entire undertaking had been planned with
that objective in mind. He noted further that no one would pay much
attention to his scholarly and rigorous analysis. He felt the "ancient
myths" were much more colorful and thus acceptable to the public.

UNION PACIFIC, DENVER & GULF

Just about everyone thinks of the Union Pacific railroad as always
having been an east-west oriented carrier. Hardly anybody is aware
that for several years it owned and operated a north-south line from
central Wyoming extending to the Gulf of Mexico. Prior to 1890 it
was a loose assemblage of subsidiary companies and until the end of
1898 they were consolidated under the corporate title of Union Pacific,
Denver & Gulf.

The oldest element in the UPD&G's structure was the Colorado
Central (See separate account of CC) and its subsidiaries. Its trackage
lay between Denver and Cheyenne, with an isolated line stretching
from La Salle to Julesburg, Colo. The CC's period of activity began
in 1870, and very little was done after 1881.

Between Denver and Pueblo the track belonged to the Denver,
Texas & Gulf, which was an 1886 reorganization of the Denver & New
Orleans (D&NO). This latter company had spiked down its rails
during 1881 and 1882, providing a second line between Denver and
Pueblo—actually a third if the Atchison, Topeka & Santa Fe, running
over the Denver & Rio Grande is counted. Never released from possession by its contractors, the overly ambitious D&NO failed, and was
brought into the UP's domain.

South of Trinidad, as far as the New Mexico-Texas border, the
Denver, Texas & Fort Worth provided a connection with the Fort
Worth & Denver City railroad to Fort Worth, Texas. Both of these

companies were backed by the Union Pacific. Accommodating its standard-gauge rival, as it had done the AT&SF in 1881, the D&RG added a standard-gauge third rail to its track from Pueblo to Trinidad during 1887-1888, allowing the DT&FtW to begin construction. The northern and southern portions of this lengthy route were joined at Alps, N.M., in 1888.

A long branch of the DT&FtW went to Martinsen in the forest southwest of Trinidad, and short ones were built to coal mines north and south of Trinidad in Colorado.

The northernmost segment of the UPD&G was the Cheyenne & Northern constructed from Cheyenne in 1887 to Wendover, Wyo. A connection with the Chicago & Northwestern at Orin Junction, Wyo., was effected later.

A direct line between Denver and Boulder (instead of the circuitous one of the CC through Golden) was completed in 1886.

The UPD&G's major undertaking was the completion of its own line between Trinidad and Walsenburg in 1895. This was accomplished by connecting several short branches and spurs to coal mines situated west of the D&RG's route. Even with this addition, the UPD&G did not possess a continuous route through Colorado. That part of the CC north of Fort Collins had been broken before 1890. Consequently, the UPD&G used UP track between Greeley and Cheyenne.

Moreover, because the route to Denver via the branch from Greeley to Fort Collins was so circuitous, the UP's much shorter line was utilized instead. (The gap from Pueblo to Walsenburg was not completed until 1911, when the Colorado & Southern and D&RG built a joint double-track.)

Having insufficient traffic to sustain it, the UPD&G went into receivership in 1894. Its reorganization was consummated at the end of 1898, at which time it was combined with the (narrow-gauge) Denver, Leadville & Gunnison to form a completely independent system, the Colorado & Southern which a decade later was brought under control of the Chicago, Burlington & Quincy's organization.

SUMMARY

AT&SF — The Atchison, Topeka & Santa Fe's main line traversed Colorado's southeastern quadrant as part of a route between Kansas City and the Pacific Ocean.

Thwarted in an attempt to extend a long line into Colorado's mining regions, the company settled for branches to Denver and coal mines south of Cañon City. By acquiring the Colorado Midland, AT&SF not only reached Leadville and Aspen, but also gained an outlet at Ogden, Utah, over the connecting Rio Grande Western.

Unfortunately, the CM was lost after a very few years of association. Subsequently, secondary lines serving the agricultural area of southeastern Colorado were added, one of them having been a direct link between Amarillo, Texas, and La Junta. The AT&SF was controlled by financiers in New England, and it does not appear evident that their interests extended beyond the business of railroad transportation on a grand scale.

CB&Q — By building a line into Denver, the Chicago, Burlington & Quincy gave that city its first single-management connection with Chicago, and by acquiring the Denver, Utah & Pacific it was in a position to build a line through the Rocky Mountains, with the expectation of reaching Salt Lake City or Ogden. The expense and difficulty of construction caused these plans to be abandoned, but meanwhile the CB&Q added a new line angling across Colorado's northeastern corner into Cheyenne.

The formation of the independent Colorado & Southern caused the CB&Q to build parallel trackage from Alliance, Neb., to the main line at Brush. The Great Northern, and Northern Pacific bought the CB&Q, then arranged for the latter to acquire the C&S and its satellite, the Fort Worth & Denver City. In recent years the CB&Q, GN, and NP were merged to form the Burlington Northern, the C&S remaining separate, but controlled. The CB&Q was managed by conservative investors, ancillary operations in land having been conducted primarily to provide sources of continuing traffic. Subsequently, the CB&Q acted as a member of the GN and NP systems.

CRI&P — The Chicago, Rock Island & Pacific should not have been built into Colorado, but apparently its management felt that the Colorado Midland could be acquired, providing a trans-mountain route toward the Pacific. Neither objective was attained, however. After the Dotsero Cutoff was constructed, this line became a freight-traffic connection with the Denver & Rio Grande Western. This was an example of ill-advised and over-enthusiastic intentions.

CC — During all but the first few years of its corporate life the Colorado Central was an instrument of the Union Pacific's Directorate, doing whatever that group wished to further individual personal interests in local politics, financial raiding, and ruinous competition.

The narrow-gauge line was truly an economic necessity for the mining industry a short distance west of Denver, but the standard-gauge line between Golden and Cheyenne, Wyo., was constructed solely to assure the failure of the paralleling Denver Pacific. The line between La Salle and Julesburg benefitted only the UP, and the extension of narrow-gauge track beyond Georgetown was an abortive attempt to reach Leadville.

Of little utility to the Union Pacific, excepting the La Salle-Julesburg track, the CC and its satellites were integrated into the UP-controlled Union Pacific, Denver & Gulf system.

DP-KP — The Denver Pacific was a project of Denver businessmen to provide a railroad outlet for Denver. Originally, it appears that the Kansas Pacific was intended more as a means of profiting from granted land than as a transportation link between Denver and Kansas City.

The branch to Swink was a quickly retracted attempt to invade Atchison, Topeka & Santa Fe territory. Jay Gould used them to enhance his personal fortune by manipulating their securities. The amalgamation of the DP, KP and UP gave the UP a virtual monopoly of transport in Colorado until new competitors appeared.

MP — When the narrow-gauge Denver & Rio Grande found itself without a friendly connection to handle through traffic, Jay Gould had his railroad build a line to Pueblo, roughly parallel to that of the Atchison, Topeka & Santa Fe, from Kansas City, Mo. This long branch was of little traffic value other than a link between the Missouri Pacific and the D&RG, which the MP later controlled, and profited from the latter's prosperity.

Using the D&RG and the Rio Grande Western as steppingstones, the MP "system" reached the Pacific Ocean over the Western Pacific, the D&RG's Western Extension. Despite financial upheavals, the MP directly or indirectly maintained its grip on the D&RG (and its successor, D&RGW) until the Trusteeship which eliminated the MP's control. Since that time the MP line across eastern Colorado has been virtually an extension of D&RGW's lines from Denver and Ogden, Utah.

UP — The Union Pacific preferred to build its main line through southern Wyoming. It then gained control of the Colorado Central, giving it an entry into Denver and the mining region in the nearby mountains.

The acquisition of the Denver, South Park & Pacific provided access to mining areas in the center of the state, competing with the Denver & Rio Grande. Jay Gould engineered the failure of the Denver Pacific and Kansas Pacific, which were merged with the Union Pacific.

A corporate rearrangement of the UP resulted in the amalgamation of several subsidiaries as the (controlled) Union Pacific, Denver & Gulf, which the UP lost in its own financial collapse. Therefore, the UP constructed only branch lines in the agricultural territory north of Denver.

There seems to be little doubt that the UP was used by its directors and officers to enhance their personal fortunes by security manipulation, rate-hiking, and unfair competition. These practices ended when a new management rehabilitated the UP, and used it as the cornerstone of a great system.

UPS&G — The Union Pacific, Southern & Gulf was an amalgamation of Union Pacific-controlled companies, forming a north-south system.

The UP lost control when the UPS&G became the major element of the newly formed independent Colorado & Southern, which was acquired by, but not merged with, the Chicago, Burlington & Quincy. Its trackage in Colorado has shrunk greatly, and it is now an unmerged subsidiary of the Burlington Northern.

About the Author

Robert A. LeMassena, who wrote the chapter, "How and Why the Railroads Came to Colorado," was elected as the 1994 recipient of the Railroad History Award, in the category of Senior Achievement, presented by the Railway & Locomotive Historical Society. The award came in recognition of LeMassena's many books and articles on North America's steam locomotives.

An accomplished design engineer, LeMassena was born in Newark, N.J., in 1914, and attended grammar and high schools in Orange, N.J. He was graduated from the Stevens Institute of Technology, Hoboken, N.J., with a mechanical engineering degree. He worked at Bell Telephone Laboratories 1936-1947 in the design of the radiotelephone and Navy radar equipment. He moved to Denver in 1948, and married Caroline Willson in 1952. He worked for Heiland Research Co. and Honeywell until 1962, then became self-employed.

He wrote and published *Colorado's Mountain Railroads* (in five volumes), 1963-1966; *Union Pacific in Colorado*, 1967. He wrote texts for 1,000 railroad-subject collectors' cards, 1970-1974; and authored *Rio Grande . . . to the Pacific*, 1974.

Also, *Articulated Steam Locomotives of North America* (two vols.), 1979 and 1991; *Colorado's Mountain Railroads*, revised 1984; *American Steam*, Vol.1, 1987; Vol. 2, 1989; *America's Workhouse Locomotive*, 1993; and *Union Pacific Official Color Photos*, 1993.

The author said a book about large steam locomotives is being published as well as a book about learning Spanish. He has also written more than 100 articles, mostly about railroad motive power, for magazines and books published by Sundance Publications, Denver, and the Colorado Railroad Museum.

He has been a member and president of the Rocky Mountain Railroad Club, and a member of the Colorado Railroad Museum, and the Railway & Locomotive Historical Society (since 1940).

"I have ridden on 200 different railroads, about 50,000 unduplicated miles," Bob recalls. "Also several 'last runs' on railroads in Colorado, including the last streetcar in Denver (July 2, 1950). I've ridden on more steam locomotives than I can remember."

MONTCLAIR

Colorado.

The Beautiful

SUBURBAN TOWN

Of Denver, Colo., U. S. A.

Montclair 1885 Prospectus from *Tom Noel Collection*

Moral Geography in Denver;

Streetcars, Suburbs & Saloons

By Thomas J. Noel

*D*URING THE DECADE after the 1859 Gold Rush, Denver was a flash in the pan. Between 1860 and 1870, the "Queen City of the Plains" gained only 10 residents. Only after the arrival of the "iron horse" in 1870 did the long-predicted boom materialize. The city's population soared from 4,759 in 1870 to 35,629 in 1880, according to the federal census.

As dozens of railroads built steel spiderwebs into Denver's Rocky Mountain hinterland, the city became a center for ore processing and agriculture, for commerce and tourism. Denverites struggled to provide every conceivable service and any merchandise that the people of the Rockies might want. Consequently, by 1890 Denver was firmly established as the regional metropolis and, among Western cities, was behind only Omaha and San Francisco in population, with 106,713 residents.

If the railroad triggered this explosion, it was the horse railway, or streetcar, that enabled the city to expand. Elevators and high-rise construction techniques were unknown in 1870; the city had to grow out rather than up. Suburbanization in Denver—as in most of America—began with the nineteenth-century streetcar, not the twentieth-century automobile. After moving to these new streetcar suburbs, many citizens began to take a critical look at the most common institution of the old frontier town—the saloon.

Saloons became the symbol and the scapegoat of urban problems which speeded suburbanization, as the following sketch of the Mile High City's streetcar growth will reveal. By 1890, Denver's population density surpassed Washington, Kansas City, Minneapolis, St. Paul, and Omaha.[1] The population boom after the arrival of the railroad made Denver a congested metropolis short on housing. Wide-awake developers saw the demand and began platting "additions," as the nineteenth century called its subdivisions.

View in 1875 from 14th and Larimer streets. From Larimer (then Denver's main street) car lines radiated to suburbs. (Wood engraving exaggerates width and skyline.)

The key to successful suburbanization, as developers soon discovered, was the streetcar. They built these street railways to carry the first suburbanites out to the new prairie tracts, and then back to the jobs, markets, and amusements of the city. When thousands of house-hungry Denverites began moving into the new additions, businesses also began to move out, just as they had rearranged themselves in the path of the stageline and the railroad. Passengers disembarking at the rural end of Denver's first streetcars soon found taverns and other businesses there.

In 1871, the Denver Horse Railway Company completed the city's first streetcar line. Its tracks ran up Larimer Street to 16th Street, along 16th to Champa Street, then up Champa to Denver's first streetcar suburb, Curtis Park.[2] At the end of the line on 27th Street stood a roadhouse. Originally called Shaffenburg Park after its founder, the tavern changed its name in the 1870s to the National Park. "None but the purest and best liquors," boasted National Park manager William Wise[3]. This amiable German, born in Stuttgart in 1835, had done a lot of traveling and, like some other westerners, was known to his creditors in the East as "worthless and behind in payments."[4] Yet Denverites liked this pipe-smoking pioneer and his German-accented tales of fighting Colorado Indians back in the 1860s. When the first home-builders settled in Curtis Park during the 1870s, they celebrated at Billy Wise's. By the 1880s, they could amuse themselves in several other saloons that moved into Denver's first suburb.

Horses or mules powered Denver's second streetcar line down 15th Street, over the South Platte River bridge and then tugged passengers up the river's steep northwest bank to North Denver. There, on a dusty, deep-rutted path known as "The Boulevard" (later Federal), the route ended on a turntable in front of the Grand View House.[5] The Grand View's elegant saloon easily outclassed the ramshackle old Highland House down by the river, but it soon found a rival in the nearby Highland Park Hotel. The Chapin brothers uncorked champagne for the grand opening of the Highland Park shortly after the first horsecar pulled up in front of the Grand View in 1873.[6]

North Denver housed little but the Rocky Mountain Brewery during the 1860s, but that changed with the streetcar's arrival. Philip Zang, who once wheelbarrowed Rocky Mountain Brewery beer over to Denver, was among the first to capitalize on improved streetcar transportation. He bought the old brewery, rechristened it Zang's, and soon made it the region's largest producer. Near the brewery and along the streetcar tracks, homes appeared and taverns proliferated. By the 1890s a business district had sprung up along 15th Street with large three-story buildings which towered over Denver across the river.[7]

Denver's third streetcar route ran southeast on 16th Street to Broadway, then swung south to Cherry Creek. After the area became accessible by streetcar, it was selected as the site of the 1882 National Mining and Industrial Exhibition at Broadway and what became Exposition Avenue. Silver baron Horace A. W. Tabor, prime promoter of this showcase for Colorado's minerals and manufactures, called the show "the grandest thing that ever occurred in this great West."[8] Despite Tabor's inflated oratory, the exhibition survived only three years. "It has done the state some good," Tabor said after losing more than $30,000 on the fair, "but to us it was a good deal of a failure." [9]

Tabor's sentiments were probably shared by the saloon proprietors who had built along the South Broadway streetcar tracks to catch Exhibition traffic. The Baron von Richthofen's beer garden was not the only resort to close.[10] Of the 11 taverns built near the Exhibition grounds, all but three had disappeared by 1886. As the short-lived rash of taverns ringing the Mining and Industrial Exhibition Hall sug-

Denver City Railway Building, right, and Union Station, left, formed Denver's transport hub in the 1880s. Denver Horse Railroad Company occupied building on right (17th and Wynkoop). Horses and mules were stabled in basement, and brought up to street level on large elevators.

gests, saloons were ephemeral institutions. Not only were bars among the first and easiest businesses to open during growth cycles, they were also one of the first businesses to close during hard times. In the boom-and-bust cycle of nineteenth-century urban development, saloons sometimes had to retreat almost as fast as they advanced out in the prickly pear cactus and prairie dog villages.

A longer-lived saloon served as the nucleus of the suburb platted by Edwin P. Harman in 1882. Situated on the north bank of Cherry Creek on a site long used as a dump, Harman Town was incorporated in 1886. In the center of town at 2nd Avenue and Murdock (now Clayton) Street, Alois and Caroline Zimmerman's brick tavern stood for years as the finest building in the area. Blacks, squatters, and transients settled along sometimes dry, sometimes flooded, always littered Cherry Creek, and made Zimmerman's beer hall their gathering place. Zimmerman's Inn and Harman Town did not begin to prosper until 1892 when the streetcar line arrived, the town hall was built, and city folk began moving out there.[11]

Although the first streetcar suburbs had welcomed saloons, a turning point came in the 1880s, when more pretentious suburbs sought to establish themselves as "saloonless" enclaves. High license fees, restrictive covenants and ultimately zoning were used to exclude saloons from selective residential neighborhoods, a practice one scholar has labeled moral geography.[12] Moral geography first came into practice in northeast Denver, the corner of the city where streetcar-line construction became most intensive during the 1880s.[13] In 1876 the Larimer Street line paralleling the railroad tracks and the Platte River was extended to the northeastern end of Larimer at 37th and Downing streets. In the river bank, railroad-track area on the northwest side of Larimer, industrial, warehouse, and wholesale plants located while new residential areas proliferated on the southeastern side of Larimer. After Larimer Street was extended, other streetcar tracks pierced the northeast Denver prairie, bringing homes and development in their wake. Lines went out East 15th (Colfax), 17th, 22nd, 25th, 29th, 31st, 34th and 40th avenues, some reaching York Street, some pushing even farther east. Saloonkeepers and other entrepreneurs hoped to capitalize on the mushrooming new streetcar suburbs. "The growth of beer dives is keeping pace with the city's expansion," noted the *Rocky Mountain News* in the late 1880s, "and there has been much complaint of injury to new neighborhoods by the persistency with which those corrupting dens are thrust in every available opening."[14] After moving into neighborhoods outside the core city, partly in order to escape urban evils such as saloons, suburbanites were distressed to find saloons moving into their new neighborhoods. Economic as well as moral considerations fueled the drive to exclude taverns, which homeowners condemned as "befouling and injurious to property values."[15]

In 1882 citizens began pressuring the board of aldermen to ban saloons within 500 feet of a school or church. The council did not cooperate until 1889.[16] Hoping to avoid the Larimer Street spectacle of bars shouldering each other in rows for block after block, voters also introduced a proposal in 1884 to limit saloons to one per block.[17] This stipulation, despite repeated efforts by neighborhood activists and antisaloon zealots, was never enacted by the city council.

More successful attempts were made to close saloons on Sundays and after midnight. By the mid-1880s, policemen rang a loud curfew bell each night at midnight to close the saloons, and inspected on Sunday morning to make sure no alcoholic spirits were being served.[18]

The 1889 measure raising annual saloon license fees to $600 would, according to its proponents, force some of the marginal, meaner bars out of existence.[19]

Despite promises of councilmen, saloon licenses were awarded in new streetcar-spawned neighborhoods. In 1889, the city council sanctioned the proposed saloon of Timothy Connor, brother of a police lieutenant, thus exciting "a turmoil in the neighborhood of 30th Avenue and Lafayette Street" in freshly developed northeast Denver.[20] Later that year, permission was "smuggled through the board of aldermen" to establish a bar in the most fashionable streetcar suburb of all, Capitol Hill.[21] By 1890, the press reported sentiment "working up to a white heat" against the movement of "beer dives into quiet residence neighborhoods."[22]

Inflamed antisaloon suburbanites the following year helped to install Denver's first reform mayor, a man promising to curb the power of the saloon. The new mayor, Platt Rogers, strove to impose moral geography on the city by excluding bars from new residential neighborhoods and confining them to a downtown area where they could be more easily avoided by upright residents and more easily policed.

If new streetcar additions to the city fretted about the invasion of "whiskey holes," some suburban developments outside the city limits were even more circumspect. In their charters, ordinances, real estate prospectuses, and newspapers, the suburban towns surrounding Denver boasted of being saloonless havens of morality, health, security, and prosperity. Suburbanites and developers who dressed up their remote patches of prairie real estate as liquorless paradises joined prohibitionists in condemning the city as saloon-infested.

These charges were difficult to deny. By 1890, Denver had more saloons per capita than Baltimore, Boston, Kansas City, Minneapolis, New Orleans, Philadelphia, St. Louis, or Washington.[23] By 1914, the Mile High City contained almost 500 licensed saloons and many unlicensed liquor outlets.[24] In the city's core, bars sat on nearly every corner. At 18th and Curtis, the Killarney Cafe was surrounded by Pat O'Brien's L-shaped saloon, which had entrances on both streets. O'Brien's, the oldtimers claimed, was so rough that the house would refund your money if you drank two beers and did not see a fight.[25] Taverns crowded many blocks of Market, Larimer, 15th, 16th, 17th, 18th, and 19th streets. As the most common commercial establishments in the core city, saloons were frequently condemned as symbols of urban vice.

Squalid sanitation problems also plagued the downtown saloon district throughout the nineteenth century. Rats occupied cellars, sewers, and the waterways by day and invaded the alleys by night, congregating around refuse dumped into back alleys. Many saloon-keepers kept cats and dogs to police the rodents, but the size and boldness of the rats frightened away the cats and terriers sent into their dark holes. At 1840 Larimer St. a rat attacked a sleeping 14-year-old lad. Awakened by screams, the boy's father found the eight-inch-long rat hanging on leech-like to his son's arm. Frantically, the father beat the rodent with a shoe into a dead and "shapeless mass."[26] In other establishments, fleas, cockroaches, and bedbugs flourished.[27] The latter problem may have been abated by the saloonkeepers' practice of paying children a penny for every cockroach they killed.

Human pests also swarmed in the dive district. "Beer dives," declared the *News*, "are the most fruitful source for breeding and feeding prostitution."[28] Although some prostitutes plied their profession in saloons, the majority operated in bordellos which featured their own bars as well as "professors" plunking away at pianos. By the 1880s, an estimated 1,000 "brides of the multitude" offered their wares along the three-block Market Street strip in the heart of the saloon district.[29]

Confidence men also worked in the bars. Most notable was Jefferson Randolph "Soapy" Smith, a Southern dandy who came to Denver in the 1880s in a black-vested suit, flashing a diamond stickpin and gold pocketwatch and chain. Setting up a soap stand at 17th and Larimer, Smith began haranguing the masses about their lack of cleanliness and promoting "the finest soap in the world, perfected in my own laboratory, and manufactured in my own factory." Lukewarm response greeted Soapy's exhortations to "wash your sins away" and that "cleanliness is next to godliness," but when he began inserting $5, $10, $50, and $100 bills into the soap-cake wrappers, the public became mesmerized.[30]

Inevitably the bills went to Soapy's confederate cappers, but the crowds never tired of hearing this slippery huckster lie through his luxuriant black beard. With proceeds from his dollar-a-cake soap business, Soapy was able to open the Tivoli Saloon and gambling hall at 17th and Market. "Caveat Emptor" was the sign Soapy put at the head of the stairway to the second-floor gambling rooms, confident that few of his customers could read Latin.

Soapy Smith was only the best-known of Denver's con men. Doc

Baggs, a soft-spoken pioneer in phony mining stock; Canada Bill, a shadowy gambler preying on gambling railroad tourists; and Lou Blonger, a saloonkeeping swindler who fleeced early twentieth-century Denver visitors, all added to the unsavory reputation of downtown Denver.

Not only was Denver increasingly filled with swindlers, vice, and vermin, it was also overcrowded with newcomers. The city reached its all-time maximum density in 1890, when 106,715 people squeezed into 17 square miles. An army of newcomers, particularly lung-disease patients, flooded into the city. According to one 1880s account, recent arrivals:

> . . . filled the hotels, crowded the boarding houses, and thickly invaded private residences. . . . They moved in thronging, encumbering crowds through the streets, and in the heated midday, they blocked with their chairs, the shaded portions of the sidewalks.[31]

Wealth-seekers came as well as health-seekers. Thousands of Mid-westerners fled dry, dusty, heavily mortgaged farms for Denver. In addition, thousands of poor immigrants streamed into the Mile High City. Sometimes the only housing they could find was in tents and shanties along the river and creek bottoms.

Rather than cope with the mounting population and problems of the core city, many members of the middle and upper classes sought to escape via streetcar. Streetcars were cheap and efficient people movers, the best way for homeowners to put space between their families and the core city. Suburban developers either built or subsidized the construction of dozens of lines, in order to populate their suburban real estate. For only a nickel, they told potential customers, one could leave the crowded city and ride out to spacious suburbia. In a matter of minutes, streetcar riders could escape the urban scene for another world.

Rapid growth of streetcar suburbs relieved Denver's population density and the downtown congestion of the late 1880s and early 1890s. In area, Denver increased from 6 square miles in 1874 to 49 square miles in 1901, when historian Jerome Smiley wrote that streetcars:

> . . . have been chiefly instrumental in distributing Denver's population over the unusually large territory it occupies, and are to a great degree responsible for the absence from the city of anything approaching a "tenement house district." Denver has nothing like that blight common to so many large cities. The system has enabled men of moderate means to acquire homes for themselves in pleasant places away from the business center, instead of being housed tier upon tier in congested localities as so many have to be in so many

other cities. The thousands of pretty dwellings and suburban cottages that line streets far away from the commercial districts would not be there under less favorable conditions for coming and going; neither would the suburban towns be there.[32]

By 1900, the outer ring of suburbs consisted of Highlands, Berkeley, Argo, Globeville, Elyria, Park Hill, Montclair, South Denver, Valverde, Harman, Colfax, and Barnum. Argo, Globeville, and Elyria, northside industrial neighborhoods of smelter, stockyard, and other blue-collar workers, welcomed saloons. Colfax, a neighborhood heavy with Russian and East European Jews on the west bank of the Platte, also housed saloons. Indeed, Colfax achieved notoriety as a sanctuary where saloonkeepers and gamblers exiled themselves during Denver's sporadic crackdowns. Although Harman tolerated the Zimmermans' long-established beer garden, most of the other suburban towns ostracized the saloon.[33]

Temperance advocate Horatio B. Pearce platted the suburban town of Highlands on his 80-acre ranch in 1871. After petitioning the legislature to incorporate his town and getting himself elected mayor, Pearce inexplicably moved into the sinful big city to the east. His town, however, preserved his dry sentiments.[34] The "secrets of Highlands' success" were revealed in the town's annual report for 1891, which claimed that rival suburban towns "can be discerned only by the aid of a field glass bringing up the rear." Primarily success was attributed to the location of Highlands:

> True to her name and nature, she stands high and sightly, where the pure air from the mountains—that God-given slayer of disease—is used first-handed by her people and swells their lungs with strength and healthfulness. With no smelters, factories or emitters of vast volumes of smoke within her borders,

the report continued, Highlands was the best sanatorium in the country.

Secondly, success was attributed to rapid transit, to the seven streetcar lines serving the town's 1891 population of 7,000. The final virtue of Highlands was listed simply as "No Saloons." By ordinance, Highlands defined liquor outlets as "nuisances" and established a prohibitively high annual license fee of $5,000. To further discourage grog shops, another town ordinance declared that no liquor license could be considered without the approval of two-thirds of the landholders living within a half mile radius.[35]

On the northwest boundary of Denver, Highlands was confronted by a column of saloons on the east side of Zuni Street border and by North Denver's huge Zang Brewery. To help prevent any seepage from these wet-goods establishments, Highlanders built on their side of Zuni Street a Women's Christian Temperance Union (WCTU) reading room.

North of Highlands stood the suburban town of Berkeley, which traced its name to the Berkeley Farm founded there by John Brisben Walker around 1880. After donating 50 acres for the establishment of the Jesuits' Regis College, Walker, like so many other town-builders, sold out and moved on. He collected $325,000 for the property he had purchased nine years earlier for $1,000.[36] Other town-boomers moved in and coaxed a reporter for *Frank Leslie's Illustrated Newspaper* to proclaim Berkeley "beyond question the most beautiful suburb of Denver."[37]

Berkeley was also saloonless. If local authorities were lax about enforcing the town's restrictive saloon license fee, two plume-hatted, black-skirted stalwarts of the Berkeley WCTU were ever-vigilant. Hearing that a druggist was selling alcohol for nonmedicinal indul-

(Photo by James Kunkle, Denver Tramway Historian; Tom Noel Collection)

Denver Tramway Central Loop, 15th and Lawrence, in 1906. All streetcars passed by or through "The Loop."

gence, this pair marched into his pharmacy. One of them complained of a cold, then bought a dime's worth of quinine and a quarter's worth of whiskey. Rather than mixing the quinine and whiskey, a legal remedy, the druggist poured the spirits into a separate bottle. The ladies triumphantly paraded their whiskey bottle to the magistrate, who fined the druggist $200.

The northeast Denver suburbs of Park Hill and Montclair were platted in the 1880s as dry suburbs for the upper crust.

Park Hill, situated on the high ground east of City Park, originated with the schemes of the hapless Baron Eugen A. von Winckler. He arrived in Denver after his discharge from the Prussian Army for disregarding a regulation that forbade an officer to fall off his horse. The baron purchased a quarter section and platted it in 1887 as Park Hill. His plans to install a racetrack and resort community ended with his suicide.[38]

After real estate interests established the Denver and Park Hill Railway Company in 1888, other developers became interested in Park Hill's future as a streetcar suburb.[39] The finest of Park Hill's subdivisions, Downington, was situated between tree-lined Colfax Avenue and Montview Boulevard and spacious Forest Avenue and Monaco Parkways. Downington was also bisected by 17th Avenue with its 100-foot-wide landscaped median, and each lot included a publicly owned 25-foot-wide setback and tree lawn. The neighborhood's lavish parkways and setbacks may be credited to Warwick Downing, a Downington promoter and a principal property holder, who also happened to be a Denver park commissioner. A prospectus for Downington boasted that:

> . . . neither Auteil or Passy in Paris, Mayfair in London, the Ring Strasse in Vienna, the Theirgarten [sic] in Berlin, Riverside Drive in New York, nor the broad avenues and "circles" for which Washington is famous equaled Downington's magnificent parkways.[40]

Downington, which successfully bans bars to this day, claimed to be Denver's largest restricted residential area, whose integrity was insured by "iron-clad restrictions" against churches and schools as well as apartments, doubles, hospitals, and stores. The assurance of "no saloons" did not have to debase the Downington prospectus. It was written between the lines. After noting that Capitol Hill, the wealthiest neighborhood for Denver's turn-of-the century elite, had been defiled by commercial and multifamily usages, the Downington promoters assured lot buyers that they would never be "held-up by the threat, either expressed or implied, to put up undesirable types of building on adjoining property." Amid Park Hill's parkways and croquet wickets, the children of Downington would "be free from the contaminating influence of down-town city streets."

Playing on parental fears, the Downington prospectus continued:

> Children with red blood in their veins resist the confining influence of cramped quarters in thickly settled districts. Are they to blame if they run out into the streets and get into bad company? Are they to blame if their delicate moral fibres are tarnished by evil associations? Is it not your duty to provide ... for healthful and harmless recreation? [41]

In Downington and other Park Hill subdivisions, children supposedly had the best chance in Denver of developing high morals, outside the specter of the saloon.

Immediately south of Park Hill lay Montclair, platted by the Baron Walter von Richthofen shortly before his friend Baron von Winckler laid out Park Hill. Richthofen, scion of the noted Junker clan and uncle of Baron Manfred von Richthofen of World War I aviation fame, came to Denver in the 1870s. After plunging into schemes ranging from selling Rocky Mountain water as "ginger champagne" to operating the Sans Souci beer garden, the baron ventured into a more temperate investment. [42]

Montclair, Richthofen declared in his 1885 prospectus for "The Beautiful Suburban Town of Denver," shall have:

> ... as pure a moral atmosphere and one as beneficial to society as the bracing air of Colorado. .... Montclair should in effect be a club of families of congenial tastes, united for the purpose of excluding all that might destroy their peace or offend their better tastes. [43]

Montclair land deeds stipulated that intoxicating liquors should never be manufactured, sold or otherwise disposed of on the premises.

Montclair's evangelical temperance folk not only banned roadhouses but provided an alternative. Sympathizing with travelers and bicyclists thirsting "for the good old days of Jacob, when there were wells dug by the wayside," Montclair built a public water fountain to serve man and beast. [44] Denver, as Montclair officials noted during the dedication ceremonies of the fountain (still standing near the junction of Richthofen Parkway and Oneida Street), contained hundreds of saloons but very few public fountains. To help keep their children close to the water fountain and away from Denver saloons, Montclair Town created its own school district. The *Montclair Mirror*, in an article probably aimed at Park Hill and Capitol Hill residents as well as locals, advised parents to send their children to Montclair High School rather than the East Denver High School "surrounded by saloons in the center of the city."[45] Parents of East High School students shuddered at newspaper stories of beer halls luring students to drink. "A sweet young girl whose winning face and graceful form made her the idol," a typical article related, "was led into a wine room which, of course, meant seduction and a life on Holladay Street."[46] After its incorporation as a separate town in 1888, Montclair established a $2,500 saloon license fee and other ordinances that kept the neighborhood saloonless.[47] Any objectors had to do their bar-hopping at the Denver end of Montclair's two streetcar lines.

South Denver, situated east of the South Platte River and south of Alameda Avenue, was invaded by saloons early. First there had been the proliferation of saloons on South Broadway with the opening of the Mining and Industrial Exhibition building. Later Pop Wyman's roadhouse, Fiskel's beer gardens, Broadway Park and other unsavory saloons went up along the South Broadway streetcar line. The Overland Park racetrack also attracted the sporting element, including Den-

(James Kunkle, Denver Tramway Historian Photo; Tom Noel Collection)

Central Power Station (15th to 14th and Platte streets) was built in 1901. (Building is now the Forney Transportation Museum.)

ver gambler Edward Chase, who set up a southside beer and betting stand. Joseph Lowe and his wife, "Rowdy Kate," a couple infamous for the saloons, dance halls and bordellos they had run in mining towns, opened the Cottage Grove in the 1880s. Nominally, a beer garden, Cottage Grove was widely condemned as a disorderly house whose lewd, drunken regulars tarnished the image of suburban South Denver.[48]

The Denver Eye, a gazette serving the new neighborhood, took a dim view of these developments. Although South Denver was "destined to be filled with the homes of our best and most prominent citizens," the *Eye* observed, property values were in danger of becoming "almost valueless because of these nuisances."[49] At the urging of the *Eye* and some leading residents, South Denver began to reform itself. The first step was setting up a local government. Although the town had been platted in 1874, it was not incorporated as a self-governing town until 1886. James Fleming, a Pennsylvania oilman who had become a Colorado mining man, contributed his mansion at 1520 S. Grant St. as a town hall, but continued to live there after he was elected the town's first mayor, a post to which he was thrice reelected. After the new government established a $3,500 annual saloon license fee, the *Eye* boasted that South Denver's "roadhouses and saloons were all cleaned out, and it has remained free from these blots ever since."[50]

On Denver's southwestern outskirts, Valverde and Barnum also used their charters and ordinances to curtail the saloons within their town limits. Valverde was laid out in 1882 and incorporated 10 years later[51] while Barnum was incorporated in 1887 and named for its promoter, circus magnate Phineas T. Barnum. Barnum claimed that two-thirds of his town's settlers "came here to die and they can't do it. The wonderful air brings them back from the verge of the tomb."[52]

By 1890, Denver was virtually surrounded by saloonless suburbs, including independent suburban towns and newer additions to Denver proper. After growing with the city along its waterways, stage lines, and railways, the saloon was barred from following the ultimate nineteenth-century city shaper, the streetcar. Between 1890 and 1915, taverns were largely confined to the core city except for a few working-class and immigrant neighborhoods. Consequently, the tremendous growth in the number of saloons between 1880 and 1915, from some 100 taverns to around 500, occurred primarily downtown. Although numerous homes went up east of Broadway and south of East 38th

Avenue, saloons were excluded from this fashionable Capitol Hill area.

In the neighborhood north of Capitol Hill, east of Downing Street and south of East 38th Avenue, only one saloon was tolerated. Bars also were banned from the northwest quadrant bounded by West Colfax Avenue on the south and Zuni Street on the east. Except for a few taverns along Santa Fe Drive, Cherry Creek, and Broadway, the south side of town was also saloonless. While the city had mushroomed to 58.75 square miles by 1902, saloons remained concentrated in the six-square mile core city of the 1870s.

After being banned in most of the Queen City's suburbs, saloons became heavily concentrated along the streetcar line. Their success as a business was often linked to a key location near the streetcar terminals or at the more popular streetcar stops and transfer points. Between 1890 and 1915, hundreds of saloons were operating each year within the square-mile central business district bounded roughly by the Platte River on the west, 23rd Street on the north, Welton Street on the east, and Cherry Creek on the south.

Within the urban ecology, the downtown saloon was often located

(Photo by Erwin Krebs; Tom Noel Collection)

Streetcars were supplanted by buses in 1950. Picture on last day of operation is in Montclair at East Colfax and Poplar turnaround.

in recycled buildings. Worn-out hotels, theaters, restaurants, grocery stores and even old schools, churches, and residences were converted to saloons. Bars were commonly the last occupants of a building. As a very flexible, adaptive institution, they frequently found homes in buildings designed for other purposes. Barkeepers were often blue-collar workers who had scraped together the minimal capital necessary for a go at entrepreneurship. They sought the cheap rent for old buildings in the less fashionable downtown blocks. Saloonists frequently remodeled other structures for their own use, a practice that has become architecturally fashionable a century later as "adaptive use."

Bars often occupied the oldest and most historic buildings. For example, the first Colorado National Bank building later became the Bank Saloon. The First National Bank building, where the state's constitution was written, became the Meskew Brothers Saloon, and the Clark and Gruber Mint was later a workingman's tavern. The Wells Fargo Express Office became a delicatessen. One of Denver's first Baptist churches became a German beer garden, Walhalla Hall.

Particularly after the 1880s crusade to enforce midnight and Sunday closing laws and the beginning of the prohibition crusade, saloons began maintaining a lower profile and often maintained an inconspicuous side or back door. Thus, on a spring Sunday in 1890, a reporter for the *Rocky Mountain News* found customers trooping into the illegally open taverns through back and side doors. "Entrance was gained in one or two instances by passage through adjoining stores," the reporter found. "The crowds of bums and hangers-on seated on barrels outside served as guides to the inquisitive passerby."[53]

Although saloons were the most common urban institution, they were frequently among the least conspicuous. Freestanding saloons were commonly diminutive structures overpowered by the neighboring hotels, business buildings, factories and stores. The great majority of bars, however, were not freestanding buildings. Rather they were tucked into the corners, buried in the basements, stored up narrow flights of stairs on upper floors, or hidden off the back alleys. Practically every hotel and major business block had a bar. Saloons could be found in the basement of the Boston Building, in the lobby of the Brown Palace Hotel, in the alley behind the First National Bank, in a corner of the Tabor Grand Opera House. Practically every corner building housed a bar.

Suburbanites pouring into the city every morning for work found the Queen City perfumed from hundreds of bar doors open for an airing. This pungent spectacle impressed suburbanites. They made sure that when Denver began aggressively annexing her suburbs after 1893, that most of the new areas would remain saloonless. Dry suburban rings surrounding a wet city were legally sanctioned in an 1893 Colorado Supreme Court decision involving newly annexed Valverde Town. The court held that liquor traffic "may be prohibited in one part of a town or city and licensed in another part, as the public welfare may require."[54] By 1902 Park Hill, South Denver, Harman, Highlands, Barnum, Colfax, Argo, Berkeley, Elyria, Globeville, Montclair, and Valverde had been annexed to Denver. Most of these suburbs had been saloonless and remained largely saloonless as Denver neighborhoods. Their incorporation into Denver significantly strengthened the city's antisaloon minority. When Denverites went to the polls in 1914 to vote on the prohibition amendment, the six older city wards voted wet while six of the ten outlying wards voted dry to bolster the narrow statewide victory of prohibitionists.[55] Suburbanites, after successfully banning the saloon at their end of the streetcar line, helped deliver all Coloradans into the dry promised land of their moral geography.

Endnotes

1. U.S. Census Bureau, Eleventh Census, 1890, 4, pt.2, "Vital Statistics of Cities of 100,000 Inhabitants and Upward for the Census Year Ending May 31, 1890," pp.3-4.

2. Jerome C. Smiley, *History of Denver* (Denver: Times-Sun Publishing Company, 1901), p. 854.

3. J.E. Wharton and D.O. Wilhelm, *History of the City of Denver* (Denver: Byers & Dailey, 1866), p.92; *Rocky Mountain News*, July 14, 1872.

4. R.G. Dun & Company, *Credit Ratings for Colorado Territory*, entry for William Wise dated April 8, 1875, Manuscript Collections, Baker Business Library, Harvard University, Cambridge, Mass.; obituary for Wise in *Denver Times*, Oct. 24, 1906, and *Denver Republican*, Oct. 25, 1906.

5. Smiley, *loc. cit.*

6. *Denver Daily Tribune*, June 25, 1875.

7. My account of North Denver is drawn in part from Ruth E. Wiberg, *Rediscovering Northwest Denver* (Denver: Northwest Denver Books, 1976), pp. 7-46.

8. Smiley, *op. cit.*, pp. 854, 859; Duane A. Smith, *Horace Tabor: His Life and the Legend* (Boulder, Colo.: Colorado Associated University Press, 1973), pp. 200-206, 264-265.

9. Smith, *op. cit.*, p. 265.

10. Louisa Arps, *Denver in Slices* (Denver: Sage Books, 1959), p. 161.

11. Smiley, *op. cit.*, p. 651; Cherry Creek Neighborhood Plan (Denver: Denver Planning Office, 1976), p. 3.

12. I have borrowed the term "moral geography" and insight into this topic from Perry Duis, *The Saloon and the Public City: Chicago and Boston, 1880-1920* (Ph.D dissertation, Univ. of Chicago, 1975). In his extensive treatment of suburbs and saloons ("Keeping Evanston Pure," pp. 823-31, and "Drying Up Cambridge," pp.832-40), Duis argues that moral geography was rooted in l) a long tradition of internal districting; 2) increasing attempts to escape the city only to be followed to the suburbs by downtown nuisances; and 3) the neighborhood vigilante tradition.

13. For information on the construction pattern of Denver's streetcars, see Smiley, *op. cit.*, pp.853-870, and the Map of the City of Denver Showing Cable and Steam Railways, Jan. 28, 1893, Map Collection, Library, State Historical Society of Colorado.

14. *Rocky Mountain News,* Dec. 21, 1889.

15. *Ibid.*

16. *Ibid.,* Feb. 3, 1882; Feb. 7, 1891.

17. *Ibid.,* April 29, 1884.

18. *Ibid.,* May 5, 1885.

19. Laws Passed at the Seventh Session of the General Assembly of the State of Colorado (Denver: Collier and Cleveland Lithographing Company, 1889), p. 126.

20. *Rocky Mountain News.* Jan. 20, 1889.

21. *Ibid.,* Dec. 21, 1889.

22. *Ibid.,* Aug. 29, 1890; see also R.G. Dill, *The Political Campaigns of Colorado* (Denver: Arapahoe Publishing Company, 1895), p. 137.

23. U.S. Census Bureau, "Vital Statistics of Cities. . . 1890," pp. 3-4.

24. *Denver Express,* Aug. 6, 1914; Letter of Executive Board of Denver Saloonkeepers' Union Number 1 to Alexander Nesbit, Denver Commissioner of Safety, Aug. 18, 1914, in Benjamin Hurwitz Papers, Western History Department, Denver Public Library.

25. Forest H. Johnson, *Denver's Old Theatre Row: The Story of Curtis Street and Its Glamorous Show Business* (Denver: Bill Lay, LITHO, Printers, 1970), p. 36.

26. *Rocky Mountain News.* Jan. 9, 1899.

27. *Ibid.,* July 9, 1870.

28. *Ibid.,* July 23, 1889.

29. Forbes Parkhill, *The Wildest of the West.* (Denver: Sage Books, 1951), p.13.

30. My account of Soapy Smith is drawn from Frank G. Robertson and Beth Kay Harris, *Soapy Smith: King of the Frontier Con Men* (New York: Hastings House, 1961).

31. *Inter-Ocean: A Journal of Colorado Politics, Society, and Mining,* Denver, June 6, 1880, p. 271, Western History Department, Denver Public Library.

32. Smiley, *op. cit.,* p. 870.

33. See "Saloons" listing in the 1900 Denver City Directory.

34. Except where otherwise noted, my account of Highlands is drawn from Wiberg, *op. cit.,* pp. 51-153.

35. *Town of Highlands: Its Progress, Prospects and Financial Condition; First Annual Report, April, 1891* (Highlands, Colo.: Highlands Chief Press, 1891), *passim,* Library, State Historical Society of Colorado, Denver.

36. Except where otherwise noted, my account of Berkeley is drawn from Wiberg, *op. cit.,* pp. 164-183.

37. *Frank Leslie's Illustrated Newspaper,* Sept. 28, 1889.

38. Manuscript biography of Baron Eugen A. von Winckler, Library, State Historical Society of Colorado.

39. Smiley, *op. cit.,* p. 864.

40. *The Road to Downington: Denver's Most Beautiful Residence Section* (Denver: Carson-Harper, c. 1907), photocopy in my possession courtesy of Richard Downing, Jr.

41. *Ibid.*

42. Except where otherwise noted, my information on Richthofen and on Montclair is from Arps, *op. cit.,* pp.155-171.

43. *Montclair, Colorado: The Beautiful Suburban Town of Denver, Colo., U.S.A.* (Denver: 1885), Library, State Historical Society of Colorado.

44. *Denver Times,* Dec. 15, 1898.

45. *Montclair Mirror.* Sept. 26, 1903.

46. *Rocky Mountain News.* May 8, 1889. A similar story telling of the luring of young boys into saloons is related in the *News,* Feb. 7, 1891.

47. Ordinances of the Town of Montclair Passed by the Board of Trustees (Denver: Coleman & Norvell, 1891), p. 36, Western History Collections, Denver Public Library.

48. J.D. Horan and Paul Sonn, *Pictorial History of the Wild West* (New York: Crown Publishing Co., 1954), p. 106; *Denver Eye,* Jan. 1, 1890.

49. *Denver Eye, loc. cit.*

50. *Ibid.*

51. Smiley, *op. cit.,* p. 651.

52. Robert L. Perkin, *The First Hundred Years: An Informal History of Denver and the Rocky Mountain News,* (Garden City, N.Y.: Doubleday and Company, 1959), p.-348.

53. *Rocky Mountain News.* April 7, 1890.

54. Town of Valverde vs. Shattuck, 19 Colo. 104, pp. 104-22.

55. Elliott West makes this point and charts the prohibition vote by urban and suburban wards in "Dry Crusade: The Prohibition Movement in Colorado, 1858-1933" (Ph.D. dissertation, Univ. of Colorado, Boulder, 1971), Appendix VI, P. 449.

About the Author

Thomas J. Noel, a member of the Denver Posse of Westerners since 1977 and Sheriff in 1989, was born in Cambridge, Mass. Tom earned a B.A. in History and M.A. in Library Science from the University of Denver, and an M.A. and Ph.D. in History from the University of Colorado at Boulder.

Tom is a professor of history and chair of the department at the University of Colorado at Denver. His many books and articles have won the Colorado Historical Society's Hafen Prize, Top Hand Awards from the Colorado Authors League, and a National Award from the American Society for State and Local History.

His books include *Richthofen's Montclair* (Boulder, Colo.: Pruett Pub. Co., 1976); *Denver's Larimer Street: Main Street, Skid Row & Urban Renaissance* (Denver: Historic Denver, Inc., 1981); *The City & The Saloon* (Lincoln: Univ. of Nebraska Press, 1982, 1985); *Denver: The City Beautiful and its Architects* with Barbara J. Norgren (Denver: Historic Denver, Inc., 1987, 1993); *Denver: Mining Camp to Metropolis* with co-author Stephen J. Leonard (Niwot, Colo.: Univ. Press of Colorado, 1990); *Historical Atlas of Colorado* with Paul J. Mahoney and Richard E. Stevens (Norman, Okla.: Univ. of Oklahoma Press, 1993, 1994). His next books, *Colorado: The Highest State* with Duane A. Smith (Niwot: Univ. Press of Colorado) and *Buildings of Colorado* (New York: Oxford Univ. Press) are scheduled for 1995 publication.

Tom writes an "op-ed" column for *The Denver Post;* is a member of the Denver Landmark Preservation Commission, which he chaired from 1990 to 1993; and a board member of the Denver Public Library Friends Foundation. He resides in the east Denver neighborhood of Montclair, with his wife Vi Sumiko.

"Ursus horribilis" by *Max Smith*

Old Mose, The Great Grizzly

by Dr. Lester L. Williams

*W*HEN OLD MOSE was killed in 1904, it was estimated he was from 35 to 40 years old. The center of his haunts was Black Mountain in Colorado. He hibernated there, he killed Jacob Radliff there, and he was killed there, so the statement he was born there makes sense.

Old Mose was probably born during the latter part of, or shortly after, the Civil War, on Black Mountain in the south end of South Park. Little is known of his early years, then reports began to drift in to some of the ranches and mining camps of a grizzly of extraordinary size who seemed to delight in rushing into the camp of some unsuspecting miner, scaring him nearly to death, then leaving—and seeming to enjoy the episode. There is no record the bear ever attacked anyone on such a foray, but the stampedes he caused were many and ludicrous.

This big grizzly killed enough domestic animals to set the ranchers after him. The first documented depredation by this very large bear occurred in 1878 when he killed a heifer on the Stirrup Ranch, at that time owned and operated by the Waugh brothers. This ranch was, and is, at the head of Cottonwood Creek between Black Mountain on the north and Waugh Mountain on the south, and lies in a nice park called Poncha Park. (Naturally the ranch's brand was a stirrup.) At one time the ranch comprised 56,000 acres and was the largest cattle operation in Fremont County.

Over the years, many stories have appeared about Old Mose. Some are factual, some are not; some are one author quoting the mistakes of another writer. In the present account, an attempt has been made to verify statements as far as possible.

Harry Epperson wrote a remarkable book, *Colorado As I Saw It*. Epperson was born in 1880 and lived a good share of his life in the south end of South Park. He knew the area intimately and qualifies as a good source of information. He recounts the story of how Old Mose killed Jake Radliff.

The *Fairplay Flume* of Nov. 29, 1883, carried a full-column account of the death of Jacob Radliff, a pioneer of Park County. Since this appeared less than a week after the event and in Radliff's home town, where he was a well-known citizen, it must be accepted as factual, and the spelling of the name as *Radliff* is accepted.

The newspaper tells that Radliff had first come to Fairplay in 1863 and was an experienced hunter, a man of deliberate action, who never lost his head in the face of danger, and who was a dead shot. He seemed to be highly esteemed in Fairplay. Radliff and Henry Seymour went to the south end of South Park to hunt, and camped on the line of Park and Fremont counties. A man named Cory joined them. On Nov. 22, 1883, they separated, for Radliff always tried to hunt alone. In an open park he discovered the tracks of a bear. The newspaper reported:

> He was not hunting for such game and would have avoided it, but suddenly a large bear came through the underbrush upon him. The contact was so sudden that the old hunter was unprepared. . . . Mr. Radliff had only time to draw up his gun and fire at random. The bear was so near that he had to push it off with his gun to prevent its ponderous claws tearing him. The random shot probably did not do any execution and he had pushed off the bear several times with his gun when the brute caught his ankle with its paw. Breaking the bones like twigs, the bear tossed the hunter into the air six feet. As he fell to the ground, the brute pounced upon him, crunching the bones of his legs, tearing his cheek, and clawing his body frightfully. Mr. Radliff was perfectly conscious. He knew his danger, uttered repeated cries, and endeavored to rise and escape, but the infuriated brute again tossed him in the air, and as he fell bit him nearly from ear to ear and tore off his scalp Then the poor torn victim of brute ferocity lost consciousness.

Seymour heard the shot and the cry for help and came running. Radliff told him he had come upon a huge bear, had fired at the animal, but the bear had grabbed his gun and broken it into bits, then attacked him. Seymour and Cory carried Radliff to an open spot, wrapped him in a wagon sheet and put him in the wagon, then drove off down the mountain to Badger Creek on the IM Ranch, where they arrived late in the evening. The Mulocks owned the ranch at that time, and Parker Mulock, his bride of a few months, and a young cowboy named John Hyssong were there. Hyssong later told that Radliff was bleeding so profusely that the wagon sheet was soaked and blood oozed on the ground.

The young bride, though unaccustomed to violence, shed some of her clothing to bind the wounds and did everything in her power to relieve the man's pain. John Hyssong rode to Platte River Station on the South Park Railroad, 45 miles distant, where he sent a telegram to Dr. Delamater in Fairplay, summoning him to attend Radliff. The doctor arrived at Platte River Station at 1 a.m., was met by Hyssong, who grabbed Delamater's medicine case, and led him out into the darkness to two sweat-caked horses tied to a telegraph pole. He assisted the doctor to mount, then said: "Let's make it snappy, Doc."

They galloped hour after hour, over ridges and down arroyos, guided in the darkness by Hyssong's instinct. At dawn the young cowboy and the doctor arrived at the IM Ranch. Doctor Delamater examined Radliff, found that he had been bitten through the back of the neck, the scalp was torn almost off, one arm was lacerated and broken and torn loose at the shoulder, both thighs torn, and one leg was broken in two places. Though in agony, Radliff was conscious. He told the story of his terrible encounter clearly and concisely, and urged Seymour to profit from his fate and cease hunting bear. It was decided to try to transport Radliff to Fairplay, and he was gently placed in the wagon for the long drive. Alas, he died on the way.

Harry Epperson concludes: "The praise of the early-day country doctor can never be sung loud enough," and I would agree, for this must have been one of the more arduous house calls.

On Nov. 28, 1883, Radliff was buried in the Odd Fellows Cemetery. The funeral services were conducted by the officers of South Park Lodge No. 10 of which the departed was a highly respected member. The funeral procession included members of the Odd Fellows Lodge, the Coleman Hose Company in uniform, the town authorities, and many citizens in carriages.

The tracks of the bear which killed Radliff measured 10 inches across, making him truly a monster. The other hunters, Seymour and Cory, did not identify the bear as a grizzly, but the size of the tracks points to this conclusion. The few settlers in the area believed the bear had lived there many years, and recently had killed a heifer of Mulocks. It is interesting to note that the 1883 newspaper account did not call the bear Old Mose, because the name had not yet been applied to the animal.

The story has been told that William Stout and M.W. Waterhouse, two of the oldest residents of the Arkansas Valley at that time, were impressed with the manner in which this big grizzly would *mosey* up to men he would happen upon, scare them thoroughly, then slowly *mosey* away; also, the deliberate manner in which he left a carcass when shot at, so they named him *Old Mose*, short for *mosey*.

Another story of the naming tells that Wharton Pigg and Henry Beecher, old-time ranchers and hunters, noticed the unusually large bear tracks around Black Mountain and called the bear Old Mose after

"Hugh Glass fights a grizzly as companions flee," by Delano

a notorious grizzly that used to range the Flat Tops in northwest Colorado, and was killed in 1882.

History tells us that Old Mose was not the only grizzly to be given a name. Other famous—or infamous—ones were Red Robber, Old Silver, Three Toes, Old Clubfoot, The Crippler, and Bloody Paws. Old Mose seems to have resisted the longest, and fought the best of all.

As a result of his killing of many domestic animals plus Jake Radliff, the ranchers made a concerted effort to be rid of this large bear. One such effort was a trap. Knowing of the bear's fondness for a bath early every morning, a trap was set in a beaver pond on the left branch of Thirty-One Mile Creek on the north slope of Black Mountain. Every morning the trap was checked. One morning young John Douglas checked the trap. Imagine his excitement as he ran back to the ranch to report the bear was in the trap. Men grabbed their guns and headed for the lake, but the bear didn't wait. His fresh tracks showed that now two toes were missing. They were found in the trap and given to Beulah Beeler. From then on there was never any question of the identity of Old Mose. His left hind foot was missing two toes.

The name Beeler brings up another story of South Park. Harry

Epperson writes about the Beelers in his book, as does Carl Mathews in a Denver Westerners *Brand Book*. The Beeler family's claim to fame was in keeping their psychotic son chained naked in a dirt-roofed log cabin behind their ranch house. Their daughter Beulah was a real beauty and much sought after by the cowboys, but her parents kept her out of sight. She eloped with a fast-talking cowboy named Evans from Texas, so became Beulah Beeler Evans.

Another trap was built by rancher C.A. Hall, consisting of a pen of logs about 4 feet high, with a steel bear trap in the narrow entrance. Hall baited the trap with the carcass of a dead cow. Three times Mose stole the bait without springing the trap. It was then discovered the wily grizzly merely reached over the log wall to take the carcass, avoiding the trap in the entrance.

Other hunters would not heed the advice of dying Jake Radliff to leave that bear alone. The story is told that James W. Asher was killed by Old Mose in almost the same manner as Radliff. Several years later a skeleton with ribs caved in was found on Cameron Mountain. Beside it was a model 1873 Winchester, caliber .38-55, with two unfired cartridges in the magazine. It was concluded the skeleton had been a hunter killed by Old Mose.

In the summer of 1903, a skeleton was found on Thirty-Nine Mile Mountain just north of Guffy. Boots and spurs marked it for a cowboy, and again Old Mose was blamed—whether truly or falsely.

Sometime, probably in the 1880s, Wharton Pigg enters this story. He had been born July 29, 1868, in Missouri and had come to Colorado in 1882, when his parents homesteaded on Currant Creek. Being an avid outdoorsman and hunter, he likely hunted Old Mose in the 1880s.

Two of Wharton Pigg's children, Mrs. Genevieve Humphrey and Howard Gordon, tell of a hunt when Pigg had tracked a sow with two cubs on Cover Mountain. He believed the sow to be Old Mose's mate. He shot the two cubs, who fell in deep brush. The sow came running at their squalls, and he shot her. Then he reached in his pocket for more cartridges, but instead found only a hole. Not being certain any of the bears were dead and thinking Old Mose might be in the area, Pigg tore off down the hill. Next day he returned and found all three bears dead. He measured his tracks and claimed his prints were 28 feet apart as he fled down the mountain from the bears!

After 1890 when Cripple Creek was booming, Pigg took a load of potatoes grown on their ranch to the gold camp to sell. He sold not only the potatoes, but also the team and the wagon. He stayed on in the mining camp, worked as a blacksmith sharpening drills for Winfield Scott Stratton's Independence Mine, and took a large share of his wages as stock at 4 cents a share. When the stock went to $4 he sold out, returned home, and bought the Stirrup Ranch. In addition to being a rancher, Whart Pigg was a hunter and a writer of animal stories, and a representative of the U.S. Biological Survey. On the Stirrup Ranch, he fenced a section of land with a woven-wire fence 8 feet high. He purchased 40 elk from Jackson Hole, Wyo., and white-tailed deer in Texas, and had them shipped to Fairplay by train. He transported them to the Stirrup Ranch in a train of wagons with very high sides, then turned them loose in the enclosure. He also had numerous black bears roaming the ranch. With herds of elk wiped out by hunting, his idea of a private game preserve for paying hunters seemed like a sound business enterprise.

About this time a dispute arose between Pigg and government officials as to whether or not Pigg should enclose government land. They sent two government surveyors to settle the controversy, and they moved into a little log cabin near the ranch house. Once while cooking their evening meal of bacon and eggs, the structure filled with smoke. When they opened the window to let the smoke out, two small bears jumped in and started consuming the meal. The surveyors made a hasty exit, left all their instruments, and never returned for them. They were eager to concede that Pigg did not have a single acre of government land enclosed.

Pigg made a study of Old Mose and probably knew the grizzly better than any other man. He was amazed and fascinated by the keen instincts that repeatedly saved the grizzly from traps set by eager hunters or angry ranchers. He learned that Mose periodically ranged widely. Every month or two he made a circuit from Jack Hall Mountain to Buffalo Peaks, and one unverified account says he ranged from the Tarryall Mountains to the Cochetopa Hills. His favorite spots were Black Mountain, Tallahassee Mountain, and Cover Mountain, all in the south end of South Park.

In his later years Old Mose was followed by a cinnamon bear of large size who had nothing to do with the killing of game, but who fed royally on the abundance of meat Old Mose left behind.

During his approximately 40 years of life, it was estimated Old Mose killed 800 domestic animals at a cost to ranchers of about $30,000. Feelings against the bear ran high. A reward was posted, and for many years there was a standing offer of $500 to the hunter who brought in the bear's carcass. Since a top hand on a ranch received $30 a month plus board, this was a tempting reward. Many cowboys and hunters were on the lookout for Old Mose, but it was said most of them secretly hoped they wouldn't find him.

The burning ambition of Wharton Pigg's life was to kill Old Mose, and may have been the deciding factor in his buying the Stirrup Ranch. Locating in this area gave Pigg ample opportunity to hunt Old Mose, and he hunted him regularly. However, fortune smiled on another hunter, James W. Anthony.

Late in 1904, *Outdoor Life* published the account of the final hunt, as written by Pigg. The successful hunter, Anthony, was never quite satisfied with Pigg's version, and three years later set down his own account in 23 handwritten pages which certainly have the ring of truth, and portions of which are quoted verbatim.

Early in 1904 Anthony moved from Boise, Idaho, to Cañon City, Colo. He wrote:

> I brought along a pack of bear dogs. When this became generally known about the first thing a new acquaintance would ask would be, "Why don't you kill Old Mose?" I heard this so often I finally declared I thought I must be the only friend Old Mose had. . . .
>
> After coming to Cañon I soon became acquainted with a number of land owners from the Black Mountain country, among them Mr. W.H. Pigg. They assured me that a big bear lived on their cattle ranges, and that he killed cattle every year. The previous summer he had killed a 3-year-old registered Hereford bull in Mr. Pigg's pasture. Also that he had killed two hunters. This sounded interesting and quite convincing.
>
> The previous year I had captured or killed 16 bear and I owned the best lot of bear dogs that I have ever seen. A bear that could run ahead of them more than a mile or longer than 20 minutes was an exception. It was tree, fight or get killed. In fact, they had killed one yearling outright and caught two others, one of which H.P. Center killed with his knife, the other I killed in the same way.
>
> Mr. Pigg invited me to come up to his ranch and hunt from there. As I had sold all my horses in Idaho and as good saddle horses were very scarce in Cañon, as indeed is usual in most places, and as Mr. Pigg knew the country and had an extra good and swift saddle horse, I did not much like to hunt with him, the country being all new to me and myself practically afoot. So I thought that my chance of being at the kill would be very slim, and I had wanted a hide such as I thought that bear carried for several years. However, I said to Mr. Pigg: "If you like I will take my dogs and go up to your ranch and hunt with you for that bear, but if we get him I want the hide." As I recollect he did not make a direct reply to this.
>
> I finally bought a horse that suited me pretty well tho' it was only a 4-year-old, and went up to the Stirrup Ranch. We rode pretty steadily for over a month before we struck the bear's track as he had not yet come on the

range. Stormy days and evenings we would talk on various subjects often telling yarns. And day and night in waking hours I would try to think out some promising scheme by which I could get a shot at Mose but the chances seemed against me for Mr. Pigg and his knowledge of the country, and his excellent saddle horse "Shan" seemed to extend completely across the horizon.

About two weeks before we struck the bear's track Mr. Pigg said to me: "If I get a chance I will shoot that bear." "Sure," I said, "that is what we are here for," but I know he meant if he killed the bear he would claim the hide.

Here we leave the story written by Anthony. Since he knew the country intimately, Pigg's account of the hunt is well-oriented geographically. Not knowing when Mose would emerge from hibernation, they began hunting about the first of April, with the Stirrup Ranch as home base. Their forays familiarized Anthony with the country. They hunted for caves and looked for evidence of bears. Pigg told how they found plenty of old sign, logs turned, ant hills dug up, and places where cubs had climbed aspen trees the previous year. They looked at rubbing trees and Anthony saw firsthand where a number of black and brown bears had left their mark, but he was mainly impressed by hairs from a silver tip left 8 feet high on a tree, and hair from a large cinnamon a foot lower.

While hunting, Anthony kept the dogs necked up in couples. Constant traveling tired the dogs, and some days they were left at the ranch for a rest. The morning of April 26 they left the dogs at the ranch and started on a three-day trip around Black Mountain. They checked the usual bear haunts around the west end of Black Mountain and the lakes to the north, probably on the upper end of Thirty-One Mile Creek. They stopped at Ed Shimmons' ranch near the head of Currant Creek for the night.

The next morning they invited Shimmons to hunt with them, but he said he had helped gather up the pieces of two bear hunters killed by their prey, and thanks, but no thanks. Shimmons had a wagon stuck in Sheep Gulch which required his attention, so Pigg and Anthony rode west toward Agate Gulch. After going about two miles they found tracks of a very large bear on dry grass. The tracks had been made since any wind had blown, therefore, early that morning. Anthony writes the tracks were nice, big, wide, and deep in the soft earth, and reminded him of old times in Wyoming. They followed the tracks for 50 yards and noted the long claws, identifying it as a grizzly, then they started back to the Stirrup Ranch for their dogs. There they ate lunch, changed horses and coupled the dogs into pairs, Ray to Penny, Ginger to Dummit, Ring with Prince, and Bowey to Buff. They headed for Ed Elcessor's cow ranch on upper Thirty-One Mile Creek, where they arrived about 5 p.m. and put up for the night.

The following morning, April 28, they separated with Anthony taking his dogs up the right fork of Thirty-One Mile Creek to where they had seen the tracks, while Pigg went up the left branch to see if the grizzly had gone toward Black Mountain during the night. Pigg found the bear had not, then cut across to meet Anthony at the tracks.

The dogs could not follow the trail because the country was very dry, and the tracks were more than 24 hours old, but Pigg's keen eyes could. The bear had avoided timber and damp places, and kept on open ground and on grass as much as possible. Pigg tracked the bear and Anthony followed afoot, leading the horse and keeping the dogs back. The hunters trailed the bear across both forks of Agate Creek, through the fence of the VVN ranch where the bear had pushed a pole off and climbed over into the large pasture, then into the small horse pasture, then where the animal headed toward the lakes, suddenly turned at right angles toward the deserted VVN Ranch house, almost through the yard, then down over the old meadow where he made another gap in the fence. The track went down Rye Slough to a gap on the west of Black Mountain, then south. They lost the trail on the bald ridges where wind was blowing hard. Pigg had followed the track about eight miles that day. They expected to intercept the trail in the lower gulches of Poncha Park, but they didn't, and as it was evening they went on about five miles to the Stirrup Ranch and stayed for the night. Pigg recalled that his eyes hurt and his head ached from the trailing and although he was dead tired, he had trouble falling asleep.

Despite fatigue, they were back at the hunt early the next morning, going up Aspen Gulch on the west end of Black Mountain. They found tracks leading up the mountain, but too old for the dogs. A brief snowstorm caught them and obliterated all tracks, so they spent the rest of the day looking over the west slope and top of Black Mountain. Toward sundown they led their horses off the extreme east point where the "signal post" (bench mark) stands, and spent another night with Ed Elcessor.

Next morning, April 30, they were out again. They circled north and west of Black Mountain again and went to the head of Gribble Creek near the place they had last seen the tracks.

Anthony's account continues:

> We rode along the skirts of Black Mountain, sometimes through aspen thickets, then across little grassy parks, again among the dark spruce. We saw

some frightened cattle, but no bear tracks. We came out of the timber near the abandoned ranch buildings (VVN). The dogs could still smell where the bear had pushed a pole out of the fence a couple of days before. We went on west and south for a mile or so inside the wire fence, then got out of the pasture and rode west. On the south side of the A.N. pasture, we found no tracks and were completely puzzled. Mr. Pigg suggested that on the following day he would ride down to the Antelope Hills about five miles east and that I might ride out Black Mountain again. It was now about 1 o'clock so we ate our lunch with the appetite that comes with exercise in the hills. I took from my saddle pockets some dried bear meat that I had prepared the year before in Idaho. I said, jokingly: "Let us eat some of this for medicine," meaning in the Indian sense of the word. We did so, then after smoking a short time, we mounted our horses and rode toward the south. Having given up this locality, we had gone perhaps a fourth of a mile and were riding across an open park when I noticed that my dogs, which usually kept close to my horse, were not with us. Looking back a couple of hundred yards, I saw them all in a bunch trailing. We had crossed the track.

I galloped back and stopped the dogs and Mr. Pigg going forward a few steps said: "Here's his track." As is my custom when about to turn my dogs loose, I passed a rope through the collar of one dog of each couple, then one man held the ends of the rope while the other man, not without considerable trouble, took the collar off each dog whose collar was not on the rope, afterwards removing the collars from the roped dogs. The dogs were crazily excited by the scent of the bear, jumping, squirming, barking, and crying to be free, and as fast as one was slipped, would disappear among the trees on the track. I had eight dogs, four couples, and by the time the last collar was off and couplings and rope tied on the saddle, the leaders had a good start of us. However the bear had wandered around before lying down so the dogs circled a minute or two and finally separated, Gale and Zephyr taking back in the direction from which the bear had come. Right here is where your correspondent made a misstatement. He said Mr. Pigg followed one bunch of dogs and I another. That is not so. I followed Ray, my best dog, paid no attention to the others, and Mr. Pigg kept with me. As soon as Ray and his following, Ring, Dummit and Ginger had the track straightened and apparently going toward Black Mountain, Mr. Pigg rode rapidly in that direction, along the ridge. This ridge was thinly covered with pine trees. I followed for a few rods, then rode to the left a few rods and stopped and listened. I was on the edge of a little cliff, and below me and a little to the right, perhaps 15 rods [about 83 yards] away, but out of sight in a dense growth of spruce and aspen, were my dogs, barking savagely. I knew they were fighting him close up, that the bear was bayed, and barring mishaps as good as killed. I took my horse down a little trail for a few rods so that in case Mr. Pigg passed above the cliff he would not be apt to see the horse. Left the horse, took off my gloves, laid them where I could find them again easily when the excitement should be over. Put a cartridge from my pocket in the chamber of my .30-40 carbine (Winchester Model '95), and went down into the thicket.

When I first saw the bear he stood nearly broadside and about four rods [about 22 yards] away. If I had had a more powerful gun, I would have shot him through the shoulders, but as I had seen the .30-40 bullets remain in elk and brown bear I thought best not to try it, so shot at his head, but the bullet went through his throat. This wound, I afterward found, bled pretty fast. In the shooting I was hindered by my fear of killing a dog. However, as soon as the dogs saw me they didn't attack the bear, seeming to say, "We have stopped him for you, now help yourself to bear."

Those dogs had helped me kill over 30 bear and evidently thought that shooting would end the trouble. The bear on receiving the shot turned and walked along the trail and ran diagonally down a gentle hill. When he was directly below me and 17 steps distant, he seemed to realize where I was and started for me. Here I fired two or three shots to turn him, as he was quite close enough, considering his reputation, and I didn't want him to rush me. The little trees were thick so one bullet, at least, struck a small spruce. We found the steel jacket in the hair on the bear's head. He also received one flesh wound in the neck. He turned and started back toward the spot where I first saw him. As he went I ran in closer and shot him in behind the shoulder, the bullet coming out of his breast at a point generally called the sticking place. He faced me at 11 steps distance and came on with his head low. I fired at his forehead, the bullet center right and left, but a little high. It unjointed his neck at the junction with the skull and followed down the spinal marrow. He sank slowly to the ground, raised himself partly up once or twice and was still except for his breathing which continued for some time, and even after he ceased breathing he seemed a threatening dangerous bulk, as in his life he had been a terrifying blood chilling destruction to men and cattle for many years.

In his account, Wharton Pigg thus described the site:

Now on this certain little ridge, in a dense thicket of spruce and aspen about 4½ miles northwest from the Stirrup Ranch stand three small spruce trees in a triangular form, each blazed on the inside. On one is written, "Where Old Mose died," and just 11 steps southwest stand two saplings bearing blazes. On one is written: "Where J.A. Anthony stood when he fired the fatal shot." Then farther up the hill, about 10 rods [55 yards], under the shade of a large rock and thick spruce is a round hole, perhaps three feet deep and five feet in diameter, beside which stands an aspen tree about eight inches in diameter with a large blaze. On this is the following inscription:

Old Mose's Last Bed.
J.W. Anthony and W.H. Pigg
Hunters
Ray, Ring, Ginger and Dummit
Pack
April 30, 1904

Anthony's account resumes:

Mr. Pigg soon came and asked if I had had much trouble to kill him. In that moment of exultation I remarked that it was as easy as taking candy from a kid. The bear deserved a less trivial remark. He was undoubtedly brave and had received education in the ways of men sufficient to know if he could get to the hunter and stop the shooting—that hunter would be to him "as clay in the hands of the potter." I still had cartridges in my magazine, as I had put in four during the fight. Your correspondent calls my killing the bear luck. It was a case of being prepared.

I had raised and trained the dogs and I knew if we pinned Mose or any other bear in ordinary country and circumstances he would be our meat. It

Wharton Pigg props up Old Mose's head shortly after James Anthony killed the bear.

seemed as if half the men in the county had hunted that bear. On speaking of this to a cowpuncher who came from Texas, but now lived in the Gorelle country, he said: "Yes, and hoping to God they wouldn't find him." Two toes were gone from Mose's hind foot and by this we knew him. The ranch men paid the $60 reward they had offered, and I gave Mr. Pigg half of it. I also loaned him a female hound from which he has raised some dogs that rounded up some bear last year. When he saw the body of the big bear, he said he had no claim to the hide. I said: "All right, then you can sell the meat." I wanted to take the hide off right away but Mr. Pigg wanted to bring him to town to show. We brought a wagon within a short distance of where he was killed and dragged him with a horse down hill to the wagon and five of us loaded him in. We hung him up in the slaughterhouse at the Stirrup Ranch and when his hind feet were swung against the roll of the beef hoist, his nose was on the floor. He hung there one day for the ranch men to view and then Mr. Pigg drove to Cañon with him, part of the way at night in a fearful storm. We hung him up in Wright and Morgan's Butcher Shop one day. Crowds of people viewed him all day and in the evening. Then about 11 o'clock Mr. Wright took off Old Mose's hide. We put the hide in the refrigerator room and sent it the next day to Professor Stainsky, Colorado Springs, who saved the hide all right. The meat, however, had not cooled, and added to the original game flavor of an old Silver Tip, that of being too well kept. The market for bear meat in Cañon has received a shock which it has not recovered from to this day.

Your Cañon City correspondent referred to me as an Idaho hunter. This is not correct as I lived in Colorado about as long as I did in Idaho, but Idaho is a grand state with many beautiful mountains and sparkling streams stocked with trout. I have hunted in a number of the Western states, mostly in Wyoming, where I lived for several years. Right now I am ready to move again and would like to know where there is a good bear country, damp enough for fair trailing, preferably in Colorado. Old Mose had been known and hunted in the Black Mountain country for about 20 years when he was killed. He lasted about 10 minutes when Ray and company were turned loose on his track. Those dogs we thought were on the back track were I am sure on track of another bear, a red bear, that was a partner of Mose. This is another story as Rudyard K [Kipling] would say. If you care to read it would write it at some future time.

So ends Anthony's account.

Wharton Pigg always referred to the hunt as his unlucky day, for he said he didn't have the honor of outwitting the giant outlaw grizzly.

Instead of the promised $500, the reward paid was only $60 which Anthony and Pigg split.

At the Wright & Morgan Market in Cañon City, Old Mose weighed 870 lbs., hog dressed—that is bled out and minus all entrails and dehydrated over two days. This probably represents 65 to 70 percent of total weight, making his intact weight about 1,200 lbs., and this at the end of the winter hibernation. Ranchers who saw the bear estimated his weight going into hibernation at about 1,400 lbs., truly a monster. From nose to tail he measured 10 ft. 4 in. and his body was 8½ ft. around. His jaw was 14 in. long. Despite his age, advanced for a grizzly and estimated at 35 to 40 years, his teeth were exceptionally good. The paws were 8 inches in diameter and equipped with claws up to 6 inches long.

The hide and head were refrigerated and then sent on to Colorado Springs to Prof. Gus Stainsky's taxidermy shop at 5½ E. Pikes Peak

Ave. where the hide was hung outside on display, then dressed. Having killed Old Mose, Anthony kept the hide and skull, and in his will bequeathed them to the Museum of Vertebrate Zoology, Berkeley, Calif. The administrator of his will, the Citizens National Bank of Evansville, Ind., displayed the hide in their lobby a few days, noted it was the oddest asset they ever held for an estate, then saw that it got to Berkeley. The museum acknowledged receipt of the hide in excellent condition with very little deterioration, although Mose had been killed 45 years earlier. The museum still has it, but it is in poor condition, even though it is preserved in a controlled-humidity refrigerated vault. Mose's skull is the second-largest grizzly skull in their collection.

Many bullets were found in Old Mose's carcass. When the hide was hung up in Cañon City, a scar was noted on one hip. Wharton Pigg advised this be covered, saying that every cowboy who saw the scar would claim he made it. Later Dann Hall walked in, said: "I took a shot at Old Mose one time up on Table Mountain and hit him too. I was close enough to know. I remember I hit him right about there, on the right hip." Hall pointed and touched the spot Pigg had covered, so this scar was credited to Hall.

About 1903 John Lyle was on a high point, saw Old Mose below him, fired a shot, and struck the grizzly in the back. He heard the animal give a grunt of pain and surprise. Pigg found a bullet lodged in the backbone and some vertebrae nicked. The bullet had been fired from above at an angle of 45 degrees, and John Lyle was given credit for the shot. A number of bullets from such light calibers as a .30-30 were found just under the skin. In places the skull was 4 in. thick, and a number of bullets had been stopped by this armor plate.

Dr. Ellsworth Lancaster, a Colorado College professor and specialist in psychology and neuroanatomy, was called in to examine the brain of Old Mose. He said, "One of the most interesting brains I have ever seen lies on the laboratory table before me. It is the brain of Old Mose, the huge grizzly which was recently killed on the hills south of Pikes Peak by J.W. Anthony."

Lancaster went on to note the most striking finding was the brain's small weight, only 15 ounces. He compared brain weight to total body weight and in Old Mose this ratio was less than 1 to 1,000. In contrast, a 150-lb. adult human being has a 3-lb. brain, ratio 1:50. The ratio in an ape is 1:30; elephant 1:747; and whale 1:22,400. Lancaster equated ratio of brain weight to body weight as a measure of intelligence, but his conclusions become a little fuzzy, for a small dog may have a ratio

Old Mose's carcass hangs on a beef hoist in Wright & Morgan Butcher Shop in Cañon City. Wharton Pigg, left, with Lee straight-pull rifle; and James Anthony, holding his Winchester Model 1895, caliber .30-40 Krag.

of 1:45. This would make the dog the most intelligent creature.

He continued, considering balance between parts of the brain, and noted that in the brain of Old Mose, motor areas were prominent and centers of smell and hearing were highly developed, but centers for intelligence were very primitive.

Regarding the armor plating of Old Mose's head, he noted:

> On opening the skull the first strange thing about the brain . . . is its location in the head. The brain of dogs and such animals usually runs forward nearly to the line of the eyes and fills the skull cavity. With this bear, the brain occupies only a small part of the head. . . . The front end of the brain was about 4 inches behind the eyes and all the intervening space was filled with a porous or cellular structure of bone, with scores of cavities large enough to insert the tips of the fingers into the cells or chambers. This is interesting to the hunter. It explains why he finds it so hard to kill the grizzly by firing a ball into the front of the head. The chances are that it would not reach the brain and a dozen bullets might lodge in those chambers and do little damage to the life of the bear. The bullet must strike between or just back of the eyes and take a downward course to hit the brain. On the sides of the head the . . . muscles are 4 in. thick by actual measurement and hence a bullet, unless fired at close range, would hardly pass through them and penetrate the skull, which slopes on the side like the roof of a house, from the top or ridge of the head down to the base. On the ridge the skull is quite thick but it is a surprise to find that the skull is only 3/16 of an inch on the sides, or about as thick as the skull of a man. Skull shape and thickness of muscles give the well-known protection to the brain of the grizzly. From the side, the bullet would tend to glance upward and miss the brain unless fired downward at an angle of 15 to 25 degrees.

With large centers for smell, hearing and motor areas, and little cortex for intelligence, Lancaster reasoned Mose was a creature of instinct with tremendous ability for keen smell and hearing. He had no moral nature, he did not reason, he did not love nor hate. If frightened, injured, or hungry the bear's instinct told him to run, to crush, and to kill, and he did just that. He lived a purely instinctive life as does every animal. It's too bad such a tremendous animal did so much damage to domestic animals on frontier ranches, arousing the anger of cattlemen, and so had to be killed. He was just doing his thing.

Afterword

The foregoing paper on "Old Mose, the Great Grizzly" was presented at a meeting of the Denver Westerners on Jan. 24, 1979, and published in The Denver Westerners *Roundup*. Several events have since occurred relating to this grizzly.

The Cañon City Municipal Museum attempted to bring Old Mose's hide back home and expressed a desire to have it mounted and put on display. After all, the grizzly's home was on Black Mountain, in Colorado, and near Cañon City. Alden H. Miller, head of the Museum of Zoology at the University of California at Berkeley, refused to release the hide, stating that, although it had been preserved in a temperature- and humidity-controlled vault, it was too brittle to ship, mount, and exhibit.

James E. Perkins of Colorado Springs became interested in Old Mose. In 1987, Perkins arranged for a tooth from the skull to be sent to the Arizona Game and Fish Department in Phoenix, where laboratory supervisor Bill Carrel studied the tooth and determined the bear was 10 to 12 years old when killed. David E. Brown, supervisor of the game branch, stated that Bill Carrel has "aged" hundreds of bear teeth and is highly proficient at such analysis. Aging is done by studying layers of concretions on a tooth, with a layer being added each season out of hibernation. (Apparently bears don't use a toothbrush.)

Clouding the waters still further, Barbara R. Stein, curatorial associate of the Museum of Vertebrate Zoology, University of California, Berkeley, wrote in a 1987 letter that the museum had no record showing the skull of Old Mose was ever examined or his teeth checked in order to determine the age of the specimen. If they are referring to the correct skull, how was Professor Lancaster [Dr. Ellsworth Lancaster, Colorado College professor] able to have the brain of Old Mose on the table before him to examine and study? To remove a brain for examination, the top of the skull must be sawed off.

If the tooth was not from Old Mose, was that grizzly a genetic sport that lived an unusually long life? Or if the correct tooth was aged, was Old Mose just the descendant of a line of very large grizzlies who lived on Black Mountain?

References

Anthony, James W. Letter to *Recreation Magazine* relating in 23 handwritten pages the "Killing of Old Mose." 1907.

Bair, Everett. *This Will Be an Empire.* Pageant Press, Inc., New York 1959, pp. 252-260.

Campbell, Rosemae W. *From Trappers to Tourists.* The Filter Press, Palmer Lake, Colo. 1972, p. 185.

Cañon City Museum and Fremont County Historical Society, slides of skull of Old Mose from museum at Berkeley, Calif., taken by Don Crimmins.

Cañon City Record. "Old Mose Dead." May 3, 1904, p. 1.

Colorado Springs City Directory, 1904.

Colorado Springs Evening Telegraph. May 4, 1904, p. 5.

Colorado Springs Gazette. May 4 and 5, 1904.

Colorado Springs Gazette Telegraph, Aug. 15, 1964. "The Terror of Black Mountain" by

George Doutht.

Crimmins, Donald R. Letters of July 28, 1977, and Oct. 10, 1977.

Deeping, John E., trust investment officer, Citizens National Bank of Evansville, Ind. Letter Aug. 22, 1977, and copies of correspondence dealing with transfer of skull and hide of Old Mose to museum at Berkeley, Calif., in accordance with will of J.W. Anthony; copy of letter from museum at Berkeley acknowledging receipt of hide "in excellent condition."

Denver Republican. May 3, 1904, p. 2. "Career of Old Mose, a Noted Bear, is Cut Short."

Epperson, Harry A. *Colorado As I Saw It.* Inland Printing Co., Kaysville, Utah, 1943, pp. 26-29.

Everett, George C.; and Hutchinson, Dr. Wendell F. *Under the Angel of Shavano,* Golden Bell Press, Denver 1963, pp. 257-261.

Fairplay Flume, Nov. 29, 1883, p. 4.

Gordon, Howard H. (son of Wharton Pigg). Letter of Sept. 19, 1977, with pictures of Old Mose, J.W. Anthony, and W.H. Pigg.

Hershey, Charlie Brown. "Colorado College, 1874-1949." Published by Colorado College, Colorado Springs 1952.

History of the Pike National Forest, No.136, p. 15.

Hubbard, W.P. *Notorious Grizzly Bears.* Sage Books, Denver, 1960. Account of "The Story of Old Mose" by Janet Sterling.

Humphrey, Mrs. William D. (daughter of Wharton Pigg). Letters of Aug. 24, 1977 and Sept. 9, 1977. Copies of Pigg's "Demise of Old Mose" and Anthony's "Report on Killing of Old Mose." Also, letter of Nov. 27, 1977. Life of W.H. Pigg.

Humphrey, Mrs. William D. "Stirrup Ranch Has Interesting History." Published in *The Daily Record,* Cañon City, Colo., Aug. 31, 1967.

Huntley, Paul L. *A Cowboy and his Horses,* published by Master Printers, Cañon City, Colo. 1977, pp. 52,53.

Huntley, Paul L. *Black Mountain Cowboys,* published by Master Printers, Cañon City, Colo. 1976, pp. 109,110 and 174-185.

Huntley, Paul L. Multiple interviews, 1977.

Kortlucke, Miss S.M., curatorial associate, Museum of Vertebrate Zoology, Univ. of California. Letter June 17, 1977.

Leasure, Robert. "The Saga of Old Mose. Giant Grizzly Turns Killer." *Colorado Magazine,* Sept./Oct. 1972, p. 10.

Leasure, Robert. *Black Mountain.* G.P. Putnam's Sons, New York 1975.

Lundberg, Nelson, Wahner and Jones. "Protein Metabolism in the Black Bear Before and During Hibernation." *Mayo Clinic Proceedings,* Nov. 1976, Vol. 51, pp. 716-722.

McConnell, Virginia. *Bayou Salado, The Story of South Park.* Sage Books, Denver 1966, p. 245.

McCracken, Harold. *The Beast That Walks Like Man.* Hanover House, Garden City, N.Y., 1955.

Mills, Enos. *The Grizzly, Our Greatest Wild Animal.* Houghton Mifflin Co., Boston and New York 1919.

Pigg, Wharton H. "Old Mose's Demise." Published in *Outdoor Life,* Vol. 14, 1904, pp. 561-565.

Queal, Cal. "The Grizzly that Terrorized Colorado," *Empire Magazine, The Denver Post,* Jan. 28, 1968.

Rocky Mountain News, June 5, 1921. Sect. 2, p. 16, "Old Mose is Famous Bear Many Years."

Schoonmaker, W.J. *The World of the Grizzly Bear.* J.B. Lippincott Co. 1968, p. 82

Squire, Bill, interview and letter.

Sterling, Janet. "Legends of the Royal Gorge," published by *Cañon City Daily Record,* 1943, p. 47. "The Story of Old Mose."

The Denver Field and Farm. Nov. 13, 1915, p. 8.

The Denver Post, May 15, 1904, p. 2. "King of Grizzlies is Dead."

The Denver Post, May 15, 1904. "What Old Mose's Brain Shows" by Dr. E.G. Lancaster, Colorado College.

The Free Press, Colorado Springs. Vacation edition, June 3, 1959. "Old Mose was Some Bear. Stirrup Impressed Him Simply as a Cafe."

The Shooter's Bible, Stoeger Arms Corp. No. 30 (1038 and No. 59 (1968).

U.S. Geological Survey Topographical Quadrangles, 15-minute series. Guffey, Black Mountain, Cameron Mountain, Cover Mountain, Antero Reservoir, and Florissant quadrangles.

Williamson, Harold F. *Winchester, the Gun That Won the West.* Combat Forces Press, Washington, D.C., 1952, pp. 68, 69 and 162, 163.

About the Author

Dr. Lester L. Williams, Colorado Springs Reserve Member of the Denver Westerners, presented his paper, "Old Mose, the Great Grizzly," on Jan. 24, 1979. The article was published in the January-February 1979 issue of *The Roundup.*

Subsequent to the writing of the article, Doctor Williams uncovered additional information about Old Mose, raising some still-unanswered questions. This information was set forth in the author's "Afterword."

A complete biographical sketch of Les Williams appears earlier in this book, accompanying his article, "C.N. Cotton and His Navajo Blankets."

Les has been a member of the Denver Posse of the Westerners since 1954, and served as Sheriff in 1971. In 1976, he helped form the Pikes Peak Posse of the Westerners in Colorado Springs, and was Sheriff of that group, as well. He is also a past-president of the Historical Society of the Pikes Peak Region, which he helped organize in 1974.

Doctor Williams is an Air Force veteran of World War II, and has practiced medicine in Colorado Springs since 1946.

"Wildlife through the lens" by *Max Smith*

A. G. Wallihan, Colorado's Pioneer Nature Photographer

by Nancy Bathke and Edwin A. Bathke

*M*R. WALLIHAN'S PHOTOGRAPHS of wild game possess such peculiar value that all lovers, whether of hunting or of natural history, should be glad to see them preserved in permanent form. The art and practice of photographing wild animals in their native haunts has made great progress in recent years. It is itself a branch of sport, and hunting with the camera has many points of superiority, when compared to hunting with a rifle. But, even under favorable conditions, very few men have the skill, the patience, the woodcraft and the plainscraft which enabled Mr. Wallihan to accomplish so much; and, moreover, the conditions as regards most of our big game animals are continually changing for the worse. The difficulties of getting really good and characteristic photographs are such as to be practically insuperable. . . . It has never been my good fortune to see as interesting a collection of game pictures as those that have been taken by Mr. & Mrs. Wallihan, and I am equally pleased with the simplicity with which they tell their most interesting stories of the ways in which they got these photographs."

These words were written by Theodore Roosevelt, a renowned champion of promoting, preserving, and partaking in nature. He penned his observations and admiration of the Wallihans' photography in 1894 and in 1901, in his introductions to both books authored by the Wallihans.

This paper intends to identify the Wallihans, certainly obscure characters in the history of photography and in the history of Colorado. Turning first to photography, the beginnings are traced back to 1839 when Louis-Jacques-Mande Daguerre of France and Henry Fox Talbot of England discovered the fundamentals of the photographic imaging process. The "new art" slowly developed during its infancy in the 1840s, when men of science considered photographs, while "pretty" or "ingenious," not to be worth serious attention. However, the concept of a "picture" being worth a thousand words appealed to people, and by the 1850s was catching on rapidly. During the second half of the nineteenth century, the profession of photography prospered and became firmly established. Extensive photo studios were common in all major cities, and itinerant photographers brought their trade to the most rural of communities.

This development of photography coincided with the settlement of Colorado. Those entrepreneurs with the capabilities of capturing people and scenes on paper cards readily provided photos to people wanting to record their locales and events, for themselves and for distant friends and relatives. Famous photographers in frontier Colorado were, first and foremost, William Henry Jackson, and then Charles Weitfle, William Chamberlain, Joseph Collier, James Thurlow, Byron Gurnsey, William Hook, and Joe Sturdevant, to name a few. These were all professionals, attempting to make a living at providing photographs to the public. The subject of this paper was essentially on the fringes of these endeavors.

And yet Allen Grant Wallihan made his mark in photographic history in Colorado, doing something no one else had succeeded in doing before. A. G. Wallihan was probably the first photographer in the world to photograph wildlife in its natural habitat. Even the premier photographer, W. H. Jackson, for all his excellent photography, used posed specimens when producing animal pictures.

The story of Wallihan is generally obscured in modern-day analysis of Colorado history. And yet when we probe into his background, his life in the early West is truly representative of frontier adventure.

Allen Grant Wallihan was born in Footville, Grant County, Wis., on June 15, 1859, the youngest of 11 children. His early years were spent on a Wisconsin farm, and in 1870 he accompanied his parents to Denver. In the spring of 1871 the family moved to Divide, and had the post office at Southwater, four miles below Monument. The book *Colorado Post Offices* lists Southwater as having been established on Jan. 8, 1872, and being in service until Oct. 1, 1878. It was moved from Bassett's Mills, which had provided service since June 15, 1869. When the Southwater office was closed in 1878, it was moved to Husted. (The community at Southwater is familiar to us as Borst.)

While Allen, the youngest child, was living with his parents in El Paso County, older siblings were making lives for themselves in Colorado. Most notable of these was Samuel. He became an editor in Denver, and, with T. O. Bigney, edited *The Rocky Mountain Directory and Colorado Gazetteer for 1871*. This very significant work among early Colorado directories was published by S. S. Wallihan & Company in Denver in 1871.

In 1876, the family returned to Wisconsin. (It appears that no long-term successor was found for the post office). But, to quote A. G., "I was too much saturated with love of the mountains to stay there so in '79 I returned to Husted and on to Leadville." That his brother George was the editor of the *Leadville Chronicle* in 1879 may have been a factor in drawing him to the silver camp.

In 1879 A. G. Wallihan was a young man of 20, away from home and on his own for the first time. He kept a diary of his adventures during this first year alone. In 1945 his widow presented that diary to the State Historical Society of Colorado. This small annual diary, measuring 3 by 7 3/4 inches, and bound in purple cloth, presents poignant insights into life in Leadville in 1880 and into the daily activities of a 20-year-old there. Although the diary was printed for the year 1879 as "The Perpetual Diary," his first entry is "Thursday, January 1, 1880: Commenced the new year by working all day at the Red Headed Mary claim at Adelaide. 1 shift."

(Author's Collection)

The Wallihans lived in the heart of big game country.

Wallihan was quite a mine laborer during January to June. He recorded the shifts he worked at each mine, sometimes working two shifts in a day. He mentions several prominent Leadville mines, such as the Iron Mine on Breece Hill, the Little Evans, the Highland Chief, the Triangle, and the Sherman. Putting in, firing, and clearing out shots in the mines were some of his mining efforts, and he reported each.

Typically, A. G. Wallihan lived in a cabin near the mines he worked in, and trips into the town of Leadville were an important part of his daily life. On Jan. 3, he wrote: "One shift. Went to town in evening. Rec'd letter from Percy. Wrote to Father. Bo't a knife and pair of overalls," and on Jan. 6, "Went to town. Deposited $12 in bank."

Wallihan was a careful manager of his money, and regularly did business at a bank. On Jan. 20, he recorded, "Took out a policy for $1,000. Deposited it in Merchants and Mechanics Bank." In January 1880 he began recording income and expenditures in the back of his diary. Entries for wages, board, the knife and overalls, oysters, stockings, payments on a revolver and cartridges, a clock, and doctor's bills are all duly recorded in January and February. Then, in March the entries are briefer, and, as is the case with most of us, and in spite of good intentions, the accounting ceased at the end of the month.

Life in the mining camp was not easy, and the entries starting on Jan. 30, 1880, indicated some of the daily travails:

"Friday, January 30. Worked in Dick's place, and was taken sick in the evening. Shivered all night. One shift.

"Saturday, January 31. Took two drinks of brandy. Got up about 11:30. George and Dr. Crook came up in evening. Doctor gave me some medicine. Ate some pears.

"Sunday, February 1. Slept very well. Felt some better. One o'clock and no medicine. Sent C. E. C. down at 7:45. Ike came with the medicine at 8.

"Monday, February 2. Took the medicine in the morning, worked all night. Took no. 2 at 12:30. King came up with Corbett at 11. Sore throat nearly gone.

"Tuesday, February 3. Got up feeling better. Throat sore again. Ate more for breakfast than I have since I have been sick. Ate some supper.

"Wednesday, February 4. Throat very sore. Couldn't get my mouth open wide enough to eat anything but spoon victuals for breakfast.

"Thursday, February 5. Feel better, sore throat nearly well.

"Friday, February 6. Well enough to go to town."

The weather was regularly commented on, such as: "Friday, February 27. A raw, cold day. Put in three shots and cleared them out. Sent letter to George [his brother]." And, "Thursday, March 4. A terrible storm," then "April 5, snowed," "April 6, snowed," and "April 7, snowed very hard." On May 8 it "snowed all night," and on May 9, it "snowed all day." After the spring, entries were often "C & C," for clear and cloudy.

Timbering in the mines was an additional task. Allen and his co-workers both cut and placed the timbers in the mines. They also surveyed, and sharpened picks and drills. But it was not "all work and no play." There were frequent trips to the saloon, at least weekly. This was not just riotous living, however. The saloon was the frontier meeting place, and here they picked up their mail and sent their letters. Still, their lives were normal: "July 4. Charlie and I cleaned out the G. L. shaft. Geo. didn't come. Charlie went to town on the stage. I got drunk. No beer. C & C." But such activity by Wallihan was infrequent.

On June 15, 1880, was the simple entry, "We all went fishing. Caught 16. No word from Geo. My 21st birthday. Clear." Hunting and fishing were a daily part of life. In the spring they often shot at snowshoe rabbits, and sometimes got one. The first mention of fishing was on May 23, on the Pacific Slope. In June fishing became a frequent activity. June, July, and August the major work efforts were cutting timbers and catching fish, which were sold in Leadville. On July 22, the entry read, "Came to town. Arrived about 9. Made the restaurant suffer. Sold our fish for 50 cents, 14 1/2 lb." On July 31, they received 45 cents for their fish. Then, on Aug. 1, the diary read, "Sunday. Did nothing. Went to circus in evening with Welty."

On Aug. 8 the group took a contract for 1,000 ties at 15 cents. By the end of the month they had cut nearly 300 ties. But it apparently was not a job they relished: "Thursday, August 13. Made 13 ties and quit. Charlie got homesick and we made up our minds to throw up the contract." By the end of August Allen had left Leadville.

On Aug. 29, A. G. Wallihan camped at Malta, south of Leadville. On the 30th his camp was below Granite, the 31st at the head of Browns Canyon, Sept. 1 at Poncha Springs, Sept. 2 below Monarch Junction, and on the 4th he returned to Maysville.

In September, the Wisconsin farm boy put the experiences of his youth to use. On Sept. 5 he recorded in his diary, "Struck a job just after leaving town at $30 per month." The next days were spent cutting and shocking oats, hauling hay, and digging potatoes.

In early October Wallihan hunted deer around Maysville. On Oct. 9 he started for Divide, and saw two mountain sheep, taking seven shots at them. On Monday, Oct. 18, he wrote; "I was sick," and on the 19th, "Still sick." Then on Nov. 1, "Came to Colorado Springs," followed by Nov. 2, "Dr. Kimball pronounced it mountain fever."

Diary entries became sparse toward the end of 1880. On Dec. 25, Allen Wallihan recorded his Christmas gifts: "Got a silk handkerchief, pair of gloves, pair of socks, and a pocket drinking cup." The last entry of the year read, "Thursday, December 31. Rec'd letter from Father containing $45." With that, any known recording of the daily activities of A. G. Wallihan ended.

A. G. Wallihan provided a biographical summary in his first book, *Hoofs, Claws, and Antlers of the Rocky Mountains*, published in 1894. After arriving in Colorado Springs following most of 1880 in Leadville, he hunted antelope for a month. Then he returned to Husted, although he didn't indicate whether any of the rest of the family lived there, or if they still had a home there. He drifted into the mountains in the fall of 1881, to Alpine in the spring, and then in 1882 settled in Lily Park, Routt County, in northwestern Colorado.

Sometime in the early 1880s, probably soon after moving to Lily Park, Allen met Mary Augusta (Higgins) Farnham and her brother, Tom Higgins. She was also a native of Wisconsin, having been born in Milwaukee County. Her father had moved to Milwaukee in 1835 from Franklin, Mass. On her mother's side she was of old Revolutionary stock of English descent, the Rawsons. In 1885, in Rawlins, Wyo., she became Mary A. Wallihan, wife of Allen Grant Wallihan.

The Wallihans lived in Lily Park until June 1885, when they moved to Sulphur, Wyo.

Their sojourn in Wyoming was brief, and in October 1885 they moved to Lay, Colo. This was to be their home for the remainder of A. G. Wallihan's life. Their ranch house was the sole building, comprising the "town" of Lay.

During the days of the U.S. Army expedition to Meeker, some troops stayed overnight in the vicinity. A Lt. McCauley of the Third U.S. Cavalry referred to the place as Lay. The lieutenant's fiancee was Miss Olive Lay of Chicago. When McCauley's superior officer asked him why the name, he replied, "Did you ever hear of the great General

Allen G. Wallihan and Mary Higgins Wallihan in later years.

Lay?" The colonel didn't want to admit unfamiliarity with history, so he said "Yes, of course," and the name was officially accepted.

Lay became a government ranch following the Army expedition to Meeker. The ranch served a double purpose, being a roadhouse catering to travelers' needs, and a post office. The Lay Post Office was established on Aug. 1, 1881. Early in 1886 A. G. was appointed postmaster, serving until his death in December 1935, being one of the longest-tenured postmasters in the nation at that time.

The young A. G. Wallihan had recorded his hunting attempts in his diary, shooting at rabbits, a wildcat, and a weasel. Between leaving Leadville and arriving in Colorado Springs he hunted both deer and mountain sheep. The hunting efforts he recorded seemed to mark him as a beginner, but when he got to Colorado Springs, he hunted antelope for a month. In *Hoofs, Claws, and Antlers*, he claimed: "While a good shot at antelope, I could not kill a deer until I had fired six shots, all less than 60 yards away and standing. I killed one, and was thereafter all right on deer shooting."

Mrs. Wallihan also related her hunting experiences in their first book. She described her father as a very good hunter of many game species. As to hunting, she wrote: "Though interested in this kind of shooting I never had an opportunity to try my skill until I came west, about the time I was married. My brother and Mr. Wallihan wanted me to learn to shoot." She fired a revolver a few times and a gun once, then tried the Parker shotgun on cottontail rabbits. At first she couldn't hold it, but soon was skillful enough to hit a goose at 60 yards and an elevation of 75 feet, pleasing all three of them. The next spring she got her first deer, and soon she was also an adept hunter.

The Wallihans lived in some of the most prolific deer and antelope country in the West. A. G. gave credit to Mrs. Wallihan for the idea of photographing wild game on the hoof. One day while crouched in the sagebrush studying a colony of ants at work, she looked up to find herself closely surrounded by a herd of mule deer. That gave her the idea of using a blind and a camera.

Mary Wallihan gazed at the deer for a long time, and then remembering her rifle, raised it, and the deer all ran off. She did bag one when they were about 100 yards away, but said, as she was dressing the deer, "If I had a camera then, I could have gotten a wonderful picture of them so close." The following summer two young missionaries on vacation stopped by, one had a camera, and Mrs. Wallihan bargained for it, paying for the camera in part with buckskin gloves she had made from buckskin Allen had tanned.

The Wallihans set out to learn the techniques of photography, not only loading, focusing the camera, and exposing the plate, but also the chemical procedures of mixing developers and fixing baths, washing and drying plates, printing proofs, and mounting finished prints on cards. After all, they were far removed in a wilderness area, with no other photography business around.

They developed their techniques, immediately realizing that a handheld camera would be useless and could only provide an image too small to be of value. So A. G. lugged around heavy tripod cameras, set up his equipment by game trails, and patiently waited. He started using 4x6½, and then 8x10 plates, and up to 1894 was using Carbutt's cut film, and then changed to Cramer's Crown plates because they were speedier—and speed was essential for animal photos. In their book, *Camera Shots at Big Game*, he describes his cameras, and refinement of necessary photographic techniques as he became more successful. That he truly became a proficient professional photographer is evidenced by the images that have survived. Not only was he

(Author's Collection)

A.G. Wallihan shot wildlife photos with heavy tripod camera.

a nature photographer, but he also recorded images in Craig and Steamboat Springs—street scenes, businesses, and building interiors.

Charles B. Roth, Colorado historian and an early member of the Denver Posse of the Western-ers, interviewed A. G. Wallihan during the early 1930s. The writ-ten responses of Wallihan to Roth's questions were published in the September 1944 issue of the State Historical Society's *Colora-do Magazine* as an article attri-buted posthumously to Wallihan, with introduction by Roth. Walli-han wrote that he made his first attempt to get close enough to shy deer to get photographs in Octo-ber 1888.

On the other hand, in the Wall-ihans' second book, *Camera Shots at Big Game*, copyrighted in 1901, Wallihan stated that he made his first attempts in the autumn of 1889. William T. Hornaday, in his 1925 book, *A Wild-Animal Roundup*, reported that "The photograph-ing of wild game received its first great impulse in America" from the Wallihans, but that their first negatives were made in October 1890. While this may seem to be a bit of quibbling about dates, the claim to being first lies in the balance. George Shiras III, noted nature photog-rapher for the National Geographic Society, wrote in his 1935 two-volume work, *Hunting Wild Life with Camera and Flashlights*, that on July 8, 1889, he tried to take photographs of deer by flashlight. Both attempts at photos were spoiled, but he refined his technique, and the next season he was successful. A photo of a deer taken in June 1890 is reproduced in the volume. Shiras did not physically take the photo himself, but rigged his camera so that the deer tripped a wire and took his own picture. From this start, Shiras went on to become the pre-mier nature photographer for the National Geographic Society. His first photos were published in the society's journals in 1906, and Shiras contributed regularly for the next 30 years.

Thus, the question of who was truly the first to photograph wild animals, free in their natural settings, can not be answered with any degree of certainty. However, it appears that the pioneering efforts of both photographers have merit and appropriately deserve recognition.

Arguments can be made giving the benefit of the doubt to the Wallihans, but regardless of the decision, their groundbreaking photography is worthy of recognition, and deserving of more credit than has thus far been given. Perhaps we can cap our case with A. G. Wallihan's own words in the September 1944 issue of *Colorado Magazine* :

> Dr. Hornaday has stated that I was the first to photograph wild game, and as far as I know the statement is true. My photographs were all taken from live wild game, as wild as game can be, not in any preserves, and further I or my wife were with the cameras and made the exposures at all times. There were not set cameras for the game to touch off the shutters by breaking a thread, nor were they baited with delicacies at any time, but they were taken by sheer skill and persistence, under all kinds of hardships, freezing cold in winter, and the hottest suns of summer days.

The Wallihans' first photographs were of deer, and mule deer were their most popular subjects. As their photo business expanded, they numbered and copyrighted the various images. Most of the printed

(Author's Collection)

Mary Wallihan's hunting skill was widely known.

captions on the negatives appear to be dated 1894, 1895, and 1896. At first, the backs of the photo cards were penned, for example, "Deer No. 21, Copyrighted, A. G. Wallihan Photo, Lay, Col." A rubber stamp was made, and a back imprint on cards of "A. G. Wallihan, Photographer, Lay, Colorado" has survived. Eventually, sales of photos attained such volume that custom-printed cards were made, and these cards listed the number of images available for each animal species. Successive orders of cards contained updates of the number of photos available. The last of these cards reads:

WALLIHAN'S BIG GAME PHOTOGRAPHS
TAKEN FROM LIVE WILD GAME

Consisting of 53 Deer, 13 Elk, 13 Antelope, 30 Mountain Lions,
1 Coyote, 7 Wild Cats, 3 Rattlesnakes, 2 Sage Hens,
3 Jack Rabbits, 1 Snowshoe Rabbit, 1 Cottontail Rabbit,
1 Grouse, 11 Bear, 2 Ducks, 1 Badger
– 141 in the Set –
53 8x10; Balance 5x8.

PRICES- 8X10 SIZE, $6 PER DOZEN 5X8 SIZE, $3 PER DOZEN.

A. G. WALLIHAN, LAY, ROUTT COUNTY, COLORADO.

The first book that the Wallihans authored, *Hoofs, Claws, and Antlers of the Rocky Mountains*, was published in 1894 by Frank S. Thayer, in Denver. Following the introduction by Theodore Roosevelt, the Wallihans presented a short biography of themselves, then proceeded to provide rich details—expeditionary, photographic and nature—on taking many of the photographs reproduced in the book.

An article in the *Rocky Mountain News* on June 30, 1895, featuring Mrs. Wallihan, described this book and stated that the Wallihans were working on a new book, for which Thayer was paying $1,000 for 24 photographs. A second edition of *Hoofs, Claws, and Antlers* was published by Thayer in 1904, and in this edition the very brief introduction was written by "Buffalo Bill" Cody.

Mary Wallihan's prowess with a rifle was becoming widely known, and two of the photo plates in *Hoofs, Claws, and Antlers* are captioned, first, "Doubles at One Shot," showing Mrs. Wallihan with the two large buck mule deer that she had bagged with one shot, and secondly, "Mrs. Wallihan's 30th Deer," showing her standing with her rifle over the fallen buck.

The Wallihans photographed practically all species of Western wild game, both large and small, but they achieved their most renowned photographs of cougars. To do this, Wallihan built two stout boxes, one for the camera and the other for the plate holders and lenses, and fitted them with padding, so that they could be fastened to a pack-horse. The packhorse would have to be led on a hot trail after the hounds and mountain lions, and the boxes had to be lashed securely on the horse so that, no matter how fast they went, or if the horse fell and rolled over, the equipment would not be damaged.

The most exciting picture that A. G. made was of a cougar leaping from a tree, the photograph catching her in midair. The dogs had treed a very wild and shy female mountain lion. The dogs were pursuing the cougar from tree to tree, and had cornered her in a small tree. The hunters reconnoitered and Wallihan found he could get very close behind another small tree. Then the three other men began yelling and throwing clubs at the cougar from the far side. The mountain lion started for Wallihan's side, he sidestepped out into full clear view, she made the leap, the camera was trained on her, and the shutter released. The cougar struck the ground so close to Wallihan that he wrote, "I could have knocked a homerun if I had been possessed of a baseball bat, and not the camera."

The photograph of the leaping cougar, taken in 1895, would be A. G. Wallihan's most famous, and for it he would be awarded a gold medal at the Paris Exposition.

The second book authored by Allen Grant Wallihan, *Camera Shots at Big Game*, was published by Doubleday, Page & Co. of New York. The first edition was printed in 1901, but the second edition had a printing date of 1904. However, the title page had a publisher's date of 1906. This rather large book, 11 by 8 inches and well over an inch thick, contains just 77 pages of text, but the inclusion of 22 stunning full-page photogravures, as well as 45 other photographic reproductions make the book a showpiece of the Wallihans' wildlife photography. Wallihan describes his camera techniques as well as experiences on the trail in acquiring the many animal images. Again, A. G.'s friend Theodore Roosevelt provided the introduction, and Teddy wrote eight pages praising Wallihan's work. Theodore Roosevelt admired the Wallihans' photography and they were friends. Roosevelt participated in two Colorado hunts. In 1901 he hunted cougars around Meeker, and in 1905 hunted bears near Glenwood Springs. Wallihan wrote to Roosevelt, asking to meet him. Roosevelt had seen Wallihan's cougar photos, and since guide Billy Wells and his dogs had been instrumental in getting these photos, Teddy wrote to Billy. But Bill Wells declined and referred Roosevelt to John Goff, another lion-hunting guide with whom Wallihan was familiar. John Goff then guided Roosevelt on both the Meeker and Glenwood Springs hunts.

(Author's Collection)
Photo of leaping cougar was Wallihan's most famous shot.

A. G. Wallihan journeyed to Meeker, where Teddy wanted to meet him. They met over breakfast, discussing Wallihan's photography, with both expressing their disappointment in publisher Thayer's addition of some posed animal pictures to A. G.'s natural animal photography in *Hoofs, Claws and Antlers*. Roosevelt did not blame Wallihan, since he wrote the extensive preface in Wallihan's second book, *Camera Shots at Big Game*.

Mary Wallihan shared in her husband's work and fame. In August 1901, she spoke at the Congress of Women at the Antlers Hotel in Colorado Springs. An extensive article in the *Rocky Mountain News* told of her life in Lay, her hunting exploits, and her contributions in wildlife photography.

Mary Wallihan died in September 1922 at the age of 85. At her request, she was buried on a rock pinnacle overlooking the ranch that had been her home for nearly 40 years. Allen married again, on Sept. 26, 1927, to a childhood sweetheart, Mrs. Essie Cook, who was then living in Memphis, Tenn.

A. G. Wallihan was ill for a number of years when Charlie Roth knew him. A. G. knew the end was not far away, and deliberately set about making plans. He constructed his own casket, and placed it in a shed for the time when it would be needed. He gave Mrs. Wallihan specific directions on how he should be buried. He wanted no preacher, but a lawyer friend from Steamboat Springs was to officiate. He selected a burial spot on a hill on his old homestead. In December 1935 he passed away, and a pioneer's funeral was conducted for a real pioneer. Allen Wallihan was laid to rest beside Mary Wallihan, on the rocky knoll overlooking Lay.

Essie Cook Wallihan moved to Los Angeles, and before her death in 1945 she gave many of her husband's possessions to the State Historical Society of Colorado. Among the items were his 1879 diary, his spurs, watch, three handkerchiefs, trunk, and an Indian blanket, as well as copies of both of his books. The previous year, A. G. Wallihan's nephew had given to the society Wallihan's large camera and tripod, hunting knife, and gloves.

Charles B. Roth also donated the .40-70 Remington-Hepburn rifle that Wallihan used, and a group of Wallihan's photographs.

With these mementos and the photographs and books of Allen and Mary Wallihan, their remarkable pioneering efforts in wildlife photography combine in a tribute to their work, and as documentation for recognition of their achievements.

About the Authors

Edwin A. and Nancy Bathke have been Colorado residents for 34 years, and have resided in Manitou Springs the past 25 years. Their interest in Colorado and the West is indicated by their hobbies of traveling, hiking, and collecting Colorado artifacts. Nancy is a collector of antique souvenir spoons, sheet music, and souvenir glass of Colorado. Ed collects old photographs and stereopticon views of Colorado, and books of Colorado. They are members of the Ghost Town Club of Colorado, the Ghost Town Club of Colorado Springs, and the Pikes Peak Posse of the Westerners. Both Ed and Nancy are past presidents of the Ghost Town Club of Colorado and the Historical Society of the Pikes Peak Region, and past sheriffs of the Pikes Peak Posse of the Westerners. Ed was the founding sheriff of the Pikes Peak Posse.

Ed became a Corresponding Member of the Denver Westerners in 1965; a Posse Member in 1970; Deputy Sheriff in 1971, and Sheriff in 1972. He was also editor of the 1972 *Brand Book* (Vol. 28).

Nancy recently became the second woman elected to membership in the Denver Posse. They are co-authors of *The West in Postage Stamps*, have had articles published in the *Brand Books* and the *Roundup* magazine of the Denver Westerners.

Ed Bathke is a mathematician, and recently retired as a computer analyst at Kaman Sciences in Colorado Springs. He holds B.S. and M.S. degrees in mathematics from the University of Wisconsin, and an M.S. in applied mathematics from the University of Colorado. Nancy is a retired elementary school teacher. Her last assignment was teaching computer skills to kindergarten through fifth grade pupils at Woodmen-Roberts Elementary School, Air Academy District 20, in El Paso County. She has a B.S. in education from the University of Wisconsin, and an M.A. in education from the University of Colorado.

Nancy is listed in *Who's Who of American Women* and *Who's Who in the West*, and both Ed and Nancy are listed in *Contemporary Authors*.

"From boots to balloons" by *Max Smith*

From Infantry to Air Corps:

A History of Fort Logan

By Earl McCoy

*E*ARLY MILITARY POSTS in Colorado were situated along the trade and settlement routes to provide safety between the towns. During the Civil War, Denver had camps for volunteer troops: Camp Weld just east of the South Platte River, Camp Wheeler where Lincoln Park is now, and the Denver Depot and Arsenal at 11th and Larimer streets in the building that later became the Lindell Hotel. Repeated requests from Denver and other cities in Colorado to have posts of the Regular Army established nearby were refused; Gen. William T. Sherman, General of the Army, expected towns to be able to provide their own troops if threatened by Indian raids. He wrote, "Denver needs no protection. She should raise on an hour's notice 1,000 men, and instead of protection she can and should protect the neighboring settlements."[1]

By 1883, when General Sherman retired and turned over the leadership of the Army to Lt. Gen. Phil Sheridan, even Sherman agreed that the "small posts along wagon and stage routes of travel [were] no longer needed." For economy, and access to railroads capable of sending troops to any given point of danger at a speed of 500 miles a day, a distance that formerly took a full month of marching, it was recommended that forts be consolidated near cities.[2]

Early in 1886, citizens associated with the Chamber of Commerce again organized a campaign to obtain a military post at Denver. Sen. Henry M. Teller introduced S. 2477 on May 19, 1886, to authorize a post and to appropriate $250,000 for construction. In July 1886, William Endicott, Secretary of War, submitted a statement in support of the Teller proposal to the Committee on Military Affairs, including these comments:

> The subject matter of this bill invites, in its consideration, the question of abandonment of numerous small posts that are no longer necessary and the concentration of larger forces at strategic points near the frontier, or at points of railroad intersection. . . .

> There can be no doubt that such a policy would prove highly advanta-
> geous to the military service, and result in greater economy, and I think . . .
> that Denver should be one of the points at which one of the permanent
> military posts of the country should be located. . . . If such an appropriation
> is made, and a military post near Denver established, the following smaller
> posts could be disposed of, as no longer needed for military purposes, viz:
> Forts Lyon, Colorado; Union, New Mexico; Fred Steele, Wyoming; and the
> cantonment on the Uncompahgre, Colorado.[3]

Other reports have also listed Forts Garland, Lewis, and Uncompahgre as posts to be replaced by the new camp near Denver. Ft.
Garland had closed in 1883; Ft. Lewis lasted until 1891. Ft. Uncompahgre (also called Ft. Robidoux) had closed in 1845; the name was
confused with the cantonment on the Uncompahgre, also called Ft.
Crawford. A letter from General Sheridan, endorsing the Denver-area
camp, accompanied Secretary Endicott's statement.

At the same time that Senator Teller's bill was being discussed,
Congress was considering an offer of land for a post near Chicago, to
be donated by the Chicago Commercial Club. The camp near Chicago
was delayed because of concerns that concentration of troops near
Chicago was related to the recent Haymarket riot and intended to
suppress the growing development of the Knights of Labor. S. 2477,
creating the fort at Denver, passed the House of Representatives on
Feb. 2, 1887; Judge George Symes, congressional delegate from Denver, told the newspaper that he had "succeeded after a heroic struggle
in securing the passage of the bill . . ." by assuring his colleagues that
troops located near Denver would be used "to suppress Indian troubles
arising in any part of the Western States and Territories . . ." and not
to control labor union activity.[4] (No one else noticed the "heroic
struggle" of Judge Symes). Although policing labor disputes and
strikebreaking were not the major reasons for approving the new post,
the Army did take on these functions from time to time until the end
of the nineteenth century.[5]

President Cleveland signed the bill on Feb. 17. It provided that a
military post would be established on a tract of land of at least 640
acres, to be donated, with the state to cede jurisdiction to the federal
government. The site was to be selected by the Lieutenant General of
the Army, with an appropriation of $100,000 for construction of
"necessary buildings, quarters, barracks and stables" (down from the
$250,000 first requested).

Members of the Denver committee, chaired by J.A. Thatcher and
including Henry R. Wolcott, ex-Senator N. P. Hill, and ex-Gov. James
B. Grant, were busy promoting the establishment of the fort that win-

ter, and after the legislation was approved the committee located 11 sites for General Sheridan to consider. The clear preference of Denverites was a tract of land adjacent to Sloan Lake, and it was pointed out that it would be easier to "keep away the saloons and other nuisances" if the camp were close to Denver.[6] On March 20, General Sheridan and his party came to Denver, and spent the next four days touring the proposed tracts. After his departure he sent a letter to the committee announcing his selection of the "Johnson Tract," about 8½ miles south of the Union Station, giving his reasons for the choice: a never-failing stream of clear and pure water running through [Bear Creek]; a railway running through the northern edge [the Morrison branch of the Denver, South Park & Pacific Railroad]; a beautiful plateau for a parade and buildings; possibilities of artesian wells; and good views of the mountains and plains.[7] Frank Hall, in his 1899 *History of the State of Colorado*, stated that "General Sheridan's object in placing it there was to prevent, as far as possible, the soldiers from coming into the city and spending their money in dissipation."[8]

(Courtesy Western History Dept., Denver Public Library)

Lt. Gen. Philip H. Sheridan endorsed "camp" at Denver.

Committees were organized to solicit funds in Denver and the area near the post to purchase the land. The cost of the property was $33,619, contributed by 104 businesses and individuals, with donations ranging from $3,000 (from the Union Pacific Railroad) down to $10. At last, on Oct. 22, 1887, Company A of the Eighteenth Infantry arrived from Ft. Hays, Kans., as the first troops assigned to the post. For some reason, the soldiers camped about a mile from the military reservation, on the Howard Ranch. The next day Company E of the Eighteenth Infantry came from Ft. Leavenworth, Kans., to join the first arrivals, and on Oct. 25 Maj. George K. Brady reached Denver from Ft. Crawford as the first commander of the "Camp Near the City of Denver." The soldiers camped in 26 tents on the bank of Bear Creek, with Sibley stoves to provide heat, as "the snow was flying in feathery clouds and the wind was whistling a tune of 'Icy, Icy, Drear and Shivery'," according to a newspaper report.

Food was prepared on cookstoves cut into the bank of the creek, with a menu of bacon, canned vegetables, fried potatoes, hardtack with bacon gravy and onions, and black coffee. Major Brady was staying at the Albany Hotel in Denver, and said that he and the troops would move onto the post on Oct. 26.[9] The monthly report for October 1887 stated: "October 31st permanent camp was made on the U.S. Military Reservation about nine miles S.W. of Denver, Colorado."

In November, Capt. Lafayette E. Campbell arrived from Ft. Leavenworth to become Quartermaster of the post and to supervise the building program. Temporary barracks were completed on Dec. 24, in time for Christmas, and the Guard House was finished Dec. 31, in time for New Year's Eve.

Frank J. Grodavent was engaged as architect to design the buildings. *The Denver Republican* on July 1, 1888, in reporting that plans for the buildings had been approved and bids for construction would be opened in a few days, stated that "the Army Post will present a fine appearance, and will become one of the leading attractions and pleasure resorts of Denver." (A 1942 history of the fort characterized the barracks and officers' quarters as "quite uninspired architecturally.")[10] The article went on to say that the post "will add certainly to the business of the city nearly half a million dollars annually, but the social attractions will also be a prominent feature." It was estimated that planned construction would require $300,000 in addition to $100,000 originally appropriated. Work on building barracks and officers' quarters began in 1888—10 barracks for six companies of infantry and four companies of cavalry, as well as duplex officers' quarters. Also in 1888 the Denver & Rio Grande Railroad built a spur line to the fort. The first infantry barracks were completed in May 1889.

Although the post was officially labeled "Camp Near the City of Denver," it had frequently been called Sheridan Post or Ft. Sheridan. Before his death in August 1888, General Sheridan indicated his preference that the post north of Chicago should bear his name. That post had been informally called Ft. Logan, after John Alexander Logan, the Illinois senator who had been instrumental in gaining con-

(Courtesy Colorado Historical Society)

John A. Logan, Illinois senator, for whom fort was named.

gressional approval to accept the donated land for the fort. Logan had distinguished himself in the Civil War, quickly rising to the rank of major general with the volunteer troops. After the war he was again elected to Congress, and later became a senator. In 1884 he was the candidate for vice president on the Republican ticket, as a running mate with James G. Blaine.

General Logan was one of the organizers of the Grand Army of the Republic in 1868, and served as the first commander of the GAR for three two-year terms. He issued an order to GAR units that May 30, 1868, should be observed as Decoration Day to honor soldiers who had died in the war, thereby establishing Decoration Day—or Memo-

(Sketch from May 6, 1897, Rocky Mountain News

Col. H.C. Merriam, Ft. Logan's first commander.

rial Day—as a national holiday.

Logan had visited Colorado in 1873. His wife wrote that "while there he joined a party of capitalists, who were making prospecting tours over the mountains and along Cripple Creek. . . ."[11] Logan invested in the Evening Star Mine at Leadville, but refused to pay a second assessment as a stockholder and consequently did not participate in enormous profits the mine later produced. In 1874 he either paid $40,000 for a one-seventh interest in the Dives Mine at Silver Plume, or paid $100,000 for 100 feet of the lode. The following summer Logan was actively involved as an attorney for the Dives Mine in bitter litigation with the Pelican Mine. He died in December 1886, and did not see the fort which would bear his name.

At any rate, on April 8, 1889, the post near Denver was named Ft. Logan. On May 1, Companies D and F of the Seventh Infantry left Ft. Laramie, Wyo., and marched 206 miles to Ft. Logan. They arrived May 16; the previous day the two companies of the Eighteenth Infantry, who had been at the post for more than a year and a half, finally moved into permanent quarters on the grounds. The decision had been made that Ft. Laramie would be closed down, and on Oct. 17, 1889, Col. Henry Clay Merriam was ordered to go from Ft. Laramie, where he had been commander, to Ft. Logan to find out if construction there would allow the remaining troops to be transferred from Wyoming before winter. Colonel Merriam became the commanding officer of Ft. Logan on Oct. 18, 1889, and served there for eight years, longer than any other commander in the history of the fort. Other troops from Ft. Laramie also came to Ft. Logan that October, but this time the soldiers marched only 22 miles to the Bordeaux station, where they boarded a train that took them through Cheyenne to Denver. The last Ft. Laramie soldiers arrived at Ft. Logan in March 1890. Among the units coming from Ft. Laramie was a band, and the Monthly Return for May 1890 reported for the first time that troops participated in a parade in Denver, this time on Memorial Day.

December 1890 saw the first attempt at military action by troops from Ft. Logan. Colonel Merriam left with six companies by train for South Dakota to participate in the Army's assignment to control Sitting Bull and the Ghost Dances. Merriam's train went by way of Omaha to pick up an additional company of soldiers from Ft. Leavenworth, and then proceeded to Ft. Sully. They were delayed in crossing to the west side of the Missouri River for several days because of ice, and consequently were too late to take part in the Wounded Knee hostilities. Colonel Merriam told the newspaper that his units did help to round up some of Sitting Bull's band of Sioux who were trying to flee after Sitting Bull's death on Dec. 15. Most of the troops returned to Denver late in January 1891. The last two companies stayed at Ft. Sully to guard 236 Indian prisoners until Feb. 6, and then left by train for Denver. They reached Ft. Logan on Feb. 10, having been snowbound at Julesburg for 24 hours.

An 1893 magazine gave a progress report on developments at the fort. Facilities had been prepared for cavalry units to be added to the fort, although the first cavalry troops did not arrive until October 1894. There were also accommodations for a "proposed Company of Indians" to be recruited among the Apaches:

> The orders are to accept only unmarried men, not over 35 years of age; but foot-soldiering has little charm for an Indian whose idea of felicity is a pony, a gun and unlimited range. As a scout, he has all these with rations thrown in; even in the Cavalry, there are advantages to counterbalance the manifest disadvantage of restraint; but so far the Infantry has seemed to offer few attractions. How these wild men, who have known no other covering than the blue sky above them, or the temporary shelter of a tepee, will conduct themselves in these, to them, palatial surroundings, is an anxious inquiry. Ladies who have known them only as cruel and relentless foes shudder and draw their little ones closer to them; officers shrug their shoulders and speak of the new barracks as the "Kindergarten," and all feel it to be a hazardous experiment.[12]

With attitudes such as these expressed, it is not surprising that the company of Indians was never organized.

Routine life at the fort included laborious drills and exercises. In

(Friends of Historic Fort Logan Collection)
John F. Hill, of H Troop 14th Cavalry, at Ft. Logan in 1902.

the summer, the garrison was on the rifle range by 5:30 a.m., and often practiced firing until noon. Signal drills with flags, heliograph and telegraph were held for all units. Classes were conducted three hours a day, eight months of the year for enlisted men who wanted to learn the three R's, or who were ordered to attend because they were "grossly ignorant." Practice marches to areas east of Englewood, to Palmer Lake, or even to Colorado Springs were included in training. Sunday evening dress parades brought visitors to the post, and occasional military balls contributed to the cultural life of the community. The post canteen in the early years provided a place for soldiers to relax with snacks, soft drinks, and beer, but efforts by temperance forces and nearby saloonkeepers convinced the Army that no alcoholic beverages should be sold on the military reservation.

The year 1894 brought more action for troops from Ft. Logan, although not the usual military engagement. On the night of March 15, five companies were sent to Denver "to have the troops in readiness to quell anticipated riot, and to protect public property." The occasion was Gov. Davis H. Waite's siege of City Hall; on the morning of March 18 the troops returned to the post. On July 2 the same five companies of the Seventh Infantry were ordered to Trinidad, Colo., and Raton, N.M., "to enforce mandates of the U. S. Courts, protect property in hands of Receivers of U.S. Courts, prevent obstructions of said property and transmissions of U. S. Mails." This was a time when the Pullman strike which had begun in Chicago had reached Colorado, and the railroads were shut down in Trinidad. The next month Company D was sent to New Castle to assist the militia.

A *Denver Post* headline in 1978 proclaimed "Fort Logan Birthplace of U. S. Air Force"—with only a bit of exaggeration.[13] The article referred to the first appearance of the Air Corps at Ft. Logan in 1894 when the fort became the base for the Signal Corps balloon, which had been kept at Ft. Riley. The balloon, named the General [Albert J.] Myer after the Army surgeon who was the first chief signal officer, was constructed in France in 1893. The covering was made of "goldbeater's skin" from the lining of intestines of oxen or cattle. It was inflated with hydrogen, produced with a gas generator, adding sulfuric acid to iron filings; compression equipment forced the hydrogen into steel storage tubes.

To handle the balloon at Ft. Logan, 28-year-old Ivy Baldwin was induced to enlist as a sergeant. Baldwin, whose name was originally William Ivy, performed as an acrobat and high-wire walker as a teenager, and joined with Thomas Baldwin to make balloon ascensions. They were known as the Baldwins, and Ivy Baldwin continued to use that name the rest of his life. He appeared in Denver in 1890 for a balloon performance at the opening of Elitch Gardens. Even as a sergeant at Ft. Logan, in charge of the Army's balloon, Baldwin continued to perform at Elitch Gardens. He was the high-wire walker at Eldorado Canyon near Boulder, after it opened as a resort in 1906, and last walked over the canyon at age 84.

Capt. William Glassford, chief signal officer at Ft. Logan in 1894, announced plans to have a second and larger balloon built, but in 1895 the Army's only balloon was destroyed in a strong wind. The Signal Corps had no money to replace the General Myer, and Captain Glassford finally persuaded the Army to make $700 available to purchase a quantity of pongee silk. Sergeant Baldwin and his wife cut and sewed the silk into a new envelope, made more air-tight with varnish, and used the basket and rigging from the old balloon.

(National Archives photo)
Army tests its Signal Corps balloon near Ft. Logan hangar, about
1897. (Ivy Baldwin is probably the man standing on the basket.)

Balloons had been used by armies in Europe since the latter part of
the eighteenth century, providing aerial surveillance of opposing forces
and territories. Observation balloons were in use in this country in the
Civil War. Telegraph wires were added along the 2,000- to 3,000-ft.
tether cables, allowing messages to be sent from the aerial observers.
Picture-taking from balloons was tried by several photographers, and
the *Rocky Mountain News* in 1897 reported on plans by officers at Ft.
Logan to take moving pictures from the balloon.[14]

The Spanish-American War began in April 1898. Troops from Ft.
Logan went to Cuba and the Philippines. The Ft. Logan balloon was
moved to the East Coast to watch for an attack by the Spanish fleet.
Sergeant Baldwin and his balloon were then sent to Tampa, Fla., to be
loaded for Cuba. Confusion reigned as troops and supplies tried to
find passage. Baldwin's balloon, now named *The Santiago*, suffered
from lying in the sun, and when it was spread out, the varnish had
melted and become sticky, tearing holes in the cloth which had to be
patched. Lt. Col. Joseph E. Maxfield of the Signal Corps reported, "It

was in such condition that had the ascents to be made in time of peace it would have been felt unsafe to use."[15]

Three ascents were made the first day *The Santiago* was used in Cuba, from a distance of more than a mile from the Spanish forces. The next day the balloon was moved forward for a closer look, and the cable snagged in trees while the basket was only 50 feet in the air. Spanish artillery punctured the already leaking gas-filled bag. Stephen Crane, New York *World* correspondent, described the result: "The balloon was dying, dying a gigantic and public death before the eyes of the two armies. It quivered, sank, faded into the trees amid the flurry of a battle that was suddenly like a storm."[16]

The balloon and basket were retrieved and returned to the United States, but the day of balloons at Ft. Logan was past. Ivy Baldwin left the Army in 1901 when his second enlistment was up.

Ft. Logan was changing with the times. In 1904, electric lights were installed in the buildings, replacing coal-oil lamps which were standard sources of light in Army posts. Army policy had denied the use of electricity at any fort until it could be available at all of them, including frontier posts far from a power supply. But, at last, electricity would "displace the dull glow of the smudgy oil lamp that has held sway over the darkness for many years."[17] Two direct telephone lines to Denver were hooked up in 1910, and from 1912 the monthly post returns were typewritten, greatly improving their readability.

Expansion of the fort grounds occurred in 1908, when $110,000 was appropriated by Congress to purchase lands adjacent to the post for additional drill grounds and a reservoir. The additional 340 acres brought the reservation total to 980 acres. But the September 1909 Monthly Returns reported: "The Post of Ft. Logan, Colo., was discontinued Sept. 2-09, and the Recruit Depot Ft. Logan, Colo., established." Ft. Logan was not a significant Army post after 1910. Its status as a recruit depot continued through World War I and until Feb. 24, 1922. When it was reinstated as a training post it had only 300 or 400 soldiers stationed there, compared with 700 to 800 in earlier years. Newspapers from time to time reported plans to expand or close the post. Among the actions recommended to retain the fort were lobbying Congress to increase the size of the standing Army and providing an all-weather road to the post.

Maj. Dwight D. Eisenhower was assigned to recruiting duty at Ft. Logan in December 1924, which would ordinarily have been "close to an insult"[18] for someone with his rank and experience. The assignment had been engineered by Gen. Fox Conner, under whom Eisen-hower had served in Panama. Eisenhower was put temporarily under the Adjutant General's office, for assignment to the Command and General Staff School at Ft. Leavenworth. With Ft. Logan so close to Denver and Mamie Doud Eisenhower's family home, it was a pleasant time for Mamie. The Eisenhowers stayed at Ft. Logan until August 1925, when Ike reported to Ft. Leavenworth.

(1890s National Archives photo)
Maj. Dwight D. Eisenhower and wife Mamie resided in Line Officers' Quarters #17 (left side) from December 1923 to August 1924. Building was erected in 1889.

Improvements in the buildings and grounds came after the Second Engineers took over Ft. Logan in 1927. During the 1930s, $1 million in WPA funds produced construction and rehabilitation, including new duplexes for non-commissioned officers. Units of the Civilian Conservation Corps (CCC), Reserve Officers Training Corps (ROTC), Civilian Military Training Corps (CMTC), and other programs were located on the grounds.

In 1939 the Eighteenth Engineers replaced the Second Engineers, and early in 1941, these units left as the post became a subpost of Lowry Field (the second coming of the Air Corps). Frame barracks and classrooms for training clerks for the Army Air Force were constructed. The post was also used for induction into the Army, and in 1944 it became an AAF convalescent center. German prisoners of war were confined on the grounds at one time. More than 5,500 persons

(1890s National Archives photo)

Field Officer's Quarters, built in 1889, is now being restored by the Friends of Historic Ft. Logan.

lived at the fort at the peak of occupancy.

As the war came to a close, Ft. Logan was a separation center. The post was declared surplus effective May 7, 1946, and much of the land was sold to private developers, or transferred to adjacent municipalities for school and park use. In July 1946, about 580 acres were transferred to the Veterans Administration, which continued to use the 326 general medical beds for veterans of all wars. The temporary frame barracks on the ground were leased to the Denver Housing Authority, to be rented to eligible tenants to help relieve the housing shortage in the area. With the opening of the new VA Hospital in Denver in 1951, and the closing of the Ft. Logan barracks as public housing, the Veterans Administration relinquished control of the land.

A variety of proposals was made by several groups for use of the facilities: veterans housing, rehabilitation center, and a tuberculosis hospital for the Bureau of Indian Affairs. In fact, transfer of part of the facility to the Indian Bureau was apparently initiated, amid protests from veterans' groups and others that a fort created to fight Indians should not be given back to them. Finally, in December 1959, an agreement was signed between Gov. Stephen L.R. McNichols and the federal government for transfer of 308 acres to the State of Colorado. This was later reduced to 232 acres with the transfer of about 75 acres to the Ft. Logan National Cemetery. The state took possession of the land and buildings on April 1, 1960, and title was given to the newly created Department of Institutions for use by the state hospital being developed—Fort Logan Mental Health Center. The first patients were admitted on July 17, 1961. Buildings were constructed for inpatient treatment and administrative and support services.

Many of the original Ft. Logan buildings remain, used as residential facilities or offices by the mental health center, by other state agencies, and by educational and human service agencies. The 32-acre parade ground remains as an open space, well-used by residents on the grounds and by youth soccer programs from the southwest metropolitan area. The nearby national cemetery, which began as a 3.2 acre post cemetery in 1889, now has 214 acres available for current and future use.

Both the Infantry and Air Corps are gone, but the name of Ft. Logan carries on.

Endnotes

(Much information is from *Returns From U.S. Military Posts, 1800-1916*, National Archives microfilm publication M-617, rolls 641-643.)

1. Robert G. Athearn, *William Tecumseh Sherman and the Settlement of the West.* (Norman: University of Oklahoma Press, 1956), p. 76.
2. *Ibid.*, p. 344.
3. *Senate Reports*, 1st session, 49th Congress, 1885-86, Vol. Xl, No. 1483.
4. *Denver Republican*, Feb. 2 1887.
5. Jerry M. Cooper, "The Army As Strikebreaker—The Railroad Strikes of 1877 and 1894," *Labor History* 18 (Spring 1977), 179-96; Barton C. Hacker, "The United States Army as a National Police Force: The Federal Policing of Labor Disputes, 1877-1898," *Military Affairs* 33 April 1969, pp. 255-64.
6. *Denver Republican*, March 4, 1887.
7. *Ibid.*, March 30, 1887.
8. Frank Hall, *History of the State of Colorado*, 4 vols. (Chicago: The Blakely

Printing Company, 1895), 4:37.
9. Denver *Republican*, Oct. 26, 1887.
10. Robert Pfanner, "Highlights in the History of Fort Logan," *The Colorado Magazine*, May 1942, p. 84.
11. Mary Logan, *Reminiscences of the Civil War and Reconstruction*, ed. George Worthington Adams (Carbondale and Edwardsville: Southern Illinois Press, 1970), p. 246.
12. Virginia Bash, "Garrison Life in Colorado," *The Colorado Magazine*, April 1893, pp. 4-13.
13. *The Denver Post*, April 9, 1978.
14. *Rocky Mountain News*, Dec. 4, 1897.
15. Joseph E. Maxfield, "War Ballooning in Cuba," *Aeronautical Journal*, October 1899, p. 84.
16. Quoted in Frank Friedel, *The Splendid Little War* (Boston and Toronto: Little, Brown & Co., 1958), p. 150.
17. *Denver Republican*, Jan. 27, 1904.
18. Stephen E. Ambrose, *Eisenhower*, 2 vols. (New York: Simon and Shuster, 1983), 1:79.

About the Author

Earl McCoy, Posse Member and Roundup Foreman for the Denver Posse of the Westerners, presented his talk on the history of Ft. Logan, "From Infantry to Air Corps," on Feb. 26, 1986.

A native of Illinois, Earl attended Illinois Wesleyan University and the University of Illinois. He worked at community centers, including Chicago's Hull House, and in 1956 received a master's degree in social work from the University of Illinois.

From 1956 to 1959, he was a volunteer with the American Friends Service Committee, directing a center in an Arab community in Acre, Israel.

He came to Denver in 1959 as program director of Auraria Community Center, and later developed a community organization project in the West Side of Denver.

From 1968 to 1987, he was community coordinator for the Fort Logan Mental Health Center, and later was additionally named Information Officer for the center. This work led to his researching the history of the old Army post. Following retirement, Earl and others, including other members of the Denver Westerners, organized the Friends of Historic Fort Logan, in an effort to preserve the history of the fort and the communities related to it. Currently chairman of the group, Earl said the organization is also working on restoration of a single-family officers' quarters, portrayed in an early-day photo in the accompanying article.

Earl's other interests include the history and culture of Native Americans, especially in the Southwestern United States.

"Barbed Wire Brings Range War" by *Delano*

The Life and Times of Frank Canton

Gunman on at Least Four Frontiers

By John Milton Hutchins

*T*HIS IS THE STORY of a gunfighter who was in more gun-fights than Wyatt Earp, although all but probably one of them were anything but heroic. He was a bounty hunter who was a more successful mankiller than Tom Horn, for, unlike Horn, he escaped the hangman's noose. He was luckier in turning legitimate than was John Wesley Hardin, for the best title that the dissipated Hardin ever acquired was "attorney at law," while this individual attained high military rank. And, in a way, the end of this violent man was more perplexing than that of Butch Cassidy. This gunman neither died in the violent manner in which most of his life was lived, nor did he enjoy his subsequent peace and respectability because of a deserving and pleasant personality.

Many students of the American West know parts of his career. They know he was born Joe Horner and died Frank M. Canton. Yet, surprisingly, there is no full-length biography of his life, although respected historian Robert DeArment is writing one. This delay in unearthing the full and accurate story is not to be wondered at. To piece the Horner-Canton story together, one must follow a tortuous trail across at least four frontiers.

Even Joe Horner's birthplace is a matter of controversy. Horner, both in an 1890 publication and in his autobiography, claimed he was born in Virginia.[1] This assertion has been accepted by virtually every historian.[2] However, it is more likely that Horner, whose physician father was a native Virginian, was born in about 1849 somewhere in the Midwest.[3] Horner, in a document filed with the State of Texas about 1877—before he had a motive to cover his tracks—apparently stated he was born in Indiana.[4]

During the Civil War, the Horners lived in Missouri, a wartime environment that bred the violent likes of Jesse James and Tom Horn. Joe Horner's father, Dr. J. H. Horner, served with the Rebel forces, dying in 1864. John Wesley Horner, Joe Horner's elder brother, also served with the South, but he survived the war, was discharged in Texas, and in 1866 moved his mother and the rest of the family to Denton, Texas.[5]

If Missouri was the frying pan, Texas at this time was the fire. Not only was the reconstructing state plagued by desperadoes and discontented white and black United States soldiers, it was also involved in vicious Indian warfare. Joe Horner left Denton County for the even wilder Jack County in 1867. Tradition holds that he joined a Texas Ranger unit about this time,[6] although it likely was an informal ranger company of the old type, unencumbered with paperwork and pay.[7]

About 1870, Joe Horner went up the trail to Abilene, Kans., with a herd of about 1,500 cattle belonging to Burke Burnett.[8] The drive encountered the typical problems: river crossings, lightning, stampedes, and surly Indians. However, the drive ended successfully. Horner, writing years later, claimed he went on another trail drive from Abilene to North Platte, Neb.,[9] but a major Indian incident Horner described happened at least three years after he was supposed to have been there.[10]

After he returned to Texas, Horner was involved in the trial of Satanta and Big Tree, for the Warren Wagontrain Massacre in 1871. Horner was selected by Jack County Sheriff Lee Crutchfield to act as one of the bailiffs guarding the Indian prisoners.[11] It was not for fear of the Indians that a man of Horner's growing reputation was selected. As Capt. Robert Carter noted in his book, *On the Border with McKenzie*, the guards were needed to insure that no vengeful Texan would assassinate the two Kiowas traveling between the jail and the courthouse.[12]

In 1871 Horner also became a partner in a ranch north of Jacksboro.[13] This was a time when many supposedly respectable ranchers were involved in criminal activity. It was not easy then to tell the lawless from the law abiding, and it probably would be impossible now to tell about Joe Horner's activities. About this time there was a gang of horse-stealing desperadoes headquartered in Jacksboro who committed "other desperate deeds" and reportedly even disguised themselves as raiding Indians.[14] Horner was reputed to have been involved with this group, according to Jesse James Benton, who was then a boy in Denton County, and actually met Horner face-to-face. (This information is found in Ramon Adams' *Cow, by the Tail,* pp. 25-26.) Horner was charged in Jack County with several cattle thefts, according to county records.[15]

Horner certainly did lead a bunch of toughs who generally left the town of Jacksboro alone, for City Marshal Bill Gilson was big enough and proficient enough to earn their respect.[16] On at least one occasion, Gilson threw Horner in the city jail,[17] and on one other occasion Horner caused a major disturbance in town. Horner also tallied his first known killings, credited to his deadly aim.

In 1873, three companies of the Tenth Cavalry were stationed at Ft. Richardson.[18] On Oct. 10, 1874, Horner was in a saloon frequented by black troopers.[19] He supposedly was informed that he would have to stand everyone to a round of drinks. Horner demurred and started shooting at some cavalrymen. At least one trooper was killed and the rest retreated to post. Joe Horner reconvened his recreational activities to the Wichita Saloon.[20]

Shortly thereafter, a white noncommissioned officer returned to Jacksboro with a detachment of six black soldiers, armed with rifles. Joe Horner and his friend Joe Watson squatted down in front of the saloon and drove the Army men back.[21]

More armed troopers joined the fray, and Horner mounted his horse and began firing with his Winchester, supposedly hitting another cavalryman. When Horner's horse was hit and went down, the soldiers withdrew to the fort.[22]

Later in the day, as Horner and one of his cowboy friends were riding the cowboy's horse back to the ranch, they got into a running gunfight with pursuing white troopers. The cowboy was wounded and surrendered. Horner, at the urging of the cowboy, made his escape to the ranch. The ranchhand, one Frank Lake, recovered and was not prosecuted. Horner, represented by Attorney Wiley, negotiated a sort of a truce with the Army and he likewise was not prosecuted.[23] At least one trooper had been killed and another was permanently crippled.[24]

But if Horner learned any lesson, it was not to cause trouble too close to home. Rumors persisted around Jacksboro that he was involved in a dirty business and was a robber and a true "bad man."[25] Horner and his bunch supposedly were responsible for a number of murders in Texas, including the deaths of an elderly couple.[26]

On Jan. 6, 1876, things started to unravel for Horner. On that day three young men robbed the bank in Comanche, Texas. As they mounted their horses to ride out of town, they shouted, "Charge this to the James Boys!"[27] Horner apparently in later years claimed he could not have been in on the robbery because he was just then romantically involved with a young lady.[28] But a resident of Jacksboro, Capt. Henry Strong, was in Comanche that day and saw Horner and his friends commit the robbery.[29]

Horner was trailed to San Antonio and was arrested. When caught, he was supposedly having a local gunsmith fabricate a bullet-proof steel breastplate.[30] Horner was tried and convicted in March 1877, and sentenced to 10 years imprisonment.[31] His motion for a new trial was denied by the District Court.[32] However, Horner and a compatriot, named Williams or Jones, soon broke out of the San Antonio jail and robbed the Blanco stage. Horner was caught again after a gunbattle and received another 10 years confinement after pleading guilty.[33]

Horner was sent to the Texas State Prison in Huntsville. At the time he was admitted, he was 27 years old, almost 6-feet tall, and weighed 138 pounds. Physically he was in the prime of life, although the prison records noted that he had "intemperate" habits.[34] On Aug. 4, 1879, supposedly with the help of a young woman, he escaped.[35] He disappeared, and Joe Horner was not seen again in Texas until 1894.

In the 1870s and 1880s, Wyoming Territory received many displaced Texans, and one suspects that they formed

(Author's Collection)
Henry Strong saw Joe Horner rob the Comanche bank. (From Strong's *My Frontier Days. . .*)

an informal but supportive network. In 1876, Fred G.S. Hesse, originally from England, moved from Texas to Wyoming. A few years thereafter, he settled in the new town of Buffalo, in Johnson County.[36] In 1879, Texan Sam Moses came up to Wyoming with a herd and stayed in the region, becoming a sheriff and stock inspector.[37] Also in 1879, a Texan by the name of James Murray drifted north into the Territory. He was hired in 1884 as a stock detective for the Wyoming Stock Growers Association; the association apparently did not care that his real name was James Dahlman and he had left Texas after shooting his brother-in-law.[38] Also about this time there appeared one Frank Canton, a man with cold gray eyes, who apparently did not admit to being from Texas.[39] Even his friends, later writing recommendations for his appointment as U.S. Marshal in Alaska in 1893, seemed unclear as to exactly when Canton arrived in Wyoming.[40] Canton was hired on as a stock detective by the Wyoming association.[41]

In any event, Canton soon earned a reputation as a ruthless manhunter. One Wyomingite who knew him claimed that "Canton was out to collect rewards. He was always looking for someone, always suspicious of a stranger, always wanting to get something on somebody.... All he thought about was guns and killing..."[42]

In 1880, by his own account, Canton secured a homestead near Buffalo in Johnson County.[43] He was still an employee of the Wyoming Stock Growers Association,[44] a fact apparently not generally known.[45] In 1882, he was elected sheriff of the county.[46] He also married a local girl, Annie Wilkerson.[47] They first set up housekeeping in a line shack, and later constructed a log house for the ranch.[48]

As sheriff, Canton's duties sometimes coincided with work for the Wyoming Stock Growers Association. For example, in January 1884, Canton chased down and arrested Haines and Baker, two cattle thieves who had taken 70 head from the Little Venture Cattle Co.[49] Canton may have confused his corporate and public duties. After the sheriff had lodged Roach Chapman in the Buffalo jail on an Idaho charge of murder and on a Montana charge of horse theft, Chapman, who had been the foreman for the Frontier Land and Cattle Co., somehow escaped, armed and on a fast horse.[50]

While sheriff, however, Canton became best known for bringing in murderer Teton Jackson. Canton dwelt at length on the episode in his memoirs. He apparently first fed the story to the press during his legal troubles, immediately after the Johnson County Invasion in 1892.[51] Most historians have related the story as an example of Canton's courage and tenacity.[52] However, a major history of the Teton Valley, published before Canton's autobiography, describes the apprehension of Jackson in detail, yet does not mention Canton at all.[53] A more recent Jackson Hole historian has concluded that Canton's claims regarding Teton Jackson are unproven.[54] Combining this information with the limited information provided by a family friend of the Cantons in Wyoming, Frank Canton's contribution to bringing to justice the notorious outlaw may have been limited to Canton, as Johnson County Sheriff, merely receiving the murderer and transporting the criminal to jail.[55]

As to the apprehension of another, although less notorious, murderer, there seems to be less controversy. A young man named Bill Booth had a disagreement in early 1885 with his employer, Jake Schmerer. Booth killed Schmerer with a club. Canton arrested Booth on June 12, 1885. Booth was convicted of murder and, on March 5, 1886, Sheriff Canton hanged the young man in Buffalo.[56]

Frank Canton was, by all indications, a loving father and husband. Two daughters, Ruby and Helen, eventually were born to the Canton couple.[57] Once, when Mrs. Canton was in her buckboard with one of her daughters, the horses ran away with the wagon. Fortunately, a neighbor, Charley Basch, stopped the runaway team before the mother and child were killed. Sheriff Canton told Basch that he would never forget that Basch saved his little girl.[58]

Canton was reelected sheriff in 1884.[59]   Also, in that year, he attended the Democratic National Convention in Chicago which nominated Grover Cleveland.[60] "In 1886," he later wrote, "I was strongly urged by the citizens of Johnson County to accept the office as sheriff for a third term. But . . . I retired from public life and moved out to my ranch with my young wife and little daughter Ruby."[61]   Once again, Canton omitted some key information. The county was starting to divide against itself over the dispute between the big ranchers and the small ranchers and Canton was defeated in his bid for reelection.[62] It probably did not help the sheriff among his constituents that, prior to the election, he was given a vote of appreciation by the Wyoming Stock Growers Association for his work against criminals.[63] Despite his electoral defeat (or perhaps because of it), Canton was named a U.S. Deputy Marshal for Wyoming Territory on Nov. 3, 1886.[64]

As statehood for the territory approached, the division between the corporate "whitecap" cattlemen and the independent "rustler" ranchers grew.   In the summer of 1889, "Cattle Kate" Watson, a suspected prostitute, and Jim Averell, her procurer, were lynched for rustling in south-central Wyoming. Witnesses to the abduction and murders, who were sympathetic to the small ranchers, disappeared and no true bill was issued by the Carbon County Grand Jury.[65]

(Author's Collection)

Joe Horner, or Frank Canton (from Canton's *Frontier Trails*). Original picture is captioned "Sheriff Frank M. Canton of Johnson County, Wyoming."

Statehood arrived for Wyoming in 1890, but peace on the range kept its distance. Frank Canton was reappointed a U.S. Deputy Marshal in 1890, just after statehood became official.[66]

Living on the Middle Fork of the Powder River was a reputed rustler leader named Nate Champion.[67] On Nov. 1, 1891, at about sunrise, he and his companions, staying overnight in a cabin, were attacked by four assailants. The four attackers were driven off, leaving a near-new Winchester rifle by the cabin. The weapon belonged to Frank Canton.[68]

An ambush on another alleged rustler, Ranger Jones, was more successful. On Nov. 28, 1891, Jones was shot from ambush while driving his buckboard home from Buffalo.[69] After his body was found almost a week later, the leading suspects were Fred G.S. Hesse and Frank Canton.[70]

Feuds are well-known opportunities for settling old scores. Living outside of Buffalo was a well-educated stockman named John Tisdale. Tisdale was a Texan who was not implicated in rustling activity. However, shortly after he arrived in Johnson County, he saw Frank Canton and almost killed him on the spot. Tisdale had recognized Canton as Joe Horner, the alleged killer of two of Tisdale's elderly friends.[71] Tisdale cooled down, but on Nov. 30, 1891, he was shot from ambush while riding from Buffalo to his ranch in his buckboard, bearing Christmas gifts for his children.

Unfortunately for Tisdale's killer, Charley Basch heard the shots on the road ahead. When Basch approached close to a buckboard that had been driven off into the brush, he saw Frank Canton watching him. Canton told Basch to move along and to keep his mouth shut.[72] Basch rode into Buffalo and thought about what he had seen. Soon thereafter word was brought that Tisdale was found dead in his wagon.[73]

Basch later was intimidated by Canton and perhaps narrowly missed assassination himself.[74] Frank Canton was charged with murder, but Basch's loss of memory at the preliminary hearing, coupled with numerous alibi witnesses, caused the case against Canton to be at least temporarily dismissed.[75] Canton left the area and went to Chicago with his family; while there his daughter Helen died of diphtheria.[76] A charge of murder was later refiled against Canton, but was apparently dismissed in the swirl of following events.[77]

Meanwhile, those events of a broader scope were coming to a head. In the summer of 1891, Maj. Frank Wolcott, a cattleman, broached the subject of an invasion of Johnson County in a talk with the president of the stock growers association, John Clay.[78] Clay later claimed that he tried to discourage Wolcott and that he (Clay) was as innocent as "an unborn babe" in the instigation and planning of what followed.[79] In any event, Clay determined to take a convenient vacation to Europe.[80]

In early March, 1892, a number of desperate cattlemen met in Cheyenne to discuss an invasion of Johnson County. A list of about 70 "known" rustlers was drawn up. Care was supposedly taken to leave off the names of those merely suspected of thievery. The list, however, included Johnson County Sheriff Red Angus and the three members of the board of county commissioners.[81] Money to the tune of $100,000 was raised to bankroll the expedition and to hire professional gunmen from Texas.[82] The governor's office arranged that local units of the National Guard could not be mustered without authorization from Cheyenne.[83]

The Texans were recruited with little difficulty by Tom Smith, a deputy sheriff from Fort Bend County.[84] The 24 Texans arrived in Denver on April 4, 1892.[85] They were met by the chosen leader of the expedition, Civil War veteran Wolcott, and they were joined by two dozen Wyoming cattleman, including Canton.[86] There was even an expedition surgeon and a Chicago newspaper reporter.[87] The invasion force, committed to secrecy, rode a special train north out of Denver. To some, it appeared that the true leader of the force was Frank Canton, for he and Tom Smith appeared to be friends and Smith supposedly had been involved in the attack on Champion's cabin.[88] Certainly the two Texans had shared some other similar experiences. In 1889, Smith, as a Texas deputy sheriff during the notorious Jaybird-Woodpecker feud between white supremacist Democrats and "black Republicans," had made a stand in a street gunfight that was every bit as bold as Joe Horner had made in Jacksboro in 1874.[89]

The invaders' special train made a brief stop in Cheyenne, then in Douglas. North of Douglas the telegraph wires were cut. The expedition left the train outside of Casper and took to their horses, heading northwest.[90] North of Casper, they ran into a boy from Buffalo named Joe Todd, who quickly took in the situation. Since Canton and the boy's father were hardly friends, Joe thought that he would be killed. However, to young Todd's surprise, Canton said, "We don't want this boy, let him go."[91]

After two days of hard riding, informants told the invasion force

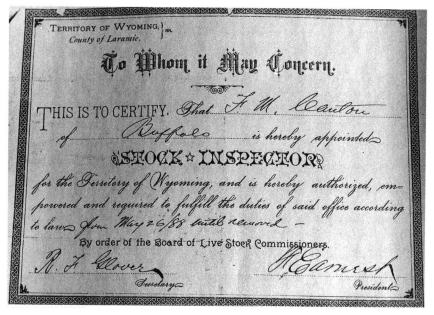

Certificate names Canton as a stock inspector in Wyoming.

that a number of rustlers had been seen at Nate Champion's cabin at the KC Ranch. Although the original plan had been to occupy Buffalo first, this tempting prize was too much to forsake. The force headed to Champion's place.

The invaders arrived at the cabin just before dawn on April 9. Two trappers had spent the night with Champion and his partner Nick Ray. When the trappers left the cabin at sunrise, they were seized by Wolcott's men.[92] When Ray appeared at the door, he was shot down. Champion dragged his fatally wounded partner into the cabin and one of the most heroic gunfight sieges of the West began in earnest.[93]

All day, the cattlemen and their hired guns blazed at the cabin, with Champion returning the fire and jotting down items in his diary. Champion wounded the young man known as the Texas Kid and a couple of others, although not seriously.[94] Ray died early in the day, at about 9 o'clock. Champion wrote in his diary late in the day that one of the attackers looked like Frank Canton.[95] Just before he was killed at about 3 p.m., Champion wrote that the house had been fired. He then closed with, "Goodbye, boys, if I never see you again. Nathan D. Champion."[96] The newspaper reporter accompanying the expedition called Champion the bravest man in Johnson County.[97]

The body of Champion was examined by the invaders. Although they left a placard on Champion as a warning to other cattle thieves, even they did not have the stomach to destroy his notebook diary. Someone, however, did cut out the name of Frank Canton.[98]

Unbeknownst to the cattlemen, the fight at the KC Ranch was their "Alamo," with the Texas gunmen playing the role of Santa Anna. They had been seen by one of the rustler faction and even during the gunbattle the word was spreading throughout the county that there was an invasion going on. In the streets of Buffalo, rifles were being handed out and riders were being sent to recruit volunteers.[99]

Knowing that they had been discovered, the invaders made their second major strategic blunder. Over the objections of Canton and Fred G.S. Hesse, who wanted to march rapidly on Buffalo, Wolcott gave in to those who wanted to take a more leisurely pace.[100] The expedition headed to the friendly TA Ranch, about 14 miles from Buffalo.[101]

What happened next is fairly well known. The invasion force, instead of finding a quick respite at the TA Ranch, was besieged by hundreds of Johnson County residents. Canton, in his autobiography, takes a somewhat heroic role,[102] and it may be justified, for Wolcott had lost effective command of his force to Canton.[103] Despite Canton's later statements that the invaders could have broken through the rustlers' lines at any time,[104] things were not going well. Fortunately, the cattlemen had their usual friends in high places, who, when they found out what had happened to the invasion, got President Harrison to send the cavalry from Ft. McKinney to rescue the besieged, arriving on April 13.[105] Amazingly, for all the gunfire during the week, the fatal casualties on the invasion side were limited to two Texans who had accidently shot themselves.[106]

The story of what followed unfortunately is not unheard of in legal annals. The invaders were nominally incarcerated at Ft. D.A. Russell for trial in Cheyenne. It was hardly "in durance vile." Frank Canton once reportedly dropped the revolver he was allowed to carry, shooting himself in the foot and he had to be carried into court.[107] The two main witnesses to the murder of Ray and the killing of Champion, trappers William Walker and Ben Jones, were kidnapped and taken out of state.[108] When Johnson County could no longer pay the bill for the incarceration of the defendants, the case against them was dropped through the means of a technical judgment of acquittal.[109]

However, the Wyoming prospects of Frank Canton were certainly dimmed. Owen Wister, traveling in Wyoming in July 1893, probably heard the popular view when a stagecoach driver informed him that the leaders of the Johnson County invasion, including Wister's friend Canton, should be killed.[110] Also, according to Canton's own assessment, the expenses of the invasion had left him broke.[111]

Canton attempted to be appointed U.S. Marshal in Alaska Territory at this time, and he received recommendations from a diverse group, including J. Sterling Morton (originator of Arbor Day), John Clay of the Wyoming Stock Growers Association, former Wyoming Gov. George Baxter, Judge John Lacey (later to defend Tom Horn for murder), and Judge Willis Van Devanter (later to sit on the United States Supreme Court). Canton was unsuccessful in his attempts to get appointed.

Canton briefly worked in Nebraska for Portus "P.B." Weare, widely known Midwestern cattleman and entrepreneur.[112] For more permanent employment, Canton turned to the Indian Territory. However, there was still the outstanding legal problem with Texas.

Joe Horner had been recognized in faraway Wyoming; he certainly

(Author's Collection)

Frank Canton (holding dog) and other Pawnee County, Okla., officials in 1892. (From Canton's *Frontier Trails*, 1930.)

would be spotted across the Red River in Oklahoma. Canton boldly went to call on Texas Gov. Jim Hogg for a pardon, supposedly taking with him a revolver so that if he didn't get a new life, Texas would at least get a new governor.[113] There is also a story that Canton asked for the pardon on behalf of the probably deceased Joe Horner, only telling the governor the truth after the pardon had issued.[114] The first story probably is apocryphal and the second one clearly is a myth. For, based upon the extensive Application for Pardon file now in the Texas State Archives, Canton's strategy was to show how a young hellion can change into a respectable citizen. The applicant, in a lengthy letter that referred to God, referred to political connections, constantly emphasized Democratic Party credentials, related his sad youth (lying about his age at the time he was arrested in 1877), and spoke about his untiring efforts suppressing lawlessness, literally begged for a pardon on behalf of his wife and child. Hogg was not an unfavorable audience even if the governor had known of Horner's life prior to the Comanche Bank robbery. Joe Horner had killed at least one black Yankee soldier, a fact which probably did not bother the governor, who introduced Jim Crow laws to the Lone Star State.[115] In any event, finding that this was "a strange case," the governor granted a "full, unconditional pardon" for each of the convictions.[116]

Canton and his family moved to Pawnee, Okla., in 1894. He hired on as a Deputy Sheriff under one Frank Lake, the same Frank Lake who had fought beside Joe Horner in 1874.[117] As was a custom of the time, he was also appointed as a Deputy U.S. Marshal, serving under E. D. Nix.[118]

Some of Canton's own statements in his memoirs, when carefully read, are revealing in demonstrating his competitiveness. For example, apparently frustrated by Marshal Heck Thomas in an attempt to collect a reward on certain desperadoes, Canton and a posse supposedly trailed Thomas, hoping to ambush him and his men.[119] Also, Canton killed, among others, one Lon McCool and one Bill Dunn. Both were shot with hidden weapons while Canton appeared to be unarmed.[120]

The killing of William B. "Bill" Dunn is a mystery in itself. Dunn, according to Marshal Bill Tilghman's wife, had himself been hired as a Deputy U.S. Marshal.[121] However, Glenn Shirley, as thorough a gunfighter historian as there is, has written that Justice Department records do not support the claim that Dunn was a lawman.[122] This seems to be in error. The annual report of the United States Attorney

General shows that one W. T. Dunn [sic] was sworn in (and "terminated") as an emergency field deputy the very day that Bill Dunn was killed by Canton, Nov. 6, 1896.[123] But whether Dunn was killed by Canton while attempting to carry out his official duties against Canton likely will never be known.

Canton, in his recollections, stated that the excitement of his job was all gone and the work had become monotonous by 1897.[124] However, historian William Hunt recently discovered that Canton, along with other deputy U.S. marshals, was implicated in an 1897 scandal over false expense claims.[125] Canton resigned to avoid the finale of the investigation. On Canton's behalf, it is only fair to say that the biographer of Bob Hutchins, another noted Deputy U.S. Marshal in the Territory, has defended the practice of claiming all the expenses to which the lawmen were entitled, even when actual disbursements were not made.[126] And, even at the time, it was well known that the deputies in the Territory were not paid any more money than the deputies in the more settled (and less expensive) parts of the nation.[127] On the other hand, Canton claimed expenses significantly larger than those claimed by such deputies as Tilghman and Heck Thomas.[128]

Also in Canton's defense, his boss, E.D. Nix, later wrote in his book *Oklahombres*, "Frank Canton established a reputation as a fearless officer that gave him an honored place in the regard of Oklahoma citizens."[129] However, this rather detached assessment came shortly after Canton had died and long after he had served under Nix.

There was one more frontier for Canton to conquer. This time, like John Wayne, he finally went "north to Alaska." Through the influence of P.B. Weare, Canton received assurances of an appointment as a Deputy U.S. Marshal, headquartered in Circle City, Alaska.[130] Also, Weare was to pay Canton an additional salary to look out for his business interests in the interior.[131] After a rugged trip to Alaska, Canton, according to his memoirs, spent at least as much time prospecting as he did with official duties.[132]

Once again, Canton's memoirs are suspect when it comes to the truth. William Hunt, in his 1987 book, *Distant Justice: Policing the Alaska Frontier*, has done a good job of researching and chronicling Canton's activities, although Hunt, unfamiliar with the true range of Canton's earlier adventures, gives Canton much benefit of the doubt.[133] On the other hand, Pierre Berton, in his 1958 book *Klondike*, accused Canton (through his alleged ghostwriter), at least in his description of the town of Dawson, of writing "sheer fiction."[134]

Unfortunately for Canton, the Oklahoma scandal caught up with him, and he was discharged from his Alaska post.[135] Canton, in his *Frontier Trails*, was again less than fully candid. "The United States Surgeon of the Medical Department," he wrote, "advised me to leave Alaska as soon as possible, and go out to the States where I could get treatment for my [snowblinded] eyes."[136] Canton had collected a mere $439.60 for his services.[137]

Canton, in relating his Alaska adventures in his memoirs, went on about his friendship with Rex Beach, who later became a well-known novelist. William Hunt, in his *Distant Justice*, has accepted this Canton-Beach connection, as has historian William Gardner Bell.[138] However, a perusal of Rex Beach's reminiscences, *Personal Exposures: His Own Story*, not only does not mention Canton by name, it obviously is a mishmash of jumbled facts and exaggerations without proper chronological divisions. Beach mentions an old Texan named Bill Joyce, who had been a ranger and had "a lean, hawk-faced frontiersman of the Remington type," but this older character does not appear to be Canton.[139] However, Beach the novelist may have left hints without being either totally honest or totally false. He may have used poetic license to mix up real characters. Thus, Beach additionally described a "desperado" by the name of Bill Dougherty. Outwardly, this individual also does not appear to be Canton; however, he was the occupant of the same bunkhouse with Beach at Rampart City, just as Canton claimed that he wintered with Beach in 1897.[140] Beach's details of Dougherty are not accurate when compared to Canton, but his basic generalities are amazingly similar. Beach recalled that Dougherty was "reputed to have 17 notches on his gun—and that was a conservative estimate." Beach said that Dougherty "was . . . deliberate and . . . calculating" and "his favorite plea was self-defense." Beach added, "More often than not he made it stick." Beach related that Dougherty had been a hired killer in a "desperate Montana mining" war. Finally, Beach made an assessment that seems to fit Canton perfectly.

> I have never heard of another bad man anything like him and he was totally unlike our present-day public enemies. He was as deadly as a fer-de-lance, to be sure, but he was no dope-crazed machine gunner and furthermore he never dodged or ran. He was a cool, calculating lone wolf who fought with his fangs and pursued his private feuds to a sanguinary finish.[141]

In the summer of 1899, Canton left Alaska aboard the steamship *Cleveland*. The voyage to the lower United States was a nightmare, the ship encountering a heavy storm and being blown off course almost to Japan before getting to Seattle.[142] Although there is no actual

Adj. Gen. Frank M. Canton of Oklahoma in 1910 (from *Frontier Trails*).

evidence that Canton met them on the voyage, Wyatt and Josephine Earp were also passengers on the *Cleveland*.[143]

Canton was on solid ground but once more unemployed. He returned for a while to Buffalo, Wyo. If things had cooled down there, he certainly had not. Canton took to drinking a lot and he was in a saloon when an old enemy, Will Foster, walked in. When Foster refused to drink with Canton, Canton drew his pistol. Foster, however, beat him to the draw and started hitting Canton on the head with his gun, almost killing him. After Canton recovered, the two met on Buffalo's main street, but neither one drew on the other.[144]

In any event, Canton and his wife returned to Oklahoma in 1900, where Canton became a law officer in Comanche County.[145] He also served as an inspector for a livestock association.[146]

Finally, in 1907, Canton obtained his long-sought sinecure. In that year he was named as the Adjutant General of Oklahoma, although he had virtually no military experience.[147] Once again, Canton was the beneficiary of having the right political connections, for his nephew or nephew-in-law was the campaign manager of Democratic Governor-elect C. N. Haskell.[148] Canton, once again, was a willing "enforcer" for the powers-that-be. A Kansas gas company had been laying a pipeline to transport Oklahoma gas to Kansas, and the governor did not want anyone getting such a natural resource unless they located in the new state. Canton immediately stopped the laying of the pipe, even though it was almost complete and had apparently been approved when Oklahoma had been a territory.[149]

Canton also participated in an official, although minor, capacity in such incidents as the manhunt for Henry Starr[150] and the so-called Crazy Snake Indian Uprising, which was ended either by the courage of Canton, by the persistence of Col. Roy Hoffman of the National Guard, or by the marksmanship of the U.S. Marshals, depending on one's perspective.[151]

In another rather ironical twist, much of Canton's services were employed to enforce state rules that, at least in his younger days, Canton would have considered prudish. In 1911, and on later occasions, Gov. Lee Cruce ordered General Canton and his guardsmen to prohibit illegal prizefighting.[152] In 1914, Governor Cruce ordered General Canton to McAlester to stop a rodeo that was scheduled to continue on into Sunday, in violation of the Oklahoma "Blue Laws."[153] In 1913, however, Canton, no teetotaler, narrowly missed the indignity of having his troops ordered to fight prohibition violations in Oklahoma City.[154]

But Frank Canton still had some of the old vinegar in his veins. In April 1914, Tulsans ignored the state bans on gambling and horse-racing and scheduled a horserace. Governor Cruce sent in Adjutant General Canton, backed up with two companies of the National Guard. Canton, ignoring a State Supreme Court injunction against the use of troops, was quoted as stating, "I will pay no attention to court orders. Governor Cruce is my commander."[155] Canton then had the guardsmen fire a volley over the heads of the horses at the starting line. The crowd believed Canton when he said the next shots would not be in the air and the races were canceled.[156]

Canton also supposedly almost "single-handedly . . . quelled 'County Seat Wars,'" according to Edward Everett Dale.[157] While county seat fights in Oklahoma were not as wild as they had been in Kansas, Canton was reported to have recaptured seized county records in a town dispute in Delaware County.[158] While he apparently did complete his task unassisted, there were no armed mobs or posses to be quelled.

General Canton retired in 1917, after attempting to assist the Oklahoma guardsmen to mobilize for duty in France, although the managerial job was just too much for his skills.[159] He died in Edmond, Okla., on Sept. 27, 1927.[160] His wife outlived him by a full 20 years.[161]

The Cantons' surviving daughter, Ruby, outlived her father by only a year, dying in 1928.[162] However, a summary of her brief life stands both as a protest of her father's methods and a monument to his tenacity. Miss Canton attended the Library School of the University of Chicago and also attended Columbia University, University of Pittsburgh, and Carnegie Tech. She served as the beloved librarian of Central State College in Edmond, Okla., from 1908 to the time of her death. In 1949, a stained-glass window in the new YWCA chapel on campus was dedicated to her, Ruby representing the essence of a young Christian woman. But she also was her father's daughter, for, when she initially was made librarian, she set out with a wheelbarrow in an effort to collect the 4,000 volumes checked out all over town. She retrieved every single book, save one.[163]

The assessments of Canton are as varied as the frontiers on which he lived. Harry Sinclair Drago wrote, "Frank Canton was a merciless, congenital, emotionless killer. . . . Even Jesse James was kind to his mother."[164]   Glenn Shirley once wrote that "Frank Canton [was a] fearless United States marshal."[165] Maurice Frink called him a "Jekyll and Hyde of the Plains."[166]   Edward Everett Dale, who edited Canton's reminiscences and supposedly would have known more about him than any other historian, said that Canton was "[h]onored and respected throughout the length and breadth of a vast region."[167] Probably the best estimate has come from the pen of Frank Prassel, who said that Canton was "[m]ysterious and somewhat sinister . . . leaving behind a multitude of legends and unanswered questions."[168]

Part of the mystery of Canton's life was assisted in no small measure by what appears to have been a historical conspiracy of sorts. Mrs. Canton, like Elizabeth Custer, seemed dedicated to protecting (and enhancing) her husband's reputation. A friendly young historian, Edward Everett Dale, was recruited to edit Canton's papers. Dale, having grown up in northern Texas just after the era of Joe Horner,[169] had to have known of him. Yet Dale, in his introduction to the first edition of *Frontier Trails*, did not mention Horner by name at all, and wrote that Canton had been "absolved of all blame" as to his "early difficulty."[170] It was only in the second edition 30 years later, after other works had exposed Canton's dirty little secret, that Dale claimed that he had discovered the Horner past.

Dale, if failing to present the whole, honest story, was at least dogged like Canton in sticking to his guns. He actively assisted historian William Gardner Bell in preparing Bell's 1964 article, and no doubt influenced Bell when Bell reminded the reader that debunkers should not judge "frontier heroes" by standards other than those that existed then on the frontier.[171] Yet, even by those standards, John Tisdale should not have been murdered.

While dedicated researchers like Shirley and DeArment will continue to bring out more of the fascinating Canton story, it is also true that some facts will always remain hidden. Novelist Rex Beach, even if he was not writing about Canton, used his wonderful skill to state an applicable summary that applies to Canton and to history.

> [T]his picturesque character [was] the most unusual and perhaps the least admirable man I ever knew. To me he was more than a killer, and outlaw; he was a lonely, laughing bandit, crowded always onward by a relentless fate. I regret now, more than ever, that he never bared his life story to me, ugly as it must have been, but I doubt if he ever told it to anybody. Even his closest associates knew only a page or a chapter of it. The rest, the inside history of the real Laughing Bill Dougherty lies to this day a secret between him and God.[172]

Endnotes

1. H.H. Bancroft, *History of the Pacific States of North America: Nevada, Colorado, and Wyoming, 1540-1888* (San Francisco: 1890), p. 792 n. 13; Frank M. Canton, *Frontier Trails* (New York: 1930), p. xvi.

2. See, e.g., D.L. Thrapp, *Encyclopedia of Frontier Biography*, Vol. I (Lincoln, Neb.: 1991), p. 221; B. O'Neal, *Encyclopedia of Western Gunfighters* (Norman, Okla.: 1983), p. 150; William Gardner Bell, "Frontier Lawman," *The American West*, Vol. I, No. 3 (Summer 1964) p. 6.

3. C.J. Crouch, *A History of Young County, Texas* (Austin: 1956), p. 223.

4. Application for Pardon File, No. 16547, Texas State Archives, Form 21 of the Texas State Penitentiaries.

5. Crouch, *loc. cit.*

6. *Ibid.*

7. Thus, Horner's name is not to be found in such works as F.I. Ingmire, *Texas Rangers: Frontier Battalion, Minute Men, Commanding Officers, 1847-1900*, Vol. III (St. Louis: 1982), p. 50.

8. Canton, *op. cit.*, p. 3; R.E. Ward, *History of the Cattlemen of Texas* (Austin: 1991), p. 77; J.M. Hunter, *The Trail Drivers of Texas* (Nashville: 1925), p. 568.

9. Canton, *op. cit.*, p. 17.

10. See, e.g., R.H. Mattison, "The Battle of Massacre Canyon," Potomac Corral of the Westerners, *Great Western Indian Fights* (Garden City, N.Y.: 1960), pp. 185-188.

11. Canton, *op. cit.*, p. 24.

12. R.G. Carter, *On the Border with MacKenzie or Winning West Texas from the Comanches* (New York: 1961), pp. 98-99.

13. I.L. Huckabay, *Ninety-Four Years in Jack County, 1854-1948* (Waco, Texas: 1979), p. 123; T.F. Horton, *History of Jack County* (n.p.: 1975), p. 147.

14. T.C. Battey, *The Life and Adventures of a Quaker Among the Indians* (Norman, Okla.: 1968), p. 239.

15. Bell, *op. cit.*, p. 7.

16. H.H. McConnell, *Five Years a Cavalryman* (Jacksboro, Texas: 1889), p. 296; Horton, *op. cit.*, p. 124.

17. Huckabay, *op. cit.*, p. 149.

18. E.L.N. Glass, *The History of the Tenth Cavalry, 1866-1921* (Fort Collins, Colo.: 1972), p. 20; A.L. Hamilton, *Sentinel of the Southern Plains: Fort Richardson and the Northwest Texas Frontier, 1866-1878* (Fort Worth: 1988), pp. 135-136.

19. O'Neal, *op. cit.*, p. 152.

20. Huckabay, *op. cit.*, pp. 109, 149.

21. *Ibid.*, p. 149.

22. *Ibid.*, pp. 149-150.

23. *Ibid.*, p. 150; Horton, *op. cit.*, pp. 121-122.

24. Bell, *loc. cit.*

25. H.W. Strong, *My Frontier Days and Indian Fights on the Plains of Texas* (Dallas: c. 1926), p. 42; R.F. Adams, *Six-Guns and Saddle Leather* (Cleveland: 1982), p. 113.

26. M. Frink, *Cow Country Cavalcade: 80 Years of the Wyoming Stock Growers Association* (Denver: 1954), p. 139.

27. Strong, *op. cit.*, p. 82. The James Gang was, of course, blamed for some crimes they did not commit. Professional courtesy among gangs would extend only so far, and blaming another gang would hardly be considered unethical.

28. M.B. Hanson (ed.), *Powder River Country: The Papers of J. Elmer Brock* (Cheyenne: 1981), p. 226.

29. Strong, *op. cit.*, p. 81.

30. *Ibid.*, p. 83. Probably proving that criminal minds work alike, it was only a few years later, in 1880, that Australian badman Ned Kelly had his own armored outfit constructed. See, e.g., Prior, Wannan, and Nunn, *A Pictorial History of Bushrangers* (New South Wales: 1968), pp. 135-136; F.M. Hare, *The Last of the Bushrangers: An Account of the Capture of the Kelly Gang* (Chicago: n.d.), p. 217. While it is unlikely that Kelly was influenced by a Texas badman, both Horner and Kelly probably heard of attempted uses of body armor during the American Civil War.

31. Strong, *loc. cit.*, p. 83; Application for Pardon File, *op. cit.*, Docket Statement dated March 15, 1877.

32. Application for Pardon File, *op. cit.*, Docket Statement dated March 17, 1877.

33. Strong, *op. cit.*, pp. 83-84; R.K. DeArment, "Joe Horner, Desperado," *Old West*, Vol. 29, No. 1 (Fall 1992); C. Parsons and G. Fitterer, *Captain C.B. McKinney: The Law in South Texas* (Wolfe City, Texas: 1993) pp. 17-18; Application for Pardon File, *op. cit.*, Copy of District Court Pleading of April 23, 1877.

34. Application for Pardon File, *op. cit.*, Form 21, Texas State Penitentiaries.

35. Hanson, *loc. cit.*, p. 226; Strong, *op. cit.*, p. 84; Application for Pardon File, *loc. cit.*

36. Bancroft, *op. cit.*, p. 792 n. 15.

37. A.W. Spring, *Seventy Years Cow Country* (Wyoming Stock Growers Association: 1942) pp. 39-40.

38. Frink, *op. cit.*, p. 93; N.S. Yost, *The Call of the Range* (Denver: 1966) p. 96. Dahlman, under his real name, later became mayor of Omaha, showing

that voters also did not care about his past. See D.D. Dustin, *Omaha and Douglas County: A Panoramic History* (Woodland Hills, Calif.: 1980) pp. 93-95; A. Sorenson, *The Story of Omaha* (Omaha: 1923) pp. 613-615.

39. See Spring, *op. cit.*, p. 39. Frink, *op. cit.*, p. 91; Bancroft, *op. cit.*, p. 792 n. 13. In his Huntsville Penitentiary Form 21, Horner's eyes were listed as blue.

40. See Application for Pardon File, *op. cit.*, various letters.

41. Spring, *loc. cit.*

42. Frink, *loc. cit.*

43. Canton, *op. cit.*, p. 34.

44. *Ibid.*

45. H.S. Drago, *The Great Range Wars* (New York: 1970) p. 262.

46. Bancroft, *op. cit.*, p. 792 n. 13.

47. Canton, *op. cit.*, p. 35.

48. Hanson, *op. cit.*, pp. 224-225.

49. Frink, *loc. cit.*

50. L.G. Flannery, *John Hunton's Diary*, Vol. 6 (Glendale, Calif.: 1970) p. 114.

51. Canton, *op. cit.*, pp. 36-42; Application for Pardon File, *op. cit.*, undated newspaper clipping perhaps from *Chicago World* newspaper, based upon a Cheyenne letter to *Chicago Herald*.

52. See, e.g., Thrapp, *op. cit.*, p. 222; Spring, *loc. cit.*

53. B.W. Driggs, *History of Teton Valley Idaho* (Rexburg, Idaho: 1970) (reprint of 1926 edition) pp. 121-123.

54. F. Calkins, *Jackson Hole* (New York: 1973) p. 116.

55. Hanson, *op. cit.*, p. 223.

56. Elnora L. Frye, *Atlas of Wyoming Outlaws at the Territorial Penitentiary* (Laramie: 1990) pp. 305-306.

57. Hanson, *op. cit.*, p. 225.

58. *Ibid.*, pp. 225, 266.

59. Canton, *op. cit.*, p. 49.

60. Application for Pardon File, *op. cit.*, letter to Joe Horner.

61. Canton, *op. cit.*, p. 77

62. Flannery, *loc. cit.*

63. Flannery, *op. cit.*, p. 107.

64. Application for Pardon File, *op. cit.*, Certificate of Appointment signed by Thomas Carr, U.S. Marshal.

65. See A.L. Mokler, *History of Natrona County Wyoming, 1888-1922* (New York: 1966) pp. 266-271.

66. Application for Pardon File, *op. cit.*, Certificate of Appointment dated Nov. 12, 1890, and signed by J.P. Ronkins (sp?), U.S. Marshal.

67. Thrapp, *op. cit.*, pp. 249-250; O'Neal, *op. cit.*, p. 55.

68. O'Neal, *op. cit.*, p. 56.

69. Frink, *op. cit.*, p. 138.

70. See H.H. Smith, *The War on Powder River* (New York: 1966) pp. 161, 167-168.

71. Frink, *op. cit.*, p. 139.
72. F.L. Bard and A.G. Spring, *Horse Wrangler: Sixty Years in the Saddle in Wyoming and Montana* (Norman, Okla.: 1960) P. 40.
73. Smith, *op. cit.*, pp. 165-166.
74. Hanson, *op. cit.*, p. 266.
75. Smith, *op. cit.*, pp. 169-173. A 1991 book asserts that Canton was assisted by none other than Tom Horn. See C. Carlson, *Tom Horn: Killing Men is My Specialty* (Cheyenne: 1992) pp. 16-17. There is a little support for this to be found in D.F. Baber, *The Longest Rope: The Truth About the Johnson County War* (Caldwell, Idaho: 1947) p. 117; and in Hanson, *op. cit.*, p. 360. However, there is evidence impeaching the affidavit that Carlson cites in Hanson, *op. cit.*, 263-265. In any event, because of shared acquaintances in Wyoming and because of shared methods of operation, it is reasonable to conclude that Canton and Horn knew each other.
76. Smith, *op. cit.*, p. 175; Canton, *op. cit.*, p. 87.
77. Smith, *op. cit.*, pp. 176-178.
78. J. Clay, *My Life on the Range* (Chicago: 1924) p. 276.
79. *Ibid.*
80. *Ibid.*
81. R.B. David, *Malcolm Campbell, Sheriff* (Casper, Wyoming: 1932) pp. 151-152.
82. *Ibid.*, p. 154; A.S. Mercer, *The Banditti of the Plain or the Cattlemen's Invasion of Wyoming in 1892* (Sheridan, Wyoming: 1930) p. 24.
83. David, *op. cit.*, p. 153; Mercer, *op. cit.*, p. 32.
84. David, *op. cit.*, p. 156.
85. *Ibid.*, p. 157.
86. *Ibid.*, pp. 133, 157-159.
87. Smith, *op. cit.*, p. 189.
88. Hanson, *op. cit.*, p. 285; O'Neal, *op. cit.*, p. 292.
89. C.L. Douglas, *Famous Texas Feuds* (Austin: 1988) pp. 169-171; C.L. Sonnichsen, *I'll Die Before I'll Run: The Story of the Great Feuds of Texas* (New York: 1951) pp. 210-212.
90. David, *op. cit.*, pp. 165-175.
91. Hanson, *op. cit.*, pp. 293-294.
92. The first-hand account from the perspective of the trappers is found in Baber, *op. cit.*, 103ff.
93. Mercer, *op. cit.*, p. 43.
94. Baber, *op. cit.*, p. 111.
95. Baber, *op. cit.*, p. 137.
96. Baber, *op. cit.*, p. 138.
97. Smith, *op. cit.*, p. 208.
98. Baber, *op. cit.*, p 138.
99. A.J. Jordan, *Jordan* (Missoula, Mont.: 1984) pp. 54-55.
100. Smith, *op. cit.*, pp. 208-209.
101. Smith, *op. cit.*, p. 211.
102. Canton, *op. cit.*, pp. 94-99.
103. Hanson, *op. cit.*, p. 285. Also contributing to Canton's assumption of power was a bitter argument that arose, when the invasion force was still on the train, between Wolcott and Canton over the

pack animals. See Jack Gage, *The Johnson County War is a Pack of Lies: The Barons Side* (The Flintlock Publishing Co.: 1967) pp. 66-67. However, the expedition's surgeon, Dr. Penrose, asserted that Wolcott reasserted command at the TA Ranch. C.B. Penrose, *The Rustler Business* (Douglas, Wyo.: 1959) p. 29.
104. Canton, *op. cit.*, p. 99.
105. Smith, *op. cit.*, pp. 223-225.
106. *Ibid.*, pp. 212, 222.
107. *Ibid.*, p. 263; Ida McPheren, *Trail's End* (Casper, Wyo.: 1938) p. 319.
108. A.E. Sheldon, "A Nebraska Episode of the Wyoming Cattle War," *Proceedings and Collections of the Nebraska State Historical Society*, Vol. V (2nd Series) (Lincoln: 1902) pp. 138-149.
109. Smith, *op. cit.*, pp. 262-264, 281-282.
110. Darwin Payne, *Owen Wister: Chronicler of the West, Gentleman of the East* (Dallas: 1985) p. 140.
111. Canton, *op. cit.*, p. 108.
112. *Ibid.*, p. 107.
113. Frink, *op. cit.*, p. 89.
114. Thrapp, *op. cit.*, p. 222; Carl Breihan, *Gunslingers* (Wauwatosa, Wis.: 1984) p. 46.
115. See T. Allen, *Those Buried Texans* (Dallas: 1980) p. 71.
116. Application for Pardon File, *op. cit.*, Governor's Letter dated July 17, 1894.
117. See Canton, *loc. cit.* Canton did not mention his difficulties in Jacksboro in his memoirs, so this is one of the few full published connections of the Canton-Lake relationship, although Glenn Shirley, *West of Hell's Fringe* (Norman, Okla.: 1978) p. 265 cryptically mentions that Lake was a "former Texas acquaintance" of Canton.
118. Thrapp, *loc. cit.*
119. See Canton, *op. cit.*, pp. 138-141; Shirley, *op. cit.*, pp. 280-282, 372.
120. Canton, *op. cit.*, pp. 117-118, 137.
121. Z. Tilghman, *Marshal of the Last Frontier* (Glendale, Calif.: 1949) p. 214.
122. Shirley, *op. cit.*, p. 270.
123. *Annual Report of the Attorney-General of the United States for the Year 1897* (Washington, D.C.: 1897) p. 280.
124. Canton, *op. cit.*, p. 150.
125. W.B. Hunt, *Distant Justice: Policing the Alaska Frontier* (Norman, Okla.: 1987) p. 80.
126. E.L. Baker, *Gunman's Territory* (San Antonio, Texas: 1969) p. 212.
127. *Annual Report of the Attorney-General of the United States for the Year 1894* (Washington, D.C.: 1894) pp. xix-xxii.
128. See *Annual Report of the Attorney-General of the United States for the Year 1897*, pp. 278-279.
129. E.D. Nix, *Oklahombres, Particularly the Wilder Ones* (n.p.: 1929) p. 80.
130. Hunt, *op. cit.*, p. 72.
131. *Ibid.*; Canton, *op. cit.*, p. 154.
132. See Canton, *op. cit.*, pp. 156-222.
133. See Hunt, *op. cit.*, pp. 81-82.

134. P. Berton, *Klondike: The Life and Death of the Last Great Gold Rush* (Toronto: 1958), p. 318.

135. Hunt, *op. cit.*, pp. 80-81.

136. Canton, *op. cit.*, p. 221.

137. *Annual Report of the Attorney-General of the United States for the Year 1898* (Washington, D.C.: 1898), pp. 234-235; *Annual Report of the Attorney-General of the United States for the Year 1899* (Washington, D.C.: 1899), pp. 318-319.

138. Bell, *op. cit.*, p. 78.

139. Rex Beach, *Personal Exposures: His Own Story* (New York: 1940), p. 37.

140. *Ibid.*, p. 98; Canton, *op. cit.*, pp. 186-187.

141. Beach, *op. cit.*, p. 98.

142. Canton, *op. cit.*, pp. 221-222.

143. Glenn Boyer (ed.), *I Married Wyatt Earp* (Tucson: 1990), pp. 195-196. Coincidentally, the Earps had also lived as renters in the cabin occupied by Beach and Canton in Rampart City. *Ibid.*, p. 166.

144. Hanson, *op. cit.*, pp. 467-469.

145. *Ibid.*, p. 469.

146. O'Neal, *op. cit.*, p. 152.

147. Canton, *op. cit.*, p. 234.

148. Irvin Hurst, *The 46th Star: A History of Oklahoma's Constitutional Convention and Early Statehood* (Oklahoma City: 1957), p. 34. There was also an early Oklahoma State Senator named Horner, who may have been another political connection.

149. *Ibid.*, pp. 33-34.

150. See G. Shirley, *Last of the Real Badmen: Henry Starr* (Lincoln: 1976), p. 173.

151. Hurst, *op. cit.*, p. 115; Tilghman, *op. cit.*, pp. 272-274; W.F. Jones, *The Experiences of a Deputy U.S. Marshal of the Indian Territory* (Tulsa, Okla.: 1937) p. 8; Thrapp, *loc. cit.*; K. Franks, *Citizen Soldiers: Oklahoma's National Guard* (Norman, Okla.: 1984), p. 14.

152. Orben J. Casey, "Governor Lee Cruce and Law Enforcement, 1911-1915," *The Chronicles of Oklahoma*, Vol. 54, No. 4 (Winter 1976-1977), p. 450.

153. *Ibid.*, p. 449.

154. *Ibid.*, p. 445.

155. *Ibid.*, p. 455.

156. Franks, *loc. cit.*; Diane B. Haser-Harris, "Horse Racing in Early Oklahoma," *The Chronicles of Oklahoma*, Vol. 64, No. 1 (Spring 1986), p. 16.

157. Canton, *op. cit.*, p. 237.

158. Breihan, *op. cit.*, p. 48.

159. See Canton, *op. cit.*, p. xiii; Franks, *op. cit.*, pp. 19-20.

160. Thrapp, *op. cit.*, pp. 221, 223.

161. Bell, *loc. cit.*

162. *Ibid.*, p. 78.

163. Jessie Newby Ray, "The 'Y' Chapel of Song," *The Chronicles of Oklahoma*, Vol. 35, No. 4 (Winter 1957-1958), pp. 470-471.

164. Drago, *op. cit.*, pp. 262, 263.

165. G. Shirley, *Pawnee Bill* (Lincoln: 1958), p. 140.

166. Frink, *loc. cit.*

167. Canton, *op. cit.*, p. xii.

168. F.R. Prassel, *The Western Peace Officer* (Norman, Okla.: 1972), pp. 145-146.

169. Edward Everett Dale, *The Cross Timbers: Memories of a North Texas Boyhood* (Austin: 1966), p. 4.

170. Canton, *loc. cit.*

171. Bell, *loc. cit.*

172. Beach, *op. cit.* p. 107.

About the Author

As noted previously, John M. Hutchins is an Assistant U.S. Attorney in Denver, following a stint with the Colorado Attorney General's office. Earlier he had his own law practice in Meeker, Colo., and subsequently was assistant city attorney for El Paso, Texas. (See earlier biography in this book.)

John, 1994 Sheriff of the Denver Westerners, presented his talk on "The Life and Times of Frank Canton" on Jan. 22, 1992. (His paper was originally entitled, "The Jekyll-Hyde Gunman of the Johnson County War of 1892.") The Canton paper was his second program for the Westerners—this time, on the darker side of frontier life, revealing his intimate knowledge of the history and the workings of the law. His first paper, "The Colorado Territorial Bench and Bar," also appears in this 50th Anniversary *Brand Book*.

The paper on Frank Canton won the Danielson Award from Westerners International, and is a fascinating change of pace for our *Brand Book*.

"The Old West Salutes the New" by *Delano*

Early Colorado Filmmaking

and The Colorado Motion Picture Company

By David Emrich

COLORADO HAS AN INTERESTING place in the history of motion pictures. Before Hollywood became the center of film production, there was considerable movie-making in Colorado. One of the more interesting chapters in the history is centered around Cañon City and two companies: the Selig Polyscope Company and the Colorado Motion Picture Company. The experiences of these filmmakers are interesting, but they also tell us something about the American West—the West of the pioneer, of dangers, and ultimately, of the success of "civilization" over "frontier."

Most people think of Hollywood as the birthplace of the motion pictures. But not all movie-making has been in Hollywood and its environs. Early innovations in film production occurred on the East Coast. During the movie companies' migration from east to west, there were stops in Colorado by many of the early production companies. Two reasons drew them west from headquarters in Chicago, Philadelphia, New York City, or Orange, N.J.

First the very low light-sensitivity—an ASA rating of approximately 8—of early motion-picture film stock demanded the bright, almost constant sunshine found in the American Southwest.

Second, the growing popularity of Westerns—starting in 1903 with "The Great Train Robbery"—demanded more realistic locations and personalities. Painted backdrops could not replace the dramatic landscapes of the Rocky Mountains.

One of the early filmmakers coming to Colorado was the Selig Polyscope Company of Chicago. H. H. "Buck" Buckwalter, a widely known turn-of-the-century Denver still photographer, started shooting movies for Selig in 1901. He filmed scenes of Denver street life, Ute Indians, mountain landscapes, and a few Westerns. Some of these titles included "Runaway Stage Coach" (1902); "Robbery of the Leadville Stage" (1904); "Bandit King" (1907); and "Montana Girl" (1907).

Buckwalter's main interest, however, was in the distribution and exhibition of the Selig movies, rather than in their production. Buck-walter worked as the western booking agent for Selig and other com-panies until 1917, but seems to have stopped shooting movies by 1907.

In the summer of 1911, a more prestigious branch of the Selig company made its way to Colorado. The troupe included Tom Mix, reputed to be one of the three great silent movie cowboy stars. Mix and his wife Olive were trick riders, not stars. Even though Tom Mix was not considered a leading man, during his three months in Cañon City, he dominated contemporary accounts. His riding—not to men-tion his off-screen activities—became legend.

In the fall of 1911, the troupe also included Joseph A. Golden as producer and director; Marshall Stedman, business manager; Myrtle Stedman, leading lady; and William Duncan, leading man. In August, they shot movies in American City, north of Central City. In Septem-ber, the company moved to Cañon City, staying until winter closed in. Here they made a number of one and two-reel Westerns (each reel was between 12 and 14 minutes long).

The company returned in June 1912—without Tom Mix—and shot in the Cañon City area until early January 1913. The shooting sched-ule was speedy, to say the least—38 titles were shot in the 9 to 10 months the Selig Company was in Cañon City. Titles such as "The Bully of Bingo Gulch," "The Telltale Knife," "The Dynamiters," "A Cowboy's Mother," and "The Diamond 'S' Robbery" indicate the style of these films.

Filmmaking in those days did not allow much concern for safety. The fast shooting pace and action-filled sequences often resulted in accidents. For instance, Myrtle Stedman was knocked unconscious when the horse she was riding bucked her off into some rocks. A top-heavy stagecoach loaded with people rolled down a 150-foot embank-ment. Rex Roselli, a "heavy" for the company, was stabbed in the leg and the *Florence Daily Citizen* of July 11, 1912, calmly reported:

> Fortunately the femoral artery was not severed and as the wound was cared for immediately, it is not thought that any permanent serious result will follow.

One accident involved William Duncan, leading man and director of the company, in late summer 1912. He instructed the film crew that, while standing in a doorway, he would raise his hand as a signal to start rolling the film. The second time he raised his hand, a man holding a shotgun was to wait a beat and then blast the door apart. Unfortunately, the instructions were not followed exactly. The man holding the shotgun fired one signal early, while Duncan was standing

Colorado Motion Picture Company camera crew sets up equipment in a car at Cañon City.

partly in the doorway. Needless to say, Duncan was in the hospital a few days.

Local residents were used as extras and as minor players and, on occasion, as leads. A couple of movies starred a local boy, Roderick MacKenzie. In one of these one-reelers, "Roderick's Ride," he rides "Pony Express style" to get a doctor to save the life of his younger sister. In another, "The Little Hero," he lowers her into a well, then lowers himself to escape a raging prairie fire. A supporting actor earned $5 a day. An extra got $1 a day. Nevertheless, the economic benefits for Cañon City interested the city fathers in the motion picture business.

Even as early as October 1911, there was talk of opening a year-round studio in Cañon City. Otis B. Thayer, the actor-turned-director of the company, let the *Cañon City Record* know that he would:

> . . . endeavor to land the proposed studio for this place. . . . That nowhere in the United States are the surroundings more adaptable for securing a wide range of pictures than here, and that fact, coupled with the unusual number of

bright cloudless days, renders Cañon City an almost ideal place for the successful prosecution of the company's business.

Yet this studio was never built. In January 1913, the Selig company
moved to Prescott, Ariz., for the winter. Although there was correspondence between the Cañon City's Businessmen's Association and
Selig, the company never returned to Colorado.

Tom Mix did come back to Colorado, though. In the summer of
1926, the Fox Company—later 20th Century Fox—came to Colorado
and shot "The Great K & A Train Robbery" at the Royal Gorge and
Glenwood Canyon.

By the end of 1913, any idea that Selig would establish a permanent
Colorado studio was abandoned. But there was still hope for Cañon
City.

Otis B. Thayer had left Selig in July 1912, for an enterprise called
the Cheyenne Motion Picture Company. They made the first movies
of the Cheyenne Frontier Days celebration in Wyoming, then apparently broke up. Obie—as he was called—then became part owner and
director for the Columbine Film Company in Denver.

Columbine's first production, shot in January 1913 in Denver, was
"The Way of the Transgressor," an apparent exposé of child-labor
conditions. This movie was in the new vein of films that were, in
themselves, an exploitation of base social issues. (Another example
was the 1913 Universal release about white slavery, "Traffic in Souls.")

"Judge Ben Lindsey's Juvenile Court" was another Columbine Film
Company movie. Denver Judge Lindsey played himself in the film.
George Creel, a *Denver Post* editorial writer, was the author of the
story. Creel later became district attorney, and subsequently headed
the Committee on Public Information, an official U.S. propaganda
agency during World War I.

The film was also a first for a couple of cowboy actors, Bud Chase
and Joe Ryan. It also starred Josephine West, an actress who followed
Obie away from the Selig company. This movie was shown at the
Paris Theatre in April 1913. As with most movies of the day, it played
in Denver for just three days.

After making some additional films, such as "The Faker and the
Bootlegger," Obie Thayer and Columbine were absorbed into a new
organization, the Colorado Motion Picture Company, incorporated on
Aug. 30, 1913.

Obie brought his actors and crew to Cañon City in October 1913,
in order to use the penitentiary for a three-reel feature film depicting

(Courtesy Western History Dept., Denver Public Library)
Denver judge played himself in "Judge Ben Lindsey's Juvenile Court."

prison life, "The Hand of the Law." Warden Tynan took a leading role in this film. None of the still photos surviving from this movie shows the warden or, indeed, much of the prison. But the *Cañon City Record* of Dec. 25, 1913 stated:

> Warden Tynan is conspicuously shown in this remarkable series of pictures, as are also other officers of the prison. The road-building camps and mountain scenery about Cañon City likewise figure in the scenes that are presented.
>
> It is thrilling throughout, and recounts the daring escape of Joe Willard, a convict who gets over the prison walls and escapes to the mountains with the officers of the law in hot pursuit. Two dogs belonging to Bill Wallace are requisitioned by the warden to help run down the refugee, and they play a marvelous role of skill and tenacity in tracking and bringing to bay the run-aways. One of the thrills of the drama is where the dogs bring the escaping prisoner to bay on the top of a high cliff and a fight takes place between the pursued and his pursuers, which ends by the man and dogs falling 300 feet down a declivity in an inextricable jumble, the dogs hanging on to the man in a vise-like grip.
>
> Another one of the reels shows Joe Willard in a daredevil act that elicits admiration by its heroism. The sweetheart of the convict on an unmanageable runaway horse dashes past one of the prison road camps where Willard is at

(Courtesy Western History Dept., Denver Public Library)

Bud Chase as Jim Webster is saved from hanging by sweetheart (Josephine West as Nell Carter) in "Pirates of the Plains." (State prison guard
tower at Cañon City is in rear.)

work, with the prospect of being thrown off and killed. Willard jumps in the
Warden's automobile, which is standing conveniently near, and, under high
pressure, endeavors to overtake her in the machine and rescue her from her
impending fate. He gradually gains on the runaway horse and eventually
overtakes it. Leaping from the automobile, he falls upon the animal's neck and
finally brings it to a standstill and saves the young woman from injury.

Two quite exciting scenes! Injuries were possible, if not inevitable,
in making such movies. (It would be interesting to know what happened to the warden's car.)

Shortly after shooting this film in Cañon City, Thayer presented the
Businessmen's Association with a proposal to move the Colorado Motion Picture Company there permanently, on the condition that $5,000
in preferred stock be subscribed to in Cañon City. The association
agreed, providing the city was represented on the board of directors

and that Thayer provided a statement of assets and liabilities.

Thayer agreed to two local board members, to serve as secretary and treasurer. He listed company assets (in equipment and film rights) at $58,300. Other officers of the company included William Foley from Denver, co-owner with Thayer of the earlier Columbine Film Company; and Courtland Dines. Within 24 hours the $5,000 in stock was sold, and the Colorado Motion Picture Company moved to Cañon City in January 1914.

The reasons for the support the company received were obvious. First, within a year, between 75 and 200 persons were expected to be employed by the company, with weekly payroll of $1,500 to $3,500.

The Colorado Motion Picture Company seemed likely to grow. Thayer had found distribution for these movies through a then-new company, Warner Features—soon to be Warner Brothers. Warner contracted for at least one three-reel film every three weeks. From mid-January through the end of August, the production company was reported to have produced between five and seven movies.

The first of these, "Pirates of the Plains," starred Bud Chase and Josephine West. Chase, playing Jim Webster, is convicted of a murder he did not commit. Josephine West, as his sweetheart Nell Owens, of course, believes in him. She finds the real murderer badly wounded, out on the plains, and hears his confession just before he dies. Nell rushes to save Webster from the hangman's noose. The priest in this movie was played by director Obie Thayer. Jack Donahoo, who played the sheriff, came with the company from Denver. He stayed on in Cañon City and later became the city's police chief.

The second film, "The Range War," was produced in February 1914 and starred Joe Ryan and Josephine West. The movie opens with Josephine West at a ball in Chicago, then continues with the traditional sheepman versus cattleman conflict. Again, the film was full of stunts. The *Cañon City Record* of Feb. 26, 1914 reported:

> In "The Range War," Joe Ryan makes some of the greatest rides of his most exciting and spectacular career as a movie star. In one scene he stops a runaway team, overtaking it on horseback and jumping from the horse to the wagon, then down the wagon tongue to the horses' heads, producing action teeming with danger and uncertainty. At another time, he is dragged by a horse going at full speed. It is apparent from the picture that he is actually dragged and that a dummy is not substituted.

Again, as so many newspaper stories recounted, there were accidents. Twice during the filming, Ryan was trampled by horses while preforming stunts. The *Record* stated that "he received enough inju-

1. Josephine West (right) puts a gun in Joe Ryan's back in "The Range War" scene. 2. In a typically hazardous action shot, Joe Ryan rescues Josephine West in "The Range War." 3. Josephine West sits as Obie Thayer directs. Cameraman is Owen Carter. 4. Josephine West and Joe Ryan promote love interest in "The Range War." (*All pictures courtesy Western History Dept., Denver Public Library.*)

ries in this picture to kill an ordinary man."

    Second, it was expected that the movies themselves would advertise the region, a concern the town fathers frequently discussed.

    Sometimes there were dangers of another kind. Perhaps the strangest story involved this film company deals with a mining war at the Chandler Mine between Cañon City and Florence.

On April 25, 1914, a gunfight broke out between striking miners and guards for the mine owners. Shortly after a truce was called, the movie company started to enact a gunfight of their own—using blanks—for one of their films. The *Fremont County Leader* (April 30, 1914) reported:

> Within a few minutes the hill between them and Brookside was bristling with guns containing sure-enough bullets. These were in the hands of strikers who were eager to learn what was going on. The mission of the picture gang was explained to them and they drew off. It is dollars-to-donuts the movies [sic] were not comfortable during the short minute of parley.

At least two more movies were shot during March, April, and May that year. Unfortunately, no titles have been found for these films. Existing still photos show the first of these was a story about mine claim-jumping. This film again starred Josephine West, and was the last Cañon City movie for Joe Ryan. Jack Donahoo and Obie Thayer again played parts.

A second—untitled—movie also starred Josephine West, in her last film for the Colorado Motion Picture Company. Edmund Cobb, the company's new leading man, arrived in late April, having worked with three of the largest early filmmakers: Lubin Company of Philadelphia; Vitagraph in New York City; and Selig, Chicago. The movie dealt with the kidnapping of Miss West by a man (bandit?) who takes her to a mountain hideout.

With each new movie, the company became more ambitious. Another film was shot during June, "Across the Border," about gunrunning along the Mexican-U.S. border during the Mexican Revolution. The cast of hundreds included two troops of the Twelfth U.S. Cavalry.

Ed Cobb played the lead. Grace McHugh, the female lead, was new with the Colorado Motion Picture Company and was an accomplished actress and horsewoman, as well as aeronaut and swimmer.

Again accidents were reported in the press. Charlie Reeves, a Cañon City resident who provided horses and acted in many small parts, was kicked in the back by a horse while setting up a shot with a group of horses killed after the explosion of an ammunition wagon.

On July 1, 1914, the company had just started to make its next film when a tragedy struck. A scene for "Across the Border," ruined in developing, was being reshot when Grace McHugh's horse stumbled as she was trying to cross the Arkansas River just above Cañon City. Panicking, she caused the horse to further lose its footing, and she was thrown into the river.

The July 2 *Cañon City Record* reported that, at first, John Keough rode into the river to help her. The newspaper quoted Obie Thayer:

> She grabbed his hands so that he could do nothing. In his efforts to break her hold so that he could grab her, the force of the water swept her away downstream. In the meantime, cameraman Owen Carter took off his clothes and jumped into the current alongside of her. He grabbed her and I saw him carry her to the sand bank.

Thayer thought that all was okay. But another witness said Carter then stumbled, hitting his head on a rock, and both he and Miss McHugh fell back into the river. Lawrence Jossenberger, also with the company, having seen them carried on down the river, jumped in and was himself almost drowned. Grace McHugh and Owen Carter were not so lucky, and both were drowned. At first, some people doubted that the two had really drowned. Owen Carter's mother, for one believed it might have been an advertising scheme.

(Courtesy Western History Dept., Denver Public Library)

Jack Donahoo and Ed Cobb confer in military movie, "A Cycle of Destiny."

"And yet, if it were, Owen would not be a party to such a thing," she told a *Denver Post* reporter. "He would have let me know. He was a good boy, and so considerate of his mother."

Owen Carter's body was found one week later, a mile downstream. Grace McHugh's body wasn't found until two weeks after the accident. Ironically, on the same day the *Cañon City Record* announced discovery of the actress' body, the paper carried a story on Ed Cobb's acting history, and the stunts he performed for "Across the Border." In one of these, "he floats down the river for a half-mile and finally comes up against the bank," the writer noted.

The movie that the company had just started filming, "A Cycle of Destiny," was begun again with a new leading actress, Gertrude Bondhill. The *Cañon City Record* reported on July 16, 1914, that the new movie was to be:

> . . . a three-reel Military Indian drama of the period of '65. Otis B. Thayer, director of the company, is showing what he can do, now that he is blessed with pleasant weather, as he made 38 scenes in two days, which is eight scenes more than a one-reel picture.

This movie also starred A. S. Lewis as the "heavy" and Johnny Keogh and Jack Donahoo as Army officers. In September, the company announced it would make another three-reel military play, "In Perilous Paths." (This movie may not have been made.)

The Colorado Motion Picture Company essentially went out of business and left Cañon City sometime in the fall of 1914. Legend is that the company was sued by Grace McHugh's mother and its officers had to fold the corporation. (This may not have happened.)

Thayer most assuredly saw William Duncan of the Selig company almost drown in the same area in the summer of 1911. Considering this and the other accidents that happened to the actors, the company was a likely target for a suit. But there is no record of any kind of lawsuit being filed in Cañon City or Golden (where Grace was from). There also was never any newspaper story nor any discussion in the Businessmen's Association's notes pertaining to a suit. Moreover, the corporation's annual report filed with the state in March 1915 noted that the firm was "entirely out of debt." Finally, the Colorado Motion Picture Company was not officially dissolved until April 26, 1918. The real reason the company went out of business may never be known.

Interestingly, a week after the drownings of Grace McHugh and Owen Carter, a movie signaling ultimate consolidation of the film industry in California was shown in Cañon City. "Quo Vadis," an epic Roman film 11 reels in length, was a tremendous hit worldwide.

It encouraged filmmakers to produce the large-scale, long movies that we know today as feature films.

The same climate factors that attracted production companies to Colorado drew filmmakers to California. While some movie companies were discovering Colorado, more were discovering Southern California. The dramatically accelerating costs of ever-larger and longer movies led to the consolidation of the industry in the "heaven" that we call Hollywood.

Obie Thayer continued making movies in Colorado for several years. First, he worked in Colorado Springs for the Pikes Peak Photoplay Company in 1915 and 1916; then for the National Film Corporation in Denver in 1916 and 1917; and finally, for his own firm, Art-o-Graf Film Company in Denver, 1919-1923. Gertrude Bondhill worked with Obie Thayer at the Pikes Peak Photoplay Company in Colorado Springs until some time in 1916. (The only other notable person to work for that company was Silver Dollar Tabor, who wrote her mother, Baby Doe, of her employment.)

Miss Bondhill then went to New York, performing on Broadway. Later she was on the radio program, "Pepper Young's Family."

Joe Ryan and Bud Chase also went to California and were in Western serials for a number of years.

Ed Cobb left Colorado for California, to work for the Essanay Company, another early major film producer. He rejoined Obie Thayer's Art-o-Graf Films in Denver from 1919 to 1923. He then returned to California, first to make serials, then features for Universal during the 1920s, 1930s, and 1940s.

Obie was the last to go, finally leaving Colorado for California in 1925. The concentration of the movie industry in California was nearly absolute. There were almost no further attempts at feature filmmaking by any local Colorado company until after World War II. Hollywood continued to come to Colorado for the picturesque locations that brought producers to the state in the first place. By getting away from the back lots of the East Coast and later the West Coast, the filmmakers were able to portray the West in a more realistic light. In the early days of the movies, people in the *background* of the action were realistic because many were portraying how they themselves had lived. Many of these extras thus relived the cattle drives and Indian fights they had experienced in their youth. The later the movie was made, the less realistic these background elements became.

Primarily, moviemaking was a business. By using the same sets, the same costumes, and the same "professional" extras, film companies could produce movies more economically and safely. The film *industry* necessitated the homogenization of the movies. But in the early, rough versions, there was a realism in the images that can never be duplicated. And again, making these movies was not unlike living on the frontier they portrayed. As the *Cañon City Record* stated in an Oct. 11, 1911, story:

> There is a large element of danger to the participants in some of these dramas that are portrayed for the benefit of the camera, and only those of the steadiest nerves and utmost bravery are chosen to take part in their presentation, for most of them delineate the "wild and woolly west" when its frontier was a buffer between savagery and civilization.

Grace McHugh is pictured on a postcard issued by the Colorado Motion Picture Company, to promote film, "Across the Border." *(From postcard owned by John Donahoo of Cañon City.)*

This brings us back to Grace McHugh's experience in the movie business. An interview with her was to have appeared in the *Rocky Mountain News* on the day of her death. While the *News* did not print the interview, they did print this short excerpt on July 2, 1914:

> Of course, to hold my job, I have to take many chances. I make it a rule to never get excited or hesitate, or even to think of the possible consequences. Often I have narrow escapes and frequently sustain physical injuries, but I never think of them at the time.

This comment is telling in that it displays the extent to which these actors pursued their craft. Grace McHugh represents the raw talent and the will of these early film actors. The Colorado Motion Picture Company expressed this same thought when it issued a postcard with a photo of Miss McHugh on the front, to promote the movie, "Across the Border." On the reverse side, the legend reads:

> The tragedy which cost Miss Grace McHugh her life in the production of "Across the Border" robbed picturedom of one of its greatest artists. Young, beautiful, talented and courageous, Miss McHugh had before her the promise of a brilliant life. She was a true actress—a conscientious worker—a woman of character and strength. Her career, short as it was, is an inspiring example of what ability and determination can accomplish.
>
> "Across the Border" is conceded by critics to be the best film of its kind yet produced, its remarkable success being due to the originality of the scenario, the realism of the pictures and the splendid acting of her role by Miss McHugh.
>
> The Colorado Motion Picture Company feels that "Across the Border" is itself a fitting tribute to the memory of Grace McHugh, than whom no more worthy star has appeared in the motion picture firmament.

These words seem to express the point of this paper. Here is a woman of the twentieth century who fearlessly portrayed and, indeed, personified the American "Wild West." But perhaps more tellingly, she represents the business that was—and is—moviemaking, for on the bottom of the postcard, are these final words:

"To be shown at the Cañon City Opera House Wednesday and Thursday, Oct. 7 and 8. Matinee Thursday."

Ultimately, Grace McHugh's death did serve as a publicity stunt.

Colorado Motion Picture Company trademark.

(Courtesy Denver Public Library)

About the Author

"Early Colorado Filmmaking and the Colorado Motion Picture Company" was presented for the Denver Westerners on Aug. 22, 1990, by Posse Member David Emrich. The paper covers an unexplored aspect of Colorado history, and represents a combination of the Emrich family history, and David's own career choice.

A fourth-generation Coloradan, David Emrich's interest in Colorado history and Western American history stems from stories told him by his parents and grandparents. He earned a bachelor's degree in economics and political science from the University of Colorado, a school previously attended by three generations of his family. He met his wife Mary shortly after graduation, and they recently celebrated their 10th anniversary.

After graduation, David decided to follow in the footsteps of his father Paul, working in the motion picture business.

David now owns a small Denver film and video editing company, Post Modern. He has worked on feature films, and TV shows for PBS, Discovery, and ESP, as well as hundreds of TV commercials and business-to-business video presentations. His "Spirits of the Rain Forest" was an Emmy Award-winning documentary.

David Emrich has been a member of the Denver Westerners since 1988, becoming a Corresponding Member after attending just one meeting, as a guest. He was elevated to the Posse in 1991. In his limited spare time, he continues to research early Colorado motion picture companies. And he dreams of some day working on a documentary on Western history.

"Disaster in Pueblo" by *Max Smith*

The Great Pueblo
Flood of 1921

By Bernard Kelly

*J*UNE 3, 1921, WAS a dark, misty, rainy day in Pueblo, Colorado. The newspaper reported that a cloudburst the day before had caused Dry Creek, just west of the city, to go over its banks, and said that two children had been drowned. Water from the rain backed up along Main Street and seeped into doorways. People talked with a mild sense of adventure about the "flood."

It was the last day of school for me. I was leaving the eighth grade at St. Patrick's School and knew I would be entering Central High School the next fall as a freshman. Oh, it was good to be out of school! Some friends and I enjoyed the scary news of high water in the Arkansas River, but my main problem was, how was I going to get a new suit with long pants to wear in high school the following September? I still had a good suit of short pants and jacket, and I knew my family thought this would be perfectly adequate for next fall!

West of Pueblo, heavy clouds boiled up over a triangular tongue of plains country half surrounded by mountain ranges. Many tributaries of the Arkansas River rise in the mountains that bound this drainage basin. Cloudbursts have cut deep channels or arroyos across the prairies. A dense black bank of clouds lay along the top and sides of the range during the morning, and about 1 p.m. it dropped down from the mountains and began to push out over the prairie. Another storm descended from the direction of Cripple Creek up north.

It began to rain. By 3 p.m. the rain had become a downpour which spread over the upper and middle parts of the valley. The water came down faster than the soil could absorb it, racing along ditches and through arroyos. It built up into walls often several feet high like sea waves about to break on a shore.

Just west of Pueblo, 12 inches of rain was measured in a concrete box. At Teller Reservoir, 10 inches fell after 3 p.m. At Skaguay Reservoir near Victor, Colo., 7½ inches. At Penrose, 7 inches. Ten at

Eight-Mile Creek, 9 at Chandler Creek. Between 3 and 3:30 p.m., 5 inches of rain piled up in 30 minutes on Boggs Flats, and the solid fall of water drowned a horse in an open field. At that time Boggs Flats was an enormous open area just west of Pueblo, and only sparsely inhabited. Boggs Flats ranchers measured 14 inches of rain that afternoon and night. A hard-surfaced road in the area was washed out to a depth of 7 feet.

The storm had begun in the foothills about 1 p.m. Friday, June 3. By 3 p.m., it had spread over the upper and middle parts of the valley. Between 5 and 7 p.m. it had gathered its might at the valley's lower end, near Pueblo.

Pueblo then had a population of 40,000. It lay at the confluence of the Arkansas and Fountaine Qui Bouille rivers. Residential areas were north and south of the Arkansas River bed, but most of the business district and railroad yards stood in the lowland that had been wrested from the streams. There had been a flood May 30, 1894, but after that the levees were heightened and strengthened, bridges raised, and the channel widened to accommodate a greater runoff than ever seemed likely. The work was completed in 1898. Now, in 1921, the river was straddled by a series of bridges, including a heavily traveled passenger, vehicular and street-railway span at Union Avenue.

Between 5 and 6:40 p.m., the river rose 8 feet in the narrow channel. At 6 p.m., the flood warning began to sound—a steam siren mounted on the North Side waterworks. Its chilling wail, rising and falling, could be heard in all parts of the city.

The Kelly house stood on a bluff overlooking the Denver & Rio Grande Railroad yards. I had a love of trains bred in me early from watching the switching operations just below our house, and from seeing the more distant passenger trains of four different railroads entering and leaving the Union Depot, about half a mile away. That bluff, they told me, was once the south bank of the Arkansas River. Now the river was contained in a narrow channel about the distance of 10 city blocks from us.

Naturally everyone was excited at the scary wail of the siren, constantly warning us. Two of my friends and I, all of us just out of eighth grade, decided to walk across a bridge near our house, go down on the river levee, and follow the levee downtown, where we were sure there was some action! My sister and her boy friend decided to go with us. We walked along that levee, and the water was only a foot or so down from the edge.

If you have smelled flood water, you know it has a dank, sort of sour smell, a combination of plants, buildings, trees and living creatures soaked in silty water. As we walked, we watched occasional trees bounding by, and being tossed in the air by the strong current. When they came past the spray would spatter on us as we walked. I don't think we ever thought of the danger. It was all too exciting. Eventually we reached the place where the river crossed the main street going downtown, Union Avenue. There were freight cars standing on a railroad siding there, and we three boys climbed up on the cars to see the action better.

A kind of holiday spirit took over the town, as if the banshee voice of the siren announced good tidings. Hundreds of Puebloans hurried from their homes to the river banks, thrilled at the sight of the angry high water. The scene was dramatic—no doubt about that. Tree trunks, lumber, demolished houses, and the bodies of animals swept by in the muddy water. The water whipped by seriously close to the levee tops, but the crowd stayed on, enchanted.

Not until 8 p.m. did we begin to take things seriously. By then, the stench of the flood was overpowering. There were reports that the river was "coming over" in places. Police drove the curious from the bridges and ordered us kids down off the boxcars. Trees hurtling down the river with the speed of express trains were hitting the bridge railings and being tossed high into the air. Water backing up into storm sewers boiled out of manholes. The crowd began to move toward high ground, slowly at first, then faster and faster.

One such safe place was about four blocks away—another bridge, or rather a viaduct, over the Union Depot yards. We started to walk toward that place. Suddenly the lights went out. All the lights. All the lights everywhere. There was a kind of murmur from the crowd, and we walked faster.

"Must have got into the power company," someone said.

There was intermittent light. An electrical storm was brewing and lightning was almost continuous. Great roars of thunder followed. We walked up onto the viaduct, and looked down into the Union Depot yards.

Two passenger trains were standing in the depot yards, the Rio Grande's No. 3, just in from Denver, and the Missouri Pacific's eastbound No. 14, scheduled to leave at 8:05 p.m. It was decided to move her over the Santa Fe bridge to the north side of the river, and she puffed out of the yards at 8:36 p.m. When No. 14 reached the

Santa Fe bridge, however, the idea of crossing was abandoned. The Arkansas was pounding at the bridge flooring.

No. 3, scheduled to go west but held up in Pueblo because of washouts reported ahead, also was moved out of the yards in the hope of reaching high ground. As the train started out of the depot yard it seemed much like the departure of an excursion party bent on pleasure. The cars were brilliantly lighted and the few passengers who remained on board were laughing and waving to bystanders. Most of the travelers, advised of the delay, had gone uptown to see the flood.

We later learned that the two passenger trains wound up stalled side by side near the river.

The Arkansas overflowed its channel at 8:45 p.m. near Main Street. The crowd on the Union Avenue viaduct saw the black water racing through the depot yards. The babble of excitement suddenly choked into a gasp. Like a blast of cannon, a crash of thunder came, then a fresh deluge of rain. The cloudburst which had pelted the plains to the west all afternoon finally had arrived over Pueblo.

We were like ants under a waterfall. It was almost impossible to breathe. Our party of five ran toward the south bank, which was the long bluff on which our house stood. We arrived home drenched, but we were able to tell the exciting story to the stay-at-homes.

"But look out there!" my father exclaimed.

Out of our front window I could see a red glare.

"That's a fire!" he said.

From this point I have to depend on later accounts, newspaper stories, government publications, and souvenir booklets. Much of this material I used for an *Empire Magazine* story which appeared in *The Denver Post* in 1956.

Most of Pueblo is, and was, on high ground and out of reach of the flood. But also many parts of the city were lower than the tops of the levees, and were quickly submerged. The rampaging waters swirled out on new courses, pouring around corners and down streets. Finally

---

On opposite page, aerial view shows still-swollen Arkansas River flowing through Pueblo's downtown channel, from lower right to upper center (looking generally east, downstream). Two-story building with cupola (at right) is City Hall. *(All photos with this article are from the collection of J.H. Young, courtesy of Jackson C. Thode, Posse Member; and the Denver & Rio Grande Railroad.)*

the swift current changed, to parallel the normal direction of the river, west to east.

At first, small objects in the city were caught up; then larger and larger pieces. Packing cases, fences, and lesser buildings were torn away, followed by masses of wreckage jammed together in rafts. Now larger frame buildings were ripped off their foundations and floated down the streets. Brick and stone structures crashed under the water pressure, adding to the terror.

Over all, the only illumination came sporadically from great jagged flashes of lightning. This permitted glimpses of appalling destruction. The screams of the frightened and the trapped and the dying sounded through the roar of the water and the crash of thunder and rain.

Suddenly the sky was an angry red. Those who saw knew fire had broken out but none could leave shelter to see where.

The water touching supplies of lime may have begun the conflagration in a lumberyard. Piles of blazing timbers raced along the street tide, starting other fires. The rain glistened and bubbled like blood in the glare.

Desperate people took refuge on roofs of buildings, only to lose their lives when the structures collapsed. Others who had delayed their departure from the downtown area too long were caught by the flood and dashed to death. The smashing of plate-glass fronts in business houses added a soprano note to the gross sound of destruction.

On Union Avenue, buildings disintegrated in rows. The wreckage was caught up and battered other buildings in turn. The weight of the wheeling, floating objects carried by the enormous thrust of the river became rams which crushed whatever obstructed their path.

In the railroad yards steel cars, laden and empty alike, were tossed aside. Wooden freight cars were ripped from their trucks, and floated along the streets like barges. Tracks and ties were torn up, and in one place were piled eight high like giant jackstraws.

Out beyond the Union Depot where the two passenger trains were stalled, courageous railroaders went through the cars trying to calm the passengers. Other crews marshalled every man they could, attempting plan after plan to save the trains and the people aboard. In the end the mad river won.

The lights in the cars went out as the tumbling water hit the battery boxes. The cars began to turn over, one at a time. The panic-stricken occupants ran forward through the trains as the cars rolled behind them. The flood gushed through the windows.

Frank Ducray, then sheriff of Mesa County, was on one of the trains. He'd seen a 17-year-old girl swept away almost within reach of his arms when heavy planks, hurtled along by the flood, crashed between them. He saw two women clinging to a house as it went by. One was singing a hymn.

"I saw a man and his daughter, and he was kneeling with her while she recited the 'Now I lay me down' of her childhood. I saw them swept away in one another's arms," Ducray said.

Eleanor Demfer of St. Louis was on a vacation trip. When the flood struck, she moved from her sleeper to a rear car which seemed safer. Suddenly it began to tilt. She seized a curtain rod as the car went over. A woman screamed for someone to save her child. She was standing on a seat, holding an upper-berth rod with one hand and a tiny baby in the other, clear of the water. She cried out that her strength was failing.

Miss Demfer worked her way to the woman and took the baby. She held it up out of the swirling blackness with the strength of youth. Rescuers finally came and took them out a broken window to a nearby building.

Ed Harrison, another passenger, jumped from his coach and swam to a floating log. He clung to it and eventually was cast up on an island far down the river. F. D. Spicer's house was torn from its foundations and floated downstream until it lodged on the same island in the middle of the Arkansas. Harrison and Spicer spent two nights and most of two days marooned there.

Most of the passengers and crewmen escaped to a coal car nearby. It began to flounder under them and they made their way to a second coal car. This one stood fast all through the night. They saw a railway employee start to crawl out of a smashed window, but he was too large to get through. He fell back and was drowned.

Meanwhile, Joseph E. Sprengle, manager of the Andrew McClelland Co., and Orrin Maddox, an employee, reported like soldiers at the company's grain warehouse to see what they could save. They were trapped inside by the flood and forced to climb to the rafters. Here they perched in complete darkness while the waters rose higher and higher. The torrent came within a foot of engulfing them.

A.J. Jackson and his wife took refuge in a tree, where he was forced to support her in his arms. He shouted for help again and again. At last his strength failed and his wife slipped from his grasp and was drowned.

At the telephone company, Mrs. Joseph E. Prior, day chief operator, and Margaret Williams, night chief operator, were marooned with
39 other girls. As long as the power held they phoned warnings to
citizens as rapidly as they could. Then the lights on all the boards
went out. The girls watched the flowing water and wreckage from the
upstairs windows. Someone started a phonograph in an effort to keep
up their spirits. They could see the dark waves rise higher and higher,
with floating objects tumbling and plunging. Houses, barns, and sheds
came along, and, worst of all, struggling forms of men, women, and
children.

Byron Thedy, the telephone company's night wire chief, went into
a first-floor room where the cable records, most important documents,
were kept. A rush of waters slammed the door behind him, and he
was trapped. The water climbed to his armpits, then reached his neck.
The weight and force of the torrent resisted his frantic efforts to open
the door. He found a length of strong board, pushed the door with all
his might until it opened a crack, and forced the board into it. Bit by
bit he wedged it farther open. At length he was able to squeeze
through with the precious records.

A big frame house slammed against the telephone company garage,
wrecking it, then came on toward the brick building. Some of the girls
knelt and prayed. Others covered their faces with their hands. A
sudden counter current toppled the marauding house and carried it
safely past. They heard a man crying for help. Across the alley, on
top of the one-story garage close by they saw him. He had in some
way cut a hole through the roof and crawled up out of the water. The
head of another man appeared through the hole, then the second head
dropped back and was seen no more. Thedy shoved a plank to the
man on the roof and he was dragged into the higher telephone building.

Through it all, the phonograph continued to play—"Ja-da; Ja-da;
Jada, Jada, jing-jing-jing."

V.Z. Haven, credit manager for Crews-Beggs Dry Goods Co., went
to his store about the time the lights went out. He and his aides started carrying things up out of the basement. The windows suddenly
broke and the fire alarms began to ring. The water poured into the
vestibule. They tried to block the flow with whatever was handy, but
the water came in so fast they gave up. By the time Haven barred the
door, the water inside was 3 to 4 feet deep.

Something struck the plate glass and in rushed the torrent. Haven and the others ran upstairs to the mezzanine floor and the water was right behind them. From there, like isolated men and women all over town, they watched. The velocity was so great that it picked up houses, safes, steel light poles, and everything that stood in front of it. They saw a fire raft floating down the street. The heavy rain was the only thing that kept the town from being burned up.

George Holmes of Holmes Hardware Co. said, looking around him, "When I built this building I figured it could withstand 16 inches more water than in the flood of 1894. When this storm broke, I thought that by putting flour sacks at the back door I could hold off 5 feet. By the time I got the sacks here, the water was rolling in the door."

About 75 persons spent the night in the Union Depot. About 20 were passengers, waiting for trains. Alex Cress, manager of the Union Depot hotel, shook his head, and told a guest, "The water came up so quick that when we put sacks of potatoes against the door, the water washed them away as fast as we set them there."

Also at the depot, B. Milton Stearns, assistant chief dispatcher, got a level rod and kept a log of the rise and fall of the flood throughout the night—probably the only such record in existence. The water rose 3½ feet between 11:30 and 11:45 p.m. It reached a high of 9.75 feet above the floor at 11:55 p.m. Because the floor of the depot was known to be at the river gauge height of 17.61 feet, it was possible to determine from his records the true high reached by the swollen river, 27.36 feet.

W.E. Kirk, later a Denver druggist, then was managing a brand new pharmacy at Fourth and Main streets. That night he had closed the doors and was arranging patent medicines on the balcony which went entirely around the upper part of the store. He looked down to see the water flowing around in the main floor and knew his escape was cut off. Kirk lost no time thinking about it. He went to an upper window and climbed out on an electric sign. He hung there until some men in a rowboat rescued him.

Hubert Abell, who was about to graduate from school, lay on the floor at his home listening to the sirens. Presently George Morrissey Jr. came by.

"Let's go look at the flood," Morrissey said. They went to the Morrissey Carriage Co. at C and S. Main streets to find George's father moving office furniture and machines up to the second floor where the Morrisseys had an apartment. The two youths lent the older man a hand with the heavier equipment, including an electric motor which they unbolted and placed on a manually operated elevator. This they hoisted, along with other valuable gear, to the second floor level. Time passed and Abell decided he'd better be getting home. But when he descended to the main-floor doors he discovered the water was already 3 feet deep and rising fast. He went back upstairs.

After the lights went out, the three stood at the apartment windows on the second floor and watched. They saw a friend across the way on a narrow parapet high above the street, working an escape from one building to another. They saw a house come hurtling down the street. It struck a flashing traffic light which, for some mysterious reason had continued to operate, and knocked it over. Then it rushed at the Morrissey building, hit it with a crash and knocked a two-story hole in it. The house whirled on and smashed into a bridge.

Then they saw a boat coming, a rowboat. In it were a man, woman, and a baby. As the boat passed close to the building across the street, the woman reached out, apparently in an effort to halt their headlong pace, and upset the boat. All three went into the angry waters.

The man somehow managed to seize the babe and throw that same arm around the woman. Using his free hand he swam toward the Morrissey building.

A dump rake the Morrisseys had outside on the curb had upended in the flood and the horse shafts protruded just a foot above the water. The man, supporting his double burden made for the shafts, miraculously caught one, and was able to stop and hold himself, the woman and baby.

Abell snatched a butcher knife and ran back inside to the elevator. He sliced off a piece of support rope—and the entire load slammed down into the water. Uncaring, he ran to the window and tossed one

---

Opposite page, upper-left picture is of Pueblo Union Depot yard. Passenger coach, off its trucks, rests amid debris. Bottom left, passenger cars lie twisted and smashed in river bottom after futile effort to move them to higher ground. Top-right, freight cars rest amid flood debris in the Walker Yard. Lower right, railroad bridges dropped from their pilings into riverbed, or were crammed with wreckage. Santa Fe bridge (on left) remained in place, but D&RG structure at right of switch engine was shifted. Wooden ties floated steel rails off roadbed, twisting and buckling trackage.

end of the rope to the man who managed to loop it around the woman so the boys could pull her up and into the second-story window. The rescuers freed her, then threw the rope back and the man fastened it to the baby. Again Abell and George began to pull, but the baby became lodged under a folded awning against the side of the building, under the water.

Young Morrissey, a large man, braced himself in the window and let Abell down by the ankles into the flood. Abell, his head completely submerged, managed to reach the baby, release it from the awning, and bring it back in his arms to the window. Then they rescued the man.

Abell knew nothing of first aid, but he could see the baby was choking. Its face was almost black. He took a pocket knife and pried the babe's teeth apart, then took a table knife and turned it in the opening to force the tiny mouth farther open. He reached in with his fingers and pulled the child's tongue forward. The little one lived.

When day dawned on June 4, 1921, a scene of the greatest desolation was disclosed to Pueblo's survivors. From the bluffs on the south to Sixth Street on the north was a sea of water, mud, wreckage, waste. For miles along the south bluff the railroad yards were littered with damaged cars at every sort of angle. Near the Union Depot, masses of junk were piled up as high as the floors of the Union Avenue and Main Street viaducts. Mud was several feet deep in downtown streets. There were gaps where buildings had been only the day before. The litter of shops and small businesses had been tossed into the street. Dead animals were everywhere in the flood area and, all too often, human bodies were to be seen in the muck.

As for me, I went to my favorite perch on the hill above the railroad yards and saw a scene that stays with me today. The railroad yard was a river. Cars and heavy engines were tossed about like building blocks. As far as I could see in both directions were wreckage and ruin.

And to add to the terror, it had begun to rain again, and the river water flowing through the yards seemed to be rising, and, indeed, it did rise.

There was another, smaller, flood the next day, Saturday, and a third on Sunday.

Today there would have been radio, television, helicopters, and fast planes to bring quick relief for the flood victims. In 1921 there was little drinkable water, no power, no gas, no telephone or electric lights.

Across the street from the Union Depot stood the Arcade Hotel and drug-store. A refrigerator boxcar proved to be an uninvited "guest" when it floated through the corner door of the building.

Railroads and highways in every direction were washed out. Isolation was complete.

No one outside had any idea what had happened in Pueblo, and no one inside could have told whether the rest of the country still existed. It was as though the world had come to an end, and every soul still living was in limbo, waiting.

To this day no one has been able to say how many died in the flood. Ralph C. Taylor, until his retirement as news director of the *Pueblo Chieftain* and *Star-Journal,* put the toll of known dead at 96, with the probability that the real loss of life was far above that. Whole families were wiped out with no survivors left to register the fatality figures. Other observers have estimated the death toll at from 156 to more than 200.

Thousands were homeless. A report from the Pueblo City Council said 510 dwellings were destroyed, 98 buildings wrecked, and 61 build-ings washed from their foundations. Property damage was estimated at $19,080,000 in 1921 dollars. The railroads suffered heavily. Of their six bridges over the Arkansas and three over the Fountain, only one stood intact on June 4. The Missouri Pacific yard and the engine terminal were cut off by a new channel and left on an island without rail connection. Some 2,000 cars in the various yards and many en-gines suffered enormous damage.

How deep did the water get? It was 14.4 ft. at First Street and Santa Fe Avenue, 13.2 ft. in the Central Block nearby, 11.9 ft. in the Electric Building, also nearby, and 5.5 ft. deep in the Post Office. My father had an office not far from the Union Depot. It was 9 feet 8½ inches deep there.

As soon as the water was low enough to permit wading, Abell and young Morrissey took their rescued baby toward the bluffs to seek medical help. On the way they saw another man struggling through the water to reach the same point. Suddenly he disappeared as though a giant hand had snatched him down. The two went on, gained the Main Street viaduct and turned the baby over to police, who sped it to a hospital. Abell, a prominent Puebloan and head of the Abell Truck & Implement Co., there today, says he never again heard from or of man, woman, or babe. He doesn't know their names or what became of them.

But he does know the fate of the man who disappeared into the water the morning after the flood. When he returned later that way he saw what had happened. There was a manhole there, uncovered. The man had been sucked down into the raging underground waters of the storm sewer.

But it is indeed an ill flood which washes in no good. That summer I got a job at a warehouse, washing the mud off tin cans of food which later were sold at bargain prices. I made enough to buy a flood-salvaged Hart, Schaffner & Marx suit, which was washed, cleaned, and pressed, and offered at a bargain price by the Taub Brothers Clothing Store. I paid $10 for it. And it had a jacket and long pants.

About the Author

Bernard "Bernie" Kelly was born on Sept. 1, 1905, in Pueblo, Colo., and as a boy of 15, went through the Arkansas River flood of June 1921. He gave his talk on the Pueblo flood at the Posse's Summer Rendezvous in 1981, and joined the Denver Westerners on the same day. A true native and lifelong resident of Colorado, Bernie says he has seen a lot of the state's history, but nothing as dramatic as the 1921 flood.

Bernie had early ambitions of being a fiction writer, and playing in a dance orchestra (banjo and string bass). He joined Charles Quaranta's orchestra, playing with the group in engagements throughout southern Colorado. He was graduated from Pueblo Junior College—now the University of Southern Colorado—and wrote their school song. (The song is still used by the school.)

Bernie Kelly sold his first story to *Esquire* magazine in 1937—he has never hit that magazine since—and wrote a great deal of fiction for such publications as *True Story* and other "Romance" magazines.

In 1940, Bernie turned to journalism, and became a cub reporter for the *Pueblo Chieftain*. Then World War II came along, and he joined the Army, seeing stateside service in public relations work. After the war, he returned home, rejoining the *Chieftain* staff.

In April 1947, he was hired as a *Denver Post* staff writer. He became an assistant editor and writer for *Empire, The Post's* Sunday magazine, serving in that position for 19 of his 28 years at the newspaper. He enjoyed several foreign assignments at *The Post*, traveling to remote spots in Africa, and elsewhere. It was while he was on *Empire* that Bernie wrote the story of the Pueblo flood of 1921—the same story appearing in this *Brand Book*.

Bernie Kelly retired from *The Post* in 1975, but not from writing. He has continued to write fiction and plays. He also collaborated with Morey Engle, writing the text for *Denver's Man With a Camera, Harry Rhoades*.

Bernie Kelly has been married for 14 years to Margaret Halloran.

"Rocky road hang-up" by *Max Smith*

Early Colorado Auto Trails

By Jack Morison

I MAGINE IT IS 1925. You are behind the steering wheel of a new Buick touring car, somewhere west of Kansas, in eastern Colorado. The sun is low in the western sky.

It has been some time since you passed a farm house, scattering chickens in all directions. Earlier in the day, you spent two hours in a mudhole and $5 to hire a farmer to pull you out with a team of horses.

You snagged your duster on a strand of barbed wire, trying to close a farm gate. A plume of dust you are raising not only follows you, but settles on everything and everyone in the car. You have ruined both spare-tire casings. The kids are unhappy. Your companions have frequently reminded you that you could have come by train.

You have traveled 80 miles since early morning, landmarks are not lining up with the guidebook, and you are approaching a fork in the road. You have that sinking feeling that you are lost. And then on the section that bears to the right, tacked to a fence post, is a sign with red-over-green bands. That's your trail marker, and you are still on the right road! With luck, you will find a tourist camp before dark, and you won't have to pitch the car tent.

Pioneer motorists had to follow marked trails across the country. There were 35 such interstate routes entering and/or leaving Colorado.

It's uncertain when the first wheeled conveyance entered what is now Colorado, but there is evidence such vehicles were coming into the area on the Santa Fe Trail at least by 1828. The Overland Stage route dipped into the state in 1849, and then by 1859 all kinds of two- and four-wheeled equipment had arrived, from fancy stagecoaches to a so-called wind wagon, which may or may not have made it to Colorado territory—or it may have piled up in an arroyo somewhere in eastern Kansas. The Kansas City (Mo.) *Times* reported a wind wagon was a "combination flying machine and go-cart." They were designed to replace bull trains on the prairies and had wheels, a deck and sails. Several wind wagons were reported to have crossed Kansas.

On June 7, 1859, the first stage arrived in Denver from the east, making the journey in 71 days. Eight years later, on June 19, 1867, the first train entered Colorado Territory, reaching the first town, Julesburg, on June 25, six days later. Before you could say Union Pacific, the rail line departed up Lodgepole Creek, going back into Nebraska. On June 20, 1870, the Denver Pacific reached into Denver from Cheyenne and for the next half-century the railroads ruled supreme.

During 1899, a couple of "rich man's toys," both electrics, were uncrated in Denver, and the auto age was on its way. A Doctor Bartholmew was the owner of one electric that was driven just 25 miles during its lifetime.

D.W. Bruntor was the owner of the other auto, a Waverly Electric. During the next three years, electric, steam, and gasoline vehicles of all makes and sizes appeared on the scene.

In the fall of 1902, 42 Denver automobile owners got together and formed the Colorado Auto Club. The purpose of the club was to promote better roads. A similar club was organized in Colorado Springs.

During that same year, the Taylor State Road was being planned from Denver to Grand Junction. The state engineer, Mr. McClure, predicted it would be the greatest thoroughfare through the Rocky Mountains. The proposed route ran from Denver to Ft. Logan, up the South Platte River Canyon, and over to Bailey, then down through Eagle River and Glenwood canyons to Grand Junction. The procedure for getting from Bailey to the Eagle River was a little vague.

As early as 1903, Dr. H. Nelson Jackson, a Vermont physician, and his chauffeur made the first transcontinental automobile crossing. The trip cost the doctor $8,000. The journey took nine weeks, and Dr. Jackson lost 20 pounds.

The railroads—seeing the auto as no threat—soon began to promote auto-train travel. A motorist could put his vehicle on a flatcar, and travel by rail to some area of interest where the horseless carriage could be unloaded and used for local touring for a few days. Then the auto would be reloaded onto another train and taken to greener pastures.

In early times, roads that autos could travel without a multitude of problems were mostly within city limits. As town-to-town traffic increased, county governments got involved. For several years, the counties had charge of all highways and since some counties did not have the financial resources of others, roads were of unequal quality.

The Colorado Highway Department was formed in 1910, with a

goal of establishing more standardized auto trails. The new department had a budget of $40,352 and spent $40,322.54, leaving a balance of $29.46 (This may have been the last time a state agency stayed within its budget.)

By now, more and more people wanted to test their mechanical wonders in state-to-state travel. The involvement of the federal government and some sort of interstate road system were not far off.

Rufus J. Morison (the author's grandfather) of Traer, Iowa, had made annual train excursions to Colorado since the mid-1890s. About 1910, he decided the family would drive. They left Traer one summer morning and headed west. The roads across Iowa and eastern Nebraska were in good shape, and the family made good time. When they reached western Nebraska, they traveled mile after mile on farm roads along section lines. It was the job of 15-year old John Morison to sit in the front seat, alighting to open and close gates. John in later years told how they would go a mile, and he would open a gate so the car could go through. Then he would close the gate, hop aboard, and they would go another one mile, only to repeat the procedure, mile after mile, hour after hour.

Gasoline was purchased in hardware stores. On the 11th day of that 800-mile trip, the Morisons could see the lights of Boulder, Colorado. Rather than camp one more night, they drove on, reaching that city about 11 p.m.

By 1911, there was such a clamor for better roads that good-road associations were formed throughout the country, The first survey of a Denver-Omaha road was completed that year. J.A. Davis of Sutton, Neb., ramrodded this project, and $6,000 was raised by people along the route to publish a trail guide and to promote the road.

During 1911, an estimated 6,000 autos from other states visited Colorado. By this time there were 18,000 autos registered in the state, and $36,767 was spent on road improvements. The main routes or trails into Colorado by this time were: (1.) Julesburg-Sterling-Fort Morgan-Denver; (2.) Wray-Fort Morgan-Denver; and (3.) Lamar-Rocky Ford-Pueblo.

The year 1914 was a milestone for automobilists in Colorado, with concrete paving of the first stretch of roadway. The November 1924 *Colorado Highways* magazine noted, "Back in 1914 there was a stretch of mud on the Morrison Road west of Sheridan Boulevard that was the bugaboo of motorists traveling to and from the Denver Mountain Parks. We have gone to the limit in trying to keep that piece of road

This group (probably an auto club) in Rocky Mountain National Park is dressed for bad weather, and rear wheels of last car are chained and ready. The road is the National Park to Park Highway.

out there by the Holstein Dairy in shape for traffic. We have reached the conclusion that the only thing to do is pave a mile of the road, starting at Sheridan Boulevard."

A marked increase in traffic over the Morrison Road was noticed. Motorists went out of their way to drive to Morrison in order to try out the pavement.

By 1915, automobile trail associations were being formed all over the nation. By 1924 there were 461 such trails nationwide, five of them initiated at Alliance, Neb. One such trail formed in Denver was the National Park to Park Highway. This route went from Denver to Rocky Mountain National Park, then on to Yellowstone, Glacier, Mt. Rainier, Mt. Hood (then proposed), Crater Lake, Yosemite, Sequoia, then back to Denver following the Midland Trail over Berthoud Pass. This trail was later shifted south to include Mesa Verde, the Grand Canyon, and other points of interest.

The first federal highway aid came in 1916 when a whopping $38,000 was allotted. By 1920, federal aid had jumped to $810,051 and the tourists were driving to Colorado.

Denver's Overland Park Auto Camp registered 7,906 vehicles that summer. Overland Park provided 160 acres of camp space with free bath and laundry facilities, reading, writing, and restrooms, a community clubhouse, grocery store, restaurant, and filling station.

In August 1921, the Colorado to Gulf Highway opened, following a route south from Denver through Colorado Springs, Pueblo, Trinidad, and eventually Brownsville, Texas. In September, the Monarch Pass road was completed.

By this time, many routes going everywhere were designated as auto trails. Each trail had a guidebook and road markers so traveler could find the way. A trail association sponsored a guidebook and markers, and saw to it that roads were maintained by interested merchants and individuals who resided along the route. In some cases there was mismanagement of money, and a few scams, but for the most part, trail associations made an honest effort to serve the traveling public.

(Author's Collection)

City of Denver maintained free Overland Park Campground for tourists.

Colorado trails deserve special comment. The 35 routes were all "interstates," each had a name, and each had its own sign or marker. Ten of the trails passed through Pueblo and 16 were routed through Denver. Several were isolated, while others overlapped as they traversed the state.

A blue band above a white band over another blue one designated the North Star Highway, shortest trail in the state. This trail started at Sidney, Neb., and terminated at Sterling, 40 miles to the south.

The Buffalo Highway marker was a brown buffalo on a white background above a brown band bearing the word, "HIGHWAY" in white letters. This trail followed a north-south route that paralleled modern-day Interstate 25.

The Glacier to Gulf did take a side trip to Estes Park by way of the Big Thompson Canyon and the South St. Vrain Creek.

The Colorado to Gulf followed the Buffalo Highway from Colorado Springs south, while the Denver, Deadwood, and the Powder River Trail came as far south on this route as Denver.

The Denver Black Hills Highway came down from Pine Bluff, Wyo., passing in Colorado through Hereford, Briggsdale, Purcell, Greeley, and then the route of present U.S. 85 through Brighton into Denver.

One trail entered the state twice. The Rocky Mountain Highway, marked with a green-bordered white triangle enclosing the green letters "R.M.," entered Colorado from Encampment, Wyo., near Walden. After nine miles of North Park beauty, the route took a sharp turn to the left and traveled nine miles back to the Wyoming border, heading toward Laramie. From that railroad paradise, the road again turned south and followed a path that paralleled somewhat the old Overland Trail through Virginia Dale, reentered Colorado, going on to Fort Collins and Denver.

The Plains Mountain Highway had to be one of the loneliest of the trails. It went from nowhere to nowhere, and not through too much. It entered Colorado from Kansas and traveled west past Two Buttes to Springfield. The route passed through the southern Colorado settlements of Joycoy, Utleyville, Andrix, Kim, Tobe, Trinchera, Laub, Abeyta, Bereja, Garcia, and Beshoar—total population of the bunch about 400 – then entered Trinidad. From Trinidad, the Plains Mountain linked the coal-mining communities to the west until reaching its terminus at Stonewall. There was hope at that time that a road would be constructed over Whiskey and Elwood passes so the highway could continue west along the southern border of the state. Stonewall was as far as it got.

The author's mother, Freda F. Morison, came to Colorado in 1919. As they came west, she remembers following the route that had all-yellow signs. These were much easier to manufacture than, for example, something with a brown buffalo. This route was the Golden Belt Highway entering the state at Burlington and continuing into Denver. Today this is basically the route of present-day Interstate 70. Several other trails coincided with the Golden Belt in Colorado.

The Blue Line (blue-orange-blue bands), Midland Trail, National White Way, Pikes Peak Ocean to Ocean, Golden Rod, and the Victory Highway all entered the state at this point. The little town of Burlington once had seven interstates! Now there is only one. Of course, I-70 now carries more traffic in one hour than those seven early roads did in a month.

By this time, auto jokes were becoming popular. Such as the only time pedestrians have the right-of-way is when an ambulance is taking them to the hospital. Or the one that related to the 35-mile-an hour state speed limit. In a Western city there was a sign reading, "4,076 died from the effects of gas. 39 inhaled it, 37 put a match to it, and 4,000 stepped on it."

The New Santa Fe Auto Trail followed the basic route of the mountain branch of the old wagon road. For the most part, so did the National Old Trails Road and the Albert Pike Highway. The Colorado route connected Holly-La Junta-Trinidad, with a few side trips here and there, and the Albert Pike going on into Pueblo.

One of the more interesting old trails was the G.P.C.—the Gulf Plains Canada. Much of the old trail can still be followed today, and the gravel portion from Vernon south of Wray to Idalia is just as it was seven decades ago. The road ran down the sidelines of eastern Colorado as far as Holly before stepping out of bounds into Kansas. At Hartman, Colo., 81-year-old C.E. Dennis remembered that, when he was a boy, the G.P.C. and the New Santa Fe Trail both passed through town. He can point out the house where gasoline was once sold. Locals still refer to the zigzag segment of gravel from Hartman on into Holly at the G.P.C.

Perhaps one of the grandest and most popular of the auto trails was the Lincoln Highway. This famous trail, later becoming U.S. 30 and now I-80, traversed Nebraska and southern Wyoming, reaching from coast to coast. The highway had a Colorado branch, from Big

Springs, Neb., to Fort Morgan and Denver, before going into Wyoming. One of the Lincoln Highway red-white-blue markers, with the blue "L" in the white, has been preserved and is on display at North Platte, Neb.

In 1925, the first transcontinental bus service was inaugurated. The route from New York City to Los Angeles followed the Lincoln Highway. The buses were painted red, white, and blue in the same pattern as the markers. For a fare of $410, a passenger could travel across the continent in only 30 days.

The Rainbow Trail also used the red-white-blue combination, starting in Colorado and heading on west. This trail went along the Arkansas River to Salida, then over the old Monarch Pass road to Gunnison. The route followed the Gunnison River to Sapinero where it climbed over Blue Mesa and Cerro Summit on its way to Montrose and Grand Junction, continuing into Utah. Today U.S. 50 follows the old Rainbow Trail and there are several places along the present high-

(Author's Collection)

Pikes Peak Ocean-to-Ocean Highway followed old Ute Pass west of Colorado Springs.

way where the old auto road is still visible. The marker showed a rainbow on a white background.

The Pikes Peak "O to O" (ocean to ocean) is one of the most interesting of the early trails. This New York-to-Los Angeles trail was headquartered in St. Joseph, Mo. As mentioned earlier, the Pikes Peak "O to O" entered Colorado and followed other trails as far as Limon, then angled off through Simla and other communities to Colorado Springs. From there the road continued to the western border of the state by two routes: the first, Cañon City-Salida-Gunnison-Montrose-Grand Junction; the other, Ute Pass-Leadville-Tennessee Pass-Glenwood Springs-Rifle-Meeker-Rangely. The Pikes Peak "O to O" had a colorful marker of a red band over white with the letters "PP" on the white. It was reported in the May 1, 1921, *Automobile Roads from Colorado Springs* that those red-and-white bands were painted on poles at turns and crossroads, and also frequently between turns—usually every fifth pole, and occasionally on telephone poles. The road ascended and descended the Continental Divide, over Tennessee Pass, on a 4 percent grade utilizing an abandoned railroad grade which had been widened and improved. This section would have been preceded by the Denver & Rio Grande rail line which went over the pass before the present tunnel was built.

West of Tennessee Pass the Pikes Peak "O to O" at times was reported practically impassable because of heavy gypsum dust covering the road. In places the dust was a foot deep and the road very rough.

In addition to Burlington as a Colorado entry for auto trails from the east, a motorist could also approach the Rockies through Julesburg on the Lincoln Highway; Holyoke on the White Way-7-Highway, and the Detroit-Lincoln-Denver; through Wray on the Burlington Highway; from St. Francis, Kans., to Beecher Island, and then on to Wray on the Northwestern Highway. Three trails through Towner, Colo., were the Kansas-Colorado Boulevard; the Hutchinson (Kans.)-Denver-Joplin (Mo.); and the Bee Line.

The Union Pacific Highway entered Colorado at Cheyenne Wells. The National Trails, the Albert Pike, and the New Santa Fe Trail entered at Holly.

Far to the south, just 10 miles north of the Oklahoma border and entering from Kansas, was the Dallas-Canadian-Denver. It entered Colorado and zigzagged its way to Lamar. From Lamar it followed the route of present U.S. 287 into Denver. Today, between the Kansas line and Lamar, the highway is still there in most places, with identifi-

This mudhole scene was common. The car license is from Oregon (1921) but getting stuck could happen anywhere.

able wide, sweeping curves at the corners.

The route passed through the now-ghost town of Wentworth, and on to Stonington. The town of Walsh did not exist until 1927, so the D.C.D. continued north through what was Blaine, no longer extant. En route, the D.C.D. crossed Bear Creek on an impressive arched bridge, still standing. The road then passed the base of Twin Buttes before reaching the Springfield-Lamar road at Verdun, now also a ghost town.

The Springfield-Lamar road mentioned above was the T.O.C., Texas-Oklahoma-Colorado, starting at Dalhart, Texas, crossing the panhandle of Oklahoma, and terminating at Lamar.

Motorists on these trails obtained much information from guidebooks, such as landmarks, cottage camps, gasoline suppliers, miles traveled, and various helpful hints. Things worth knowing included:
— To keep your windshield clear of mist on rainy days, rub a sliced onion over the glass with an up-and-down motion.

— While you may not believe in signs, it is safe to assume that "Caution" and "Danger" warnings are not erected for the mere amusement of those who took the trouble to put them up.

— Roads were made to travel on, not to burn up.

— The most obnoxious animal in the world is the road hog. He is as objectionable as any other hog, and you can't eat him.

— Pure vinegar will clean celluloid windows in curtains of your car.

And quoting directly from the *1926 Rand McNally Road Atlas*, "Women drivers of motor vehicles should be given special consideration . . . and watching."

Speaking of women and driving, in 1925 Mrs. Myrtle Roe, a teacher from Sterling, Colo., submitted the best lesson plan for teaching street and highway safety. The U.S. Chamber of Commerce sponsored the contest and 75,000 teachers from every one of the 48 states submitted plans. Mrs. Roe received a check for $500 and a trip to Washington, D.C. (This same lady achieved a much lesser claim to fame by being the author's principal during his first three years of school, a wonderful person.)

The Spanish Trail, the D.L.D. (the Detroit-Lincoln-Denver), the Midland Trail, and the Victory Highway all deserve much attention. Following are just some of the highlights on these trails.

The Spanish Trail started at Walsenburg and went west to Utah. It traveled over La Veta Pass to Alamosa, and then more or less followed the route of present U.S. 160 to Wolf Creek Pass, Pagosa Springs, Durango, and Cortez. From Cortez it went north to Dolores, then west again to Dove Creek and into Utah.

The D.L.D. was at first called the O.L.D.—the "O" being for Omaha. Except for a mile or two, this road can still be followed as originally routed from the Nebraska state line into Denver. Much of the roadway was and still is graveled. At the old Merino Crossing of the South Platte River, the D.L.D. marking can still be seen on the end of the bridge. The portion between Fort Morgan and Hudson, now Colorado 52, is still called by local farmers the D.L.D. Approaching Hudson from the east, a hill is topped and suddenly the whole Front Range of the Rockies lies revealed. The view is breathtaking today, as it must have been in the heyday of the auto trails. Present I-76 gives no such experience. The author has two parcels of land along this highway. One tract is a half mile west of Fleming, Colo., on a paved section (now U.S. 6). The second is one-half mile along a graveled portion that today is a farm road, but at one time was part of an

This tourist has pitched his tent close to car for shelter on the Colorado-to-Gulf Highway, south of Pueblo.

interstate highway. As one stands along this quiet stretch of road, it is not hard to imagine the multitude of tourists—dust and all—who once passed this way.

The Midland Trail started in Washington, D.C., and terminated at San Francisco Bay. At Colorado, this trail split into several branches, giving the tourist a wide choice of routes. The main highway was via Berthoud Pass. In descending the pass westbound, the trail guide recommended that the motorist "try brakes, shift to intermediate, and cut off ignition for run down hill."

From Kremmling west, this route skirted Gore Canyon to State Bridge, then south to Wolcott and on down the Eagle River. Quoting the 1916 guide, from Gypsum west to Glenwood Springs, "This canyon road is now being made into a 22-foot rock-surfaced boulevard, by men serving penal sentences, who work without armed guards upon their honor not to escape. Owing to heavy rock work and blasting, tourists may not pass the scene of work after 7:30 a.m. or before 4:30 p.m. Time the run accordingly, drive slowly, sounding horn until finished road is reached." The Midland Trail had for its road marker an orange-black-orange rectangle.

The Victory Highway (No. 35 if you have been counting) followed a route which today is U.S. 40: Burlington-Denver-Berthoud Pass-Rabbit Ears Pass-Craig, and on into Utah. In May 1922, in order for the Victory Highway Association to maintain this more than 400 miles of road from the Kansas border to Utah—crossing the Continental Divide three times—the Colorado Highway Department graciously donated the use of a heavy truck. The association was to provide a crew to keep the truck in operation.

The goal of the Victory Highway Association was quoted in 1925 by a leading newspaper: "When the Victory Highway is completed it will constitute the greatest monument in all history. From the pyramids to the Peace Palace at The Hague, there is nothing that compares with the gigantic enterprise of proclaiming our part in the World War by means of a paved roadway crossing the continent and linking the two oceans with a concrete chain 3,300 miles long."

Life-sized bronze eagles were to be placed on Colorado markers at each county line, with tablets listing the names of those who gave their lives in the Great War.

The legend read, "Starts in New York City-Baltimore, following mainly the Old National Road. Through Colorado via Berthoud Pass and Rabbit Ears Pass to Salt Lake City-Sacramento-San Francisco.

"We must prove our remembrance in the present and send on this message in bronze to all the coming years, 'The United States of America Does Not Forget.'"

The number of these markers actually placed in Colorado is not known. As early as 1922, the markers were becoming a problem. In some places they were too numerous while in other areas they were missing entirely. The markers were not uniform in size and were very costly.

An association had to choose whether to spend money for signs and guidebooks, or road improvements. Chester Paulus of Denver remembers, as a lad, a woman in Nebraska who lived beside the D.L.D. The traffic and the dust it created made her so angry that, each time markers were erected near her home, she promptly tore them down.

By 1926 when Colorado had a grand total of 191 miles of paved roads, a nationwide standard type of sign had been adopted. By August of that year, 1,500 new U.S. highway markers had been posted along the main interstate trails. The shield-shaped markers bore "Colorado" across the top, a large "U.S." in the center, with the number of the highway.

Markers for U.S. 40, 6, 160, 85, 50, and so on were much easier to follow, cheaper to produce and maintain, uniform in style and size, and more modern. But what sounds more interesting and exciting? "I crossed Colorado on I-70," or "I traversed the state on the Pikes Peak Ocean to Ocean Highway."

(Author's Collection)
Early-day postcard touts travel up Big Thompson Canyon.

Afterword

This article began with a 1925 Conoco road map belonging to my nephew, Darryl L. Morison of Fleming, Colo. Several years ago, my brother Kay D. and son Darryl restored a vintage Conoco delivery truck dating back to the 1930s. Then they began collecting early-day

Conoco memorabilia. Several months ago, a friend found the road map at a Kansas auction, and obtained it for their collection.

I was shown the map and, at first glance, it looked interesting. I soon realized this was a real treasure filled with historical information. The year 1925 marked the last use of the auto-trail system before the nation adopted the U.S. Highway designations still used today. As I studied the map, I counted 35 interstate auto trails or highways entering Colorado.

Several years ago, I purchased a copy of *The Midland Trail*, a 1916 booklet reprinted by the University of New Mexico Press. Also I remembered, years ago when I was about 12, looking through two or three trail guides that my Aunt Frances Morison had saved from several early trips to Colorado from Iowa. I was fascinated by the directions given in these guides. For example, ". . . turn right at the red barn . . . ford the creek with the left ruts . . . get a run for the next hill. . . ." and so on. I knew at once that this map could be the basis for hours of research on what looked to be an unknown topic, so I made some copies of the original, and was on my way.

From the start, my wife Erma and I discovered that material on this subject was very rare. Our first stop was at the Western History section of the Denver Public Library. This bulwark of Western knowledge had nothing on Colorado auto trails, as such, but we were later able to obtain some information from early issues of *Colorado Highways* magazine. Our next stop was the Colorado Historical Society, and again we came up empty-handed. We then went to the Colorado Department of Highways—and "Strike Three." All of the sources mentioned that they would love to have a copy of the map.

I have been a member of the Denver Posse of the Westerners since February 1956 and in that period of membership, the topic of Colorado auto trails has never been covered. I now was really excited, because we had a brand new, unexplored—and as far as we could tell—area of Colorado history to unearth.

My wife and I have now interviewed many old-timers who remember the trails; we have driven hundreds of miles tracing the early roads; and searched through antique shops that might have early trail guides. (One dealer said he hadn't seen one for 30 years, and the rest had not heard of them.)

We visited local museums, libraries, and courthouses, and spent several hours looking through related information. This paper covers some of our findings on this interesting and exciting topic. During our years of having Western history as a hobby, we have concentrated on railroads, wagon roads, ghost towns, mining, and early Denver. Not for one moment did we have any interest in the auto highways of this state, other than that they keep improving so that we don't have to fight the increasing traffic. Now, because of a 69-year-old map, we are off on another tangent.

With many questions unanswered and miles of roads yet to travel, we present the results of our investigation of "Early Colorado Auto Trails, 1915-1925."

ACKNOWLEDGMENTS

I would like to acknowledge some people who have been of great assistance to me:
— First and foremost, my wife Erma who, in reality, is my co-author. She has helped in research, the interviews, tracing the trails, and has done all the typing.
— Kay Morison, for providing the 1925 map and a 1924 U.S. Atlas.
— Fellow Posse Member Ed Bathke, for opening up his auto-trail collection for my research, and for contributing some display items.
— Cindi Trombley and Ardie Schoeninger, for lending several items from the 1920s.
— Carl Carlson, for the use of a reprint of a 1927 U.S. Atlas.
— Bob Lewsader, for providing a useful map of Utah.
— Merle and Audrey Dorsett, who traveled many a mile with Erma and me in the search for old highways.
— Maggie Stephens of the Fort Morgan Public Library, who was of great help, and who provided several very useful maps.
— Virginia Bussell, librarian for the Baca County Public Library.
— Freda Morison and C.E. Dennis, Chester Paulus, and others for their contributions of personal experiences.
— And lastly, Warren Schmidt of Fleming, Colo., who discovered the Conoco map at a Kansas auction.

Sources and References

City and County of Denver, *Municipal Facts Bi-Monthly*. Denver: March-April 1922.
Colorado State Highway Department, official monthly publication. *Colorado Highways*, Denver: 1922-1930.
Denver Daily Doings. [A weekly visitor's guide.] Denver: July 24-31, 1922.
Denver Tourist and Publicity Bureau. *Come Up to Colorado.* Denver: 1923.
Denver Tourist Bureau. *Colorado Travelog.* Denver: 1923.
Motor Club of Colorado, Highway Publishing Co. *Official Tourist Information.* Denver: 1929.
Rand McNally. *Auto Road Atlas.* Reprint Chicago: 1926.
Rand McNally. *Auto Trails Map of Colorado.* Chicago: 1925.
Rand McNally. *Commercial Atlas of America, 55th Edition.* Chicago: 1924.
The Rio Grande Press, Inc. *Midland Trail Tour Guide 1916.* Reprint. Glorieta, N.M.: 1969,
Wiley, Marion C., State Department of Highways. *The High Road.* Denver: 1976.

About the Author

Jack L. Morison presented his paper, "Early Colorado Auto Trails," before the Denver Posse of the Westerners on Nov. 28, 1990. The work constitutes research and exploration of a facet of Colorado history not previously investigated on such a scale. And it is all "vintage" Jack Morison, in this careful attention given to a contemporary subject. Jack has also spoken to the Westerners on, "Steamboats on the Yukon."

Posse Member Jack Morison is a native Coloradan, and has had a lifelong fascination with the history of his native state. He retired as a math teacher, after 33½ years with the Denver Public Schools.

He served as Sheriff of the Denver Posse of the Westerners in 1993, having joined the organization as a Corresponding Member in January 1956. His wife Erma is a Corresponding Member.

Jack's other principal interests have been the railroads and ghost towns of Colorado. He is a charter member of the Ghost Town Club of Colorado. He is also a member of the Rocky Mountain Railroad Club, the Front Range Antique Power Association, and the Wally Byam Caravan Club.

Jack and Erma have two children, Charles and Linda, both Denver-area residents; and are proud grandparents of John and Jackie Kimmel.

"East Face of Longs Peak" by *Max Smith*

Tragedy on Longs Peak

By Carl A. Blaurock

O NE OF THE SADDEST events in my life was climbing to the upper stretches of Longs Peak to help bring down the body of a very dear friend. Miss Agnes Vaille, a strong sturdy woman, an active and experienced climber of the Colorado Mountain Club, had lost her life three days earlier in a winter climb of the East Face of Longs Peak. She and Walter Kiener, an experienced Swiss alpinist in this country only a year and a half, started for the East Face from Enos Mills' Timberline Cabin about 9 a.m. Sunday, Jan. 11, 1925.

The day was mild and pleasant when the pair started, but as they advanced well up toward the summit, a strong wind came up and the temperature dropped far below zero. They climbed all day and night, reaching the summit about 4 a.m. Monday. On the descent of the North Face, Agnes slipped, fell, and rolled more than 150 feet down a steep stretch. She landed in a snow bank near the eastern tip of the snowfield known in the summer time as "The Dove" from its resemblance to a flying bird.

Here, after traveling a short distance, she was completely exhausted. Her fingers were frozen, and she was unable to continue. Kiener helped her to a large rock, which gave some shelter from the strong wind. He then went on alone to meet a rescue party which he surmised would climb to the Timberline Cabin to search for the climbers, now missing for 24 hours. He also was severely frost-bitten and near exhaustion, but reached the cabin shortly after the rescuers had arrived.

Perhaps not long after Kiener left her, Agnes evidently started on but went only a short distance, then fell forward on her face, arms stretched forward. She probably quickly became unconscious, and perished. This is how rescuers found her.

I was a member of the search party and this is the story of the fourth and tragic attempt by Agnes Vaille and Walter Kiener to climb the East Face. Here is the background of their dramatic climb and the events preceding their successful—but fatal—effort.

One day in October 1924, Agnes and Walter started their first attempt to climb the East Face. They did not have an ice axe with them

View of East Face of Longs Peak shows frequently used route.

and soon realized the hard snow and ice would be difficult and dangerous to traverse without one. Therefore they gave up the attempt and
retreated.

A few weeks later near the middle of November, Agnes phoned and
asked to borrow my ice axe.

"Agnes," I said, "you're not going to try to climb again, surely?"
Agnes: "Yes, we are." Carl: "Don't do it, Agnes, you know how
quickly storms can come up in winter and temperatures drop precipi-
tously." Agnes: "I think we can do it." Carl: "You probably can but
I don't think it wise to try it in winter. If you wait until late spring or
early summer you will still have as much snow and ice to contend with,
but much less chance of bad storms."

My entreaty did not dissuade her and I then contacted Walter
Kiener. My efforts and arguments were no more effective with Kiener
than with Agnes. He insisted they would go ahead with their plans.
After this rebuff by Walter, I called Agnes again. I knew that she was
aware that I had climbed the East Face two years earlier and was
familiar with the route.

"Agnes," I said, "I know you and Walter are adamant about going, but would you object if I went along? I think the three of us have a better chance of success than just two." She replied, "I'd be delighted if you would come along."

So the die was cast. On Sunday morning Nov. 16 the three of us started our climb. The day was sunny and mild, with practically no wind. When we reached the long steep snowbank extending down from near the upper slopes of Mt. Meeker to the foot of the cliffs of Longs' East Face (usually called Mills Glacier) we decided to ascend this to where it intersects Broadway, rather than to chop ice all the way up Alexander's Chimney. Broadway is the name for the horizontal ledge about half way up and cutting across the East and North Face of Longs. It varies in width from a few inches to 4 or 5 feet and is a good ledge from which to attempt various routes on the upper slopes of that part of the peak.

We proceeded uneventfully along this ledge until we reached the long snowbank that reaches down to Broadway from the "Sharks Mouth," a gash visible from Estes Park. We found this snowbank was covered with several inches of powder snow lying on top of crusted packed snow underneath. This seemed to indicate a potential avalanche danger, so rather than cross it to reach the cliffs on the other side—which is the usual route—we decided to go directly up the cliffs on the east side of the Notch.

Picking the most likely looking chimneys, or couloirs, we ascended these cracks to upper ledges, working our way ever higher toward the summit ridge. Finally when about 50 feet from the top ridge, we were stymied by a smooth granite wall on which we could not find footholds or handholds by which to continue. As it then was 5 p.m. and beginning to get dark, we decided to give up and climb back off the peak. After descending one or two ledges we found ourselves on a ledge still quite a distance above Broadway. As it was now dark we could not discern our footprints on the Broadway snow, nor could we decide which chimney we had ascended hours before. We wanted to be sure to descend that same one because if we tried an unknown one in the dark we might get down part way and find it impossible to go farther, and perhaps have difficulty climbing back up. Besides, a slight wind had come up which blew snow up the chimneys and into our faces, obscuring the character of the chimney.

Knowing that a nearly full moon was due to rise and shine on our location about 9 p.m., we decided to wait it out on this ledge and eat what little food we had. We knew that by moonlight we could identify the couloir we had ascended. I have forgotten what we had to eat, probably a sandwich or two and maybe an orange. I do recall that the water in my small canteen was frozen, so we had no liquids.

After the moon rose we soon found our chimney and roped down it without incident. Once on Broadway, our difficulties were behind us. We had only to follow its snowy ledge to Mills Glacier, slide down that to the base and follow the trail back to Timberline Cabin for more food and a rest.

After a short stop at the cabin we proceeded down to our car and headed for Denver, arriving around daybreak just in time to clean up, change clothes, and go to work. In view of this abortive attempt, I told the others I would not make another try that winter, but if they waited until spring I'd be glad to go with them again.

(Photo by Author)

Scene along "Broadway" on Longs Peak climb.

In December they got the urge to try again and headed for the Peak. This time the weather turned bad before they reached Broadway. They gave up and returned to Denver.

On Saturday Jan. 10, 1925, Agnes and Walter left Denver, taking Elinor Eppich along, and arrived at Timberline Cabin about 3 a.m. This gave them only a few hours rest before daylight, with poor sleeping conditions. At 9 a.m., Walter and Agnes left the cabin for Chasm Lake and Elinor left shortly thereafter for Longs Peak Inn to await the climbers' return. Thus the fourth, successful but tragic trip began.

After 24 hours passed with no word from the climbers, Elinor became concerned and at 9 a.m. phoned Mrs. Enos Mills at Estes Park. Mrs. Mills contacted Herbert Sortland, inn caretaker. He and Jacob Christian, Hugh Brown, and his son Oscar—all of whom worked for the inn—left to make the rescue effort from Timberline Cabin.

At 1 p.m., Elinor phoned her father in Denver, who contacted several Mountain Club members. Edmund Rogers and Roger Toll drove to Estes Park, and shortly thereafter I joined William Ervin and George Barnard to drive to the Park in Barnard's car. At dark we reached Lyons and phoned Elinor at Longs Peak Inn. We learned that Kiener had returned to Timberline Cabin and had met the rescue party. He informed them that Agnes was alive but exhausted and that he had left her in a sheltered place on the Boulder Field. Immediately Hugh Brown, Christian, Sortland, and Kiener started up the trail for Agnes. Our Barnard party meanwhile returned to Denver, believing all was well on the mountain.

Edmund Rogers and Roger Toll, having reached Estes Park, started up the road for the inn. After bucking considerable snow, they abandoned the car and walked the final four miles, arriving at the inn about 11:50 p.m. This was just after Christian and Brown had come down from Timberline Cabin with news of Agnes' death.

At 12:45 a.m. Edmund and Roger started up the trail, carrying food for those at the cabin. They arrived there at about 4:30 a.m., and found Walter Kiener, Tom Allen, Jack Moomaw, and Walter Finn. Allen was assistant superintendent of Rocky Mountain National Park, and Moomaw and Finn were Park Service rangers. They had gone up Monday afternoon immediately after Elinor had phoned the alarm. High winds by now had come up, making travel above timberline very uncomfortable and difficult.

The first rescue party alerted by Mrs. Mills arrived at the cabin a short time before Kiener walked in. With Kiener as guide, they immediately started back up for Agnes in the face of severe winds and snow. Oscar Brown was to remain at Timberline Cabin to keep a fire going. In about half a mile at a point just above the last timber, Hugh Brown gave up and turned back to the cabin. He sent his son Oscar down to the inn to report Kiener's story. It was the son's report to Elinor that reached our group telephoning her from Lyons. This resulted in our return to Denver.

After proceeding about a mile, Sortland found he could not go on against the severe storm and turned back with the intention of going down to the inn. He never reached it. Somehow he stumbled into a ravine and died. The windblown snow covered his body, which was not found until late spring when the snow melted. This left only Christian and Kiener to continue.

They had a very difficult time proceeding in the wind and severe cold and finally reached Agnes about 4 or 4:30 p.m. She had gotten up and apparently tried to go on but in her exhausted state only went about 100 feet or so, fell forward face down, and perished. At this discovery, Kiener almost collapsed. After all he had been out continu-

(Photo by Author)

Agnes Vaille, dead at 35.

ously for more than 30 hours without rest or sleep, and was ready to drop from exhaustion. It was with great difficulty that the strong Christian was able to keep him going and get the two of them back to the cabin—really a superhuman effort.

They arrived at the cabin about 7:30 p.m. where they found Hugh Brown waiting. The National Park Service men arrived there about 10 p.m. Shortly thereafter Brown and Christian departed for the inn where they carried the story of Agnes' death, which was then transmitted over the press service wires.

Rogers and Toll reached the cabin about 4:30 a.m. and found Kiener and the Park Service rangers. They decided to wait until 9 a.m. and then, if the wind did not abate, they would go down as it would be impossible to reach the body. About 10 a.m. they left for the inn.

Tuesday morning we in Denver awoke and learned of the tragedy from a front-page story in the *Rocky Mountain News*. Later that morning, I joined Ervin and Barnard for a return trip to Estes Park. A second car carried James G. Rogers, Richard Hart, and, I believe, Henry Toll. Frank J. Haberl of the Stanley Hotel invited the entire group to stay there at no cost, an invitation we thankfully accepted.

On Tuesday afternoon and Wednesday a search party of 13 men went to Timberline Cabin and combed the area where Sortland had disappeared. They searched all possible shelter and some deserted cabins but found no trace.

Late Wednesday afternoon, the Denver contingent, plus park personnel and others, went to Longs Peak Inn. We hoped the storm would abate overnight and that we could go up for Agnes on Thursday. In the morning the wind had died down, and with skis and a toboggan, all except Hart started up the trail about 5 a.m. We reached Timberline Cabin about three hours later and found there was practically no wind even above timberline.

Progress up the trail was slow as each of us was heavily loaded with clothes, food, skis, and other rescue paraphernalia. After a short stop at the cabin we went on, pulling the toboggan and spreading out over a wide area searching for Sortland as we advanced. Bill Ervin and I were the first to reach Agnes' body at 13,300 ft. elevation about noon. In a short while, the rest of the party arrived. The toboggan was left at the edge of the Boulder Field for later use.

Skis were lashed together, with ski poles crosswise for supporting the body which was then lashed to the skis. With six persons at a time carrying the burden, we returned to the toboggan, where Agnes' body was lashed to it for transport to Longs Peak Inn. The party reached Timberline Cabin about 4:15 p.m. and the inn two hours later. There we found Edmund Rogers had arrived with Otis Weeks, brother-in-law of Agnes. Most of the party then returned to Estes Park for the night and Weeks accompanied the body to Denver.

Walter Kiener had been sent to a hospital in Denver on Tuesday. He eventually had to have one or more joints of each finger amputated, except for the right index finger which remained whole. In addition, all the toes on one foot, and at least two on the other foot were removed. For a long time after his recovery, he worked in the park on botanical research and spent many days on the Broadway ledge doing his work. He, too, passed on many years ago.

Carl Blaurock, at time of rescue attempt.

What a price to pay for a stubborn and, I think, foolish venture! Two lives lost and a survivor crippled. Tremendous endurance and courage were demonstrated throughout by many persons and Kiener's efforts, alone, were almost superhuman. Courage and stubbornness are one thing and can be admirable, but it is regrettable in this instance they were not tempered by better judgment. Agnes Vaille was a woman of great persistence and will power, and whatever she undertook she usually carried through in spite of all obstacles. At only 35 years of age, her death was a great loss to the community and to her friends.

About the Author

Carl A. Blaurock, author of "Tragedy on Longs Peak," appearing in this 50th Anniversary *Brand Book*, died Feb. 1, 1993, in Aurora, Colo. At the time of his death at age 98, he was the oldest member of the Denver Posse of the Westerners, and the last surviving founder of the Colorado Mountain Club, organized in 1921. He was preceded in death by his wife Louise, who died Feb. 28, 1992, also at age 98.

A longtime Posse Member, Carl received the Denver Westerners' Lifetime Achievement Award in 1990. His paper, "Tragedy on Longs Peak," was presented to the Westerners on June 24, 1981.

Carl Blaurock was born in Denver in 1894, attended public schools, and was graduated from North Denver High School, and the Colorado School of Mines. With a background in metallurgy, he went to work for his father, manufacturing dental goldwork and refining precious-metals scrap. He continued in that work until retiring in 1972.

An avid outdoorsman, Carl was a devoted mountaineer and was the first person to climb all of Colorado's 53 "fourteeners" peaks, a feat he accomplished by 1921. He climbed Pikes Peak in 1909 at age 15, and climbed his last peak, Notch Mountain, in 1973 at age 79.

[On Dec. 31, 1922, five Colorado Springs men reached the summit of Pikes Peak. In March 1923 they formed the AdAmAn Club, and thereafter would "add a man" a year. In 1923, the first man added was Carl Blaurock. —Edwin A. Bathke]

Blaurock's paper, "William Henry Jackson, Pioneer Photographer," appeared in Vol. 31 of *The Brand Book*. He was co-author with Walter R. Borneman of *Climbing Guide to Colorado's Fourteeners*, and collaborated with Barbara Euser in his autobiography, *A Climber's Climber.*

Sheriffs, Deputy Sheriffs of the Denver Posse of the Westerners

	SHERIFF	DEPUTY SHERIFF
1944	Herbert O. Brayer (Acting)	(None)
1945	Edwin A. Bemis	Edward V. Dunklee
1946	Forbes Parkhill	Arthur Zeuch
1947	Charles B. Roth	Judge Wm. S. Jackson
1948	Arthur H. Carhart	Henry W. Toll
1949	Dabney Otis Collins	B. Z. Woods
1950	Dr. Levette J. Davidson	Walter Gann
1951	Walter Gann	Fred A. Rosenstock
1952	Fred A. Rosenstock	LeRoy R. Hafen
1953	Dr. Philip W. Whiteley	W. Scott Broome
1954	LeRoy R. Hafen	Fletcher W. Birney Jr.
1955	Ralph B. Mayo	Maurice M. Frink
1956	Maurice M. Frink	Francis B. Rizzari
1957	Judge Wm. S. Jackson	Francis B. Rizzari
1958	Harold H. Dunham	W. Scott Broome
1959	Fred M. Mazzulla	Dr. Lester L. Williams
1960	Fletcher W. Birney Jr.	Charles S. Ryland
1961	Charles S. Ryland	Robert L. Perkin
1962	Erl H. Ellis	Robert L. Perkin
1963	Robert L. Perkin	Herbert P. White
1964	Numa James	Kenneth E. Englert
1965	Nevin Carson	Guy M. Herstrom
1966	Guy M. Herstrom	Richard A. Ronzio
1967	Dr. Arthur Campa	Wm. E. Marshall
1968	Wm. E. Marshall	Robert L. Brown
1969	Robert L. Brown	Wm. D. Powell
1970	Dr. Nolie Mumey	Dr. Lester T. Williams
1971	Dr. Lester T. Williams	Edwin A. Bathke
1972	Edwin A. Bathke	Richard A. Ronzio
1973	Richard A. Ronzio	Jackson C. Thode
1974	Jackson C. Thode	Davidson G. Hicks
1975	Davidson G. Hicks	Dr. Robert W. Mutchler
1976	Dr. Robert W. Mutchler	Wm. H. Van Duzer
1977	Wm. H. Van Duzer	Ross V. Miller Jr.
1978	Ross V. Miller Jr.	Merrill J. Mattes
1979	Merrill J. Mattes	George P. Godfrey
1980	George P. Godfrey	Thomas (Mel) Griffiths
1981	Thomas (Mel) Griffiths	Alan J. Stewart
1982	Ray E. Jenkins	Stanley W. Zamonski
1983	Richard A. Cook	Robert D. Stull
1984	Robert D. Stull	Richard D. Akeroyd Jr.
1985	Richard D. Akeroyd Jr.	Eugene J. Rakosnik
1986	Eugene J. Rakosnik	Dr. Henry W. Toll Jr.
1987	Dr. Henry W. Toll Jr.	Hugo G. von Rodeck Jr.
1988	Hugo G. von Rodeck Jr.	Thomas J. Noel
1989	Thomas J. Noel	John F. Bennett
1990	John F. Bennett	C. R. (Bob) Staadt
1991	C. R. (Bob) Staadt	Rev. Jon R. Almgren
1992	Rev. Jon R. Almgren	Jack L. Morison
1993	Jack L. Morison	John M. Hutchins
1994	John M. Hutchins	Theodore P. Krieger
1995	Theodore P. Krieger	Kenneth L. Gaunt

In Memoriam

      Records of the Denver Posse of the Westerners are inadequate in enumerating the deaths of members. A quick estimate shows that more than 40 in the Posse have died since the 1976 *Brand Book* was published. This number includes many of those early members who worked so diligently for the organization. No comprehensive list is possible, and some worthy members would inevitably be omitted. However, this 50th Anniversary volume must pay tribute to at least some of those who are gone. The intent is to honor some—but to slight no one. We apologize for this admittedly partial listing:

Ellis M. Altfather
Carl A. Blaurock
Donald B. Bloch
Herbert O. Brayer
Dabney Otis Collins
Perry Eberhart
Robert A. Edgerton
Erl H. Ellis
Thomas Hornsby Ferril
Thomas Melvin Griffiths
LeRoy R. Hafen

L. Coulson Hageman
Davidson G. Hicks
Numa L. James
Eugene T. Lindberg
Ralph E. Livingston
Fred Milo Mazzula
Dr. Nolie Mumey
Richard A. Ronzio
Charles S. Ryland
Bennett M. Wayne
Herbert P. White

Index

Clear Creek Canyon (Colorado) 236, 291, 292
Clearwater battle (Idaho) 267, 280
Clearwater River (Idaho) 268, 269, 271
Cleveland (steamship) 391, 392
Cleveland, President Grover 362, 382
Coalmont, Colo. 297
Cobb, Edmund 409, 411, 412
Cochetopa Hills (Colorado) 330
Cochetopa Pass (Colorado) 15, 133
Cody, William F. ("Buffalo Bill") 224-226, 228-230, 242, 355
Colfax (Denver suburb) 313
Collier, David C. 149, 151
Colliers magazine 89
Collins, Catherine Wever 250, 251
Collins, Col. William O. 250
Collins, Lt. Caspar 250
Colorado & Southern Railroad (C&S) 289, 299, 300, 302
Colorado As I Saw It 325
Colorado Auto Club 434
Colorado Bar Association 149, 152
"Colorado Brown Stain" 139
Colorado Central Railroad (CC) 236, 289, 291, 292, 295, 297-299, 301, 302
Colorado City, Colo. 15, 286
Colorado College of Dental Surgery 140
Colorado hospitals and sanatoriums (1876-1900) 125
Colorado Highway Department 434,
Colorado Highways 435, 447
Colorado Magazine 137, 251, 354
Colorado Midland Railroad 287, 289, 290, 300
Colorado Motion Picture Company 401, 404, 406, 407, 409, 411, 413, 414
Colorado Mountain Club 451, 455
Colorado Mountain Railroads 286
Colorado Railroads — Chronological Development 286
Colorado Seminary (Denver) 231
Colorado Springs, Colo. 19, 74, 124, 125, 133, 135, 139, 140, 145, 286, 289-291, 337, 341, 350, 351, 358, 368, 412, 434, 437, 438, 441
Colorado State Dental Association 132, 134, 138-140
"Colorado State Library" 163
Colorado Supreme Court 156, 158, 163, 164, 321
Colorado to Gulf Highway 437
Colorado Volunteers 16, 117
Colt's Single-Action Army revolver 70, 210
Columbine Film Company 404, 407
Colville Reservation (Washington) 281
Comanche County, Okla. 392
Comanche, Texas 379, 380, 389
Comanches 3, 4, 6, 7
Commissary storehouse, Ft. Laramie 54, 55
Conejos, Colo. 18, 123, 157
Conejos County, Colo. 157
Confederates 161, 191-203, 254
Congress 12, 69, 71, 149, 150, 152, 155, 362, 365, 371
Conner, Gen. Fox 372

Connor, Brig. Gen. Patrick E. 218
Connor, Timothy 310
Continental Divide 28, 274, 441, 445
Converse Minstrels 171
Cook, Captain 196, 199
Cook, Charles 193
Cook, Mrs. Essie 358
Cook, Richard A. 263, 283
Cook, Sam 194
Coolidge, N.M. 74, 77
Cooper, Congressman William C. 69
Corregidor Hospital in Manila 44
Costilla Creek (Colorado) 11
Cosmopolitan magazine 89
Cottage Grove beer garden (Denver) 318
Cotton, Barbara (Seymour) 83
Cotton, Charles McGugin 62
Cotton, Clinton Neal 61-65, 67-81, 80-83
Cotton, Fred 62
Cotton, John Bowman 70
Cotton, Liberty Leslie 61
Cotton, Mary Alice Crain 62, 67, 81
Cotton, Mary Neal 61
Cottonwood Canyon, Neb. 209, 210
cougars 356, 357
couloirs (chimneys) (Longs Peak) 453
Council Bluffs, Iowa 26, 35, 131
Cover Mountain (Colorado) 329, 330
Covered Wagon Women 247
Cow, by the Tail 379
Cow Island (Montana) 276
"Cowboy's Mother, A" (movie) 402
Coyle, Joe 9
Crain, Mary Alice Cotton 62, 67, 81
Crane, Stephen 371
Crazy Horse (Oglala Chief) 207, 249, 252
Crazy Snake Indian Uprising 393
Crazy Woman's Fork (on Bozeman Trail) 249, 252
Creede, Colo. 137
Creel, George 404
Cress, Alex 425
Crestone, Colo. 11
Crews-Beggs Dry Goods Co. (Pueblo, Colo.) 424
Cricket Hall (Denver) 174
Cripple Creek, Colo. 124, 134-136, 140, 289, 329, 366, 417
Criterion Concert Hall (Denver) 174
Crocker, Dr. Eugene A. 129, 131, 132
Crocker, George F. 162
Crook, Doctor 348
Crook, General 249
Crow Indians 249, 251, 271, 276
Cruce, Gov. Lee 393
Crutchfield, Sheriff Lee 378
Crystal, N.M. 74
Culebra Creek (Colorado) 11
Culp, David W. 131
Curtis Park (Denver suburb) 306, 307
Custer Battlefield National Monument (Montana) 253
Custer, Elizabeth "Libbie" 225, 229, 233, 241,